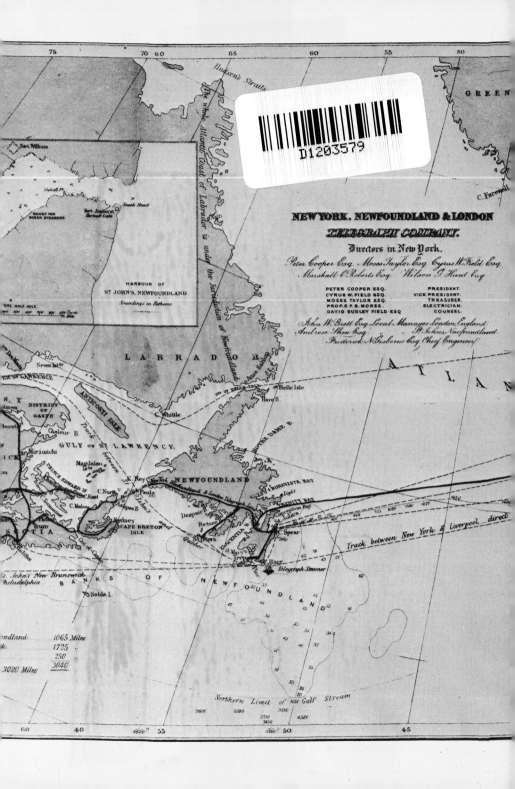

CYRUS FIELD

→→→✕←←←

Man of Two Worlds

CYRUS FIELD:

MAN OF TWO WORLDS

\>\>\>\>\>\>\>\>\>\>\>\>\>\<\<\<\<\<\<\<\<\<\<\<\<

Samuel Carter III

G. P. Putnam's Sons   New York

FOR ALISON

...cependant

Acknowledgments

➤➤➤➤➤➤◄◄◄◄◄◄ In spite of his care and thoroughness in business matters, Cyrus Field left few accounts of his personal life and not much beyond the bare statistics of his undertakings. While his daughter Isabella Field Judson mentions and sometimes quotes notes which he kept for an intended autobiography, this was never written, and the notes themselves are disjointed and often undated. He left no sustained diary and was not a prolific letter writer. Day-to-day records were kept in the form of columnar statistics, such as his personal log on the *Great Eastern* or his mileage and expenditures in South America with Frederick Church. Beyond these sometimes exhaustive figures, Field was not anxious to reveal himself in anything he wrote.

Apart, then, from published accounts of his life—and these (even Isabella's) are few and generally sketchy—one must rely on manuscript sources for much information on the man himself. However, accounts of the laying of the Atlantic cable are plentiful enough, and most libraries contain material on Field's activities (in politics and the elevated railways, for example, if not his private life). I have deliberately omitted footnotes or numbered references to this material in the belief that a reader should not have to look elsewhere in a book for facts essential to the story.

By far the largest collection of Field papers (twenty-one boxes in all) is in the Manuscript Division of the New York Public Library, and my thanks go to its cooperative staff. Perhaps the second most important collection is at the Library of Congress, catalogued not only under Cyrus Field's name but also under the names of his correspondents, notably Presidents Lincoln, Johnson, and Grant and Samuel Morse, Alexander Bache, William Evarts, Hamilton Fish, and Matthew Maury. Additional correspondence with Maury is in the Naval Observatory records in the National Archives at Washington.

Worthy but smaller collections are in the libraries of Duke University, Yale (Sterling Memorial Library), and Williams College; the Henry E. Huntington Library at San Marino, California; the Gisborne papers at the Boston Public Library; the Justin Smith Morrill Foundation of Strafford, Vermont; the Westfield (Massachusetts) Athenaeum; and the Vermont Historical Society at Montpelier. Copies of the diaries of Frederick Church, concerning his South American trip with Field, were kindly made available by David C. Huntington of Northampton.

I have relied considerably on the shelves of the New York Chamber of Commerce and the guidance of its librarian, George H. Ginader, as well as the New York Historical Society, the Genealogical and Biographical Society of New York, Cooper Union, and the Society Library; and more remotely the Halifax Memorial Library in Nova Scotia and the Newfoundland Public Libraries Board at St. John's. The Burndy Library at Norwalk, Connecticut, was a valuable source of reference, and its founder, Bern Dibner, a human encyclopedia of information. Useful material was also found in the Field Room of the Stockbridge, Massachusetts, Library, where Mrs. Graham Wilcox is a gracious and obliging hostess.

For information on Field's paper merchandising days, Winthrop Crane 3d, of Dalton, Massachusetts, kindly made available the files of Crane & Company, with which Field was actively concerned, and Edward Wilkes of the Crane Museum helped present these in order and perspective. Harry F. Lewis, Curator of Museums of the Institute of Paper Chemistry at Appleton, Wisconsin, was also very helpful. Further material was found in the Bella Landauer Collection of the New York Historical Society and in the files of such trade publications as *Paper Dyelines,* published by American Cyanamid Company, and *Superior Facts* (later *The Paper Maker*) published by the Hercules Company at Wilmington, Delaware. Robert P. Vivian of the Great Northern Paper Company was a friendly adviser in this research.

Abundant material was found in England on both the Atlantic cable operation and Field's friends and associates, and I must thank Mrs. Joan St. George Saunders for her help and guidance in my London research. The British Museum was, of course, a basic fountainhead of information, along with its Newspaper Library in Colindale. Equally helpful were the Institution of Electrical Engineers with its excellent compilation of John Brett papers; the files of Cable & Wireless Ltd., in Electra House; and the facilities of Submarine Cables Ltd. (successors to the Telegraph Construction & Maintenance Company) in Greenwich, where Rodney St. John Fancourt made available the log of the *Great Eastern* and the records of the company's cable-laying operations.

My greatest debt in England, however, is to Gerald R. M. Garratt, Keeper of the Science Museum in South Kensington, who reviewed the entire manuscript and made invaluable corrections and editorial suggestions. Without his advice I would have been much handicapped.

Members of the Field family who have been helpful far beyond the call of courtesy are Mrs. Cyrus Field Judson, Jr., of Hastings-on-Hudson, New York; Captain Wells L. Field of West Hartford, Connecticut, who kindly reviewed the chapters on Field's early life; Field Curry of Pittsburgh, who offered many valuable suggestions; Rear Admiral Andrew Mack of Stockbridge, Massachusetts; Mrs. Reginald Belknap of Madison, Connecticut; Mrs. Frank McCoy and Mrs. Alice Jones of Washington; Mrs. Thorold Field of Duluth; Mr. and Mrs. Daniel Lindley of New York; and—in England—William Musgrave of Epsom, Surrey, John Hayes of Canterbury, and Mrs. Arthur David Musgrave of East Grinstead, Sussex.

A word of thanks is due to Mr. and Mrs. W. Wallace Ryan for a guided tour of the Cyrus Field mansion at Ardsley, which still stands well tended in their care.

I am indebted also to Malcolm Stearns, Jr., of Haddam, Connecticut, who made available his personal collection of Field memorabilia, and to writers who have worked on subjects germane to Field's lifetime and who offered friendly counsel—namely, Arthur C. Clarke, Allan Nevins, Bern Dibner, James Dugan, Paul Sarnoff, William Swanberg, David Huntington, Frances Leigh Williams, and Jean Lea Latham. To Mrs. Irene Donahue, librarian of the Baker Library at Dartmouth College, my gratitude for the extended loan of reference material.

Thanks for indispensable editorial assistance and direction go to Andrew Bluemle of G. P. Putnam's Sons, as well as to Professor Broadus Mitchell, who so carefully reviewed the manuscript. I am also indebted to Malcolm Reiss and Phoebe Larmore of Paul Reynolds, Inc., whose guidance and advice were of immeasurable help.

Above all, to Charles W. Ferguson I owe more than could be properly expressed here. This book, while undeserving of his worth as mentor, would never have seen the light of day without his friendship, interest, and encouragement.

CONTENTS

Illustrations will be found following page 160.

The world as yet does not know how much it owes to you, and this generation will never know it. I regard what has been done as the most marvellous thing in human history. I think it more marvellous than the invention of printing, or, I am almost ready to say, than the voyage of the Genoese. But we will not compare these things, which are all great. Let us rather rejoice at what has been done, and I will rejoice that you mainly have done it.

—JOHN BRIGHT
to Cyrus W. Field, November 23, 1866

Science *having developed the principles, and* art *having devised the means for the practical accomplishment of the desired end, there was still wanting a man of enthusiastic temperament, enlarged views as to the importance of the object, persuasive powers to convince others; business talents of high order; persevering industry and indomitable energy. All these requirements have been found happily blended in Mr. Cyrus W. Field, and he has been the chosen one to complete an enterprise which marks an epoch in the history of civilization.*

Mr. Field has not in his unparalleled efforts been actuated by the mere hope of pecuniary gain, but by the cherished feeling of a noble mind, the desire to serve and obtain the approbation of his fellow-men, to honorably connect his name with history and to live in the memory of the good when he shall have finished his career upon earth.

—JOSEPH HENRY
November 12, 1866

CYRUS FIELD

>+>+>+<+<+<+<

Man of Two Worlds

1

Without God, Nothing

➤➤➤➤➤➤◄◄◄◄◄◄ With the publication in 1556 of John Field's *Ephemeris,* or Latin almanac, the universe—as it was then imagined —ceased to exist for Tudor and Elizabethan England. The planets which had remained comfortably fixed for centuries now joined the earth in its rotation around the sun, while the hitherto revolving stars assumed more permanent positions. And it was by these newly arrested stars that the astronomer's descendants navigated to America, to plant the fruitful family of Field on New World soil.

There is every reason to believe, however, that Field was an old and honored name before John etched it into history. "Probably not a dozen families in England can prove so high an antiquity," Frederick C. Pierce wrote in his *Field Genealogy.* The original spelling of De la Field, along with the fact that the name was hereditary— which was uncommon in England before the Norman Conquest— points to a Norman ancestry that seems well documented. It appears that the family came originally from the Alsatian town of Colmar and the Château de la Feld, where Count Hubertus traced his ancestry as far back as the sixth century. Hubertus, a hotheaded warrior by nature, joined William the Conqueror in his invasion of England in 1066 and for this service received vast tracts of land near Lancaster. In the fourteenth century, as a result of Britain's wars with France, the French prefix to the name was dropped and the spelling Anglicized to Field.

Through nearly five post-Conquest centuries the line led down to John Field, the astronomer, "a man of substance and of generous and liberal mind," also a man who fought for his convictions. From his Yorkshire home in Ardsley, John introduced the Copernican heliocentric theory to the British Isles, thereby challenging the system of Ptolemy that had ruled the world for 2,000 years. "Attacking so boldly the general belief of mankind," wrote Pierce, "the new system made its way very slowly among the scientific men of Europe, and is proof at once of the clearness of mind of this English mathematician and of his intellectual intrepidity, that he so quickly saw its truth and at once stood forth in its defense."

John was perhaps the first of the Fields to advance a proposition that banged into the rocks of public skepticism. To the *Ephemeris* he dedicated his life, and the effort—along with its slow acceptance—all but killed him. He turned to farming as a solace for his countrymen's neglect. But before he died in 1587, recognition overtook him when a royal patent added to Field's coat of arms a crest with "a red right arm issuing from the clouds and presenting a golden sphere, intimating the splendor of the Copernican discovery." Beneath a shield displaying sheaves of wheat alluding to the name appear the words *Sans Dieu Rien*—"Without God Nothing"—a conviction shared by succeeding generations.

John Field had eight sons, all marked by an individuality and independence common to this family. His "disloyal and loose-lived son Richard" he cut off with nothing but a silver spoon, and "if not satisfied with that may he lose the benefit of it." To two other sons he bequeathed "all his plate and jewels of gold and silver." The rest were presumably left on their own—including his namesake, from whom descended a grandson, Zachariah. Perhaps because of religious or political dissent, Zachariah was the first of the Fields to leave for America, around 1630, in the wake of the *Mayflower* Pilgrims.

He settled first in Dorchester but later followed the Reverend Thomas Hooker, a leading Colonial theologian, in his mass migration to the Connecticut River valley. From this point on, the Fields, along with other New England pioneers, were involved in a running battle with the Indians, yet in Northampton, Zachariah built his home outside the stockade to maintain his independence. He would either fight the Indians or trade with them, depending on their predilection. He did a little of both—serving sometimes with a conscripted army of defense and sometimes as friendly proprietor of a trading post that was frequented by Pequots. In this dual, but diplomatic, role he managed to survive attacks that decimated many of his companions.

His grandson Ebenezer married Mary Dudley, bringing the distinguished name of Dudley to the family for the first time. Ebenezer had met Mary in Guilford, Connecticut, after fleeing his home in Deerfield, one jump ahead of the marauding redskins. But other Fields who remained in Deerfield suffered bloody consequences in the Indian massacres of 1675 and 1704. Ebenezer's uncle Samuel Field was shot dead in his cornfield, and his sister left a widow by the murder of her husband. Another uncle, John, saw a daughter scalped before his eyes, while his wife and other children were hauled into the wilderness as hostages. All were ransomed but the daughter Mary, who, for some spirited reason of her own, "became enamored of the wild, free life of the woods," married an Indian chief, and could not be persuaded to return.

There was by now, if indeed there had not been before, a strain of resolute determination in the bloodstream of the Fields, a willingness to cope with sacrifice and hardship, a faith in the Divinity that served them well in generations yet to come. These qualities were evident in Ebenezer's eldest son, David, who decided it was time to stand fast, put down roots, and establish a world of strength and durability. He wanted a rock on which to build his home. At Madison, near Guilford, a few miles inland from Long Island Sound, he found a monolithic rise, on which he constructed a house of hand-hewn beams and solid planking. Known as Field Elders it still stands, gray-weathered after two and a half centuries, unpropped and barely altered, until recently inhabited by Field descendants.

Here, with the aid of three successive wives, David raised eleven children. The eldest, by his third wife, Abigail Tyler Stone, was Timothy, who inherited Field Elders when his father died. Timothy was a man of "vigorous physique and reckless courage," who served under Washington during the Revolution, rising to the rank of captain and later attending the general at his inauguration in 1789. This honor seems to have affected him for the balance of his life. Although he returned to his role of Guilford farmer and married a local belle named Anna Dudley, he never removed his silver-buckled shoes, bright Army tunic, and Continental cocked hat except, presumably, to go to bed.

In keeping with the outsize families that regularly blessed the Fields, David and Anna had six daughters and two sons—the younger of the latter being David Dudley, born in 1781. In David Dudley the family motto of *Sans Dieu Rien* reached rich fulfillment, if indeed it had ever lain fallow. He assuredly walked with God as soon as he could walk at all. A schoolmate recalled that when they went hiking in the woods, young David would mount the first convenient rock and "preach" to his companions for as long as they would consent to listen. When no congregation was available, he would head for the beaches of Long Island Sound and deliver his sermons to the waves.

Bent on the ministry (as was his older brother Timothy), David was tutored for college by the Reverend John Elliott of Guilford and, at seventeen, entered Yale, where he taught school in his spare time to help meet expenses. In New Haven he shared rooms with Jeremiah Evarts, father of William Maxwell Evarts, a later Secretary of State, for whom David's sons would have a warm respect. At Yale, David was inspired by the eloquence and intellect of President Timothy Dwight (whose "extreme sensibility to the beauty and sweetness of always doing right" had made him shun the practice of law and turn to education) and was graduated with high honors in 1802.

No theological seminaries existed at that time. To prepare himself further for the pulpit, David went to nearby Somers to study under Dr. Charles Backus, whose religious tract *The Nature and Influence of Godly Fear* had had a wide circulation in Connecticut. At Somers he acquired something else besides religious education—a wife with the unlikely name of Submit Dickinson.

Known as the "beauty of Somers," Submit was one of eleven children of Captain Noah Dickinson, who had served under General Israel Putnam in the French and Indian War and later with distinction in the Revolution. Being of the same rank as David's father, Noah balanced the list of warrior forebears in the genealogy of Fields.

David's letter announcing his engagement to his parents assures them that "the person, I flatter myself, will merit your cordial approbation," and "this match is not the effect of youthful enthusiasm, but of cool deliberation. Marrying now, I am persuaded, will not injure me respecting my prospects in life, but the contrary. . . . Her parents are respectable . . . they are able to support her."

The matrimonial picture conjured by this letter, like the name Submit itself, is a misleading preface to a rich and lively marriage. Submit did anything but what her name implies, though her production of ten children led to ribald jokes in that direction. It was a partnership of divided labors and responsibilities, but hers was the spirit that brought light and cheer into the home. Although David Dudley had the sharp arresting eyes and granite countenance of a masterful Jehovah, he was remembered by his grandchildren as appearing almost "mousey" in the presence of his small, but animated, wife, whom he addressed as Mrs. Field. And those who were questioned about the Puritanical austerity imposed on the family by Field were wont to say, "Ah, but don't forget Submit!"

After receiving his license to preach in 1803, David occupied the Somers pulpit for some months but, remembering that a prophet is not without honor save in his own country, shortly accepted a call to the Congregational Church in nearby Haddam. Dr. John Elliott, his Guilford tutor, felt the event sufficiently important to attend and deliver the ordination sermon, in which he advised his former pupil: "Be thou an example of the believers, in word, in conversation, in charity, in spirit, in faith, in purity," adding a footnote that the fledgling pastor must have welcomed: "Let no man despise thy youth."

It was not a pleasant location, the rough and rocky village, almost a frontier town, which made its dusty living from the quarries of the Brainerds—the "seed family" of Haddam. "No general revival of religion had reached the place," David Field wrote in retrospect. The meetinghouse was a drafty barnlike structure, which served also as the town court; the parsonage, a small frame house, with, wrote Evelyn Brainerd, "a tiny yard separating it from the street, a heavy stone chimney peering over the short front roof, and within, one of the finest corner cupboards." That the cupboard was often bare and the chimney often smokeless for want of firewood might also have called for note. But to this dubious community Field brought, along with his bride, dynamic energy and faith.

He had already mastered a fire-and-brimstone approach to the Gospel that was both expected and relished by his flock. They came from miles around to hear him—the children barefoot, carrying their shoes to put on when they entered church. Many brought picnic baskets to enable them to spend the day; the Connecticut riverbank looked like the camping ground of a gay invading army. In his granddaughter's record of the family, there is a gentle account of these meetinghouse services, in which "the bass viol took a gruff but animated part, the tunes or hymns were led with a tuning fork, and the pretty girl singers wore silk mantillas, dimity gowns, and shirred silk bonnets; they slyly nibbled fennel and dill as they flirted surreptitiously behind their palm leaf fans with the village beaux."

Against this innocent background the young pastor loomed as a gaunt and menacing prophet, "tall, erect of carriage with keen piercing steel gray eyes set in his typically Puritan stern Old Testament type of face." He was a man without compromise; he saw no shades of gray between the black and white. Like a character in an early morality play, he was in constant perspiring battle with the devil. Yet it was not perspiration wasted. If his congregation complained that with his ringing, penetrating voice, he preached at them instead of to them, it was duly noted by local chroniclers that his pastorate ushered in "a period most memorable in the history of the town" and "left its impress on more than one generation."

Life was rugged in the riverside community. Although the Fields were able to move later to a more commodious house on higher ground, they could afford no help. Submit, frail and delicate, did all the household work, cooking, scrubbing, sewing, making beds, and dusting furniture, also weaving and dyeing the cloth her husband wore, churning the butter, salting the meat, putting up preserves, and tending the small garden that provided them with meager vegetables. The community helped out with contributions of potatoes, pork, and firewood. The total of these, plus cash donations, was supposed to equal $500 annually, but David Dudley later told his sons, "I never saw a hundred dollars in my life."

Yet Submit and David had seven children while they lived at Haddam (one of them died shortly after birth): David Dudley junior, Emilia, Timothy, Matthew, Jonathan, and Stephen—with Stephen's name taken, shortly after his untimely death, by a seventh child born one year later. To support this brood, the minister labored around the clock, shirking no midnight calls to the distressed or sick, making the daily rounds, not only of the homes of his parishioners, but also of the local schools, to see that they properly taught the Word of God beside the word of man. In the chill front parlor of the parsonage he wrote his sermons at a stand-up lectern ("as behind a breastwork in the fortress of Divine truth"), possibly, as his grandson felt, because he was thus able to practice his delivery on his feet. He had something to pound on as he tested his resonance against the bare walls.

He worked with a quill pen and wrote in a clear, ornate calligraphy on six-by-eight-inch sheets, noting on the back of each collation the date and place of invocation. Several of his sermons became pamphlet pieces for distribution beyond Haddam, one in particular, delivered at the execution of a drunken wretch, named Peter Lung, who had hacked his wife to death.

According to the grim custom of the time, a condemned man was brought into church before mounting the scaffold, forced to stand before the congregation at the pulpit, while the preacher addressed to him words that would prove a lesson for the community. In this harrowing procedure, Field's nature left no room for conciliation where evil was concerned. "What you have done," he told the doomed man, "subjects you to ignominious execution. From this there is no escape. . . . Pray God, then, if perhaps your sins may be forgiven you. Cry to him, God be merciful to me, a sinner! and continue those cries till death shall move you hence."

Yet he was not without his warm and human side. The ministers of the neighborhood, who gathered by horseback at one another's houses for the only social life available in early-nineteenth-century Connecticut, found a special hospitality at Haddam. This was heightened by the lively presence of Submit, who "furnished the side-board with a goodly array of decanters, containing wine and brandy, of which all partook to refresh them after the fatigue of their rides, and sharpen their zeal for theological discussion." When theological discussion was over, the children recalled listening with wonder "at the peals of laughter which shook the place of convocation," remembering "their father's stories, and how he sometimes fairly exploded with mirth, and laughed till the tears ran down his cheeks."

It was a hard task raising half a dozen children on a parson's pittance, feeding and clothing them and caring for their illnesses. Since the local school was rudimentary, they were taught at home, where their father schooled them in the Bible and the Greek and Latin classics. The minister's intellect was wide of range, and he had the ability, inherited by a sixth son, Cyrus (not yet born), of pursuing a variety of interests simultaneously. While actively concerned with diverse problems of the present, he was keenly interested in New England's past. He delved into the background of the towns and churches of the valley and the genealogy of local families, and wrote and published the first *History of Middlesex County*.

Submit was the heartbeat of the family in both practicality and piety. Everything was homemade—from the clothes they wore to the jam they ate and the tallow candles that they studied by. She heard their prayers and tended them in sickness, with never a flickering of faith. Her children remembered her as a warm ember on the hearth, a comforting buffer between inexorable heaven and the practical demands of earth. Devout she was. She knew her Bible from Genesis to Revelation, except for the "begats." She applied its teachings with a human understanding that perhaps escaped her husband.

The liberal preachings of Dr. William Ellery Channing, contemporary advocate of spiritual freedom, troubled David Dudley greatly—troubled him because he was unable to admit to his church anyone subscribing to those views. Perhaps not many did, for during his years at Haddam more than 200 new members received "his good right hand of welcome" to the congregation. Submit was surely a tempering influence on the harsh discipline of his uncompromising conscience. She was never fully subject to her husband's intransigent attitude. When a visiting evangelist publicly berated a townsman for his drinking habits, Submit urged Field to bring the interloping preacher to her. "I'd just like to give him a piece of my mind," she said.

After fourteen years at Haddam, David evidently felt the urge to test his mettle against a more challenging assignment. It was characteristic of the Fields, once an objective was achieved, to hanker for new areas of conquest. His youngest son, Henry, recalled: "He read about the emigrants from Connecticut and Massachusetts going out into the wilderness. Why should he not go out and preach to them? He was just in his prime, but thirty-seven years old! Who could endure hardship better than he?" In 1818 he requested a dismissal from his post and, under the auspices of the Missionary Society of Connecticut, embarked on a preaching mission to the undeveloped West, leaving Submit to care for the house and children, with the faith that "they were safe under the eyes of God."

The Far West then meant western New York, from the banks of the Oswego to Lake Erie, and here he went alone, on horseback, with his books and clothing strapped behind the saddle. Like the itinerant evangelist of Colonial times, he preached to whoever would listen—most of them, as it turned out, Indians of the Iroquois and Algonquin nations—and talked to them wherever they would listen, in tents and cabins and under the shade of trees, standing on rocks or ricks or on the stirrups of his horse.

He slept on the open ground or in the isolated cabins of obliging settlers, and on the way back to Haddam, since taverns were not appropriate for preachers, stopped at the parsonage of Dr. Stephen West at Stockbridge, Massachusetts. Dr. West, feeble and aging, had all but retired, and invited Field to preach to his congregation on the following Sabbath. David not only obliged, but also stayed to conduct the services on two succeeding Sundays. He was well liked. Dr. West's parishioners found him "thoroughly orthodox" with "no liberal loopholes" in his thinking. As a result, on his return to Haddam, he received a call from the Stockbridge congregation to become its pastor.

It was a tempting offer: $700 a year along with the promise of 121 sleighloads of firewood and ample supplies of cabbages and potatoes. To parents of six children, these fringe benefits were important. And some sort of change was on his mind, for Fields were not apt to stay content forever. On his return from Stockbridge he had gone to New Haven on the invitation of Dr. Benjamin Trumbull, a well-recognized Connecticut historian, who was about to retire and thought that David would be an admirable successor. But it would mean quitting his calling before he could regard it as fulfilled. To make his decision easier, the Stockbridge community offered to supply the means of transportation to the Massachusetts village, an important factor in that period of ill-defined roads over rolling wilderness. Field accepted.

Of this trip Henry Martyn Field wrote:

> The moving itself was no small affair. Teams were sent to Connecticut—a journey of several days—to bring the household furniture. There were beds and bureaus, tables and chairs, and most weighty of all, boxes piled with books, for my father had accumulated a large library. Thus laden, the heavy wagons took their long, toilsome journey over the mountains . . . to our new home among the Berkshire Hills.

Hooting and singing hymns, they made their triumphant entry over the Small Plain and across the double Oxbow of the Housatonic, to the frame house Field had rented from a family of Morgans on the slopes of Glendale.

Cyrus West Field was born on November 30, 1819, two days after the Thanksgiving turkey had been sacrificed. He was named in discreet respect for the town banker, Cyrus Williams, and for Dr. West, Field's distinguished predecessor. The first few days of his life were touch and go. Neighbors cheerfully predicted that Submit would never be able to raise the child, that he had no "constitution." When he reached toddling age his frail body had to be supported by a frame, in which he could roll around the room.

His mother's devotion was augmented by anxiety. Visitors observed that Cyrus was the "squirmiest" child they had ever seen. He would never have the stalwart physique of his brother; he would run on nervous energy—but he would always run, as if he had got off to a slow start and were trying to catch up.

Three years later the last of the brothers, Henry Martyn, was born, and by the time Submit was carrying yet another child, David Dudley decided the Glendale home was too small for his brood and moved the family to a modest gambrel-roofed house on the Stockbridge village green. Here Mary Elizabeth came into the world, last of nine children: two daughters, seven sons.

The family had barely grown accustomed to their new home before the older children, returning from school, saw a cloud of smoke and found their house in flames. Neighbors—for as long as they could stand the heat—threw books and possessions from the windows and Submit stood weeping in the street, while the old manse was reduced to ashes. David Dudley took the fire philosophically, observing of a flaming barrel of his sermons: "They give more light to the world than if I'd preached them." But he suffered acute distress when volunteers carried out the stand-up desk at which he composed his sermons; the drawer flew open and spewed on the lawn a shower of playing cards he had confiscated from his older children.

The family settled in with neighbors, while Field, with singular purpose, began to write his Sunday sermon, choosing his text from the Book of Lamentations: "It is of the Lord's mercies that we are not consumed." The congregation was so deeply moved that a meeting was held immediately afterward, and funds raised to replace the devastated dwelling. Within a few months there rose a plain, square, red-brick house, now known as the Old Parsonage, which still stands, with some later alterations. It was in this house that the Fields established their identity with Stockbridge, among the oldest New England settlements, isolated, self-sufficient, proud, and staunchly Puritan in faith. It bore in the character of its county families the mark of the evangelist John Sergeant, who had made it in the preceding century a missionary outpost to convert the Housatonic Indians. He was followed by Jonathan Edwards, who "found in the shades of the forest that perfect rest so needful for the tranquil mind of the philosopher." And finally there had been Dr. Stephen West—perhaps not up to the stature of his predecessors, but still a man of influence in shaping the theology, not just of his community, but also of New England. From this religious heritage there were those who looked upon the village and its valley as "the garden of the Lord."

It was a beautiful spot from any viewpoint—without what the present residents refer to as its cemetery loveliness—a vale of deep pine woods and sloping meadows, through which the untroubled Housatonic flowed. To the south loomed Monument Mountain like a brooding sentinel. The industrial age had scarcely touched the village (though paper mills were springing up in Lee and Lenox); no daily papers reached it; the east-west railroad had not yet been laid. Yet for all this idyllic insulation, it boasted old and cultured and aristocratic names: Pomeroy, Ashburner, Dwight, Sergeant, Seymour, Hopkins, and Sedgwick. Even the crickets in the fields (legend had it) chirped, "Sedgwick, Sedgwick, Sedgwick." Wrote Emilia Field: "A love of the soil is bred in the bone of all New Englanders, but there seems to be something deeper for Stockbridge itself."

The meetinghouse, built on Prospect Hill at the close of the Revolutionary War, overlooked the valley to the north and south and west. "It was of a primeval order of architecture, standing four square to all the winds of heaven, with tall pulpit and high-backed pews." Surrounding it were the pine groves where parishioners, who, as at Haddam, came from great distances to hear their preacher, could rest and picnic and then return for "the second blowing of the Gospel trumpet." For the indefatigable minister held three services on Sunday, with several more by candlelight on weekdays, and lost no opportunity to celebrate holidays with worship. It was he who established the Sunrise Meeting every New Year's morning, which lasted as a village institution for 100 years.

Among his congregation was a young man named Mark Hopkins, who, on becoming president of Williams College, recalled these multiple services and especially their moderator:

> In respect to feeling he was not demonstrative, and some thought him cold. No mistake could have been greater. On sitting near him I remember to have been struck by noticing the big tears rolling down his cheeks when he came to the more touching part of his discourse, while there was scarcely a sign of emotion in his voice or the lines of his face. Perhaps intellect predominated. Probably it did; but he was a man of deep feeling, and under the impulse of it, as well as of principle, he was a faithful, earnest, laborious pastor.

Laborious he was indeed. The parish was large, the seasons rugged, and his was the only church in that widespread community. On horseback he scoured the countryside in search of "lost sheep," left no home unvisited, brought consolation to the sick and dying. He was fond of saying, "It is better to go to the house of mourning than to the house of feasting, for that is the end of all men, and the living will lay it to heart." In a similar vein he often reminded his disciples: "We are strangers and sojourners, as all our fathers were."

Behind all this labor, originating and sustaining it, was the nature of the man himself. His youngest son wrote:

> If the creed of the Puritans was an iron creed, it formed an iron character, a firmness and intrepidity which have produced the greatest effects in the history of both Old and New England. His faith was one in which there was no enfeebling doubt—none of that subtle poison diffused by much of the scientific teaching of our day, which penetrates so many intellects, and emasculates their strength. To him the Bible was the Word of God—the one absolute and infallible test of truth, from which there is no appeal.

How much his teachings and example influenced his sons is hard to measure. Certainly they all professed religious principles, but their destinies were guided by those principles in varying degrees. Only one followed his footsteps to the ministry, and to his credit, David Dudley did not try to influence his sons unduly. He may have recognized a new breed of American, a borderline generation caught between Puritan New England, with its strict code of ethics, and a dawning age of freedom, opportunity, and industrial wealth. His sons surely subscribed to the motto of *Sans Dieu Rien*—but possibly with the secret thought that God, too, might be handicapped without the Fields. It was a partnership from which all sides would benefit.

2

Stripling in Stockbridge

>>>>>><<<<<< When Cyrus was ten, he was forced by duty to join Henry and Mary in making dandelion chains. Young Cyrus, inept at fitting one stem into another and irked by the taunts of his younger brother and sister, as their chains grew longer and faster than his own, told them wrathfully:

"Just wait! *Someday* I'll make a chain long enough to go clear around the world!"

It was more a mystical resolution than an idle boast. And it expressed an impatience, a sense of urgency, that haunted him all through his youth. He was always competing—mostly with himself. His ambitions outdistanced his capacities, but he would not yield. What he lacked in talent, he would make up with persistence. And to make the job more challenging, he would set his goals high. There would never be any final victory, for victory prescribed another goal ahead to keep his destiny perpetually unfulfilled.

He was the oldest of the dwindling family at home now. David Dudley junior had been through Williams College, which he had entered at the age of sixteen, and was starting in the legal profession in Henry Sedgwick's office in New York. His older sister Emilia had married the Reverend Josiah Brewer and, to Submit's extreme distress, had gone to Smyrna, Turkey, with her missionary husband, taking her brother Stephen with them, it being considered a proper education for a youth with missionary tendencies to visit foreign lands. Timothy, reputed to be the most brilliant of the brothers, had received at the age of fifteen a commission in the Navy through the influence of Congressman Henry Dwight of Stockbridge. Matthew was employed at a paper-manufacuturing plant in Lee, while Jonathan was an undergraduate at Williams.

Of home in Stockbridge, Henry, given to sentimental descriptions, wrote:

> But what a dear home it was, and how lovingly and happily did we nestle in it! At first we slept under the eaves, where we often heard the rain patter on the roof—that delicious sound that lulls to slumber with the sweet sense of security. Afterwards my brother and I had a small room at the head of the stairs, where he slept in a bed a few inches higher than mine, and I in a "trundle-bed" which was shoved under it. It was a bird's nest indeed, in which we put our little heads to sleep; but never did a bird on any swinging bough sleep more tranquilly under the protection of Him without whom not a sparrow falls to the ground. Never did we close our eyes that mother did not come to fold us up tenderly, and give us her last kiss, and hear us repeat "Now I lay me down to sleep. . . ."

As had his older brothers, Cyrus got his earliest education from his father: Greek and Latin and such English classics as *Pilgrim's Progress,* from which he memorized a favorite line: "To *know* is a thing which pleaseth talkers and boasters; but to *do* is that which pleaseth God." He was not a natural student or an avid reader. And his father's library, while large, was circumscribed. Wrote a literary-minded visitor to the parsonage: "Of tales and romance there are none; of the English classics little; and of poetry just three books—Milton's *Paradise Lost,* Young's *Night Thoughts,* and Watts' *Psalms and Hymns!*"

As soon as he was old enough, he attended the two-room elementary school on Elm Street, on the second floor of which was the more advanced Stockbridge Academy. Here he pursued the conventional subjects of reading, spelling, geography, and mathematics.

While there is no indication that Cyrus aggressively sought or cultivated leadership among his playmates, leadership was evidently thrust upon him. This may have been a recognition of his generally buoyant confidence and his sheer delight in obstacles. Along with these was his ability to organize activities and solicit their support. Swimming meets in the Housatonic and sleigh rides and skating parties in the winter took place often largely owing to his promotion.

Being the oldest child remaining, although only ten, he inherited the chores his brothers had relinquished—weeding the garden, helping cut ice in winter, milking the cows, feeding the chickens, tending the sheep, and caring for the horses.

If he had any faults at this time, and he surely did, they might well have included a brusque impatience and intolerance of those of his companions who did not measure up to his own standards. His insistence on rule and rectitude approximated tyranny. And he did not take kindly to defeat. When beaten by a competitor in a footrace on the village green, he suggested that the contest be rerun while each participant ate a pocketful of salted crackers. Not only did this handicap even up the odds, but in a queer way it also stimulated him. Obstacles, he found, discouraged competition, and raised the level of his own performance.

In an English anthology entitled *Lessons from Noble Lives,* designed to inspire British youth to high ideals, Cyrus West Field was the only American example:

> From the first, however, unlike his brothers, he showed no ardent affection for book-learning, but excelled in all active and athletic pursuits. And he was well fitted to succeed in these for his frame was lithe and wiry, his physical strength remarkable, his courage undoubted, and his enterprise indefatigable. Whatever he undertook, he carried through. No obstacles could daunt him; indeed, they seemed to intensify his steadfastness of purpose.

All true—except that there were no organized outdoor activities in the village, only those he organized himself. In fact, David Dudley Field had discouraged many popular diversions, deploring the "vulgar and barbaric practice of horse racing," along with any form of dancing for "its known tendency to dissipate the mind, and unfit it for reflection." He had publicly declared, "The shooting of turkeys, etc., as an amusement, is continued in some places, and attended with some disorder and with the brutalizing of the feelings of those who allow themselves in the cruel and barbarous indulgence."

Each day began and ended with the family assembled in the parlor for prayers and Bible reading. Chapter by chapter, the children and their parents read a verse in sequence till the end of Revelation led them back again to Genesis. Following this, they knelt in prayer—all but David Dudley Field, who chose to address the Deity while standing. The childish buttocks thus aligned were often an invitation to a surreptitious pinch, followed by an outraged squeal. Then the pastor's voice broke like a suddenly stilled bell whose gong goes on reverberating. There was no rebuke—only a dreadful silence that fell like an awesome unforgettable chastisement.

In Stockbridge, as in other New England towns, the Sabbath began at sundown on Saturday, and while there were those who held that midnight might be satisfactory, Field was not so liberal as they. When the sun reached its zenith and inclined toward the west, he would caution his children: "My sons, we are on the borders of holy time." As Henry noted of the release at the end of the long day:

> At sunset the gates were shut down rigidly on the labor of the week, and for twenty-four hours it was as if the current of life had ceased to flow. The next day, as the afternoon wore on, and the Sabbath "began to abate," there was a painful time of waiting for the last moment to expire. How many, many times did my brother and I go out in front of our door, to watch for the sun's going down! Why did it linger so long? At length it touched the rim of the hills, and slowly sunk behind the ridge of the pines that stood up against the Western sky. Lower and lower it fell, till the orb was below the horizon. We did not wait for the glow of sunset to fade into twilight, and the shades of evening to gather; but instantly, with a sense of joyous freedom, bounded away to play. It was as if a heavy weight had been lifted off our young breasts, and the blood began to flow again in our veins. My mother took her knitting; the usual topics of conversation, from which we had religiously abstained through the day, were resumed; and life went on as before.

On Sundays at the meetinghouse the two youngest children shared the pulpit with the preacher; the next youngest flanked their mother in the congregation. During the "Lastly," or closing prayer, each parent could thus keep a hand on the adjoining heads to make sure they were still there. It was a sensible precaution. The prayer, "which manifested both Godliness and endurance," lasted a full hour with the congregation standing.

Cyrus was not overawed by his father's strict adherence to religious ritual. When, in the frugal parsonage, a much-prized rattrap disappeared, Field instructed Cyrus to look for it, not to give up until he found it and to bring it to him immediately no matter what the time and place. Cyrus found the rattrap while his father was preaching at vespers. He raced to the meetinghouse, up the aisle between the congregation, waited for a suitable pause in the minister's delivery, and announced, "Your rattrap, father!"—dutifully placing it on the pulpit.

He brought the same somewhat pixielike humor to his household chores. When one of the brooding hens was sitting on her eggs, Cyrus was assigned to watch out for the hatching chicks. He did so reluctantly. Waiting was intolerable to him. When, by happy coincidence, the family cat had kittens in a nearby corner of the barn, he put the kittens under the setting hen, raced indoors and called to his parents to come out and see the newborn chicks.

His only anxiety in those early days was Submit. She still drove herself relentlessly. It is doubtful that any of the family wore store-bought clothes when she could weave the fabric from their own sheep's wool, color it with butternut dye, and turn it into jackets, dresses, shirts, and trousers. For all her drive, Submit was far from strong, and suffered frequent sicknesses, some close to fatal. During one serious spell, Cyrus spent all his days and evenings in her room—until Submit said abruptly, "I think I'm all right now," and got out of bed. "And you know," said Cyrus years later, "all of a sudden she was well!"

Whether she was ill or well, her spirits remained irrepressible. It was she who, when her strength was sound, helped organize the moonlight sleigh rides and the summer picnics with their basketloads of boiled eggs, sage cheese, loaf and raisin cakes, dried beef and capers, jams and pickles. She rode a horse to gather provisions or accompany her husband on his parish rounds. And she kept her sense of balance between piety and earthly occupations. When she succumbed to justifiable complaint and was told by her husband, "Mrs. Field, remember—the Lord reigneth over all," she snapped back, "Mr. Field, I don't care whether the Lord reigneth or he doesn't; we need help around here!"

In spite of his arduous professional activities, Field completed his *History of the County of Berkshire,* a 500-page volume published in 1829. While his writing was clear, precise, and thorough, his manner of address was often baffling to his family and parishioners. One ringing expression he was apt to spring on Cyrus was that the Lord would "overturn, overturn . . . until he come, whose right it is," and a text he was fond of quoting left young Cyrus memorably puzzled: "Parbar westward, four at the causeway and two at Parbar." The minister never felt that these strange expressions called for any explanation.

For the children, former homes in Madison, Guilford, Haddam seemed to run together. They often spent summers with their aunts and uncles in the house on the rock. On the shingle Cyrus hunted shells and pebbles with pigtailed Mary Bryan Stone, the daughter of neighbors. He seems to have had a curious interest in shells and fossils and souvenirs of nature's past, a curiosity about what was at the roots of nature, what was the hidden meaning in a feather or a stone. The sea itself he saw as grimly hostile, stretching too far from home and offering no promise. He decided that, unlike his brother Timothy, he would never go to sea.

In Stockbridge his acquaintances were many, but he was cautious about making intimate friendships. His only close companion was his brother Henry, who wrote of that period (Cyrus begrudged the time to keep a diary):

> Next to my father and mother, my earliest recollection is of my brother Cyrus. As he was the nearest to me in age, we grew up together; and from childhood until I was twelve years old, when I went to college (he, a few months later, went to New York), we were inseparable. And yet never were two brothers more unlike. He was, as I have said, distinguished by a nervous restlessness and incessant activity . . . was very fond of the outdoor sports of the country. . . . But in our childhood days there was hardly anything in which we were not together. Together we trotted off to school every morning; together we went berrying or chestnutting in the woods. On the hillside back of the village there stood then a grove of hickory trees, where we gathered nuts and set traps for squirrels. It was two lives in one, till years brought the inevitable moment of separation.

Essentially, though, Cyrus was moody and something of a lone wolf, and when the chores were done, especially on Saturdays, he would take to the woods by himself to hunt for arrowheads or birds' eggs, sometimes stopping at a friendly farmhouse for the traditional meal of salt pork and potatoes. Mark Hopkins' widowed mother lived a mile and a half from the village, and young Field called on "Aunt Mary" almost every Saturday to spend the afternoon at Cherry Cottage. He was a particular favorite of the elderly lady.

As he advanced in school, he moved upstairs to the Academy, supervised by Jared Curtis, a former Army major who had become a stern and noted teacher in that Berkshire neighborhood. No record survives of his academic progress, beyond some indication that he excelled in mathematics. He appears to have been fond of the exactitude of figures, fond of reducing subjects and problems to irrefutable conclusions. To this end he carried about a handy capsule history of the universe that he had copied down in school.

ESSENTIAL DATES

The Creation	4004 B.C.
The Deluge	2348 B.C.
Babel built	2347 B.C.
Moses born	1671 B.C.
Destruction of Troy & Rape of Helen	1184 B.C.

He was an inveterate list maker, keeping track of everything—from chores to be done and the time they took to the number of eggs each hen laid or the dates when the first tomato buds appeared. Recognizing this bent, his parents, before he was fully twelve years old, assigned the keeping of the family accounts to him. In a parson's economy, this was an important function. Little cash was exchanged in the community, and when a farmer brought a side of beef and a housewife a pound of butter or a dozen eggs, they had to be carefully appraised and credited against the pastor's $700 salary. For four years he dutifully kept books and the habit of reducing records to statistics stayed with him throughout his life.

Besides his aptitude at mathematics, Cyrus inherited from his father an instinct for good diction and for rhetoric, talking too rapidly perhaps, but with a cultured Massachusetts accent. Unlike the average youth, he was never frightened to appear in public, he was too enthusiastic about any project to give way to shyness or a naturally retiring nature. At the Academy Exhibition in the fall of 1834 he delivered a discourse on the life of Washington, proclaimed "The Imagined Speech of John Adams on the Declaration of Independence," and performed the part of Deacon Littlesoul in the school morality play. The following spring he settled for a lighter role—that of Mrs. Hardcastle in *She Stoops to Conquer*.

Stockbridge left a strong stamp on his character. But it was not strong enough to hold him. For all its pride and culture, it was essentially a poor community where there was little industry. The town was, in fact, little more than a way station between the coastal cities of the East and the expanding country to the West, with the Stockbridge Inn a stagecoach stop for changing horses.

Henry left for Williams at the prodigious age of twelve. Cyrus, now sixteen, was suddenly left alone. His sister Mary, whom he dearly loved and toward whom he maintained a sense of guardianship all their lives, was hardly an adequate companion for his restless energy. Now more than ever he felt left behind.

Given to taking inventory, he considered his position in relation to his brothers. David Dudley junior was so successful at the law that he was able to aid the family financially. Jonathan having been graduated from Williams, was now studying law with David in the Sedgwick office. Timothy, a midshipman, had had to resign from the Navy because of a lung condition, but was on a voyage around the world aboard a merchant vessel. Matthew was working in the Columbia Paper Mill in Lee, owned by the Laflin family, and Jonathan had written to his father from New York: "I saw Mr. Laflin a few days since, he spoke in the most exaggerated terms of Matthew. He thinks him one of the most promising young fellows of his age with whom he is acquainted." And young Henry Martyn, two years Cyrus' junior, was at Williams, getting on well and known affectionately as *Agra Parva,* "Little Field."

And where was he, Cyrus? He had not, he knew, the patience or the penetrating mind for law, he felt no call to the church, and both required time for preparation that he could not spare. He had no manual dexterity, no artistic talent or creative bent, and was trained in literally nothing. All he had—all he ever had, in fact—was a keen and curious mind, an inextinguishable optimism, and an inordinate amount of drive.

In spite of the family's straitened circumstances, Cyrus could have gone to Williams, for Stockbridge boys were offered special dispensations because Jeremiah Williams, father of the college's founder, had been a Stockbridge man. Again, Cyrus was too impatient. Purely by order of birth, he was, he felt, already too far behind his brothers. He had no time for Williams.

He was subject to fits of despondency that sprang from an awareness of his lack of direction. He never completely conquered them. To compensate, a resilience in his nature allowed him to recover quickly from depression, to rally from dark moodiness to confident exhilaration. Basically he did not doubt himself because he never doubted others. It was a treacherous sort of innocence, and often it betrayed him; but throughout his early years it was worth whatever grief it cost.

He had an asset in his family. From the local deference shown his father—even by the aristocratic Sedgwicks, Seymours, Pomeroys, and Dwights—he must have sensed that he was of a special stock. He knew that his family was behind him in whatever he decided and that he could count on the backing of his brothers.

In their *Stockbridge, 1739–1939, a Chronicle,* Sarah Sedgwick and her sister, Christina Marquand, made this prophetic comment:

> Throughout the century, Stockbridge's significant men and women fell into three groups: those who attained distinction after they had gone out in the world; those who acquired it while remaining at home; and those who arrived already garlanded. The Fields and the Hopkinses are bracketed in the first category. More than their destiny a natural affinity links them; plain living, high thinking and a plenitude of ability, set in relief by scarcity of cash. In a fluid society still to be moulded by vigorous hands, the American tradition of success could flourish. Ability inevitably rose to the top.

This had already proved true of David Dudley and was proving true of Jonathan and Matthew. Jonathan, miserably homesick, wrote Cyrus frequently, begging for news from Stockbridge, and advocating patience. "And in the meantime you must pay a great deal of attention to spelling, writing, and arithmetic. If you intend to become a merchant you will require all of these . . . you must prepare yourself."

Cyrus was indeed considering becoming a merchant in New York and he found David Dudley junior at his side. David had connections; he offered to get Cyrus an apprenticeship at A. T. Stewart's, the city's leading dry goods store. There were one or two other Berkshire boys employed there, including Marc Goodrich, son of a wealthy Berkshire family. In three years Cyrus would graduate into the booming world of merchandising. He could live with David until he found quarters of his own.

It was as much a wrench to leave Stockbridge as for his family to let Cyrus go. Restraining tears, Submit packed his portmanteau with the shirts, stockings, coats, and jackets she had made for him, and added some sage cheese and quince jelly sandwiches for the journey. Equally stoic and practical, Field gave him $8 from the family's thin savings; Cyrus protested, till his father assured him he could pay it back in small installments. He told Cyrus, "You have never shirked any of your obligations, no matter what tempted you to do so, and I have faith in whatever you decide to do."

Then, in his study, he asked Cyrus to kneel and pray with him, as had all his departing sons. It was the only possible parting for a man of faith, and Cyrus remembered it to the end of his days: the smarting eyes; the feeling of love for this venerable man, whose voice was beginning to falter with emotion and advancing age. Rising, the minister selected two books from his precious library: the inevitable Bible and the copy of *Pilgrim's Progress* Cyrus had long cherished.

From Stockbridge to New York was a twenty-four-hour journey—by coach across the Berkshires to the seafaring town of Hudson (fare $1.75) and down the waterway by Hudson River sloop, a broad two-masted affair fifty feet long with passengers and livestock crammed on deck or wherever they would fit below.

Aboard that ungainly vessel, cold and homesick, he was unknowingly coursing down a sort of Glory Road—preceded and shortly to be followed by many young men like himself in quest of fame.

3

Apprentice in New York

✦✦✦✦✦✦✦✦✦✦✦✦ It was a "queer little city," the New York of 1835, a bustling hive of 250,000 persons crowded in avenues and alleyways that stretched north from the Battery to Canal Street. On both sides of Manhattan stood the tall masts of square-riggers bringing wealth and merchandise from Europe and the Orient. Up the Hudson the Erie Canal had opened the promise of the fast-expanding West. Broadway and the Bowery were lined with the stately homes of merchant princes, while the cobblestone avenues were crossed by dirt streets where pigs still rooted. To a boy from Stockbridge, everything was startlingly unfamiliar: horsecars and gaslights; oyster bars and brothels; and the swarm of multilingual immigrants who brought fresh life, fresh hopes and dreams, to the community.

Cyrus' first stop was at David Dudley's quarters on suburban Broadway and Canal Street. Dudley (as he was now known, having dropped the David to avoid confusion with his father's name) was married to Jane Lucinda Hopkins, a cousin of Mark Hopkins', and would shortly be moving to a more spacious home farther down the avenue; but he was able to put Cyrus up and brief him on what he could expect. The backbone of Manhattan was New England. Many of the top names in the areas of finance, trade, and commerce—Phelps, Morgan, Griswold, Peabody, and Howe—were from western Massachusetts and Connecticut, and a common after-dinner toast at that time was to "New England habits! Industry, enterprise, and shrewdness!"

The next day Cyrus checked in at Stewart's, then at 257 Broadway, south of Warren Street. Alexander Stewart was a quiet, generally considerate man, with a gentle manner covering a hard core of astuteness.

He subscribed to the merchant's code of the time—that his clerks "should abstain from drink of every kind, from theatres, from late hours, and from houses of ill-fame." Beyond that, he insisted that they be prompt, well mannered, and presentable. Cyrus more than measured up to these requirements. Although he was to start as errand boy, it was understood that he would shortly be promoted to the selling counters.

Starting out, like Cyrus, young and almost penniless, Stewart had gambled on a small store down in Chambers Street. When it failed, he sold his remaining stock at a loss and started again. When he considered the moment right, he staked his last cent on a marble palace on the "wrong side" of Broadway, an establishment promptly christened Stewart's Folly. He put his clerks in full dress, bought for cash alone to undersell competitors, and relied on honest value to produce results.

It did. In the 1830's and thereafter, Stewart's was the cathedral of the dry goods business in New York—the prototype of the later department store. It catered to the carriage trade, mostly to women seeking frocks and fabrics from abroad. Stewart was a man of taste, of consciously acquired manners, and of wily salesmanship. He dressed like a clergyman, his upper lip clean-shaven, his beard devoutly trimmed. Greeting his customers with an Old World deference, he set a high standard for floorwalkers, whom he introduced into the New York retail scene.

That evening Cyrus found lodgings in a boarding house on Murray Street, just around the corner from the store. In the square drab room with faded wallpaper, sparse pine furniture, small fireplace for heat, he unpacked and stowed his homemade woolen underwear, cotton shirts, and linen collars; hung up his Sunday clothes and straw hat, dirtied by the journey; stacked his copies of the Bible, *Pilgrim's Progress,* and assorted penny magazines; looked out his window at the brownstone fronts across the rutted street and must have thought of the April green of Stockbridge.

He could hardly wait for Sunday at Dudley's for the midday meal of Yorkshire pudding and roast beef, and to be with the family. His longing and loneliness were so apparent that Dr. Hopkins, also a dinner guest, felt called upon to write his parents (who had worried so much about him that they thought of urging his return): "I would not give much for a boy if he were not homesick on leaving home."

He received prompt letters from his father, his sister Mary, and his brothers Jonathan and Henry. His father sent him a genealogy and record of the Fields, to serve as a sort of vade mecum. Cyrus thanked him, adding, "But I wish to know also from whom we are descended on my mother's side." Always it was Submit. "Take good care of mother," he pleaded in one letter; "tell her she must not get overdone."

Cyrus was financially handicapped from the start. His pay at Stewart's was just $50 for the first year. His room and board were $2 a week. Somehow he felt compelled to send his accounts back home, along with suitable explanations. Most of the items were concerned with keeping up appearances:

To hair cutting	12½ ¢
To one vial of spirits of turpentine (to get spots out of coat)	6¼ ¢
To get shoes mended	18¾ ¢
To one pair of shoe-brushes	25 ¢
To one box of blacking	12½ ¢
To two papers of tobacco to put in trunks to prevent moths getting in	12½ ¢
To one straw hat (the one that I brought from home got burned and was so dirty that David thought I had better get me a new one)	$1.00

Of his only indulgence he quickly repented—namely, "Paid to David for Penny Magazines, $2.00 (I am not going to take them any longer)."

He continued to get his clothes from home and when he was promoted from errand boy to clerk, he became permanently careful of his dress and appearance. "Mary wrote to me to know of what color I would have my frock-coat; tell mother instead of having a linen frock-coat that I would prefer another linen roundabout, as they are much better in a store." In a subsequent letter he told his mother, "I wish you would make for me, as soon as convenient, a black broadcloth *coat with skirts,* and covered buttons, and as I wish it for a dress-coat the cloth must be *very fine and made extremely nice.* You cannot be too particular about it."

He observed his long work hours dutifully. In a journal that he later kept (though intermittently), he noted: "I always made it a point to be there before the partners came and never to leave before the partners left. . . . My ambition was to make myself a thoroughly good merchant. I tried to learn in every department all I possibly could, knowing I had to depend entirely on myself."

In keeping with this ambition, he often worked late into the evening; this took care of otherwise lonely hours. Stewart would sometimes work all night. He knew that dry goods deteriorate from lying on the shelves, and was given to holding cost sales and advertising them:

> Mr. A. T. Stewart, having purchased a large amount of goods soon to arrive, is obliged, in order to make room for these, to dispose of all the stock he has on hand, which will be sold at Actual Cost, beginning Monday at eight A.M. Ladies are requested to come early and avoid the crush.

Prior to such events, he and Cyrus, along with other clerks of Field's bent, would take down everything in the store, and Stewart would mark it at a price that he was confident would move it quickly. When Cyrus noted that he often put the price *below* cost, he became somewhat alarmed.

"The business is in keeping the stuff moving. Never have anything dead on your shelves," Stewart told him.

When Cyrus wondered why his employer did not advertise the fact that he was offering merchandise below cost, Stewart said: "Young man, you must tell the customer only what she will believe. The actual truth is for ourselves."

Cyrus had little time for recreation that first summer. A surreptitious visit to the theater, where a designated area was reserved for prostitutes, was something that he carefully omitted from his letters home. Mostly he would wander over to the Hudson River banks, then as green as those of the Housatonic, and watch the white-sailed traffic on the river.

He went upriver to New England as often as he could—to Stockbridge, to his aunts in Guilford, to his brother Matthew in Lee. With only Sundays off, it meant a night's ride both ways, without sleep, but it was worth it. Between visits he implored his family to "tell me of all things that happen at home in good old Stockbridge."

That October he wrote to his mother: "Brother Timothy sailed the day that I got back from Southwick; I received a letter from him a few days ago. He sent his love to you, father, and all friends, but had time to write only a few words as they passed a vessel. He says the captain is a pious man, and that they have prayers morning and evening." A few months later news came that Timothy had shipped out from New Orleans on a schooner bound for South America. The vessel was never again heard from, but such was the faith of the Fields that it was many years before they would accept the grim fact that Timothy was lost at sea.

When winter evenings hung on his hands, Cyrus was happily directed to the Mercantile Library Association, in the Clinton Hall on Nassau Street. To a considerable extent, the Association helped make up for the college life Cyrus missed. Few of the other clerks were college graduates but fewer still, only about 200 at the time, were taking advantage of this gaslit little center of learning—offering a reading room, a lecture and debating hall, and a library (which excluded "all works of an immoral or irreligious tendency"). It also sponsored lectures by such eminent speakers as Longfellow, Emerson, and Horace Mann.

In a society not much given to reading, against a background of limited exposure to books, Cyrus found in the Mercantile Library much to widen his horizons. Here he read Cooper for the first time, Irving's *Sketch Book,* the works of Dickens that were coming over by packet in installments. He discovered the writings of Thomas Paine and William Ellery Channing, and his narrow Massachusetts world became that much diminished. Where once the Bible and the classics, with a smattering of mathematics, had been the limits of his education, he was now exposed to contemporary life and thinking.

He also joined an informal discussion and debating group known as the Eclectic Fraternity, which met every Saturday in a fourth-floor room above a leathershop. Here he polished his facility for public speaking. He was basically an extrovert, forthright, gregarious, and generous.

All around him at that time and in that city, forces and circumstances were determining his future. The Erie Canal had opened up the West; the railroad was on its way, as was the telegraph—both symbols of a new inventive fever in the land. Jeffersonian optimism and prosperity were in the air. Philip McDonald later noted: "The typical American predilection for action, exploitation, and progress was demonstrating itself." There was no conceivable way for anyone to go but up.

Even disaster was somehow stimulating. Cyrus pridefully recorded that the fire of 1835 was "the largest ever known in this country" and made a list of the losses, which included 674 buildings burned and thirty acres "of the richest part" destroyed. Though it was bitterly cold and windy, he threw himself into the action, getting drenched and frozen in the bargain. On Christmas Day he wrote to his father: "I was up all night to the fire, and last Sunday was on duty with David as a guard to prevent people from going to the ruins to steal property that was saved from the fire and laying in heaps on the streets."

The city rallied quickly; new construction temporarily revived the business boom. With many of his competitors put out of business, Alexander Stewart prospered; Field's salary, by previous agreement, was doubled to $100 annually as his second year began.

Whenever he was able to put aside a little money, his first thought was to visit Stockbridge, the fare by steamer to Hudson being all of 50 cents. He had become friendly with Marc Goodrich, his fellow clerk from Berkshire County, and finally invited Marc to join him. This pilgrimage to a common shrine cemented their relationship, with the result that they moved into joint lodgings when they got back to the city. In their new quarters, he told his father, "Goodrich and myself take turns in reading a chapter of the Bible every night before we go to bed . . . we have got as far as the 25th chapter of Genesis."

The arrangement lightened his expenses, made him more independent of the family and Dudley. He hated being in debt or being unable to repay any and all favors with interest. When he sent his family, at their request, some goods from Stewart's valued at $8.27½, he wrote: "Father has let me have $25 00 since I have been in New York, and if he wishes me I will pay him the above amount and then I shall be indebted to him $16 62½. I will send the balance in money or obtain that amount of goods for him here at any time." But his conscience was not satisfied. A few days later he sent his father a silk handkerchief, "which I wish you to accept for interest on the $25 you lent me."

He began to show a concern for politics, which never left him. While he was a part and almost a product of the Jacksonian era, he was by instinct and heredity a confirmed Whig; all good men of Massachusetts were. In a letter written to his father in April, 1837, he noted: "The election was closed and the Whigs have elected Aaron Clark as their candidate for Mayor by a majority of 5,000 votes. Good." Contrary to the national pattern, Clark was subsequently elected in November, and diarist Philip Hone observed: "New York has broken her chains and stands erect, regenerated." While too young, of course, to vote, Cyrus at the time leaned politically toward Clay and Webster.

He was now a senior clerk at Stewart's, acquiring polish and self-confidence in handling difficult customers. Stewart had all the manners of a parson and all the astuteness of a rogue. He was a master salesman, and Cyrus quickly acquired much of his technique. Young Field enjoyed being able to present and sell the critical qualities of products he believed in, and Stewart's merchandise was good.

Writing in *Valentine's Manual of Old New York,* John Crawford Brown recorded: "One of the rare and valuable qualities of a businessman—that of being able to select the right man for a position—was possessed in the highest degree by Mr. Stewart. He never put a round peg into a square hole." His intuition made Cyrus something of a favorite on the staff.

A contemporary writer, Matthew H. Smith, observed of Mr. Stewart that he was intolerant of any idleness among his clerks and, when not in his office, was found "walking about the store, with a quiet tread, as if his foot was clothed with velvet—up stairs and down stairs, all around, with a keen, quick, vigilant eye, searching in all places and all departments, taking in everybody and everything as he passes." It fell upon young Cyrus to devise some method of forewarning his associates of these incursions. Jackson Schultz recalled years later: "Mr. Field was in the habit of watching the old gentleman, and by a sort of tick, tick, giving notice to his fellow-clerks of the fact that he was coming, so that every man was in his place; and from that simple idea Mr. Field got the idea of telegraphing, which had made his fortune." It was a tongue-in-cheek conclusion, which Alexander Stewart, generally aware of what was going on, liked to keep alive by telling people, "Perhaps you don't know that *I* taught Cyrus everything he knows about telegraphy."

Hours were strictly observed at Stewart's; any clerk who was late to work or spent too much time at lunch was fined, and Stewart directed that the accumulated fines be donated to any charity the clerks selected. By popular vote, Cyrus was elected treasurer of this fund. When the first round of fines had been collected, he called the group to a meeting to decide on the charity. The meeting place was a popular oyster bar on Broadway, and the first motion carried was to deduct the price of the dinner from the fund, as an administrative expense. Cyrus then promoted a resolution that there was no more needy or deserving charity than the clerks at A. T. Stewart's. A motion was passed unanimously to distribute the remaining money equally among the staff, after which the meeting adjourned in the early-morning hours.

Cyrus recalled:

> Some one of the clerks or waiters told Mr. Stewart of what had occurred, and we were all requested to remain at the store the next evening after business hours, when Mr. Stewart called me up and asked me to give an account of what had been done with the funds paid to me the previous evening. I told him the exact truth in regard to the matter, when he dismissed us, saying that in the future we should be very careful in selecting the object of charity that this fund was given to.

That Stewart's ire was tempered by admiration is suggested by his raising Field's pay to $300 annually at the beginning of his third and final year.

In spite of his popularity with Stewart's staff, the companionship of Goodrich, and homelife from time to time with David Dudley and his wife, Lucinda, Cyrus never completely overcame his homesickness. The malady was sharpened by a temporary break in his ties with Stockbridge. Early in 1837 Cyrus' father was recalled to Haddam, "where the church had become divided, and it seemed probable that he alone could unite them." He asked for dismissal from his post in Stockbridge and returned to the parish where he had been ordained; at about the same time he received the degree of Doctor of Divinity from Williams.

To Cyrus the move was something of a blow; so much of his past and so many of his memories were linked to the village and the parsonage. But if the break were to be made, he wanted it complete, with no mnemonic traces left behind. He wrote to his mother late in January: "I am sorry that father is going to leave that beautiful place Stockbridge, but when you do move to Haddam I hope that you will take everything, even the old and good dog Rover."

A few months later, when the panic of 1837 struck, Cyrus was only a sideline observer but it taught him at least one unforgettable lesson. As Professor Robert G. Albion noted, the crash not only ushered in a five-year economic slump, but also "concentrated attention upon the importance of determining the soundness of credit." As Cyrus witnessed the failure of seven out of ten established businesses, he must have concluded that respect for credit was a basic platform of success. Five years later, in business on his own, there hung above his desk a single sign, asking his interviewers before they could state their proposition, "Are you Insured?"

Whether the panic influenced his next move is hard to say. One thing is certain: he was not content, although he had learned a lot from his apprenticeship. The sense of urgency had never left him. Almost a quarter of his life had passed; he had to hurry! He started studying at night with "writing masters" who advertised courses "after candlelight" in bookkeeping and penmanship. He also developed a writing style that had the grace and sharpness of a fine engraving.

He had always kept in close touch with his older brother Matthew, who had married Clarissa Laflin, a niece of Matthew Laflin, who, in 1824, all but blew up the town of Lee when his powder mill exploded. He rebuilt the mill, but was persuaded by apprehensive neighbors to convert it into paper manufacture and thus became, along with Zenas Crane of Dalton, one of the pioneers who made the region along the upper Housatonic the center of the papermaking industry in the United States. He also became a pioneer in wearing apparel made of paper by producing, among other manufactures, paper bonnets for young ladies.

There were now two Laflin mills in Lee. One, the Columbia Paper Mill, where Matthew Field had started, was built in 1826 on the site of the explosion. A second mill was built the following year, a little farther upstream. When Laflin's sons inherited the second mill, young Matthew Field was able to buy the Columbia plant with a partner, named George Phelps, who manufactured tinware in the town of Lenox.

There was only one thing wrong. Matthew was no businessman. His father had marked him out to be a farmer; he was husky and broad-shouldered and liked working out of doors with his hands. Too, he had natural mechanical ability, but papermaking had not yet been mechanized. That he managed to become one of the leading paper manufacturers in western Massachusetts was due more to the booming nature of the business, which was almost self-propelling, than to any managerial ability. He knew he needed help. And it was agreed between them that Cyrus would join the firm as bookkeeper and general assistant.

Early in 1838 Cyrus informed his father: "I expect to go to Lee to live with Matthew on the 1st of March. He will give me two hundred and fifty dollars ($250) the first year, and my board and washing." A short while later he noted in his intermittent journal:

> I have been very busy for the last five or six weeks in the evening attending Mr. Wheeler's school to obtain a thorough knowledge of bookkeeping by double entry, so as to be able to keep Matthew's books when I go to Lee. . . . I have made arrangements with Matthew so that I shall not commence my year with him until the 1st of April.

Though he would have liked an interval at Haddam with his parents or at Stockbridge with his friends, he was careful to finish out his full apprenticeship at Stewart's. When Stewart urged him to stay on—even offering a good increase in salary—he refused. It was time to head off in a new direction. Dudley wrote to his parents shortly after Cyrus' resignation: "Cyrus has, as you will see from his letters, etc., left Stewart's, with the best of testimonials of esteem from all his employers and associates. He is a noble young man—and I am proud of him."

In his last week at Stewart's a dozen of his associates, "anxious to show their respect and esteem," tendered him a dinner at Delmonico's. At the same time he received a packet with a note from one of Stewart's senior partners:

> Dear Field—you will accept the accompanying trifle as a token of esteem and sincere friendship, and whatever may be your future pursuits, to know that they are successful will be a source of much gratification to
>
> William H. Bunours

The package containeed a diamond stickpin, which Cyrus wore for more than a quarter of a century.

There was a peripatetic interlude before he left for Massachusetts. For Dudley, who had some legal matters that required nonprofessional attention, he went as far west as Michigan, rode on a railway for the first time, acquired a fondness for traveling that surprised him. Up to now travel had meant leaving home. Now he found wheels were like dynamos recharging his own batteries. He came back tired, but somehow refreshed, and on April 1, 1838, went up by riverboat and stage to Lee.

4

Making of a Merchant

➤➤➤➤➤◄◄◄◄◄◄ In the 1830's, paper mills were springing up all along the Housatonic. But demand continued to exceed supply; room for expansion was unlimited. Field had chosen well when he joined his brother's operation. As bookkeeper and general assistant—one of eight men and twenty women—his salary was less than he would have got had he remained at Stewart's, but it included board and lodging. When the Columbia Paper Mill had been built, the Laflins had also erected a brick boardinghouse, "divided into four tenements, sufficiently large to accommodate twenty persons in each tenement." It was hardly cozy; but it kept expenses down, and for the first time Cyrus was able to save money.

As at Stewart's, he learned the business from the bottom up. Paper-making was a craft in those days, starting with the pure air of the Berkshires, the pure water of the Housatonic. Except for mechanical rollers to mat and dry the sheets, the whole operation was manual, and the pulp was made entirely from rags—either the remnants of New England textile mills or, more important, domestic wastes. Women were urged to sell their cast-off fabrics to the manufacturers for reasons of profit, patriotism ("Support Your Local Industry"), or sentiment—being reminded in advertisements that the shawl or handkerchief protecting maidenly bosoms would return to them as Valentines.

It was a family industry and remained so for decades to come, as the sons and daughters of its proprietors intermarried. This did not preclude a ruthless competition. To build a mill upstream of one's competitors was to take advantage of purer water and, to some extent, contaminate the water used by downstream millers. Although he was successful (it was hard to be anything else), Matthew, whose plant was downstream from one of the newer Laflin mills, was thus at something of a disadvantage from the start. And other mills were springing up so rapidly—there were more than 100 on the upper Housatonic—that competition took a quick and heavy toll.

Field's experience at Stewart's served him well. He had learned how to mix with people; his sincerity and natural enthusiasm generated confidence. Matthew quickly lifted him from his desk and sent him on the road as sales representative for Phelps & Field. Perhaps the greatest benefit young Cyrus gained from this experience lay in the friendships he established. He came to know such New York wholesale dealers as Elisha Root, Jeremiah Cross, and Chandler White. And he became acquainted with other New England paper-manufacturing families: Smiths, Hulberts, Cranes, and Churches.

Samuel Church had established one of the first mills in Lee, which was currently being operated by a grandson, Leonard Church. Leonard had a nephew, Frederick, some years younger than Cyrus, who aspired to become an artist. Though living in Hartford, Frederick Church spent much time in the neighborhood of Lee, looking for subjects for his pen and brush, and he and Field became close friends. Cyrus had little or no sense of art, but was fond of accompanying Church on Sunday walks around the countryside, and even persuaded Church to go to Madison and sketch his grandfather's home on the rock—a work that lies buried among Church's treasures at Olana on the Hudson.

Field found another close friend in Zenas Marshal Crane, some years his senior and a man to whom he could turn for advice. Zenas, along with his brother James, had inherited their father's mills in Dalton, roughly twenty miles from Lee and Stockbridge. Zenas and Cyrus began to visit each other frequently and, possibly violating his position with Matthew, Cyrus performed services for Zenas on his travels:

Lee, July 17, 1839

FRIEND CRANE:

 I expect to go to New York the last of next week and will purchase any article for you with the greatest of pleasure. *Do* come down and see a fellow on Sunday. I want to have a long chit-chat with you.

Ever your sincere friend,
CYRUS W. FIELD

All hands on deck for
September A.D. 1839.
A great year this —

The postscript referred to Zenas' forthcoming marriage to Caroline Laflin, an in-law cousin of Cyrus by virtue of Matthew's marriage to Clarissa. It further cemented their relationship. A few weeks later Cyrus wrote to "Dear Friend Crane: Cousin Caroline told me on Saturday that she had received a letter from you and that it was your wish that I should stand up with Miss Loomis, or some other young lady at your wedding."

For reasons he promised to explain but never did, Cyrus declined the wedding honor in a sentimental letter: "You are soon to be united in the holy bands of wedlock to one of the most beautiful and lovely Young Ladies on earth. May She long continue to be Your Guardian Angel of happiness—and may You always be with peace and plenty."

In a more practical vein, he engaged the carriage and team to take the couple on their honeymoon, and assured Zenas: "If there is anything I can do for You, let me know and I will do it with the greatest pleasure." He added with customary concern for his sartorial appearance: *"Don't forget the white Satin Stock."*

The "chit-chat" which he had mentioned was probably one of the many that he had with Zenas on the outlook for his future. Phelps & Field was falling behind the competition. Cyrus could see the writing on the wall and was thinking of purchasing a modest mill and going into business on his own.

No great investment was required. Costs had gone up since Zenas Crane had established his first mill in Dalton with less than $200 of capital, but a few thousand dollars was still good enough to buy a plant. Cyrus was told of a property in Westfield, known to the trade as Ruinsville. Perhaps the disreputable status of the mill appealed to him. He obtained a loan from the Westfield Bank, largely a Laflin institution, and bought the mill with the plan of putting it in order. But he never got it into operation.

One of the joys of working in the Housatonic Valley was that traveling for the company, especially to Hartford, gave him a chance to visit Haddam, Madison, and Guilford, where his parents, aunts and uncles were. At Guilford he again met Mary Bryan Stone, the pigtailed, bonneted companion of his summer days in Guilford. Pigtailed and bonneted no longer, Mary had bloomed with a haunting, Dresden-china kind of beauty: dark hair, luminous brown eyes, and a softly molded figure.

Her father had died in 1822, and the family being in straitened circumstances, she had been brought up by grandparents. Eventually she taught school for her living. It was not precisely a satisfying life for someone with a sharp, determined mind, impatient temper, and insatiable ambition. Undoubtedly she fell genuinely in love with Cyrus, as he did with her, but she may also have seen in Cyrus a passport to a new and wider world.

Hartford, not far from Guilford, was a leading book-publishing center and paper market. This gave Cyrus an excuse to see Mary often and a chance to come to terms on marriage. Probably it was because of Mary and the sudden need for an established income that he made what could have been a serious mistake.

On his trips to New York for Phelps & Field, he frequently saw Elisha Root, a wholesale paper dealer, whose commission house was one of several outlets for their products. E. Root & Company was strictly second-rate; the Cranes, for example, would have no dealings with it. But Elisha saw in Cyrus' inexhaustible energy, persistence, and attractive presence something he needed to survive. Root & Company had suffered badly in the crash of 1837; it was heavily in debt —which Cyrus surely did not know—and was only hanging on from day to day, hoping for some transfusion of new blood.

Elisha offered Cyrus a junior partnership in Root & Company. It seemed, on the surface, to tender more stability and income than the incipient Westfield mill could promise. And it was in New York, where Mary longed to live and where he chose to be. He accepted the offer and wrote during the week of his twenty-first birthday:

New York, November 25, 1840

MY DEAR PARENTS,—I have only time to write a few lines and will come to the point at once.

The writer of this intends to be joined in the bonds of matrimony to Miss Mary B. Stone one week from this day, that is, on next Wednesday morning, December 2, 1840, at 10 o'clock A.M., and requests the pleasure of meeting you both, with sister Mary, at the house of Mr. A. S. Fowler in Guilford, at the above-mentioned time. David and Stephen will be there. We expect father will perform the ceremony. I shall leave here Tuesday in the New Haven steamboat, and you will find me Wednesday morning at Bradley's Hotel in Guilford, where you had better all stop.

There will be *only* a *very* few friends at the wedding. Shall leave immediately after the ceremony is over for New Haven, and from there come to this city.

If Henry is at home bring him with you, and send to Middletown for Mary.

With much love to all at home,
I remain your affectionate son,
CYRUS W. FIELD

It was a quiet wedding. Cake and wine were served, after which the couple drove to New Haven to spend the evening with Mary's cousins and her brother, Joseph Stone.

Typically, Cyrus dispensed with time off for a honeymoon, and Mary evidently agreed with this. They left New Haven the next day by steamer for New York and moved into lodgings that Cyrus had prepared at Mrs. Mason's house on Broad Street. Here Mary set up housekeeping—bravely making the best of brackish water from the corner pump, firewood purchased from the vendor's cart, and all the other unfamiliar inconveniences of city life. Cyrus faithfully kept a day-to-day accounting of expenses, of which their first week's record is a sample:

To bill for board for 2 months	120	00
To bill for vaccination	1	00
To figs and crackers		17
To oysters and laudanum		22
To doctor's bill—one visit	1	00

Their total outlay for that first year, including everything from a box of pencil leads to repairing a silk hat, came to $1,467.12. But the most significant item, appearing that autumn in the ledger, was $2 for a willow cradle. The first of their four daughters, Mary Grace, was born in October, 1841.

Some months before Cyrus paid for the cradle, he had suffered a rude and unexpected blow. Root & Company finally succumbed to the aftereffects of the 1837 panic and went bankrupt. Of the catastrophe, he later noted in his journal:

> In six months E. Root & Co. failed, with large liabilities, and though I was not the principal of the firm, yet on me fell the loss and the burden of paying its debts. Such was the condition in which I started in life, without capital or credit or business, and with a heavy load of debt upon me. We were for many months afterwards getting the affairs settled. I dissolved the firm immediately and started on my own account. Some of the creditors came to see me, and those that did not come I went to see, and on the best terms I could settled and compromised and got released.

The self-pitying tone rings false. He was certainly not obliged to assume the "heavy load of debt," which was discharged from the remaining funds of Root & Company. And while it is true that he was "without capital or credit," he was not without a business. By settling the obligations of his former employer—for thirty cents on the dollar —he established himself in the trade and overnight acquired enough stature to create a business of his own.

He opened offices at 9 Burling Slip under the name of Cyrus W. Field & Company. The "& Company" referred to his brother-in-law, Joseph F. Stone, whom Mary had urged him to take into partnership. It was one of many concessions made to Mary, and the best that can be said for it is that no harm was done. Stone was a likable, ineffectual man, little more than an understudy in the company's affairs.

More astutely, Cyrus hired—along with his own nephew Heman, Matthew's son—a young nephew of Zenas Crane, Wells Laflin, as a fledgling clerk. This was almost certainly a bid to cement relations between Crane & Company and Field's new firm. Whereas neither of the Crane brothers had favored Elisha Root with any business, they now began sending paper down in wholesale lots to Cyrus and conversely started buying much of their supplies—rags, bleaches, dyes, and wire netting—through Field's office.

Neither Field nor Crane had an exclusive contract with the other; both dealt with outside firms. But the relationship was so close that the offices on Burling Slip became almost an adjunct of the Dalton mills. And everything worked in Field's favor. Crane concentrated not so much on newsprint as on fine book and business papers. This gave Cyrus a certain status that Root & Company had never had. His first transaction, dated March 1, 1842, was the sale of "a small lot of Domestic Rags, sent you this day, by steamboat Columbia, which I hope will come duly to hand, and if you like them, will send more." The bill was $42.79—the first money he had ever earned in his own right.

With a second child on the way, Cyrus and Mary looked for more substantial quarters. Business was still bad and rents were low. They took a house at 87 East Seventeenth Street near Third Avenue, then considered practically suburban. Dudley Field complained that it was too remote for the families to get together often, then moved his own family from their house downtown to one that was back to back with Cyrus'.

There were no servants, but the opening of the Croton Aqueduct saved Mary from hauling water from the local pump. She still did all the housework and made and mended her husband's clothes. And Cyrus still kept an exact accounting of the family's expenses. Some of the items for that year are a study in frugality:

June	12, to cutting coat, vest, 2 pair pants	$ 1.75
"	15, to soap, 8 cents; pepper, 5 cents; tobacco and linen	.32
July	4, to Niblo's Garden, M. E. F., M. S., and C. W. F.	1.50
"	6, to Dr. Paine, $1; pill, 6 cents	1.06
Aug.	7, to letter to and one from Mrs. Field	.25
Oct.	1, to W. H. Popham, 7 tons coal	37.75
Nov.	18, to shoestrings, 5 cents; tacks, 19 cents	.24
"	22, to *Tribune*, 2 weeks	.18

Total family expenditures for the year amounted to $1,482.79, and it is interesting to note that for the following year, 1843, they were $13.74 less.

The item recorded on July 4 was a celebration at Niblo's Garden, a place of genteel entertainment at Broadway and Prince Street. The initials M. E. F. stand for Mary Elizabeth Field, his younger sister, toward whom he continued to feel protective. Mary was studying to become a writer, and came to visit them as often as Cyrus could persuade her to, during which time she and Joseph Stone became warm friends.

Field spent little time in the new house, leaving the household cares to Mary, who by now had another daughter, Alice Durand, born in November, 1843. He worked like a man possessed, breakfasting by candlelight and leaving for the office before sunrise, taking his midday dinner with him and staying long after Joe Stone and the staff had left. Factors within the industry were working for him, too. There had been a tremendous boom in the demand for paper—especially for the quality papers which Field handled.

Wrote William O. Stoddard:

> The paper business was itself in its infancy. From that time on the demand and consumption were to increase with marvellous rapidity. So were all the machinery and appliances of manufacture and the sources of supply of varied materials. It was with reference to this development of the business he had selected that the peculiar faculties of Mr. Field came out in strong contrast with those of some

of his slower-footed competitors in the paper trade. He grew with the growth of the demand, meeting it with shrewdness and enterprise.

With Field & Company a going concern, Cyrus bought back the full rights to the Westfield mill, and spent some money getting it in shape. In midsummer, 1844, he wrote to Zenas: "The mill at Westfield will soon be in good running order, and I should like to sell it to You. Will meet you at Westfield any day *next week* that you may name. All of you come, and we can trade."

He could not resist a typical bit of salesmanship and flattery: "I have several offers to purchase or rent the mill: but they are from Strangers, and I should prefer to deal with some one that I know."

Apparently Zenas was not interested, but Field managed to sell the mill to unrecorded purchasers and at once reinvested the money in 180 acres of land upriver from this property, with a grist mill on a waterfall. He again looked to Zenas as his most likely prospect:

> I have sold all my interest in the Westfield Paper Mill, and now own the Water Power on Westfield River—known as the "Great Falls." It is in the town of Russell, Mass. and twenty miles *west* of Springfield. The Western Rail Road runs within a few rods of the Falls. The water power is very great, there being a fall of over thirty feet, and *all* the water can be used for manufacturing purposes. . . .
> Do you know of anyone that wishes to purchase this property? I will sell it low.

He thereupon chartered one of the wood-burning locomotives of the Western Railroad and offered to take prospective buyers to the site by special train, with the promise of a free meal when they got there. Again, Zenas did not accept; but the property was sold to Charles O. Chapin and Henry Gould.

The relationship between Cyrus Field and Crane & Company flourished, and Cyrus was able to report at the beginning of 1845 that "business is very good here." The bill accompanying the notice was for a substantial $1,435.60 for rags, nails, wire, powder, and ultramarine. He was not only supplying a large part of Crane's raw materials, but when Zenas imported skilled labor from abroad, it was Field who arranged for passages with the Cunard Line and directed the immigrants up to Dalton. Whenever they came to the city, Zenas and Caroline stayed with the Fields on Seventeenth Street. Cyrus now felt entitled to service other clients, and these included such giants in the industry as the Smiths, Hubbards, Carsons, and Hollisters. Of his relations with the Hollisters, the trade journal *Superior Facts* observed in retrospect:

> Field was a very clever merchant and it was said of him that when he bargained he would close his eyes; and if he closed but one eye the one with whom he was dealing might get by; but should he close both eyes the other man did not have a chance in the world. Evidently in dealing with the Hollisters he had both eyes closed very tight, for they contracted with him November 20, 1844, to take the product of the [Hollister] mill and gave a $5,000.00 bond secured by a mortgage on their mill to pledge the fulfillment of the contract. The mill was destroyed by fire December, 1846, with a reported loss of $12,000 and insurance amounting to $8,000.00. They settled with Cyrus Field on June 14, 1847, and the contract was cancelled.

At the time of the settlement, Field could not resist writing to Zenas: "I did not lose a cent on this transaction."

The incident suggests how well he had learned his lesson from the fire of 1835, during his first year in New York. According to a friend, Jackson Schultz:

> He had peculiarities then as he has always had. One I recollect was, he had over his desk "Are you insured?" For no one that is not insured could get credit of him. He could not afford, he said, to insure himself and others too. Thus in all his transactions he had ideas and principles to carry out, but always good principles and ideas.

Field had been in business on his own for only two years; he was barely twenty-five; yet he was able to demand and get substantial guarantees from leading paper manufacturers *before* he agreed to handle the output of their mills. In addition, he was selective about the types and qualities of paper that he would handle.

He had learned, for example, the sales appeal of color, in fabrics and in merchandise displays. Colored paper, though not new, was in limited use. He now urged Crane to concentrate on tinted papers.

> We have bartered with the Hubbards for a large amount of their coloured papers this last year *besides* selling them Rags, Powder, etc. etc. . . . But if you should decide to make coloured papers and make me the Agent for them I should of course discontinue my trade with the Hubbards, so far as buying their papers are concerned. . . . I am confident that it would be as *well* for you to have one agent here for then we could fix a fair price and never deviate.

He then specified that Crane was to make colored papers that were either better in quality or the same quality at a lower price to meet the Hubbard competition. Crane replied affirmatively, and Field began shipping dyes to Dalton in almost every color: green, orange, yellow, pink, buff, brown, and blue. When the colors came out on paper somewhat differently from what he had expected, he gave them exotic names: peach, corn, salmon, pear, tea—and even black tea and offered his customers a "Super blue," a "Super-fine blue," and an "*Extra* super blue."

The promotion of color proved profitable. To Crane & Company he wrote: "We are getting your paper introduced and are selling to persons daily who had been using Hubbard's." Later: "I never knew of so good a demand for paper—it sells quick and at good prices." Still later: "You will see by our sales that we are doing well with your paper. It is bad for you that your assortment has been so broken— but in future we hope you will be able to do better." The reference to sales applied to a 50 percent increase, from roughly $43,000 to $65,000, in the first three months of 1846.

He was now somewhat in the position of a merchandising counselor and did not hesitate to insist that his advice be followed. He forwarded a precept that they both should adopt: "To make a *good paper,* to make it *always one quality,* & *one weight,* & always to have it sold for *one price.*" He suggested adding, to their line of colors, glazed or glossy-coated paper: "I do think that you can make a good glazed paper & one that will pay you well." When Crane responded by making and sending the requested stock, Field wrote enthusiastically: "We have got the customers. Let us know if we can depend upon you for all the glazed paper we can sell."

He ran his business with respect to Crane as if he were a functioning part of their operation. "We have in stock some prime white rags 5¾ ¢. How many tons shall we send you?" Frequently he let fall the name of a competitor as a fillip: "You will of course give us an order for your winter's stock of bleaching powder—price only 4½ ¢ per lb. Messrs. D. Carson & Sons have had them, and can inform you of the quality."

Even though the Field brood was expanding (another daughter, Isabella, was born in 1846), Cyrus spent little time at home except on Sundays. They regularly attended the Central Presbyterian Church on Broome Street, where Dr. William Adams preached. Adams was a

Massachusetts man, later to be regarded as perhaps the leading Presbyterian clergyman of his time. He became active in the Evangelical Alliance and the Board of Foreign Missionaries, as well as a founder of the Union Theological Seminary. He appears to have taken a deep interest in Cyrus and Mary, for as time went on and Field's widening horizons took him far from home, Adams followed his progress with a personal concern expressed in frequent letters to them both.

Life was moving fast, and Field was running to keep up with it. Change was the order of the Fabulous Forties. Railroads were booming, spreading from the Eastern seaboard to the Middle West. Steam was replacing sail in coastal and transatlantic trade. Imports from Europe could reach Dalton in a third less time than when Field had opened his office. This accelerated pace was like adrenalin to Cyrus, speeding up not just the company operation, but his own expenditure of energy. He never shared responsibility with Joseph Stone and never delegated work if he could possibly handle it himself. "All business entrusted to me," he wrote, "was done promptly and quickly. I attended to every detail of the business, and made a point of answering every letter on the day it was received."

In spite of the pressure of work, he began to expand the range of his interests. There was less need for strict economy now, and he started collecting paintings, especially those of the Hudson River school, which his friend Frederick Church was following. He also continued the interest that he had in fossils when he and Mary collected shells as children. When he read that W. H. Pease of Albany was offering for sale a cabinet containing 1,500 specimens of rock and fossils, he promptly bought the collection, enjoyed its novelty for several weeks, and then presented it to James Hall, professor of zoology at New York University.

Perhaps from his days of signaling the clerks by code at A. T. Stewart's he also acquired an interest in the new invention of telegraphy, the most significant development of that decade. Along with the electric telegraph, mechanical improvements in printing were boosting the number and circulation of books and newspapers. Horace Greeley's *Tribune* now vied with James Gordon Bennett's *Herald* in New York, and the penny daily came into its own.

While Field handled little or no newsprint, this general awakening of news and information media sent the entire paper business soaring. And the telegraph itself—reaching from New England to the Mississippi—was an invention that had special appeal to him. It meant speed, it satisfied his need for hurry, and it expedited business. The New York *Journal of Commerce,* itself benefiting by the new invention, told its readers: "The telegraph enables New York merchants to order paper in Massachusetts at any moment, and receive the return, manufactured and even ruled, by almost the next steamer."

In balancing his books for 1847, Cyrus reported to Zenas, as he evidently felt obliged to do: "Our business is large, safe, well-established and profitable, and we are daily adding to our capital. Our sales last year were $354,432.60, and our bad and doubtful debts together do not, as far as we can ascertain, amount to over one half (½) of one per cent." He noted that the firm had cash reserves of $67,807.27 and that his life was insured for $10,000, and he expressed the hope that Crane and Field would continue to function as a mutually profitable team. He followed this up with a more personal communication: "We have this day sent you by Wells & Co. express one basket of peaches which accept as a present. You had better obtain them from the express at once as they will not keep well in this hot weather."

By 1848, the Mexican War, which had added a vast southwestern territory to the nation, had been advantageously concluded. Gold was discovered at Sutter's Mill in California. Adhesive postage stamps promoted letter writing and increased the sale of paper. Steamers began running regularly between Liverpool, Southampton, and New York; the Harlem and the Erie railroads now extended well into the hinterland. People began to hum the tunes of Stephen Foster, and Christy's Minstrels came to town. The works of Dickens, Thackeray, Macaulay, and the Brontë sisters occupied the literate. Mary and Cyrus welcomed another daughter, Frances ("Fanny") Griswold and the sales of Field & Company reached an all-time high of more than $438,980. This brought total sales, for a three-year period beginning with 1846, to well over $1,000,000—an extraordinary volume by the standards of the era.

With the vast expansion of American business, paper on which to issue bonds was being produced by Crane & Company and marketed by Cyrus. (Bond paper was, in fact, so named from this use.) Now Crane moved into an area they were later to monopolize: production of bank note paper. It caused no great flurry in the trade, but Field's own position was appreciably strengthened by the receipt of one short document signed by Zenas:

We agree to supply C. W. Field & Co. with our regular qualities of Bank Note Paper, what they can sell, on the following terms, viz: C. W. Field & Co. . . . are to put the article into the market at $12.00 per 1000 and as fast as the paper is sold pass it to our credit at $10.00 per 1000, free of commissions.

With this in his pocket, Field was probably in as strong a position as he would ever be, although his business was assured of growth. But the achievement had taken its physical toll. His daughter Isabella later wrote: "The excitement and work of the past fourteen years had told very decidedly upon him, and perfect rest was imperative." On the advice of his physician, Dr. Paine, he agreed to a trip abroad with Mary, and they arranged to put the children in the care of Mary's sister in New Haven.

Undoubtedly he was somewhat appalled at the idea of taking months off from his work; but his sister Mary and his brother Stephen were in Paris, and that was some attraction. Also, he probably sensed that the time might shortly come to head off in a new direction. Accordingly he booked passages on the new 860-ton *Victoria*. It was an understandable choice, for although he had complained in a letter to his father (who had been abroad the year before with Stephen) that the packets were too slow compared with steamers, the *Victoria* was something special. When her captain was asked why no ship up to now had been christened in honor of the English Queen, he gallantly replied that up to now there had been no vessel worthy of her name.

Typically Cyrus could not let these five months be wasted; it was a unique opportunity to make connections with the European paper market. He took one of the unused ledgers from Field & Company stock and began filling page after page with exercises in French, beginning with *Avez-vous le pain?* and progressing to more advanced queries, such as *Vôtre ami cherche-t-il le miroir que vous avez ou celui que j'ai?* If he were going to do business with a bunch of foreigners, he had better hurry up and learn the language.

5

The Grand Tour

⤔⤔⤔⤔⤔⤚⤚⤚⤚⤚⤚ Their trip to Europe was supposed to be, for Cyrus, a rest and relaxation. It could not have been less of one. From the moment they landed in Plymouth, their itinerary read like a satirized Cook's Tour: England, Ireland, Scotland, France, Switzerland, Italy, Austria, Germany and the Rhineland, Belgium, back to England—all in five months. Field later confided to a friend that the one word he learned in every language, upon crossing international borders, was "Faster!"

Europe itself was in a state of turmoil. Following the Year of Revolutions, the Continent was a still-burning coal in the ashes of its conflicts. It was a tumultuous time for the Fields' initial trip abroad. England alone was tranquil, and in London people seemed moving, rapidly and surely, toward prosperity and progress. The railroads, telegraph, mills, and foundries seemed far more advanced than in America. And geniuses like Michael Faraday, "with sparks and flashes at his finger tips," were introducing Britain to the electric age.

It was an age of new, extraordinary products to arouse Field's curiosity. Dr. William Montgomery had introduced a rubberlike substance from Malaya known as gutta-percha. It could be molded into plastic dolls, caps for cabmen, handles for surgical appliances, and railway conversation tubes. ("With these marvellous tubes passengers can converse in so soft a whisper as not to be overheard even by a fellow traveller. They are portable and will coil up so as to be placed inside the hat.") His Grace the Duke of Devonshire had one installed in church, running from the pulpit to his pew, so he could listen to the sermon without straining. More important, men like Michael Faraday had found in gutta-percha an effective form of insulation for telegraph wires—water-resistant, durable, and pliable. There was even fabulous talk that two brothers, John and Jacob Brett, aided by a young engineer named Willoughby Smith, were projecting a submarine cable across the English Channel by benefit of this new insulating substance.

Everywhere Field went, it was the same—optimism, progress, innovation and everywhere he felt at home in England. He was instinctively drawn to this kind of country. Fed by the riches of an empire, the whole island was a dynamo. If a great project were to be undertaken, this would be a land to turn to for support.

Cyrus and Mary both still looked surprisingly young, evidently too young, too interested in each other, to be readily accepted as a married couple. Attending service at a church in Scotland, an elderly lady next to them saw Mary brazenly sharing with her husband the same book of Psalms. "Remember that you are in a house of God!" that guardian of morals told her sharply.

On the Continent, they found conditions disturbing. Louis Philippe's regime had fallen—rocked by such scandals as the Praslin murder case, in which Henriette Desportes, by this time in New York and secretly being courted by Field's brother Henry Martyn, had played an incriminating role. Although Cyrus and Mary could afford to and did stay at the best hotels—the Meurice in Paris, the Hotel d'Italie in Florence, the Erzherzog Carl in Vienna, the D'Allemagne in Rome —they were never far removed from violence and terror in the streets.

If there was one thing that struck Field with indelible effect, it was the realization of how little America was aware of what went on in Europe. How remote it seemed to those who scanned the *Herald* or *Tribune,* confined to reading the dead history of far-off countries. It made him anxious to get out of the secure domestic nest that he had been living in, and somehow to establish some rapport between the Old World and the New.

There were American reporters on the scene, of course. But what they sent back lost its vitality, its impact in the journey and was presented by each editor like a coroner's report. One such correspondent was his younger sister, Mary, writing now for the New York *Observer.* Mary had come to Europe the year before with her father and brother Stephen—the seasoned traveler of the family. Dr. Field had since returned, but Mary and Stephen had remained in Paris. Cyrus and his Mary joined them there, and they were together for the balance of the trip, going by train to Geneva and over the Simplon Pass by Swiss government diligence to Milan.

They encountered conflict everywhere they went, and Field must have been impressed with how fragile and inadequate were the channels of communication that might establish better understanding between nations.

In spite of his absorption with this view of history in the making and in spite of Dr. Paine's advice, Field was unable to put business matters completely from his mind. While in England, he noted the slowly spreading threat of cholera, and he wrote to Stone to prepare for a shortage of bleaching powder, which was widely used at the time as a disinfectant. He advised Stone to ration his existing stock and increase prices. Stone promptly wrote Crane & Company to double the previous quotations on the chloride compounds, adding, "Should you neglect to order and not be able to get any afterwards at any price you must not blame us."

One of Field's greatest business concerns had always been European competition. In the area of quality papers there was a snobbish preference in the United States for French and English watermarks. American papers, such as those produced by Crane, were easily as good as those imported from abroad. Their undiminished whiteness and enduring texture, evident today, are ample testimony to this fact. But the prejudice was there, and less scrupulous companies were selling their domestic papers under phony European labels. Field saw an opportunity to counter this threat by supplying his clients with the materials and tools of foreign manufacture to bring their products close, in formula at least, to those imported from abroad.

To this end, he scoured London for large quantities of East India hides and cuttings and arranged with the leading firm of James Muspratt & Sons to become its exclusive agent in New York for bleaching powders. In Paris he made a similar exclusive contract with the firm of Guimet for its line of dyes. During his travels around the Continent, he shipped to Field & Company some fifteen loads of rags from Italy and central Europe, the advantage of these materials being that they were free of cotton content.

From Vienna he mailed a letter to Joseph Stone to be transcribed and relayed, over his signature, to Crane & Company: "We are now prepared to supply you with Foreign Rags, French and German Ultramarine, Tennants and Muspratts Bleaching Powders, Soda Ash, Smalts, Alum, Feltsnips, Twine, Wirecloth, Screens, or any Article used by Paper Manufacturers of the best quality." He added in closing that these would be reserved only for "friends whom we Know are A No. 1."

From Vienna the party went to Frankfurt and down the raft-cluttered Rhine by steamer to Cologne, then on to Brussels, where Mary and Stephen left them. Cyrus and his Mary crossed to England to catch the new Cunarder *Europa* at Liverpool. The crossing was made to New York in a near record twelve days. Had there been cable and telegraph connections at St. John's, in Newfoundland, with Boston and New York, news from Europe would have reached those cities in six or seven days. There was already talk of such a link (telegraphy was spreading rapidly), but to Field at this point Newfoundland was just a barren island somewhere in the fogbound North Atlantic.

He was returning home more aware of the forces in Europe that affected the destiny of the United States, aware of the need for international understanding through improved communication. Never again would his boundaries be confined to Berkshire County and New York. The silver cord with Stockbridge and its Puritan conservatism had been broken.

On the passage back, in spite of frequent bouts of seasickness, he made two significant acquaintances. One was George Bancroft, whose *History of the United States* he had read in the Mercantile Library while a clerk at Stewart's. Bancroft was something of a visionary, conscientious but unorthodox, and his was a challenging mind for Cyrus to encounter. He was a spokesman for the dawning concept of America's Manifest Destiny—the categorical imperative that was to turn the minds of men beyond the limits of the then United States to the undeveloped countries north and south and to the Caribbean islands. Bancroft's broad view of history in the making "transcended the sectional mind of New England" and persuaded Field that his own destiny, his own pursuit of greatness, might lie beyond the areas of New York trade.

The other was Marshall Roberts, who had started life modestly in New York in 1834 as a shipchandler and had become active in Hudson River transportation and railroad and steamship promotion. With the aid of a government subsidy, Roberts was now running a steamship line to Panama and, having received word of the discovery of gold in California, was hurrying home to anticipate the flood of passengers westward. (Dudley Field's advice of three years earlier had been: "If I were a young man, I would go to California." Stephen Field was to be among those passengers in October of that year.)

Roberts was a man with a Puritan upbringing like Cyrus' own, but with the instincts of a gambler. In their conversations he spoke of America's future as one of infinite expansion. He talked of their personal futures in terms not of modest, obvious opportunities, but of taking chances when the stakes were high enough, trading security for the probabilities of greater gain. Field had heard this point of view from an acquaintance he and Roberts had in common, Moses Taylor, who had already parlayed his clerkship in a New York importing house to become head of that now multimillion-dollar firm. It may have occurred to him and Roberts that with people such as Taylor and a scattering of others like the invention-minded promoter Samuel Morse—not to mention brother Dudley as a leader at the bar—they had the world in their collective hands.

Back in New York it was only a matter of days before Field moved his offices into two adjoining buildings on Cliff Street, one primarily a warehouse and the other for transacting business. Since the emphasis was now to be on imports, he adopted a marketing device. It cost money to remove the cargo from a ship, cart it to his warehouse, store it until the time of sale, and then rehaul it to the train or river steamer for delivery. Why not remain the middleman for the sake of the commission, but ship directly from the importing vessel to the buyer?

This procedure had all the earmarks of a favor to his clients, since it enabled him to offer lower prices. But it also added to his profits by reducing costs. From now on, his correspondence with Crane & Company, proffering imported materials from France and England, would include such price quotations as "6¼ ¢ per lb. at the warehouse, 6¢ direct from ship." When he was obliged to keep merchandise in store, he followed the policy, learned at A. T. Stewart's, of speeding it into the market by a drastic price reduction, rather than let it deteriorate on the shelves.

The drive to expand his life applied to the family as well. A few years earlier Samuel Ruggles had opened up the exclusive Gramercy Park Square to carefully selected residents. Peter Cooper had settled there, along with the publisher James Harper, one of Field & Company's clients. Field contracted for a plot of land at what was later 123 East Twenty-first Street, and he and Mary drew up plans for a house that was to reflect their greatly improved circumstances. The exterior would be brick, simple and solid, but the inside was to include a massive library for Cyrus and one of the first greenhouses in New York for Mary. She had never outgrown her childhood love of flowers, and lately had been having them shipped down from Connecticut, to be translated by her brush into delightful watercolors that survive today.

Meanwhile, Cyrus had finally decided that his life would no longer be chained to a desk. He took his family on excursions to the Elysian Fields across the Hudson and to Long Island. In January, 1850, his first son, Arthur Stone, was born. That autumn he hired a buggy and a covered wagon for supplies, and took the entire family on a four-week pleasure tour of Connecticut and the Berkshires.

He could well afford to spread himself a little. At midcentury Cyrus W. Field & Company was one of the largest—if not the largest—wholesale paper firm in the city. He was extremely jealous of his relations with Crane & Company, and watched carefully for any violations of their New York-Dalton axis. In June, 1850, he indignantly wrote to Dalton:

> Did not your Mr. Crane make a mistake this morning, in ordering a Case of French Ultramarine from another House, instead of from our store? We saw White & Sheffield's Cart go by, with a Case of French Ultramarine marked Crane & Co. Ballston Spa, and we felt satisfied that Mr. Crane had made a mistake in giving his order.

The fact that the case was marked Ballston Spa indicates that it was intended for Zenas' brother, Lindley Crane, who had married a Ballston Spa, New York, girl and gone into paper manufacture in that city with his father-in-law. That the two operations were separate did not mollify Cyrus. Lindley was still a Crane, and the Cranes did business only with the Fields. He thought of cutting Lindley out of the axis altogether and wrote a rather pompous letter to Zenas inquiring if Zenas thought he should give his brother credit. Was Lindley really reliable if he did business with a man like Sheffield, one of Field's competitors?

His real resentment was toward Sheffield for intruding on his clients, and the feud was bitter. A certain amount of correspondence was required between New York paper dealers, but Field refused to open Sheffield's letters or reply to them; he turned them over to Stone, who passed them on to a clerk, who sent them back to the writer, unacknowledged.

This battle of the giants was resolved when Elizur Smith, a prominent Berkshire paper manufacturer, sent Field a young man who was looking for a job. Henry Hulbert was to become a leading merchant in his own right, but Field had no opening for him and suggested he look elsewhere. Hulbert did. He was hired as a clerk by J. B. Sheffield, and assigned the task of delivering Sheffield's letters to Field and standing by until that gentleman opened and acknowledged them. Perhaps the ridiculous humor of this situation overtook Field; in any event, the channels of communication between him and Sheffield were reopened, and the animosity subsided.

In spite of these displays of spleen, Field was mellowing with age (he was nearly thirty-one). He took no exception to his partner Joe Stone's courtship of his sister Mary, who had now returned from Paris. He eased up on the disciplining of his employees, who responded by presenting him with a silver pitcher at the dinner he gave the staff at the close of every year, "as a faint token of our esteem."

Field would always be impatient, addicted to punctuality, exasperated by delay; to one delinquent correspondent, he wrote: "My dear Sir: If it takes four weeks *not* to get an answer to a letter, how long will it take to get one?" (The answer was seventeen years, three months, and seven days, by which time the addressee had found Field's unacknowledged letter in an attic trunk.) But his impatience, when it was not with himself, would be more with circumstances than with individuals.

Frederick Church, now a member of the National Academy of Design, whose president was Samuel Morse, was a frequent visitor, and Field took him through the rising shell of the new Gramercy Park house. Church was duly impressed. He too had a dream home, which he had projected for a Hudson River mountaintop, near where he lived in Catskill. But he was not yet ready to settle down. Rivers were almost an obsession with him. He had "done" the Hudson, and he thought now of the Mississippi. He proposed to Cyrus and Mary that they tour the Eastern states and see, while he painted them, some of the natural marvels of the country. The idea appealed to Cyrus; he had never been farther south than Baltimore or farther west than Michigan.

In the spring of that year, 1851, they went by train to Virginia, staying with friends at a plantation on the James, near Lexington, while Church set up his easel at the Natural Bridge. Cyrus accompanied him on these painting sessions. He was so anxious that Church should present the bridge with photographic accuracy that he climbed around the limestone cliffs collecting specimens of rock to guide Church in his choice of colors. When Church disdained these props in favor of his own perception, Field pocketed the rocks to take back to New York. He aimed to check Church's finished product with his samples; if they matched, he would buy the painting. They did, and he did.

From the Natural Bridge they went on to Kentucky's Mammoth Cave. In the scores of miles of twisting tunnels they were like young boys back in Stockbridge, exploring the caverns of Ice Glen. Each became fascinated by the small white sightless fish that thronged the underground streams, so sluggish one could catch them by hand. For a moment art was forgotten while they collected these creatures to take home in glass containers. Church wrote Field some weeks later: "I am telling marvellous stories here of our adventures to gaping audiences, and exhibiting my blind fish with tremendous effect."

The big adventure that they both looked forward to was the Mississippi, which they joined at Cairo, Illinois. Church found the river disappointingly serene. Happily, on the trip upriver they were treated to a typical Mississippi steamboat race. When their captain called for extra pressure and the fires were stoked with everything available including cargo, the stewardess assured them there was no need to worry about exploding boilers. It was the vessel's last voyage anyway! Some of the drama of the race, the blazing funnels and clouds of smoke, was captured by Church in a memorable painting. And some of the glamour was re-created five years later, when the riverboat *Grey Eagle* raced to St. Paul with the first telegraph message from the newly laid Atlantic cable.

The race ended at St. Paul, then little more than a steamboat landing, although capital of the newly formed Minnesota Territory. Church was anxious to hurry east, and left the party to pursue his long-anticipated painting of Niagara Falls. However Field had heard of an impending treaty with the Indians, who were ready to cede a large portion of the Sioux lands to the white man. He hired a boat for $400 to take him and Mary to Traverse on the Minnesota River, where the signing was to take place. Since there was plenty of room in the boat, he suggested the captain sell tickets for $10 a head to other passengers. He came out even on the trip.

As they approached Traverse, with smokestack blazing and whistle shrieking, the Sioux chiefs, always suspicious of the white man, took to the woods, and only after the boat had withdrawn downriver and Mary and Cyrus had hiked on foot to Traverse did the ceremony continue. It was memorable to the onlookers—and to the Sioux. They were paid partially with muskets and ammunition, and they discovered that the loss of their hunting lands resulted in near starvation; their rebellion some years later resulted in the Sioux War of 1862.

Heading east, the Fields picked up Church at Niagara Falls, staying at the Clifton House, where they listened clandestinely to Jenny Lind rehearsing for the night's performance; then on by barge and Hudson River steamer on a homeward voyage in stifling heat that commended itself to Frederick Church as a remedy for overweight.

6

Manifest Destiny

＞＞＞＞＞＞＜＜＜＜＜＜ On their return to New York Cyrus and
Mary found the Twenty-first Street house ready for them. Dudley
Field, observing the pattern of following Cyrus around the city, had
moved in next door. By common consent, the first step was to chop
through the intervening wall and insert a first-floor passageway between the houses, making them almost a unit.

Cyrus had now achieved success, wealth, and status. According to
Moses Beach, editor of the *Sun* and publisher of the first financial
Who's Who in America, Cyrus Field—worth more than $200,000—
was among the 33 richest men in the city. This placed him easily in
the ranks of 170 financiers whose wealth, exceeding $100,000, num-
bered them among the socially acceptable. In a young and hetero-
geneous society in which there were few settled values, wealth was as
good a criterion as any.

He began to look the part. In place of the linen roundabout which
had been his working costume for years, he now modishly dressed in
black frock coat, starched shirtfront, and high-standing collar, with
a neatly folded satin stock embellished by the stickpin he had received
at Stewart's. In these early years his crop of luxuriant reddish hair was
long and continued in chin whiskers around his face.

The new house was a fitting background for his broadening life.
Militantly simple on the outside, except for the tall railed stoop that
mounted to a framed door gleaming with highly polished brass, it was
exquisitely furnished inside by a Frenchman named Baudoine, whose
services a connoisseur neighbor, George Templeton Strong, had
longed to acquire but could not (he complained) afford. In fact, it
was the first house in New York to have had a professional decorator,

and it showed it. "Peace and plenty prevail, beauty and quiet are everywhere," wrote a visitor.

The tall-ceilinged spacious rooms were crowded with Louis XIV furniture, Italian draperies, Greek statuary, Persian rugs, and marble mantels. The walls, no doubt on Field's insistence, were incongruously hung with stormy landscapes of the Hudson River school. The only other concessions to the personalities of the owners were Mary's solarium and Cyrus' library, which he modestly referred to as his study.

It was a lofty, well-proportioned room, running the length of the house, with carved stone fireplaces at each end and a frescoed ceiling, to which shelves of books extended from the floor. Over the mantels hung inevitably the works of Frederick Church, among them the recently completed watercolor "View of West Rock near New Haven." According to *Valentine's Manual:*

> The library overlooks a city square where Magnolias blossom in the Spring, and flowers under arching trees bloom all the summer through. To one who enters here, the quiet stretches of the square and the sky beyond seem suddenly and somehow to belong to libraries, so great is the sense of repose and refreshment they inspire.

Behind the house was a stable for the carriage and the horses; Mary and the children would no longer have to ride the horsecars. Abram Hewitt's son remembered, "When his coachman washed Mr. Field's carriage the water ran across the sidewalk, down the gutter, and all the way to Third Avenue." The Fields also engaged an English butler, whom the children grew to hate intensely; he imposed the upper-class British rule that younger members of the family dine at separate tables from their parents.

Gramercy Park became in a sense like Stockbridge, shaping and cradling the second period of Field's career as Stockbridge had molded him in boyhood. There was the same sense of a closely knit community, well bred, cultured, and a little bit apart. On summer evenings neighbors chatted easily with neighbors from the high stoops, strolled in parties under the leafy maples and willows in the square, hired a watchman to restrict unruly playing on the green that might disturb their peaceful haven.

Old habits die hard, however. Field still was up at six and in his library by seven. Here he made the customary list of what he had to do that day, whom he would see, and where he would be. This he placed in his hat before he breakfasted. He often worked till dinnertime, then dined downtown to return to his office afterward. At home he was punctilious about sitting down to meals; once at the table, he began to eat. Chided for not waiting for the others, he reminded them that ten minutes of waiting meant seventy minutes lost per week, or sixty hours in the year—the equivalent of two and a half full days.

He never opened telegrams received at night. "If they bring bad news I won't sleep if I read them," he explained. "If it's good news it will keep till morning." When remarks were addressed to him to which the answer might be awkward or embarrassing, he became conveniently deaf. Letters that were indiscreet or might cause pain to others, if revealed, were burned. He wore hypothetical blinders, not to evade reality but to keep his attention focused on what was first and most important, the constructive thing, the goal.

His neighbors were men of influence and wealth—among them, Samuel Tilden, the Sage of Gramercy Park, later a Presidential candidate; James Harper, head of the publishing dynasty; George Templeton Strong, the diarist; Abram Hewitt, Peter Cooper's son-in-law; and Peter Cooper, who had bought a square brick house next door to Cyrus, with garden and stables in the rear.

Like Cyrus, Cooper had come to New York as a teen-age youngster, lacking only the settled family roots that had so well supported Cyrus. He had had no education and no formal training but, through ingenuity and a variety of occupations (storekeeper, hatter, shoemaker, brewer, and farmer, "sometimes all at once"), had risen to found an immensely successful glue and gelatin factory in the city, was engaged in iron manufacture in New Jersey, and had dabbled in telegraphy at the instigation of its promoter Samuel Morse. By 1849, Cooper's ironworks were turning out telegraph wire "in large quantities," and he had become involved in two telegraph lines extending from New York to Buffalo and Boston.

Thus Cyrus and Mary became automatically a part of a distinguished coterie of knowledgeable, very bright New Yorkers, who had either inherited wealth and position or acquired them through labor, shrewdness, and imagination. The guests whom Mary regularly entertained were a cosmopolitan cross section of the city and its hinterland: Mark Hopkins and the Sedgwick brothers; the writers Harriet Beecher Stowe and William Cullen Bryant; the publishers George Putnam, Robert Carter, and Charles Scribner; the scientist Edward Youmans;

politician William Maxwell Evarts; and the theologian Dr. William Adams.

Although the new Calvary Episcopal Church was almost next door, Cyrus and Mary had remained loyal to Dr. Adams and had headed a move by his congregation to reinstall the minister in the Madison Avenue Presbyterian Church, overlooking the park where Cyrus and his neighbors grazed their cows.

There was an open door policy between the two Field homes, and Dudley, now generally described as "fat and prosperous," spent almost as much time in Cyrus' household as in his own. Jonathan had returned to Stockbridge and a house he called The Homestead to practice law and enter Massachusetts politics. Stephen had headed west to participate, not in the gold rush, but in the legal complications it would bring.

Henry, however, was very much in evidence. After five years of preaching in St. Louis, during which he had made several trips abroad, he had put together a small book called *The Irish Confederates*. James Harper was about to turn it down when Cyrus stepped in. The Harpers were clients to Field & Company with adjoining offices on Cliff Street, and James was a Gramercy Park neighbor. Besides these congenial persuasions, Cyrus offered to pay for the plates and contracted for the cost of publishing the work, thereby launching Henry on a literary career. Henry became something of a family Boswell, as well as a writer of somewhat oversentimental travelogues.

But Henry was attracting attention for a more disturbing reason. He was known to be courting a teacher of French at Miss Haines' Academy for girls, across from the Fields. Henry had even brought Henriette Desportes down to Harper's and she had helped choose the cover for his book. She was more than presentable, she was hauntingly attractive; but the fact remained that two years earlier, in Paris, she had been acquitted of complicity in the murder of the Duc de Praslin's wife. Although pronounced an innocent witness in her role of governess to the Praslin children, she had been followed by the suspicion of guilt to New York. She was referred to by Field's wife only as "that murderess," and Mary vowed that Henriette would never be accepted in her home.

It was the first time any real acrimony had intruded on the solidly knit Fields. At one of many family conferences held in Cyrus' library, it was decided by Dudley that Henriette should write to the Paris

judges who had acquitted her, asking for a confirmation of her innocence. Henry rightly resisted; Cyrus quietly demurred. Love was not
subject to legal scrutiny. Dudley persisted, and Henriette sent the letter, one of the most moving documents ever written by a woman. It
read in part:

> My heart has been heavy with the terrible secret which hangs over
> my life. But today it is happiness that is offered me, and I have not
> the strength to turn it away without making one final effort to over-
> come my sorrowful destiny. The generous man who offers me his
> name and his hand knows my whole story. He trusts me completely,
> and if it were only he I had to consider I would not need any
> human witness. But he belongs to a wealthy and respected family
> who would not see him unite his life to mine without distress, and
> who have a right to a more convincing testimonial than my tears
> and protests. . . . Monsieur, could you not in good conscience tell
> them that I was not the infamous intriguer who was branded as such
> by the contempt of the world? I am not asking for your pity, but
> rather for the sake of an honorable man I am appealing to your sense
> of justice. The happiness of my whole life depends upon the words
> you write. . . .

On receipt of a heartening reply from Victor Cousins, one of the
judges at the trial, Henry and Henriette were married, and perhaps
to atone for his officiousness, Dudley gave them a complete set of
household furnishings, from upholstered chairs and mahogany tables
to silverware and china for their home in West Springfield, Massachusetts.

As the bells of Manhattan rang in the year of 1852—a year that
promised booming business, rising costs and prices in a city of 500,000
persons—Cyrus made an inventory of his position. Retiring to his
study, he wrote to Zenas in his precise and flowing hand a letter that
set forth both his financial standing and business philosophy with regard to Cyrus W. Field & Company:

> By the most untiring exertion and constant attention, early and late,
> our *sales* and *net profits* have *increased* every year since we com-
> menced business, and on the 1st day of January 1852, after charging
> to Profit & Loss every claim which we considered bad or doubtful,
> we had a Capital of two hundred and forty six thousand, six hundred
> and seventy one and 42/100 dollars ($246,671.42) all of which was
> made by ourselves.

Our facilities for doing a large and safe business have each year increased, and were never so great, as at the present time.

Our sales would have been much larger the past year, had we taken such risks as were considered fair, but we prefer to sell only to those whom we deem A, No. 1—unless we have a good endorser, or other undoubted security.

Actually his sales had more than doubled in the past five years, during which he had become the uncontested dean of New York paper merchants. In notes for his never completed autobiography, Field wrote of this period:

There was no luck about my success, which was remarkable. It was not due to the control or use of large capital, to the help of friends, to speculations or to fortunate turns of events, it was by constant labor and with the ambition to be a successful merchant; and I was rewarded by seeing a steady, even growth of business.

The only bit of self-deception here would seem to be his reference to friends. Certainly his friendship with Zenas had been a factor in his success. But it is true that he never took undue advantage of that friendship, never asked for a loan or credit, always tried to render services in kind. When Zenas casually told him that the foreman of Smith & Company in Russell, Massachusetts, a man named West, had lured away some of his best men, Cyrus promptly charged into the fray. Indignantly he wrote to Smith:

If you want any man that Mr. Crane has in his mill, go to him frankly and tell him so. Mr. Crane is and has been an old and personal friend of ours, and we are not willing that Mr. West or any one should do anything dishonorable towards him. Please write us all the facts. We earnestly desire that you may be able to live on the most friendly terms with all the manufacturers near you.

Smith replied: "We will try not to interfere with any man in Mr. Crane's employ hereafter. If any of our neighbors hire any of our help, we shall fill their places again without complaining to our New York friends about it."

Field was continuing to act as merchandising consultant to his clients, encouraging them to introduce new products and new packaging. While he had looked askance at the firm of Beach & Crane in Ballston Spa since their temporary defection to Sheffield (and had never quite forgiven Zenas' brother for separating from the Dalton family complex), he now encouraged that firm to manufacture tissue paper, a new product in the industry. Not to appear disloyal to Zenas, he insisted that bills, correspondence, and so forth be cleared through Dalton—*i.e.,* Zenas' office.

Also at this time, he introduced the modern convenience of boxed stationery, writing Zenas during the Christmas holiday season:

> We think of selling Writing Papers only by the case after the first of January which we think will be beneficial to the manufacturers as well as ourselves. If we induce our customers to take Cases instead of a few reams, would it not be worth your while to allow us to sell from 2½ % to 5% cheaper to make sales heavier, and by not opening the cases, it would prevent the paper from getting soiled, which often has to be sold at a lower price.

Bank note paper seems not to have added greatly to his business at the time. Envelopes were another matter. In the first half of the century a letter consisted of a single sheet of paper, folded three times and sealed. If the message, written in straight lines across the paper, could not be finished on a single sheet, it was continued by writing perpendicularly across the lines already written. Postage was charged per individual sheet. With a change in the postal rates, by which a letter cost according to its weight, several sheets could be sent together. Cyrus advised Zenas to go heavily into envelope production and make his writing paper light in weight. And he still held out for color, the more extravagant the better. "Your sample of Gold envelopes looks well," he wrote commendingly.

In June, 1852, his sister Mary married Joseph Stone, in Stockbridge, where Dr. Field performed the ceremony. The aging minister had given up his pastorate in Haddam at the urging of his sons, and Cyrus and Dudley had bought the Stockbridge house for his retirement. It was badly in need of repair, and since the year to come would mark their parents' golden anniversary, Cyrus and Dudley conspired, not only to do the whole house over, but also to add a wing, or Anniversary Room, to one side. This was to be a surprise. While "repairs" were going on, Cyrus arranged for his parents to stay at a cousin's home in Stockbridge and warned the cousin: "I do not think my mother is well enough to go into her own house during the time repairs are being made."

To Mary and Joe, the newlyweds, he made a present of the Seventeenth Street house where Mary had been living since Cyrus moved his family to Gramercy Park. He was thinking of doing even more for Mary's husband, although he had not yet confided this to Stone. He had brought Field & Company to the top of the paper merchandising hierarchy in the city; perhaps it was time to turn it over to his younger partner. There was no further challenge to him in the business. His net profit in 1852 exceeded that of any other year, and the gross sales figures showed a record of inexorable growth:

> 1847—$354,432.60
> 1848—$438,983.90
> 1849—$503,750.98
> 1850—$723,080.33
> 1851—$725,679.78
> 1852—$812,267.82

He was now worth personally more than $250,000, an immense sum for that period, and the firm had capital on hand of more than $300,000. These facts led to some soul-searching and he noted in his journal:

> I then turned to my books for a list of the old claims which I had settled by compromise ten years before, found the amount which my generous creditors had deducted from their claims, added to each one interest for that time and sent to every man a check for the whole amount principal and with seven per cent interest, a sum amounting in all to many thousands of dollars.

Legally he had cleared himself with honor by the settlement of ten years past. But his daughter was undoubtedly right in saying, "He felt that in reality he was still their debtor, and one of the chief incentives to his intense devotion to business in the years following his fresh start was the hope of clearing off the debt, so that no man should have lost by trusting him."

Early in March he started sending out the checks, including three to banks which still held notes against E. Root & Company, and released two of his own debtors of their obligations. Needless to say, the reaction did much to enhance his reputation. One letter from Walter Laflin represents the sentiments of everyone who wrote him:

> This act, entirely voluntary on your part, exhibits moral honesty, that all fair men approve, but few make known by their acts. I value it the more because it exhibits in my friend a conscience alive to

right. You have made this present (for I have no claim) not because you considered I needed it, but because the ability that did not exist in 1843 does exist in 1853, and the act itself would be carrying out the principles of the Golden Rule. Please accept my warmest thanks for this token of love and friendship. May peace, prosperity, and happiness attend you all your days.

Samuel Woodruff, head of a Hartford papermaking firm, acknowledged receipt of Field's check:

with no ordinary feeling of satisfaction, for in these degenerate days it is in truth a rare occurrence to find men who like yourself—as is evidenced by this act—are honest from principle, and who never consider themselves morally quit of a just debt, even though legally released, until the debt is paid in full. We would now express to you our thanks for the sum enclosed, not so much for the value thereof in currency as for the proof it affords that "honesty still dwells among men."

The settlement of his debts also marked the turning of a page. He added to his biographical notes:

I now wished to retire from business altogether, but at length I yielded to the solicitations of my junior partner so far as to agree to leave my name at the head of the firm and to leave in the business a capital of $100,000. But this was done with the express understanding that I was not to be required to devote any time to it.

Actually he had no intention of retiring from business altogether, and he never relinquished full responsibility to Stone (his daughter notes that he "for one week succeeded in staying away from his office in Cliff Street"). He simply wanted freedom to determine what came next. Certainly there were splendid opportunities for buying into railroads, steamship lines, and real estate. But for what purpose? If he were to invest, it had to be in something with which he was personally involved, in which he had a stake and some authority. He was acquiring a growing social consciousness; making money out of money added nothing to the welfare of mankind.

In addition to money in his pocket, he had time—a precious thing that he had never owned before—time to catch up on reading he had missed. It was no accident that led him to such works as Matthew Fontaine Maury's letters in the *National Intelligencer*. He was looking, not for entertainment or even intellectual self-improvement, but for matter that would feed the mill which was grinding out his future.

Maury's series, "The Amazon and the Atlantic Slope of South America," written above the pen name Inca, was sound grist. It came at an opportune time, concerned (as the publisher proclaimed) with "one of the most important commercial questions of the age." The ringing phrase of that age was Manifest Destiny. Among the wags of the fifties this high-sounding concept was lampooned in a popular toast: "To the United States—bounded on the north by the aurora borealis, on the south by the procession of the equinoxes, on the east by primeval chaos, and on the west by the day of judgment." To the sober-minded citizen, regardless of political party, it meant simply that the commercial future of the country had no boundaries, and since the Old World had been pillaged by its errant wars and waste, the lands of the New World were a preserve of the United States.

There were other writers or politicians who promoted this ambitious concept, John Louis O'Sullivan for one, but Matthew Maury aimed it at the valley of the Amazon. A naval lieutenant whom an early injury had forced to a desk, he had become the nation's leading advocate of ocean exploration and of oceanography as a science and he strongly advocated the opening of major waterways to all the maritime countries. To this end Maury bitterly fought the Brazilian emperor's policy of barring the Amazon to navigation by United States ships. In 1851 he had persuaded Secretary of the Navy William A. Graham to send a two-man expedition to reconnoiter the mighty river from the Andes to its mouth (one of the men was Maury's brother-in-law, Lieutenant W. L. Herndon), and it was on their observations that he based his own in the *National Intelligencer*.

The series must have made fascinating reading to Field, as indeed it does to anyone today. Maury presented the Amazon valley as a nineteenth-century Mecca and compared the waterway to the Mississippi as a future correlated artery of commerce—"these two rivers unite at our feet, and pour their wealth along our shores." He depicted mountains of emeralds and gold and other precious metals, lands of incredible fertility, and potential exports more precious than those yielded by the China trade. All this was documented by intriguing vignettes such as: "The children here wash the earth in the streets for gold, and diamonds are sometimes found in the crops of fowls." Here, in short, in an area of millions of square miles, more accessible to the United States than to most of South America itself, was a "safety valve" for the exploding energies and population of the Union, a region utterly neglected by the European powers, which had no right to be there anyway:

> From the statements which I have already made, all must admit that the valley of the Amazon is not only a great country, but it is a glowing wilderness and waste, which, under the improvement and progress of the age, would soon be made to "blossom as the rose." We have, therefore, but to let loose upon it the engines of commerce —the steamer, the emigrant, the printing press, the axe, and the plough—and it will teem with life.

Manifest Destiny! It was the same ringing cry Field had heard from the lips of George Bancroft on the voyage home from Europe, defined by the *Democratic Review* as "our manifest destiny to overspread the continent allotted by Providence for the free development of our yearly multiplying millions." True, the word "continent" might not apply strictly to the Southern Hemisphere, but that was quibbling. The areas were connected by the Isthmus.

Maury was not above considering the dollar value of his proposition. "Had you not rather be 'cock of the walk' in a market place where fifteen or twenty millions of produce are bought and sold annually, than to be one of half-a-dozen competitors for trade with Europe?" Not that he advocated selling Europe short; "far from it— for if we can get both, so much the better. . . ."

To a calculating merchant with a visionary outlook, these were heady words. It was as if Providence had dropped the answer to Field's future in his lap. He resolved to see and appraise this new Utopia for himself. However, he was modest enough to know that he would need others to confirm his findings and share in their interpretation.

He thought at once of Frederick Church—not only as a proved traveling companion, but as one who could arouse enthusiasm for the subjects that he painted. While he himself could collect the facts and appraise the land commercially, Church could present the country visually to millions of prospective viewers; he could paint the travel posters for investors looking for adventure. Church was uniquely able, as one critic has since noted, to "communicate the dream to the masses and even add a touch of glory to it."

Having just returned from the wilderness of Maine, Church felt he had exhausted the great scenic possibilities of North America. He too had read Maury's South American eulogies. And the mountains of the Andes, the waterfalls and mighty rivers, and the multicolored jungles of the tropics were precisely what appealed to him.

Field then approached Chandler White, who had retired a few years before, having, like Cyrus, made his fortune in the paper trade. Field thought that White might be a source of capital for any plan evolving from the expedition. White was not anxious for adventure. But Field had already acquired powers of persuasion that, along with his contagious enthusiasm, were often irresistible. White agreed to go along, first cautiously checking with Matthew Maury: "I am about to embark for South America . . . on an excursion of pleasure and commercial exploration. Where can I get an account of Lt. Herndon's trip?" He was not going to take Field's word for everything.

There was a side purpose to the expedition in the back of Field's mind. Ever since his brother Timothy's disappearance in the Gulf of Mexico in 1836, the family had maintained a heartbreaking hope that Timothy was still alive. This had been fostered by a ship captain's rumor, somewhat callously relayed to Dr. Field, that Timothy had married in South America and settled there as "a very wealthy planter." There had been no word from Timothy; letters of inquiry to South American consulates had yielded nothing; Cyrus had even advertised and offered rewards for information on Timothy's whereabouts, with no results. The only hope remaining was for someone to go down there and investigate.

7

Search for Utopia

>>>>>><<<<<< Embarking on their South American expedition, Field and Church were anxious to avoid the crush of gold prospectors headed for the Isthmus. Consequently they decided to sail directly to New Granada (now Colombia) on the timorous brig *Viva*.

Chandler White put no trust in sailing vessels. He would follow by steamer via Panama.

Cyrus boarded the brig with Church on the evening of April 7, 1853. It was his first trip on his own, away from his family, and there was some mutual apprehension about how he would get along. Late that night the Gramercy Park household was awakened by a coded ring which sounded so familiar that the children called to Mary, "Daddy's back!" He was indeed. The brig had been held up by the tide till sunrise, and he had returned to spend the interval beneath his own roof.

The brig arrived at Savanilla on April 28, after a three-week passage blessed by calm, fine weather. The only wharf at the seaport was hemmed in by cliffs so steep that there was no point docking at it. On the captain's advice they rowed ashore to a more hospitable landing place, and hired horses for the trip to Barranquilla; there were no roads, only bridle paths. Field was used to riding from his Stockbridge days, but the heat was 95 degrees, and their mounts were "the sharpest boned horses that you ever saw." When they arrived at the Barranquilla guest house, they were barely able to sit down to their first South American dinner of roast chicken, boiled beef, fried plantains, beans, yams, preserved mangoes, rice, and coffee.

Church's diary, half in Spanish, half in English, is the only record that remains of the trip. This he illustrated with impromptu sketches later used for finishing paintings. Cyrus knew no Spanish. He had made a point of mastering the one phrase *Más rápido!* but nobody hurried in New Granada. They had already missed the boat for the interior and would have to spend ten days or more in Barranquilla waiting for the next ship.

Cyrus and his companion took advantage of this interval to look around and while they saw no gold dust in the streets, they found a land run riot with fertility. Thatched huts were dwarfed by giant cactus. Vines and tropical fruit trees, coconut palms and plantains crowded in upon the footpaths. Lizards scampered away at their approach, and turkey buzzards clogged the streets as if they owned them, welcomed as self-sustaining garbage disposal units.

Field made a point of visiting and taking inventory of the marketplaces, comparing the prices of native products with what they probably cost at home. Many were new to him, and these he weighed and pinched and tasted. The native rice especially pleased him ("the grains are small and dingy but the flavor is vastly better than the rice in the United States"). He sent home samples for further appraisal and comparison. Owing to his open trust and lack of Spanish, he was cheated extravagantly, but for this expedition he had budgeted $1,600, which was more than he would spend.

On May 10, with no news of Chandler White, they started by steamer up the Magdalena River against six- to eight-knot currents, battling jungle heat and mosquitoes, living on rice and chocolate. There was plenty of diversion. They found a tarantula in their cabin, killed it, and saved the carcass as a specimen. They later came across a scorpion and sent its cast-off skin to Church's sister ("You will notice the curved sting terminating the tail"). When the river current rose to twelve knots, the little *vapor* gave up. They went ashore, got a canoe, and tried to paddle the rest of the way to Honda.

The river had begun to flood. They left their luggage at the miserable village" of Conjeo, and decided to cut across the hills on foot. Their guide, a New Granadan named Banin, was mortally afraid of tigers and distressed that Field and Church were unarmed. At nightfall they came across a mud hut, where Banin insisted that they seek protection. Disgusted, Field and Church acceded and, after a supper of corn cakes and hot molasses, tried to get some sleep.

Deep in the night Field heard the shout of "Tiger!" and felt strong talons on his throat. He fought and twisted, and finally sprang free—

only to be attacked by Church and pinned against the wall. Banin lay battered and bleeding on the floor. It seemed he had dreamed the sleeping Cyrus was a tiger and had taken the offensive. The bewildered Church had thought that Field was the villain of this Mack Sennett farce. They got no more sleep that night, but cooked more corn cakes and hot molasses, and at dawn trudged on to Honda.

There is an old Spanish proverb: "Never leave a river before you or possessions behind." The baggage that they had thought would follow was stranded by the flooded river at Conjeo; they would have to wait for it interminably. There was no sign of White. Field had all but given up on him, although Church for some time continued to note in his diary optimistically, "We expect him on the next boat." Field used this delay to explore surrounding rubber forests and gold and silver mines. At one mine he got the foreman to explain the operation to him fully and had Church make sketches to take home for reference.

When their baggage was finally brought up by mule, they continued their four-day trek to Bogotá, battling through jungle underbrush and thickets of insects. High altitude and exhaustion took their toll of Field, but he would not admit it. Instead, he raised the battle cry of *Más rápido!* and they spurred their mules to greater speed until they had lost their peon guide completely. H. T. Tuckerman, writing of Frederick Church, recounted: "The bridle paths were dangerous without a guide; not a sign of human dwellings was visible; the hootings of owls and the howling of beasts increased the horrors of darkness."

Exhausted, they finally climbed to the top of a tree "and long shouted in vain." This maneuver gave the mules a chance to slip away, at which point they gave up and, "worn out by fatigue, found temporary repose on an ant-hill." The next day they miraculously found both guide and mules by following their track and, in sheer exuberance at this good fortune, galloped the remaining miles to Bogotá.

It was a busy city of 50,000 assorted races, strangely civilized. Wrote Church: "It looked very odd after being so long accustomed to the straw hats and *ruanas* (ponchos) or native cloaks of the country, to see people dressed in broadcloth and beaver hats, of course only the foreigners and wealthier citizens use them."

Field who hated violence found the bullfights "miserably cruel affairs." Even more shocking to him, remembering his father's ban on turkey shoots in Stockbridge, was the native variation of this sport. Church described it in a marathon, unpunctuated sentence: "A cock is buried in the ground and a person being blindfolded is handed a long sword and being removed some distance from the cock walks carefully in the direction where he supposes the cock to be and makes great sweeps with his sword hoping to decapitate the unfortunate cock in which case he is rewarded with his body."

Near Bogotá they visited the Falls of Tequendama, subject of a famous landscape by the artist. After several days of climbing, crawling, and hacking their way through the tropical growth around the falls, Church finally decided on the best view for his painting. They hired an army of peons in Bogotá, brought them to this jungle wilderness, and put them to work with axes and machetes, felling trees and clearing out dense undergrowth. Ordinarily indolent, the peons worked like demons, for this must obviously be the beginning of some mighty project of the *patrones,* a castle perhaps, a magnificent monument to God, a stronghold of national defense. When sheer toil had cleared an area the size of a Bogotá plaza, the peons turned in trembling anticipation to watch the white man squat in the center of the clearing, take out his pad, and sit there quietly till darkness fell.

Like Field, Church was imbued with Presbyterian conscience. God was in everything he painted—a sublime divinity and exaltation that makes such works as the "Falls of Tequendama" and "South American Landscape" monuments in nineteenth-century art. He never worked or even wrote on the Sabbath. Yet he turned out more sketches in this brief period than a less prolific artist would account for in a year. Some of these he gave to Cyrus, others became the subjects of later canvases, and many he simply inserted in the margins of his diary as reminders.

In fact, for what Field had in mind, Church worked out very much as he had hoped. Church not only had the reportorial instinct for communicating what he saw, but also was not above sketching mundane objects—native products of tin and silver, mining implements, methods of harnessing waterpower, details of bridge construction, segar manufactures, means of transportation, marketplaces.

Their curiosity throughout the expedition was insatiable. Sometimes their interest was commercial; sometimes, almost childlike fascination. Visiting the Volcano of Purace, they tasted the water in the nearby stream and found it "delicious, with a fine flavor, being sufficiently charged with acid to be agreeable." Deciding that, with sugar added, it would make good ersatz lemonade, they put some in bottles to take back. From the various marketplaces Field shipped home samples of grain cereals, chocolate, sweetmeats, fruits, nuts, artifacts of tin and straw. He collected different kinds of mining ore, exotic vegetables and seeds, plumages of birds, and shearings of native sheep. The huts they slept in were overrun with insects, which they carefully mounted to take home as specimens; they included a New Granada cockroach "of uncommonly large size."

Somewhat surprisingly Cyrus was never homesick. His interest in the goings-on around him was too absorbing. Also, he took with him the best parts of home in the observance of significant traditions: prayers before every meal; church on Sundays followed by a roast beef dinner; proper Yankee dress on all occasions; and a New England attitude of courtesy toward peons and aristocrats alike. Above all was his scrupulous observance, wherever he was, of American holidays and anniversaries.

On the Fourth of July he rounded up all English-speaking people in Bogotá for an Independence Day dinner. The forty guests, as it turned out, were mostly British. Fortunately they "seemed to be as patriotic as any others," and the affair, according to Church, "went off very well." There was only one thing missing. Field was dissuaded from the fireworks display he had intended, and the authorities also ruled out firecrackers. He learned the reason later from Courtland Cushing, American chargé d'affaires in Ecuador. A July Fourth pyrotechnical display the year before in Guayaquil had signaled an attack by an invading horde of filibusters, who had used the noise to mask their rifleshots.

The projected route from Bogotá to Quito was an arduous one, at high altitudes along the inverted ridges of the Andes. They shipped home everything they did not need, and to handle the remainder, Field hired a disengaged bullfighter, named Tomás. Tomás had a fourteen-year-old son, Marcos, whom he insisted on including in this package deal. Between them they could form a rear guard for the expedition.

Field decided he would take Marcos to New York, educate him according to Protestant lights, and return him to his people as a sort of prophet or messiah. Church bowed to the extravagant idea, noting laconically that "the boy is as efficient as most people here." He also found Marcos a convenient model for a number of his portraits.

They crossed the Cauca River, which, reads the diary, "flows over sands of gold richer than those of California," observed that the scenery "in some places might resemble New England but for the tropical foliage," and climbed to the suspended valleys of the Andes, ranging the earth's latitudes from jungle heat to frosty mountain peaks. In the lower valleys Field had suffered from intermittent fever; in the higher altitudes he sometimes had to be supported and propelled by guides, far above the snowline, to face west or east from the Pacific to the great Atlantic slope.

Three hundred miles away began the mighty concourse of the Amazon, flowing to "the dark blue ocean that washes the shores of our own dear land." At close range, Church recorded much of it on canvas, and wrote of the outlook: "My ideal of the Cordilleras is realized." The Andes taught him, as Professor David Huntington observed, "geographical determinism—first hand."

The peons and the Altiplano Indians regarded the mule-borne caravan as a free traveling circus. Field and Church were like creatures in a mobile zoo. If they sought privacy in a wayside hut, the natives followed them inside and, Church complained,

> deliberately stared at us whether eating or doing anything else, and as seldom any of the huts have windows we were often much annoyed by their blocking up the door. . . . They seem particularly amused at our pertinacity and temerity in washing our faces and hands, an act of ablution which they seem to consider entirely novel and dangerous.

The local gendarmes were also curious—and apprehensive. Field's foreign dress and manner and his habit of prying into everything aroused suspicion. At Cali the constabulary arrested him, and took him before the alcalde, "the most potent official in the place." His lack of Spanish left him helpless; it was no use shouting *"Más rápido!"* at these sullen guards. Not until Church was also taken into custody and, flourishing his sketchbook in their faces, demanded of the alcalde "what he meant by arresting important officials bearing dispatches from the U. S. Government" were they finally released.

In connection with his search for the lost brother, Timothy, Cyrus carried letters of introduction to leading citizens and many officials. He learned nothing at all of Timothy, but he saw the haciendas of the wealthy, rubber and coffee plantations, diamond and emerald mines in the Andean foothills, orange groves, and sheep farms. The two men were entertained royally, joined sometimes by as many as fifty aristocratic guests. On their last night at Quito, Church wrote: "Spent the night at Sr. Larrea's house where was a very handsome entertainment. I regret much to leave such friendly people."

Late in September they began their descent from the plateaus of the Andes to the warmer western lowlands and to the Rio Guayas, leading down to Guayaquil. Once river-borne, they met the fate of Alexander on the Indus. As they moved downstream, an incoming tide swept up to meet them and forced the little ship to anchor. Impatient as always, Field summoned a canoe from shore, and he and Church bucked the tide by poling on to Guayaquil, which, Church noted happily, "has a great reputation for the beauty of the ladies."

From Guayaquil they shipped their accumulated baggage home around the Cape; it was longer but cheaper than across the Isthmus; they themselves would return by way of Panama. This lightening of the load left room to take on more, and Field frequented bazaars that sold spider monkeys, jaguars, pumas, snakes, talking birds, and tropical fish. His selections were turned over to young Marcos for companionable custody until they sailed; he seemed to foresee his Gramercy Park living room as a sort of "Peaceable Kingdom."

They were way behind schedule. This was September 23. Cyrus was due in Stockbridge on October 28 for his parents' golden wedding celebration, and an anniversary was sacred. They would have to catch the earliest steamer north for Panama, meanwhile packing and taking stock of what they had accomplished.

From Church's standpoint the trip had been productive. He was bringing back some of his best work, which would indeed, as Field had hoped, arouse enthusiastic interest in this southern continent. Cyrus, being honest with himself, had failed of any positive objective. He was hard and tanned and healthy—and a good bit wiser, but his failure to meet up with Chandler White had somewhat handicapped his ardor for the Amazon commercial venture; he needed someone of White's understanding and experience to share and bolster his enthusiasm. And of course, his failure to locate any sign of Timothy was a disappointment. It would be a harsh report to take back to his mother on her wedding anniversary.

But the impressions he had gained were infinite, and some, although disturbing, were significant. One was the disunity of South America, the lack of communication between towns and countries that made neighbor suspect to neighbor and kept this corner of the world in turmoil. It was Europe of 1848 all over again, on a more primitive scale. While Church complained about the lack of mail from home —few towns served as postal stations—Field was more conscious of the lack of newspapers, highways, telegraph systems, and railroads. The only channels of trade and intercourse were the innumerable rivers flowing east and west from the cordilleras, and the trunk line of them all, the Amazon, was all but closed to traffic from the outside world. That key to his dream of empire, his master plan of bringing Yankee blessings to this unexploited land lay in the pocket of the Emperor of Brazil.

Field and Church sailed north on the steamer *Bogota,* "very comfortable and even elegant," with Marcos and the animals in the hold. Since the railroad across the Isthmus was only partially completed, mules carried them from Panama as far as Cruces, a day's ride over "shocking" roads. The following day they went on to Aspinwall, named for the builder of the railway and since renamed Colón. An Aspinwall journalist who interviewed them provided a postscript to their travels. To Field's certain pleasure, it read like a press promotion for South America:

> They say that the scenery in some parts of the Andes is grand and beautiful beyond description; and that words cannot express the kindness and hospitality with which they have been treated; that gold in large quantities can be obtained in Antioquia, and from the beds of many of the small streams that run down the Andes into the Pacific or the Amazon; and that the soil on the plains of Bogotá and in the valley of the Cauca is very rich; and that they have been so much pleased with their journey that they plan soon to return to the land of beautiful flowers and birds, and to the continent for which the Almighty has done so much and man so little.

The prediction was right about Church. He would return in 1857 to resume his production of superb Andean landscapes. Field would never revisit this multicolored land of promise.

After six days of impatient waiting they sailed for New York on the *Ohio,* a steamer of the Law Line managed now by Marshall Roberts. It was a name familiar to Cyrus and was destined in a few weeks to be bracketed with his. "The voyage was pleasant, but every day's run was studied with nervous anxiety by Mr. Field," wrote a shipboard companion, who was aware that Cyrus had a late October date in Stockbridge. The steamer was delayed by stormy weather and he did not reach New York until October 29, 1853.

Field's arrival with the knife-belted Marcos in tow, a score of screaming parakeets and a live jaguar on a leash, was something of a sensation. He himself was something of a sensation when he jokingly went to call on Joe and Mary Stone in a native costume made of grass, attracting such a band of hooting followers that he had to take refuge in the doorway of a startled neighbor. But the real sensation of the neighborhood was Marcos, about whom Cyrus' daughter wrote with some restraint:

> Marcos was an imp. It was with almost magical rapidity that he could plan and execute mischief. He succeeded in breaking the collar-bone of the cook living in the family of Mr. David Dudley Field, and his delight was to lay snares in dark halls and passages, and if he was opposed he did not hesitate to seize a carving-knife and flourish it frantically about.

Isabella concluded with eloquent understatement: "A civilized life was not attractive to him." Marcos was subsequently disposed of during Cyrus' absence and shipped back to his family in New Granada, to follow the footsteps, not of God, but of his father in the bullring.

When the family foregathered at Stockbridge all the brothers and sisters, except Stephen, were assembled with their offspring. The Anniversary Room that Cyrus and Dudley had added to the parsonage appropriately resembled a small two-story chapel with a stained-glass window at its eastern end. Cyrus had also had the house refurnished.

Submit, now over seventy, was dressed in a new gown purchased by her sons for the event and was forbidden to enter the kitchen, where, for once, the dinner was being prepared by outside help. This restriction was too much for a woman who had given her life to seeing that the home ran smoothly. Her granddaughter recalls surprising the venerable lady crawling on hands and knees, under the table and between the legs of seated guests, to see what was cooking on the stove and whether the kitchen staff was operating as it should.

Henry was present with his controversial French wife, Henriette, and Matthew's granddaughter, Rachel Field, in *All This and Heaven Too,* gave a discerning portrait of the family seen through Henriette's detached eyes. There was a common strength in all their features and a nervous, driving energy in most of them. Physically they were much alike, the men broad-shouldered, tall, red-bearded and red-haired, with almost Viking profiles; the sisters slightly Irish-looking, sloe-eyed, and mischievously modest, with the tantalizing bloom of the perpetual colleen. Henriette felt irresistibly overwhelmed by "these generations that filled the rooms with the great press of life. Tomorrow they would all be scattered again; today they lifted their voices in the

Doxology and bowed their heads as the old minister rose to give them his blessing."

In view of later events, it was provident that Matthew returned with Cyrus to New York; they were both at respective crossroads. After leaving the Laflin mill at Lee, Matthew and Clarissa had led an almost gypsy existence in the South as Matthew moved from one construction job to another, gaining proficiency as an engineer and ultimately building bridges, dams, and railroads that were lasting testimonies to his skill. Now, being, like Cyrus, an incurable New Englander, he had brought his family north for good and settled them on Clarissa's family farm in Southwick. Meanwhile, he would need to work—at what, he did not know. He was too independent to accept his brother's and Mary's hospitality and stayed at the Astor House on Broadway where sooner or later one met everybody who was anybody.

Undoubtedly Cyrus talked to Matthew about his South American dream. Matthew was someone he could talk to without fear of ridicule or skepticism, for he believed, as Cyrus did, that any wild, improbable idea might be tomorrow's miracle. His sympathy, if nothing else, encouraged Cyrus to pursue it further. A note had come from Courtland Cushing, expressing a noncommital interest in the exploitation of the Amazon and proffering his personal but unofficial backing. Cyrus now wrote to Matthew Maury, asking him to come see him and discuss the matter. Maury replied that he would like to hear of Field's experience and have the benefit of his suggestions for the Amazon, but added that "if the pleasure of making your acquaintance depends upon my going to New York I fear I shall not for sometime have that gratification."

Cyrus promptly went to Washington, a grueling trip at that time, where he found that Maury had switched from his specific interest in the Amazon to the broader goal of an international scientific conference of nations. He was working with the newly formed American Association for the Advancement of Science to urge all the leading maritime countries to pool their meteorological observations for the common good. In a way this set the precedent for the modern International Geophysical Year. Maury was too absorbed in this to give much time to any of Field's commercial propositions; all the visit accomplished was to make them sympathetic friends.

Field returned to New York no surer of his future than he had been before. The enormity of being idle overwhelmed him, and he drifted back to the Cliff Street offices and poked around in a sort of make-work routine. There was one distraction early in December, 1853: the Great Harper Fire, which some compared to the holocaust of 1835. Starting in the basement offices of James and John Harper, it destroyed the properties of that publishing empire to the amount of $1,115,000, only a fraction of which was covered by insurance. Field immediately called on James Harper to offer his personal loan of $10,000. It was a characteristic gesture although a biographer of the Harpers, Eugene Exman, pointed out that the firm was a large consumer of paper.

Harper's was indeed a good customer, as well as the largest publishing firm in the country and one of the largest in the world. It had also been willing, albeit with some financial leverage, to help Cyrus launch Henry on his writing career. But Cyrus had never solicited business by concessions or favors—beyond the basket of peaches shipped to Zenas Crane. Money was something to be put to use, and the helping out of friends and members of his family, was one good use. It was not the answer to his problem now, which was what to do with the fortune he had acquired. If he made any New Year's resolutions at the start of 1854, it was to try to find that answer.

8

"A Bold and Visionary Scheme"

>>>>>><<<<<< "I never saw Cyrus so uneasy as when he was trying to sit still," his brother Matthew wrote to the family in January, 1854.

It was an apt comment; Field was at a loose end. With no encouragement on his South American venture, he was shrewd enough to know that he could do nothing on his own. Furthermore, emphasis was now on California and the goldfields. Why look beyond the United States when there was so much wealth waiting in the West?

Field & Company was doing splendidly without Cyrus in spite of the fact that Joseph Stone was ailing from a chronic lung infection. Sales for 1853 had totaled $931,629.65—an increase equal to that realized in his last year with the firm—and would easily exceed $1,000,000 for the current year. In his well-run household and his well-run office his presence seemed almost unnecessary.

Matthew was having his own trouble trying to sit still. He was waiting at the Astor House for something to turn up and meanwhile comforting his young son Heman, who was working in the offices of Field & Company. Heman was suffering from the endemic Field complaint of homesickness. Matthew's complaint was inactivity—after his seven-year success in building bridges, including a mighty span across the Cumberland River at Nashville, Tennessee, which the Confederate Army would eventually destroy in its retreat.

It was in the congenial Astor lobby that Matthew struck up an acquaintance with a tall, rawboned, weather-beaten engineer from Canada, named Frederick Newton Gisborne, who was at more than loose ends. He was on the threshold of disaster. He welcomed a sympathetic listener, especially a fellow engineer in whom he could confide his story.

As a youngster in England, he had accompanied an uncle to Tahiti, to investigate that island as a possible source of gutta-percha which had hitherto been imported solely from Malaya. On his return to London, Gisborne sailed for Canada and for two years earned a living by farming in Quebec. From that point, he made an extraordinary jump to the post of chief operator of the Montreal Telegraph Company. In this capacity, he supervised the construction of telegraph lines connecting lower Canada with Nova Scotia and New Brunswick.

That was in 1846. Five years later, with the moral and vocal support of Bishop J. T. Mullock of Newfoundland, he organized the Newfoundland Electric Telegraph Company with a nominal capital of £300,000 in shares of £100 each.* It proposed to establish what was referred to as an intercontinental system of communication between London and New York, but its plans contained no proposals for a transatlantic cable. Rather, it would consist of "a line of Electric Telegraph from New York to St. John's, N.F.L., partly on poles, partly laid on the ground, and partly through the water, and a line of the swiftest steamships ever built, from that point to Ireland." This combination would shorten by three days or more the time required for messages to pass from Europe to the eastern cities of America.

Gisborne had been in London when the Brett brothers had laid their wire across the English Channel in 1851; he knew the Bretts, and he knew that a submarine cable across Cabot Strait to Nova Scotia was a possibility. If it failed, small packets or carrier pigeons could shuttle back and forth across the intervening water. The Newfoundland legislature granted Gisborne exclusive telegraph rights for thirty years and the necessary land to lay his wires, and even gave him £500 for a preliminary survey. With this endorsement, he got the necessary financial backing from a New York syndicate, headed by financiers H. B. Tebbetts and Darius B. Holbrook.

Thereupon Gisborne laid the first real submarine cable in North America, across Northumberland Strait to Prince Edward Island, a modest distance of nine miles. This was child's play compared with what lay ahead: the spanning of Newfoundland. There was, and is, no more rugged territory in the hemisphere—dense with forests,

* The English pound, throughout most of Field's lifetime, remained stabilized at $5.

slashed by rocks, pitted with bogs, and smothered in mists and fog. Caribou, bear, and wolves could find a home there, but it was no place for man. Even on the survey probe, Gisborne had to exchange his crew of half-starved white men for a handful of Indians, who in their turn deserted him.

By the spring of 1853 he was ready to start hacking his way south-westward from St. John's with a crew of 350 workmen. It had been his plan to lay the wires underground, but the earth was still too frozen—even for digging postholes. Poles had to be supported be-tween rocks piled on the surface. Before forty miles of line had been extended, Gisborne ran out of funds to pay his men. He appealed to New York, where Tebbetts and Holbrook refused to provide further support. Charged with fraud, he was arrested and stripped of every-thing he owned, and arrived in New York virtually a fugitive.

As an engineer, Matthew Field saw both the possibilities and the problems. The immediate need was for new backers and new money, and he saw a logical solution. Cyrus was doing nothing and he had money at his disposal. That evening he got his brother's permission to bring Gisborne to the house on Gramercy Park.

Cyrus was at once attracted to the Canadian promoter. Here might be the answer to his present sense of uselessness and inactivity. He listened, nodded, but was noncommittal. In fact, he was not sure where Newfoundland was in relation to surrounding territory; he did not know how the land lay between eastern Canada and St. John's. He knew nothing whatever about telegraphy, except that it was new and fast and that a great deal of money had been made and lost in its development.

After Matthew and Gisborne had left his study, he went to the globe on his desk and turned it slowly, following the line from the Maritime Provinces to Newfoundland and letting the globe spin clear around to Ireland. The next morning he sent word to Matthew to meet him at his home. Again he had the globe before him. Measuring the distances with his fingers, he pointed out that by the time a line had been extended from New York to St. John's, it would reach more than a third of the way to Ireland. Why not keep going and lay a cable all the way across the North Atlantic? Then they would have some-thing big, something worth investing in.

Matthew knew the idea was not altogether new. Samuel Morse had prophesied it, others less qualified had seen it as a remote dream of the future; but here was a firm proposition. As he hesitated, Cyrus assured him that he was not asking Matthew to become involved unless he wanted to; he was only asking, Could it be done?

Years later when Wells Field, Matthew's grandson, was asked by his teacher to tell the class about his uncle's laying of the cable, he said simply, "My pa told Uncle Cyrus he could do it, so he done it."

Matthew's answer was all that Cyrus needed. Since the Bretts had spanned the Channel, an 80-mile cable had been laid from Dover to Ostend, but the North Atlantic—that was something quite different. More than 1,600 miles of deep sea divided the two nearest points of land. Here indeed was a Herculean task, a challenge too superb to reject.

His precise mind recognized two separate but related problems. One concerned oceanography—the nature of the sea floor to be spanned. The other concerned physics. Could a wire 1,600 or 1,700 miles long actually carry an electrical impulse underwater?

That morning he applied directly to the best possible sources for his answers. He sat down and outlined the idea in separate letters to oceanographer Matthew Fontaine Maury, head of the Naval Observatory, and to artist Samuel F. B. Morse, the visionary intrepreneur whose advocacy had led, in spite of his lack of mechanical knowledge, to the establishment of the electric telegraph in America. Maury, of course, he knew, from their correspondence and discussions about the Amazon. Morse he knew only by reputation.

Some mental telepathy must have flashed between Field and Maury who replied: "Singularly enough, just as I received your letter, I was closing one to the Secretary of the Navy on the same subject." In confirmation, he attached a copy of what he had written to Secretary J. C. Dobbin. It proved that Maury did endorse the project in unequivocal words, basing his conclusions largely on deep-sea soundings made by Lieutenant O. H. Berryman, of the U. S. brig *Dolphin,* just one year before:

> This line of deep-sea soundings seems to be decisive of the question of the practicability of a submarine telegraph between the two continents, *in so far as the bottom of the deep sea is concerned.* From Newfoundland to Ireland, the distance between the nearest points is about sixteen hundred miles; and the bottom of the sea between the two places is a plateau, which seems to have been placed there especially for the purpose of holding the wires of a submarine telegraph, and of keeping them out of harm's way. It is neither too deep nor too shallow; yet it is so deep that the wires but once landed, will remain

forever beyond the reach of vessels' anchors, icebergs, and drifts of any kind, and so shallow, that the wires may be readily lodged upon the bottom.

The waters surrounding the "beautiful plateau," Maury went on, were as quiet as a millpond and because of this lack of current or disturbance the floor was largely powdered shell, with "not a particle of sand or gravel" to abrade a cable. (Maury's "Telegraph Plateau" was later identified as the northern foothills of the Mid-Atlantic Range, an apron fortunately marked by no deep crevasses or sharp peaks.) He estimated the maximum depth as between 1,500 and 2,000 fathoms. Considering the primitive state of oceanography at the time, he was not far wrong in any of these observations. But he prudently qualified them by adding that he did not "pretend to consider the question as to the possibility of finding *a time calm enough, the sea smooth enough, a wire long enough, a ship big enough, to lay a coil of wire sixteen hundred miles in length. . . .*" Possibly as a concession to Field, but more charitably as a genuine incentive, Maury proposed to the Secretary of the Navy that a prize be given to the company which first laid the cable and successfully transmitted a message through it.

Almost by the same post, Field received a reply from Samuel ("Finley" to his friends) Morse. Morse suggested that since Poughkeepsie was no great distance from the city, he come down to visit Cyrus, and they could go over the whole thing in some detail.

This new enterprise was the beginning of a more human and social approach to all Cyrus' activities. Field and Morse made a contrasting combination: Field still young, lithe, good-looking, and idealistic; Morse gaunt-visaged and white-haired, marked by adversity, "not handsome, but lighted up and intellectual." Yet as Morse's biographer Carleton Mabee wrote, they "could talk each other's language. They were alike sons of New England pastors of Old Testament fear in the Lord; they were alike hardheaded."

Morse was more than hardheaded. Since his days as a young and competent artist, he had had a combative nature different from Field's aggressiveness. It was personal and antagonistic. Though he had been first president of the National Academy of Design, he had failed to win recognition as a great painter. He felt that he had been slighted in the choice of artists to do paintings for the Capitol in Washington, but this, in his view, was due to the faulty judgment of others, not to his own deficiencies. Art, he complained, had jilted him.

When Field was still at school in Stockbridge, Morse had become obsessed with the idea of electric telegraphy (an idea by no means new), which came to his notice while returning from a visit to Europe aboard the packet *Sully*. Recognition of his work in this field had been slow in coming. His rights to the invention were disputed; others claimed legitimately to have had the same idea; his patents had been swamped with controversy. Full recognition had not come until the completed Washington-Baltimore telegraph line in 1844 transmitted the message "What hath God wrought!" Some years before, Morse had written to John C. Spencer, Secretary of the Treasury, that "a telegraphic communication on the electro-magnetic plan may with certainty be established across the Atlantic. Startling as this may now seem, I am confident that the time will come when this project will be realized."

Listening to Field's proposition, Morse was both confident and enthusiastic. But it was the enthusiasm and confidence of a man unfitted and untrained to appreciate the technical problems which would have to be overcome. Field, himself untechnical, could hardly estimate the lack of depth and understanding in his colleague's background. However there were few, if any, men at that time who possessed the knowledge and experience to advise on an undertaking of this nature.

At this meeting Field anticipated the use of Morse's patents on some reasonable basis and the forging of some sort of link with Morse's now unified telegraph system in the eastern states. Without such a link, the Atlantic cable would be seriously restricted.

With the endorsement of Maury and Morse, Field felt he was in a strong position to look for capital. He at once consulted Dudley, and thereafter the door between their homes was rarely closed. Dudley agreed wholeheartedly to handle any legal matters that came up— obviously there would be many—and he realized that his name and reputation, added to those of Cyrus, would be an important influence in raising money.

Cyrus felt that he would need at least ten men of wealth to help him launch the project. Logically, he turned to his friend and neighbor Peter Cooper. Cooper believed that "wealth is a trust, carrying paramount duties and obligations." And he was now absorbed in making a dream come true: the establishment of Cooper Union. Although he was a wealthy man, there were many reasons why he might be unwilling to invest in any new enterprise.

At first Cooper was reluctant, but his oblique interest in telegraphy, along with an almost mystical faith in electricity as the "manifestation of God's power in the universe," made him open to persuasion. Cooper related his reaction to Field's proposition:

> It was an enterprise that struck me very forcibly the moment he mentioned it. I thought I saw in it, if it was possible, a means by which we would communicate between the two continents, and send knowledge broadcast over all parts of the world. It seemed to strike me as though it were the consummation of that great prophecy, that "knowledge shall cover the earth, as the waters cover the deep," and with that feeling I joined him . . . in what then appeared to most men a wild and visionary scheme; a scheme that fitted those who engaged in it for an asylum. . . . But believing, as I did, that it offered the possibility of a mighty power for the good of the world, I embarked on it.

Cooper made his support contingent on Field's success in getting others to participate, but his name alone helped start things rolling. Cyrus called next on Moses Taylor—the New York importer, later to become president of the City Bank—whose "continuous accumulation of wealth," starting with his clerkship in a countinghouse, matched Field's success in business. As Cyrus recorded the interview: "I shall never forget how Mr. Taylor received me. He fixed on me his keen eye, as if he would look through me: and then, sitting down, he listened to me for nearly an hour without saying a word." By the time that Field stopped talking, Taylor was convinced. Although he too made it contingent on others' coming in, Field was confident of Marshall Roberts, whom he had met on his return voyage from Europe five years earlier. Roberts was a gambler by instinct. His ships had made a substantial fortune carrying prospectors to the California goldfields, and he had risen to be head of the United States Mail Steamship Company running to the Isthmus.

All the men who supported Cyrus in the beginning had started life from humble circumstances and made their way up by seizing every opportunity in any field that opened to them. If they were sometimes ruthless in their methods, they were both products and promoters of midcentury America. They had the imagination to see the possibilities in the project, they all had courage, and all thought in larger-than-life terms.

Chandler White was down as number four on Field's list. After the (for him) abortive South American expedition, White might well have been wary of any further schemes that Field advanced. Indeed he was, but Cyrus at length prevailed.

Throughout this marathon recruitment, Field kept in touch with Peter Cooper and Cooper at this point suggested that "If ten men can carry out the project, so can five." Accordingly Cyrus arranged for the group to get together with Gisborne, during the first week in March, 1854, at the Clarendon Hotel. Thereafter, for four successive evenings, they assembled in Field's study, where Gisborne with the aid of maps explained the progress already made in Newfoundland, while Cyrus outlined the proposed extension of the cable based on Maury's surveys.

When Daniel Huntington started his magnificent painting of "The Atlantic Cable Projectors," now hanging in the New York Chamber of Commerce, he asked Field, Morse, and others available at the time to reassemble and reconstruct the meeting for his benefit. Huntington remembered:

> Mr. Peter Cooper took the seat he usually occupied as chairman. Mr. Field stood as he often did calling attention to charts and maps on the table. A large globe was at hand for a study of the ocean paths. . . . They were a grand set of men—with striking variety of character, grouped around the large table, some sitting—some standing, and earnestly engaged in the great idea.

Huntington's collective portrait rightfully includes Dudley Field, who, although not a director, was present at the meetings, and Wilson G. Hunt, who succeeded Chandler White after the latter's death in 1856.

The first organizational step was obvious: to take over the rights, obligations, and charter of the Newfoundland Electric Telegraph Company. For all practical purposes, Gisborne was its sole representative, having been abandoned by his associates. He gladly surrendered the charter with the understanding that his debts of roughly $50,000 would be paid. A new company was tentatively formed, with all those present (except Gisborne, Morse, and Dudley Field) as directors. The name was to be the New York, Newfoundland and London Telegraph Company.

The next step was to obtain a new charter from the Newfoundland government, preferably one with broader rights than the earlier charter and certainly one that would include provisions for the transatlantic cable. From current resources the group raised $22,000 for expenses and voted to send a delegation to St. John's to talk to Newfoundland officials. Since Field's time was his own, as was Chandler White's, they agreed to make the trip, but suggested that Dudley join them to render legal services. Gisborne completed the party of four; he had his affairs to clean up, and it seemed likely that whatever work was undertaken from now on would involve him.

The group left New York on March 14 for Boston and from there to Halifax on the steamer *Merlin*. It was not a cheerful voyage, as Dudley's account suggests:

> In the darkest night, through which no man could see the ship's length, with snow filling the air and flying into the eyes of the sailors, with ice in the water, and a heavy sea rolling and moaning about us, the captain felt his way around Cape Race with his lead, as the blind man feels his way with his staff, but as confidently and safely as if the sky had been clear and the sea calm; and the light of morning dawned upon deck and mast and spar, coated with glittering ice, but floating securely between the mountains which form the gates of the harbor of St. John's.

In spite of the miserably rough weather Dudley spent the three days in his stuffy cabin drafting a new charter. When the wan and shaky group descended the gangplank at St. John's, they were met by Edward Mortimer Archibald, attorney general of the colony, who took them at once to Governor Kerr Bailey Hamilton. Both officials gave a warm welcome to the new proposal when they learned that the New York company would take care of the debts that Gisborne's group had left behind.

So generous and exclusive was the charter which Dudley had conceived that London later reported: "Her Majesty will be advised not to give her ratification to the creation of similar monopolies." It included an outright grant of fifty square miles of land in Newfoundland, with exclusive landing rights for fifty years, and fifty additional square miles to be allotted to the company when the transatlantic cable was completed (later even more generous rights were granted by the legislature of Prince Edward Island). Along with this went a guarantee of interest on £50,000 worth of bonds, along with £5,000 in cash for building a road across Newfoundland along the line of the telegraph, plus the waiving of all duties on material imported for the task.

Although it was Dudley's acumen that won the company strong rights from the start, William Howard Russell, an impartial London reporter, accorded a generous share in the success to Cyrus:

> Long ere the Company had been placed in possession of such beneficial rights, and obtained such a large amount of favour, Mr. Field, who threw every energy of body and mind into the work, and was entrusted by his brother directors with the general management of affairs, proceeded to carry out the engagements the Company had entered into with the local legislatures. It has been said that the greatest boons conferred on mankind have been due to men of one idea. If the laying of the Atlantic Cable be among these benefits, its consummation may certainly be attributed to the man who, having many ideas, devoted himself to work out one idea with a gentle force and patient vigour which converted opposition and overcame indifference.

Actually, Cyrus did not wait for the approval of the charter by the legislature. Dudley and Chandler White could handle that. Field took the *Merlin* back to Halifax, where he purchased the steamer *Victoria,* which became the flagship of the company's operations on the East Coast. In New York he arranged with the other directors to send $50,000 to Chandler White at St. John's to pay off the debts of the old Newfoundland Electric Telegraph Company. This was not only obligatory, but also timely. A St. John's newspaper reported: "We look upon the readiness with which these claims are liquidated as a substantial indication on the part of the new Company that they will complete to the letter all that they have declared to accomplish in this important undertaking."

In harmony with this, the Newfoundland legislature approved the new charter, with all its grants and rights, almost unanimously—only one vote in dissent. Dudley Field and Chandler White remained just long enough for the inevitable ceremonial banquet and then hurried back to New York, arriving on Saturday, May 6. There was now no time to lose. The directors were summoned to the Field home on Sunday at precisely 6 A.M., "and as the first rays of the morning sun streamed into the windows, the formal organization took place." It took just fifteen minutes to accept the approved charter, subscribe $1,500,000 worth of stock, and elect officers: Peter Cooper, president; Chandler White, vice-president and secretary; and Moses Taylor, treasurer. It was recognized that Cyrus' duties as the guiding genius of the enterprise would keep him shuttling between New York, Maritime Canada, and Europe, with no time to attend to routine business.

Of significance later, is a paragraph from the *Telegraph Manual,* by Taliaferro P. Shaffner, published in 1859. "Tal" Shaffner was a free-lance telegraph promoter. In the back of his *Manual* appears a biographical note on the author allegedly written by "a friend." It reads in part:

> Early in 1854, Mr. Shaffner visited New York city, to aid in the reorganization of the Newfoundland Telegraph Company, the secretaryship of which had been offered to him with a salary of twelve thousand dollars per annum. The new company was organized, having as proprietors some ten members, of whom Mr. Shaffner was one. Not satisfied with the administration of the company's affairs, he withdrew from the company forever.

Shaffner was probably unknown to Field at the time, was not, as he liked to claim, directly associated with Morse in his inventions, and was certainly not invited to join the company (consisting of "ten members" in his version), with salary or without. He sniped at the company from the sidelines, exerting a substantial nuisance value in the years to come.

But what of Finley Morse and his relations to the newly-formed company of which he was occasionally called vice-president? There is no record of Morse's being elected to any office, but the matter of title is unimportant. Cyrus insisted that Morse be included in the operation as advising electrician, and Morse was granted a tenth interest in the company for $10,000. More important, Morse agreed to use his influence in obtaining the use of the Morse patent telegraph lines from Canada's borders to New York, with messages to be carried at half rates when the cable connection with Europe had been established. He also, in a grandiose gesture, threw in his "rights to the bottom of the Atlantic Ocean," which nobody save Neptune owned.

Just three months had passed from Field's first conception of a telegraphic link with Europe to an organized company with capital to bring that link about. But he was still much farther from his goal than he could have realized. Fourteen years later he was to remark, "God knows that none of us were aware of what we had undertaken to accomplish." As his brother Henry noted, in records he began to keep of this endeavor:

Well was it for them that the veil was not lifted, which shut from their eyes the long delay, the immense toil, and the heavy burdens of many wearisome years. Such a prospect might have chilled the most sanguine spirit. But a kind Providence gives men strength for their day, imposes burdens as they are able to bear them, and thus leads them on to greater achievements than they knew.

Henry himself had an achievement in mind. It was to be the Boswell of the enterprise.

9

One Battle Lost

→→→→→←←←←← Late in May, 1854, Cyrus' brother-in-law and partner, Joseph Stone, died, leaving the firm in good condition but without a chief executive. Cyrus considered closing the business, but foresaw a need for further capital for his new project. Using black-bordered mourning stationery, he wrote to his suppliers on June 1: "The business will be continued by Cyrus W. Field, Edward D. Jones, Augustus Waterman, and David Conger, under the same name, and it will give us pleasure to receive your orders." And added: "If we should have the cholera here this summer bleaching powders will go up pretty high. Be sure and order in time."

Dual responsibility to the cable project and the paper business was to go on for six years, but he had the capacity to switch his mind and energies from one to the other without difficulty. He kept in close touch with Matthew Maury, anxious—as he had been with Finley Morse—that Maury should be an ex officio partner in the cable project. He offered Maury a financial interest in the company, which was declined on the ground that this would prevent Maury from using "any official influence which I might possess with the government, in order to further a scheme in which I am privately interested," but he added, "I have the success of the enterprise much at heart and would be glad to do what I rightfully may to forward it." Maury also asked Field for details of his plans for the cable so that he could present them to the American Association for the Advancement of Science, which was meeting that spring in Washington.

Field's plans called for a two-pronged offensive. The first was to complete the Newfoundland telegraph and to lay the submarine cable to Cape Breton that would then be connected with the telegraphic system in New England and throughout the country. The second, of course, was the transatlantic cable to Ireland, connecting, by newly laid wires under the Irish Sea and English Channel, with London and the whole of Europe. To get the connection established between St. John's and New York was a complex operation to be undertaken in three separate stages: the spanning of Newfoundland; the bridging of the Gulf of St. Lawrence; and the 140-mile extension link across Cape Breton.

Chandler White was put in charge of the office in St. John's as general agent, while Matthew Field, with Frederick Gisborne as consulting engineer, was to organize and supervise the actual completion of the Newfoundland telegraph from that city to Cape Ray. Cyrus would arrange for the submarine cable across the Gulf of St. Lawrence but would concentrate on the North Atlantic span. Theoretically both operations would continue simultaneously, but Matthew was ready to go to work at once. His task was scheduled for completion first—certainly by the following year. Actually, while both projects were separate, Matthew's was in many ways the more arduous, as Cyrus recognized:

> It was a very pretty plan on paper. There was New York and there was St. John's, only about twelve hundred miles apart. It was easy to draw a line from one point to the other, making no account of the forests and mountains and swamps and rivers and gulfs that lay in our way. Not one of us had ever seen the country or had any idea of the obstacles to be overcome. We thought we could build the line in a few months. It took two years and a half, yet we never asked for help outside our own little circle. Indeed I fear we should not have got it if we had, for few had any faith in our scheme. . . .

The distance from St. John's to Cape Ray was about 400 miles. Gisborne had earlier completed about 40 miles, starting from St. John's; but this was by far the easiest part, through inhabited and relatively level country. For the remainder, they would have to follow the irregular coastline because the central territory was too dense with forests, too difficult to supply. Materials and food would be brought ashore along the way from the steamer *Victoria,* while along the shoreline, weaving around gorges and estuaries, "a good and traversable bridle-road, eight feet wide, with bridges of the same width" would have to be built.

Matthew had enlisted an army of 600 workmen, which "moved forward in a great camp," guided by compass, through the wilderness, living in tents and huts or in the open. It was a mighty problem in logistics. The little steamer *Victoria* "was kept plying along the coast, carrying barrels of pork and potatoes, kegs of powder, pickaxes and spades and shovels, and all the implements of labor." These were dumped on the shore, to be carried inland to the moving bivouacs. "It was a wild and picturesque sight," wrote Henry Field, "to come upon their camp in the woods, to see their fires blazing at night while hundreds of stalwart sleepers lay stretched on the ground. Sometimes, when encamped on the hills, they could be seen afar off at sea. It made a pretty picture then."

It is doubtful if either Henry or Cyrus actually saw that pretty picture. Cyrus was in New York working on details of the Cabot Strait and North Atlantic cables. Peter Cooper's firm in Trenton was supplying Matthew with wire for the Newfoundland telegraph and its Canadian connections, but there was no firm in America then capable of making submarine cable. However, Gisborne knew the Bretts in England and many of the engineers and scientists connected with the laying of the Channel cable. He had purchased in London the line which he had laid from Nova Scotia to Prince Edward Island. It was obvious that Field would have to go to England for his Gulf and ocean cables, and Gisborne advised him to write ahead for samples to be ready for inspection.

Meanwhile, Field enlisted the help of Matthew Maury in procuring a ship suitable for laying the cable. Maury had to write: "I don't think that you can get the government to furnish two large steamers to lay the wires for it has them not. I have asked the Secretary to fit out the *Dolphin* again but the [Crimean] war in Europe absorbs attention here and I don't think it at all likely she will be fitted out for the present, at any rate."

Field's trip to London was put off by a second tragedy. Late in August his four-year-old son, Arthur Stone, died. The loss of the only boy in that family was a crushing blow and Cyrus slumped into a fit of depression. He fought it in the only way he knew how—by prodigious work. Almost every evening the available directors met in the Gramercy Park house to struggle with the problem of the Newfoundland operations. With fall approaching the ground was frozen; the men were cold; supplies were difficult to transport. Matthew's demands for money were increasing, and aware of Gisborne's previous failure because of lack of funds, nobody questioned his insistence.

Draft after draft was drawn by Chandler White on New York banks, until expenditures had reached $500,000 and were obviously going higher for what had been thought of as a minor phase of the whole enterprise.

In spite of everything there was no diminution in the pace of social life in the adjoining houses. In early January, 1855, George Templeton Strong noted in his diary:

> Last night to our neighbor David Dudley Field's, where we were invited "socially" to meet two hundred and fifty people; a soirée talkative, with a slight infusion of the saltatory elements toward its finale. A chaos of ill-assorted people and a babel of clack—enough to unsettle one's intellect permanently. I got through it well enough myself.

After the holidays Field sailed for England, the first of more than fifty transatlantic crossings he would make in behalf of his cable interests. He was seasick on every one, and midwinter was no time for an ocean voyage. He knew no one in London, apart from his connections in the paper trade, but he had had some correspondence with Küper & Company, the cable manufacturers, and Gisborne had given him a note of introduction to John Watkins Brett.

Oddly enough, of the two Brett brothers, John had made his money as an antique dealer, while Jacob had initially been the one with scientific inclinations. When Jacob applied to John for funds for his electrical experiments, John switched to electrical engineering and telegraphy. He enlisted government interest by installing a system of electric bells throughout the Houses of Parliament, to summon members to appointments, and in 1845 he submitted to the British government a plan for linking, by oceanic and subterranean cables, "the most distant parts of the United Kingdom or of the Colonies."

Nothing came of this scheme until Field's appearance in 1855. But in 1849 the brothers had obtained ten-year landing rights in France for their cable to Calais and had formed the General Oceanic Telegraphy Company—the first electrical telegraph firm ever registered in England. People ridiculed the undertaking as a madman's fantasy and charged that the wire would electrocute the Channel fish. During the cable's construction, which of necessity took place on open ground near Greenwich, visitors kept hacking off sections to take home as souvenirs.

The Bretts succeeded in laying a cable from Dover to Cape Gris-

Nez in August, 1850, and transmitted one garbled message to Louis Napoleon before a Boulogne fisherman hooked and hoisted up the line. Thinking he had discovered a new kind of seaweed with a core of gold, he cut out a lengthy section. ("It is believed," a London *Times* reporter wrote, "that this *pescatore ignoble* returned again and again to search for further specimens of this treasure of the deep.") The following year, Brett succeeded in laying a heavier cable, with strong wire armoring containing four separate telegraph lines. This cable continued in use for many years, although there were many who thought that signals were transmitted by tugging on one end to make a bell ring at the other.

Brett, now head of the Magnetic Telegraph Company in England, welcomed Field cordially and helpfully. He took his visitor down the Thames to visit the various cable manufacturers. The inner core containing the conducting wire and its insulation was made by one company; the outer armoring was made and laid around the core by another.

For the Gulf cable, Brett advised Field to select from the prepared samples a strand made up of three copper wires individually insulated with gutta-percha, wound with rope yarn, and covered with another sheath of gutta-percha, the whole thing then being protected with a covering of iron wire. It was arranged that the completed cable would be loaded, ready for laying, aboard the 500-ton bark *Sarah L. Bryant* and taken to Port aux Basques, Newfoundland, which would be one terminus of the line. Samuel Canning, a young British engineer who had laid cables in the Mediterranean, was engaged to meet the vessel when it arrived and to supervise the operation.

John Brett was the only Englishman to invest in the St. Lawrence cable. He became, in fact, Field's British advocate and sponsor in these early years, and Cyrus badly needed one, for the time would come, he knew, when he would have to rely greatly on British technical assistance, capital, and the cooperation of the Crown. On his part, Brett remarked of Field: "I rather like these Americans—they're so intensely serious about things."

Returning home in March, Field bombarded poor John Brett with letters and commissions. Küper & Company informed him that "the cable is progressing most favourably" and would be finished by the second week in June, but as for the actual paying-out machinery, "[we] would advise you to get it made on your side if possible." Cyrus promptly wrote to Brett: "Now I wish you would have made and shipped with the cable . . . all the necessary machinery for paying out, for it will be almost impossible to get it made in Newfoundland, and I am fearful that it would not be made well here, as we have had no experience in such matters."

He kept in continual touch with Matthew Maury, pressing on him a financial interest in the New York, Newfoundland and London Telegraph Company in return for Maury's services; he seemed intent on spreading his anticipated fortune and success among as many friends as possible. Maury again declined, but did make the modest request that his Naval Observatory might have the privilege of using the Atlantic cable, as soon as completed, to check the longitude of Washington with that of Greenwich. Field promptly called the directors together and persuaded them to pass a resolution offering Maury the right not only to use of the wires, but also to use them freely and free of charge.

Of his brother Matthew, Cyrus inquired impatiently how long his job was going to take and Matthew replied:

> How many months? Let's say how many *years!* Recently, in building half a mile of road we had to bridge three ravines. Why didn't we go around the ravines? Because Mr. Gisborne had explored twenty miles in both directions and found more ravines. That's why! You have no idea of the problem we face. We hope to finish the land line in '55, but I wouldn't bet on it before '56, if I were you.

The delay was costly and exasperating, but there was no reason to hold up laying the Newfoundland-Cape Breton cable on this account. Word came that the eighty-five mile cable had been shipped from England aboard the bark *Sarah L. Bryant*. All that was needed now was a ship to tow the *Bryant* across the Gulf of St. Lawrence, while the cable was payed out and laid itself along the bottom. Field, in an expansive mood, decided to charter a luxury coastal steamer belonging to the Charleston Line and invite the directors, their wives and children, and any merry-hearted friends to come along.

Peter Cooper and his family accepted the invitation for the trip to Newfoundland. So did the Samuel Morses with their son. The Field family was well represented, with Cyrus' two older daughters, his brother Henry and wife Henriette, and Dr. David Dudley Field from Haddam to act as chaplain on the voyage. Mary could not join the party; she was still nursing their sixth child, Edward Morse (the Morse for Samuel Finley Morse), born just a month before. Completing the gathering of more than fifty were Frederick Gisborne; Dr. Gardiner Spring, pastor of the Brick Church in New York; attorney Robert W. Lowber, who acted as social director; and assorted couples and young ladies of society. Matthew Maury had been urgently invited and arrived at the dock with his wife and two oldest sons but, discovering that the cruise might take as long as two weeks, was forced to decline and to return to Washington.

It was the morning of August 7, 1855. The ship was beautiful, the sky clear, the sea a millpond, and spirits were high among the passengers. Crowds gathered at the pier to see the sleek, flag-decked *James Adger* off. Field was paying $750 a day for the fast side-wheeler, which offered all the modern comforts: two ample saloons and outside private cabins, mahogany trim, and carpeted companionways. And she was powerful enough to tow the *Sarah L. Bryant*.

Once under way and cruising up the sound, Finley Morse brought his portable telegraph up on deck and gave a demonstration to the passengers. Peter Cooper, making his first ocean voyage, "expounded his religious views" on deck with Dr. Spring. Men in white ducks brought out their guitars and strummed to the crinoline-garbed ladies in the deck chairs. Surrounded by many of his family, Dr. Field looked like a white-bearded prophet in his muffling greatcoat; while Henry's Henriette looked glamorous and almost wanton with the sea wind in her hair.

When thunderstorms struck the ship that evening, induced, the guests said jokingly, by Morse's apparatus, they went inside and sang and danced to the tunes of Christy's Minstrels. The weather turned wretched and made Cyrus seasick, but failed to damp the generally high spirits of the voyage. Stopping briefly at Halifax, where several of the passengers, by prearrangement, left the ship for home, they sailed on up to Port aux Basques, where, from the bow of the *Adger,* Cyrus scanned the horizon for the three masts of the *Bryant*. There was no sign of the bark; nor was she hidden in the harbor when they got there. Samuel Canning rowed out to the steamer and reported no word of the *Bryant;* she had obviously been delayed by weather.

Field ordered the captain to go on to St. John's; they could pick up the *Bryant* on the way back and meanwhile pay a call on the provincial government authorities and further cement the good relations that already existed. At the St. John's pier they were met by a delegation of barking, wagging Newfoundland dogs that at once engaged their hearts. The passengers bought them at prices ranging from two to ten dollars, according to age and quality.

Field hired a local band and entertained the St. John's city council aboard the *Adger*. In return the visitors were invited to a ball on land. The following day 200 city locals were taken on a cruise aboard the ship, and that night it was time to sail. As the steamer pulled away, the Newfoundland dogs on the dock, seeing their companions leaving them, jumped in and pursued the ship, and Cyrus ordered ladders lowered to bring another and by now unwelcome pack aboard.

A surprise salute attended their departure. Part of the construction plans to make St. John's a port of call for deep-draft transatlantic steamers was the dynamiting of a large rock at the entrance to the harbor. Just as the *Adger* passed, the dynamite was touched off, and the rock exploded, startling passengers, panicking the dogs, and showering the decks with shrapnellike fragments of stone.

Returning to Port aux Basques, they found the *Bryant* waiting but badly battered by severe gales and in need of repair. The cable machinery had not been assembled. Disgusted, Cyrus and Samuel Canning spent the intervening time reconnoitering the area for a suitable landing place for the cable. They decided on Cape Ray Cove, a few miles to the west, whose sandy bottom promised a comfortable bedding for the wire.

There was no shelter at Cape Ray to house the telegraphic crew and instruments. Field ordered the *Victoria* to bring lumber from Port aux Basques, so that the crew could build a shack, but the *Victoria* could not get close enough to unload the cargo on the beach. It was decided to float the lumber ashore in rafts, with one man to a raft to guide it. The plan seemed sound except for the surf, which looked deceptively tranquil from a distance. As the rafts approached the breakers, they began to fly apart, scattering men and beams, planks and shingles, in a massive flotsam on the waves.

It was then that the Newfoundland dogs justified their purchase. Bayard Taylor of the New York *Tribune* wrote:

> ... the dogs rendered capital service—plunging boldly into the sea and seizing upon every stick which they could manage. Sometimes two of them would take a plank between them, and watching the proper moment with a truly human sagacity, bring it to the beach on the top of a breaker and there deliver it into the hands of their masters. It was really wonderful to behold the strength, courage, and

industry of these poor beasts, who, when but few fragments were left, fought savagely for the possession of them and even tried to drown each other.

The shack was almost completed by the end of the day. By the next morning fog had moved in and the cable laying had to be postponed for two days. When a rising breeze cleared the fog, the *Adger* took the bark in tow, but the *Bryant* was unable to raise her anchor and was forced to slip it. Both vessels started drifting toward each other, with their captains yelling futilely, "Back up!" The steamer collided broadside with the *Bryant*'s bow, carrying away her shrouds and quarter rail. Captain Turner of the *Adger* cut the hawser connecting the vessels and steamed off, leaving the bark holding helplessly to one end of the cable. The *Bryant* cast out her remaining anchor to keep from drifting on the rocks, immediately lost it, and was forced to cut the cable, hoist sail, and head out to sea to save herself.

In one account, Captain Turner was accused of deliberately ramming the bark in an attempt to sink her. Certainly Turner was in an ugly mood. He resented taking orders from a passenger, even though Field was in charge of the expedition, and he had felt ignominiously slighted when Dr. Spring had usurped his rightful place at the head of the table. His truculence became apparent in the second attempt to get the cable underway, after the necessary repairs had been made aboard the *Bryant*. Peter Cooper wrote:

> Before starting our engineer, who had charge of laying the cable, gave the captain instructions to keep constantly in view a flag placed upon the telegraph-house and bring it in range with a white rock upon the mountain, which would give him the exact lines upon which to steer. As soon, however, as we got off, I saw the captain was going out of the way, and as president of the board I told him so. The answer was, "I know how to steer by my compass." I said, "Your instructions were to steer by the flag and the rock on the mountain." "I steer by my compass," was all I could get out of him. He went on steering in that manner until I found he was going so far out of the way that I told him I would hold him responsible for all loss. This had no effect. I then got a lawyer who was on board to draw up a paper warning the captain that if he did not change his course we should hold him responsible for the loss of the cable. He then turned his course and went as far out of the way in the other direction.

By this time the breeze which had cleared away the fog had turned into a gale. Owing to the captain's going around in circles, they had payed out twenty-four miles of cable and were just nine miles from shore. Not only had kinks developed in the wire from this circuitous course, but the captain had also refused to regulate his speed according to that of the machinery aboard the bark. The *Bryant* finally ran up a signal flag; she had been forced to cut the cable before it dragged her under.

Sighting this melee, a patrolling British warship, the *Argus,* came to their rescue displaying a hugely lettered sign: "Can we render you any assistance?" When Turner typically refused to answer, the *Argus* flashed another sign: "Answer—yes, or no!" In joint consultation, Field and Cooper lettered "No" on the side of the smokestack. They believed they could get to Sydney, Nova Scotia, with the bark in tow, and meanwhile, even in those high seas, somehow managed to get Samuel Canning off the *Bryant* and onto the *Adger.*

While Canning was below, changing into dry clothes, Cyrus called all the passengers into the after cabin and then escorted the English engineer to stand before them. He wanted to explain how much the company appreciated Canning's efforts and admired his persistence, how the failure was in no way his responsibility. Canning all but wept.

Cyrus was brokenhearted. What had started out so gallantly, with every promise of success, had been an utter failure. Cooper reminded him that this was only the beginning; they had lost a battle but would win the war.

From Sydney, where the *Sarah L. Bryant* unloaded her remaining length of cable to be put in storage, the *James Adger* headed for New York. The guests remained festive, danced the polka and the schottische, and held a costume party on their last night aboard. The following morning, bleary-eyed from lack of sleep, they assembled to pass a resolution expressing their gratitude to Cyrus Field and Peter Cooper "for the munificent hospitality to which we are indebted for the delightful and interesting voyage which is now drawing to a close —a voyage which has made us acquainted with places little known, enriched our minds with a store of valuable recollections, and cheered us with the warmth of social intercourse." Dr. Field closed the ceremony with "an impressive prayer."

Tallying up the expedition's score, the company had lost a total of $350,000, about a quarter of their capital, on only one phase of the project and had nothing to show for it. But they had learned never again to use two ships for a cable-laying operation, and never again to use a sailing vessel. From now on, steam would be required.

What of the cable? About forty miles of it lay on the bottom of the Gulf of St. Lawrence, and Peter Cooper observed that it was fortunate the ships were not there, too.

What of the recalcitrant Captain Turner? Years later Peter Cooper wrote his epitaph: "We had spent so much money, and lost so much time, that it was very vexatious to have our enterprise defeated by the stupidity and obstinacy of one man. This man was one of the rebels that fired the first guns on Fort Sumter. The poor fellow is now dead."

What of the Newfoundland dogs? Bayard Taylor wrote his mother: "I have brought you a fine dog . . . he is of the Newfoundland breed, wolf-colored and web-footed, and will make a capital watch-dog for you. His father was the best watch-dog at Cape Ray."

10

English Alliance

>>>>>><<<<<< With his customary resiliency, Field soon recovered from his depression. Cooper persuaded the directors to buy more cable to replace what they had lost, and before they could change their minds, he contracted with Küper & Company to make and lay the cable at its own risk, using its own steamer, the *Propontis,* with Samuel Canning as the engineer in charge. Field did not want his own people involved in another fracas like the last. "It was in great measure due to the indomitable courage and zeal of Mr. Field inspiring us that we went on and on until we got another cable across the gulf," Cooper generously acknowledged.

Both Field and Cooper realized, however, that the St. Lawrence cable would be of little value unless it was joined to a network covering the entire country. The rights which Morse had guaranteed them, for the wire from Maine to New York, were not enough, and the lines that radiated from New York to the Middle West and South were owned and operated haphazardly by a number of different companies. Some used Morse's patents; others used patents which Morse contested. Independent operators like Tal P. Shaffner regarded telegraphy as territory to be acquired by a swift and ruthless attack. Shaffner contracted for lines to be erected in a hurry, in advance of competitors, whom he threatened to shoot on sight if they came within his range.

There was urgent need for a homogeneous network using a single system of telegraphy under a unified management to link all the major cities of the country. Field had no wish to become involved in domestic telegraphy, but it was clear that he had little choice. Proprietors of the cable would have to be able to relay messages to and from the originators and recipients. Peter Cooper agreed with Field that some form of unity between the cable and the telegraph interests was essential.

A new form of telegraph transmission had been evolved since Morse's early days. A printing device which translated electrical impulses into letters, it had been invented by Royal E. House, of Vermont, and improved by a professor of music named David Hughes. Field and Cooper bought the rights from Hughes for $100,000, obtained possession of the House line running from New York to Boston (later on to Halifax), and formed the American Telegraph Company —to lease or buy existing lines throughout the country and to build a system of their own. Whichever they had to do, Field believed that the Hughes patent would prove a valuable asset. The company was incorporated on November 1, 1855, with a nominal capital of $200,-000 and with Peter Cooper as its president. Wrote Edward C. Mack: "A formidable power had come into the telegraph field, which, after a four-year war of nerves, was to control all the lines along the Atlantic seaboard."

The purchase of Hughes' patent and the use of House lines were a sacrilege to Morse, who considered that his invention covered every conceivable method of transmitting messages by wire. And when he heard that the American Telegraph Company was thinking of supplanting the Morse lines with wires of its own, on the flimsy excuse that Morse's rates were too high, he was outraged—this time with some justice. His indignation was fanned by his patent agent, Amos Kendall, who wrote: "Field & Co. are shrewd business men not unfriendly to you or me but more friendly to themselves."

It was the beginning of a temporary schism between Morse and Field, but for a while Morse continued as honorary electrician in the group. There had been changes however. Chandler White had died, and Robert Lowber, the attorney aboard the *Adger,* had replaced him. Wilson Hunt, a friend of Cooper's and former candidate for mayor of New York, had joined the board of directors, although curiously confessing that he "did not feel much interest in the project."

Field had finally agreed to accept the title of vice-president, although it made no difference in his duties, which were now almost entirely concerned with the cable. During the next few months he hardly saw the Cliff Street offices of Field & Company, pausing there only long enough to write to Zenas Crane to explain that fifty bales of Turkish rags aboard the clipper *Fortitude,* purchased in behalf of

Crane & Company, had gone back to Gibraltar when the vessel sprang a leak. He did not fail to remark, however, that with the price of Turkish rags increasing day by day, the cargo would be worth more when it finally arrived.

Meanwhile, work on the two landlines—the one across Newfoundland and the second down Cape Breton—was gaining momentum, and Matthew could now assure him they would be finished by midsummer. But the cost had mounted to $1,000,000—two-thirds of their capital! Cyrus called a meeting of the directors, who decided on an issue of bonds to raise further capital and subscribed for the entire issue among themselves. By now Field's personal investment was about $250,000. He began to wonder if Maury's appraisal of the ocean floor was foolproof. It was based on surveys made *before* an Atlantic cable had been seriously projected. Since then, new techniques for taking soundings had been developed.

He questioned Maury and far from taking offense, the sailor-scientist agreed that more work should be done. In May, 1856, Maury wrote to Secretary of the Navy Dobbin requesting three naval vessels to make further deep-sea soundings, which "would answer many interesting questions in physics but also encourage the Atlantic cable laying." Peter Cooper, as president of the company, also wrote to the Secretary, asking for his support in men and ships to back the project. To both of them, Dobbin replied evasively that while he would like to help in the "laudable enterprise," neither the ships nor the men were available.

Without realizing it, Field was becoming a victim of one of the many personality feuds that were to plague him during his promotion of the cable. This one was between Matthew Maury and Alexander Dallas Bache, superintendent of the Coast Survey, a department distinct from the Navy. Bache contended that all ocean sounding surveys rightfully belonged to his department, and had already swayed Secretary Dobbin to agree. "As a result of Bache's determination to replace Maury as the man supplying Field with oceanic information, there now developed a secretly maneuvered episode that created open wrangling and damaged the prestige of American science at home and abroad," Francis Leigh Williams wrote.

Field was at first completely unaware of this maneuvering. But it resulted in Bache's man, Lieutenant O. H. Berryman, being dispatched by Secretary Dobbin on the steamer *Arctic* as commander, to make the necessary soundings in the cable waters. There was some thin excuse for this. Berryman had worked with Maury when the latter made his survey of the telegraph plateau. Now Maury was outraged at being bypassed. He put Field squarely in the middle by asking him to board the *Arctic* before she sailed and to demand to see Berryman's orders.

It was a discomforting request. Field was not anxious to take sides in any controversy or alienate anyone of influence in Washington. But he went aboard the *Arctic,* checked Berryman's orders, and took a copy back to Maury. Finding them authentic as he must have known he would, Maury was nevertheless preconditioned to reject and discredit any findings Berryman should bring back.

By remaining honestly neutral, Field kept Maury on his side, while his "dedicated enthusiasm and pertinacity" (in Maury's words) endeared him to the naval scientist.

Little by little, from Maury and Morse and everyone he talked with, Field was learning something about the technical side of submarine cables, although he never made it his first line of business. He was an entrepreneur, not a technician; and for him the task ahead was one of organization and promotion. So far the New York, Newfoundland and London Telegraph Company had been a local operation, financed by a handful of American investors. It was time now to get government support in the United States and government support, along with English capital, from London.

Field was ready to carry the crusade to England. He felt that he would need technical support, and he asked Finley Morse—with whom he had become reconciled—to accompany him on the *Baltic,* sailing early that July. Morse was unable to join him on the *Baltic* but agreed to follow some weeks later. Cyrus then invited his wife and his sister Mary to come along. Mary was still somewhat distraught over Joseph Stone's death, as a result of which her health had declined, and he felt the change would do her good.

It was the last pleasant crossing he was to enjoy for years. The weather was benign, the sea calm, and above all, the cable project seemed to be progressing. The additional cable for the Gulf of St. Lawrence was on its way from England. And Samuel Canning, assisted by a young man named De Sauty, would be in charge of the laying.

It had been a considerable achievement to obtain exclusive landing rights in the only British possessions that were practical for an Atlantic cable, and it placed Field in a strong position. Only he and four others had furnished the capital. "Our little company," he recalled some years later, "raised and expended over a million and a quarter of dollars before an Englishman paid a single pound sterling." He neglected to say that they had intentionally kept the circle small and had shown no eagerness to share the credit—or the burden.

In London, Field took rooms for himself and both his Marys in Jermyn Street, close to Whitehall and to John Brett's home in Hanover Square. As head of the Magnetic Telegraph Company in England, Brett was certainly the best man to interest influential Englishmen, and the shareholders in his company seemed to be likely prospects for helping finance the transatlantic cable.

Equally in support of Field's goal was young Charles Tilston Bright, engineer for the Magnetic Telegraph Company. Field was discovering that many scientists had dreamed of oceanic cables long before he had undertaken his crusade—Morse and Brett and Bright, among others. He recognized in Bright a kindred spirit, a man even younger than himself, who at twenty-three held more than two dozen patents for electrical inventions, and who coupled a gentlemanly modesty with nervous energy and drive. He had just completed the extraordinary feat of laying telegraph lines beneath the streets of Manchester, all in a single night, without disturbing traffic or even making the population aware that such a job was being undertaken.

Of his first meeting with Cyrus Field, Bright reflected some years later: "He was a man of destiny . . . you couldn't escape him." But at the time he quickly appraised Field as "rapid in thinking and acting, and endowed with courage and perseverance under difficulties—qualities which are rarely met with." They made a good team.

With John Brett, Field and Bright held the last of several meetings in September, 1856, to sign the following agreement: "Mutually, and on equal terms we engage to exert ourselves for the purpose of forming a Company for establishing and working of electric telegraphic communication between Newfoundland and Ireland, such Company to be called the Atlantic Telegraph Company."

So far, so good. They had the nucleus of an organization, but aside from Field's monopoly of landing rights in Newfoundland, little else. There remained to get: first, the necessary cable for the ocean link; second, government recognition on both sides of the Atlantic, along with ships and subsidies to help defray the cost; and finally, financial support from investors in Great Britain and America.

Maury's advice to Field on the building of the cable had been based on his knowledge of physical oceanography, not practical experience with telegraphy. Charles Bright, on the other hand, had actually laid most of the underground wires throughout England, as well as the submarine cable in the Irish Sea. Probably he, more than anyone else, determined the specifications to be followed, although other authorities—such as Professor William Thomson of the University of Glasgow—were consulted.

Thomson, with his quiet manner and rich Scottish accent, was to become one of the outstanding men of British science. At twenty-one he had been appointed professor of natural philosophy at Glasgow University and, moving into physics, established the first experimental science laboratory in Great Britain. He was, wrote Arthur C. Clarke, "a unique bridge between the laboratory and the world of industry. . . . It would not be unfair to say that if one took half the talents of Einstein, and half the talents of Edison, and succeeded in fusing such incompatible gifts into a single person, the result would be rather like William Thomson."

It was decided that the cable's core, nine interwoven copper wires sheathed in gutta-percha, would be manufactured by the London Gutta Percha Company, while the 2,000 miles of outer covering, consisting principally of eighteen woven strands of iron, would be split between two manufacturers: Glass, Elliot & Company, which had since absorbed the Küper Company and had made the cable for the Gulf, and R. S. Newall & Company, of Birkenhead. There was an element of risk in this division of labor, but it would not have mattered if the order had been sufficiently explicit. Unfortunately, however, although it described precisely the gauge and number of the armoring wires, it omitted to say whether the wires should be laid with a right- or left-hand lay, and with the perversity of fate, one firm chose one direction, the other the opposite! This unfortunate discrepancy introduced considerable difficulty whenever it became necessary to join a length of Glass, Elliot's cable to one covered by R. S. Newall.

More serious were the doubts of men who claimed that an electric current would, in effect, leak out; the signals would be slowed and weakened and become indistinct over such a distance. Three hundred miles was the maximum that a message had so far been sent. The philosopher-scientist Michael Faraday claimed there would be a marked delay in sending signals through that length of wire.

Field called on Faraday in his laboratory at the Royal Institution

and asked him to undertake experiments to determine the extent of
that delay.

"I know already," Faraday said. "You just won't get any instanta-
neous message."

"How long will it take?" asked Field.

"Oh, perhaps a second," Faraday concluded.

Cyrus still needed proof that the cable would work. Morse, who had
by now arrived in London, agreed to put the matter to a test. Obtaining the facilities of Brett's Magnetic Telegraph Company, during the
night, when they were not in normal use, he connected together a
network of 2,000 miles of subterranean wire, "a distance you will per-
ceive sufficient to cross the Atlantic Ocean." His signals traveled the
distance at an increasing rate of 210, 241, and finally 270 a minute.
Morse checked a second time and reported the results to Cyrus,
adding:

> In one word, the doubts are resolved, the difficulties overcome,
> success is within our reach, and the great feat of the century must
> shortly be accomplished.
>
> I would urge you, if the manufacture can be completed within the
> time (and all things are possible now), to press forward the good
> work, and not lose the chance of laying it during the ensuing summer.

The ensuing summer was what Field had in mind, but he still had
to find the ships for the task. It happened that Lieutenant Berryman,
aboard the *Arctic,* had arrived at Queenstown, Ireland, having completed his favorable survey of the ocean floor between Newfoundland
and Ireland. Field made a hasty trip to talk with him and bring his
findings back to Brett and Bright. On the return trip to London via
Wales, he shared a compartment with a man whom he easily recognized and to whom he introduced himself: Isambard Kingdom Brunel.

The "Little Giant," standing only five feet four, with his clenched
cigar and beaver hat crammed full of memoranda to himself, was considered easily the greatest engineer of nineteenth-century England.
He had thrown railroads over continents, tunneled under rivers, ex-
perimented in jet propulsion, and now, at Millwall, was building the
largest ship the world had ever seen, to be known as the *Great Eastern.*

Their talk turned naturally to the cable project. Field showed
Brunel a sample section of the cable being laid in Cabot Strait, in
which the conducting core was formed of seven twisted strands of
copper. "Why not have the outer covering of the Atlantic cable

formed of twisted strands as well as the conductor?" said Brunel. "By that means you'll have a stronger, lighter and more flexible cable than if you make the outer covering of solid wire." It was a suggestion Field and his associates adopted (and which the manufacturers confounded in construction), and it brought Brunel into their circle of consultants. On their return to London, Brunel took Field down to Millwall to see the massive skeleton of the *Great Eastern* rising on the riverbank. *"There* is the ship to lay your cable!" said Brunel. Whether he meant it or not, Brunel's suggestion regarding the *Great Eastern* was sound; it was certainly more practical to have a single vessel lay the cable but right now there was no ship big enough to carry such a massive load. The *Great Eastern* would not be completed for another year. To Field, a year was an insufferable time to wait.

Ships and crews could not be had by private means; they would have to get them from the governments involved. Field, with Finley Morse, paid a visit to Lord Clarendon, the Foreign Secretary. Would Clarendon persuade the Admiralty to supply some naval vessels for the project? Clarendon listened sympathetically but asked, "Suppose you try and fail, and the cable is lost at sea—what do you do then?" Field replied, "Charge it to profit and loss, and go to work to lay another."

He left Lord Clarendon with the assurance that the British government was on his side; the details would come later. With that encouraging development, Field took his ailing sister Mary and his wife to Paris for a brief holiday. There Mary died on the night of their arrival. It was the third death in the family within twenty-four months, and it again pitched Field into depression. He put his wife on a steamer for America and returned to England, where he was able to retire quietly for some days to James Wilson's home in Bath.

Wilson was Secretary to the Treasury, one of the many influential government officials to whom Field had been introduced by John Brett. Seeing his young guest too despondent even to discuss the cable enterprise, Wilson decided to take steps of his own. When Cyrus returned to Jermyn Street, he found that Wilson had intervened with Clarendon and other Members of Parliament and that Her Majesty's government was ready to cooperate with Field and his associates on certain reasonable terms.

The British government would not only provide ships to help lay the cable, but would assign the frigate *Cyclops,* under Captain Joseph Dayman, to make additional soundings of the ocean route. They also agreed to subsidize the cable to the extent of £14,000 a year (4 percent on the £350,000 capital investment). The only condition placed upon this subsidy was that the Crown should have priority in sending messages by the cable, unless and until the United States should join the pact—in which case both countries should have equal rights.

Field at once sent Peter Cooper a full draft of this agreement. He pointed out that although both ends of the cable would be in British territory, the English claimed no exclusive privileges, but simply wanted equal rights with the United States. What could be fairer? He suggested that Cooper and the other directors draft a letter to President Pierce, saying in effect that the company would enter into a contract with the government of the United States on the same terms and conditions as it had made with the British government.

Without further ado, the Atlantic Telegraph Company was registered in London in October, 1856, with Brett president, Field vice-president, Bright chief engineer, George Saward secretary, and Dr. Edward O. W. Whitehouse, electrician. Whitehouse, a former Brighton physician, had carried out electrical experiments as a diversion from his normal occupation. His appointment was perhaps the only dubious selection.

Publicity regarding the new company brought attacks, opposition, and ridicule—not universally, by any means, but to an extent that was certainly disconcerting. No less an authority than the Astronomer Royal, Sir G. B. Airy, hastened to point out that "it was a mathematical impossibility to submerge a cable at so great a depth" and that "if it were possible, no signals could be transmitted through so great a length."

Field's mail was swollen with letters from clergymen, housemaids, engineers, actors, sailors, artists, and gentlemen of leisure offering procedural suggestions. One was to hitch the cable to aquatic parachutes and let it hover just below the surface of the ocean or suspend it above the surface from balloons. Another was to attach it to a transatlantic chain of buoys, to which passing ships could tie up and send or receive messages. Even Prince Albert suggested that the entire length of wire be protected by a glass tube, quoting Pretonius Arbiter as his authority. One man offered to do the whole job single-handedly, if they would give him a small boat and a marlinspike.

The most important task remaining was to raise the capital, which the company had set at £350,000. Once again Brett's Magnetic Telegraph Company provided indispensable leverage and support.

Its shareholders presented a presold market, and the Magnetic Company's offices in London, Glasgow, Manchester, and Liverpool provided outlets for the sale of stock. As vice-president, Field prepared an informal prospectus outlining the company's objectives and potential, but it was his personal salesmanship, sincerity, and charm that got results. He visited each of these cities and talked to the people individually and in groups, adapting the emphasis of his presentation to the interests of his audience.

In Liverpool he encountered a wealthy country squire who professed no interest in the cable; his passion was for raising outsize beagles. Field is said to have accepted an invitation to inspect the breeder's rangy animals and inquired innocently of his host if he could imagine a dog so large that it reached from England to America. The man suggested Field was crazy.

"I simply wondered," Cyrus said, "if you could *imagine* such a dog."

"Certainly, sir; I could *imagine* anything!"

"Well, the project of which I've spoken and tried to interest you in is essentially just such a dog. If you pinch his tail in Liverpool, he'll bark in New York."

Among the private subscribers were Lady Byron and William Makepeace Thackeray, who, as Arthur C. Clarke observed, could not have shared the literary attitude of Thoreau toward telegraphy. Two years earlier the Walden Pond philosopher had written:

> We are in great haste to construct a magnetic telegraph from Maine to Texas; but Maine and Texas, it may be, have nothing important to communicate. We are eager to tunnel under the Atlantic and bring the Old World some weeks nearer to the New; but perchance the first news that will leak through into the broad, flapping American ear will be that Princess Adelaide has the whooping cough. . . .

Within two weeks the entire issue of 350 shares, at £1,000 a share, had been subscribed—oversubscribed, in fact. Field and Brett had set aside a certain quantity for themselves but, when the books were closed, had to settle for a smaller amount. Even so, with 88 shares in his name—approximately $440,000 at the going rate—Field's interest was one-fourth of the company's entire capital and almost five times that of John Brett, the second largest investor in the company.

It was not Field's intention to keep this stock for himself. Having seen how it had been pounced upon in England, he was confident that he could sell a good part of his holdings in America. It was important to him that he should—and not simply to relieve his personal finances. So far, except for himself and Peter Cooper, all the money behind the Atlantic cable project was English. "He thought," wrote Henry, "that one fourth of the stock should be held in this country, and he did not doubt from the eagerness with which three-fourths had been taken in England, that the remainder would be at once subscribed in America."

Before leaving London, he gave some thought to matters at home. The Cabot Strait cable had been successfully installed; there was direct communication between St. John's, Newfoundland, and New York. However, it would be a year at least before the overseas link with Ireland was established—a year which could not be wasted. He employed a London firm to print and distribute a thirteen-page pamphlet entitled *Statement of Some of the Advantages Which Would Result From Making St. John's, Newfoundland, a Port of Call for Transatlantic Steamers.* His idea was that if he could get existing packet services to drop off messages at St. John's, these could be wired to New York; this in turn would interest people in the whole idea of getting faster news from Europe by telegraphy.

He pointed out that St. John's was ice-free most of the winter because of high tides, that the harbor was adequately deep and sheltered, that coal supplies were readily accessible. He went on to say:

> Nothing, however, has given more importance to St. John's as a port of call, than the establishment of the line of electric telegraph between that port and New York, which is now completed, supplying news, both commercial and political, between the American Continent and all Europe, from three to five days in advance of any other present means of communication.

As a further attraction, the New York, Newfoundland and London Company would *pay* the steamship lines $1 each for messages delivered to their lines!

He returned to New York thoroughly tired, on Christmas Day, 1856. The city was blanketed with snow, and Gramercy Park, with its holly wreaths and candles in the windows, looked like a scene from a Dickens novel. But Cyrus was too depressed by his sister's death and by utter weariness to care. He reported at once to Peter Cooper and his brother Dudley, and Dudley reminded him of something he should have thought of earlier. The exclusive landing rights obtained in Canada applied only to the New York, Newfoundland and London Company. They did not apply to the Atlantic Telegraph Company which Cyrus had just organized.

Exhausted as he was, he stopped only long enough to drop the gifts he had brought and to wish the children Merry Christmas, then was on his way to Boston and to St. John's via Halifax. The voyage was wretched, matching his own spirits. He stayed in the pitching cabin throughout the journey, too sick to leave it. But before he collapsed completely in St. John's and was put in the care of a physician, he managed to set the wheels in motion to ensure that the provincial legislature would grant the English group the same rights it had offered to the New York company.

As soon as he heard of a steamer leaving for New York, nothing could restrain him. Against the advice of his doctor, he set out and was back at Gramercy Park after an absence of three weeks. In London, T. H. Brooking, vice-chairman of the Atlantic Telegraph Company, had his directors pass a resolution commending Cyrus for "the most determined perseverance, and the exercise of great talent, extraordinary assiduity and diligence, coupled with an amount of fortitude which has seldom been equalled."

If Field later had occasion to think kindly and with some degree of partiality of his British associates, it was not without good reason.

11

Flags at Half Mast

>>>>>>><<<<<< On his return from Newfoundland, Field spent only a few days in the Gramercy Park house. He was always surprised, on these periodic visits, to find his daughters growing up and his family expanding. Mary was coping valiantly but she complained that "life with Cyrus was like riding on the top of a Fifth Avenue charabanc." She was again pregnant, and in two more months their brood would number six. If it should be a boy, they planned to name him Cyrus.

Late that month, January, 1857, Field received encouraging reports from Matthew and from Samuel Canning. All the land and submarine lines from Newfoundland to New York were operating well. Although Field's promotional pamphlet on St. John's as a port of call had led to nothing, the English House of Lords observed that the Newfoundland-New York telegraph connection would permit "British mail packets between Liverpool and the United States to receive and throw overboard off Cape Race and off Queenstown cases containing telegraphic dispatches, to be picked up by the telegraph company's own vessels." Actually, this relay system was never extensively used.

In Washington, President Franklin Pierce had received favorably the letter and presentation that Field had prompted while in London. Senator William H. Seward, of New York, had drawn up a bill which he presented to Congress as "An act to expedite telegraphic communication for the uses of the government in foreign intercourse." It conformed basically to the English contract, with a promise of ships to help lay the cable and an equivalent subsidy of $70,000 a year. Writing about Field's "assiduity and patience" in promoting passage of the bill, Seward noted later: "The President and Secretary of State individually favored his proposition; but the jealousies of parties and sections in Congress forbade them to lend it their official sanction and patronage."

Therein lay the seeds of trouble that were going to call for more exertion than Field realized. A letter from Matthew Maury urged him to come to Washington and lend a hand in these negotiations, offering him a room at the Naval Observatory. "Bring Morse, Mr. Cooper and a few others. I think that by waiting on the President in a body we might render all the world . . . some service."

Ill as he still was, Field decided to go. But Peter Cooper, otherwise engaged, assigned to his junior partner, Abram Hewitt, the task of bombarding Congressmen with letters urging their support of the cable. Cooper was more immediately concerned with establishing a unified domestic network through the American Telegraph Company and was trying to arrange a conference of representatives of leading companies to achieve this before the cable was laid. By midsummer he would have his network, consisting of the "Six Nations" of telegraphy: the American Telegraph Company, the newly formed Western Union, and four other companies operating in the West. In preference to the use of Morse equipment, all would use the Hughes instruments, which received the electric signals and delivered the messages in the form of printed text on paper tape.

Samuel Morse continued to fume at what he considered treachery on the part of his associates. But his resentment was directed more at Cooper than at Field, perhaps because Cooper was titular head of the American Telegraph Company. It was Field who made a more practical gesture toward peace. While in England, he arranged to have Morse elected an honorary director of the Atlantic Telegraph Company with Morse's purchase of a $10,000 share in the new company at par. It is typical of Morse's chameleon nature that in spite of his resentment he wrote to the Secretary of the Navy, insisting that he should go along on any cable-laying expedition.

Before Field could get off to Washington, he received an unexpected jolt. Late in January the packet *Arago* arrived from Liverpool with a report that promptly circulated in New York and Washington: "Great dissatisfaction exists in London at the manner in which the Atlantic Telegraph has been gotten up, and a new company has been formed to construct a telegraph direct to the United States."

Shocked and incredulous at first, Field quickly appraised this as an insidious rumor, nothing more. He wrote to the Washington paper which first ran the story: "I believe no such company can have really been organized in London, as represented, because none of my letters by the same steamer, from directors and parties largely interested, even allude to such a movement, which must of necessity have been made public and well known to them if true." He also pointed to the hazard of financing a cable half again as long, over a route not yet deemed practicable, compared with the projected cable over a much shorter route that had been already surveyed and found most advantageous.

He was not seriously worried about this rumor but he realized it might delay acceptance of the project in this country and thereby encourage England to consider undertaking the project alone. In the House of Lords no less influential a member than Lord Redesdale had proclaimed that it would have been better for Great Britain to underwrite and control the entire project rather than share it with a foreign government. Field felt it was important to get the bill through Congress before the waters became further muddied. He left for Washington immediately.

All during the dreary month of February Field, hollow-eyed and preoccupied, strode from office to office of the Congress winning converts to the cause with his intense sincerity. "The Atlantic Cable has had many a kink since, but never did it seem to be entangled in such a hopeless twist as when it got among the politicians," wrote his brother Henry.

The extraordinary opposition in America came as a surprise to Field, as did the whole cumbersome operation of democracy. In London it had taken only James Wilson's letter to set the wheels in motion and get the project approved by the Lords of the Treasury, normally "a graveyard of lost hopes." Any subsequent debate in Parliament was a mere letting off of steam. In Washington he was faced by a battery of diverse and seemingly irreconcilable opinions, any one of which could wreck the project.

He ran up against a solid bloc of Southern Anglophobes, headed by Senators James C. Jones and Robert M. T. Hunter—the former expressing the sentiments of all: they didn't "want anything to do with England or with Englishmen." Others protested the "enormous" subsidy of $70,000 which would benefit only a few Northern capitalists and an army of investors in Great Britain. Hunter argued that the cable would be simply a link between two British possessions, a facility over which America would have no control in time of war and one that could be even turned against her in the event of conflict with England.

This specter of war haunted the debate. In combating it, Field had the decisive support of Senators Seward; Thomas Jefferson Rusk, of Texas; and Stephen Douglas, the "Little Giant" of Illinois. Seward's argument was:

> In regard to war, all the danger is this: There is a hazard of war at some future time, and whatever arrangements we might make, war would break them up. No treaty would save us. My own hope is, that after the telegraphic wire is once laid, there will be no more war between the United States and Great Britain.

Douglas added: "I am willing to vote for this bill as a peace measure —but not as a war measure; and when war comes, let us rely on our power and ability to take this end of the wire and keep it." One lone Southern voice, that of Senator Judah P. Benjamin, of Louisiana, presented the clinching argument that should England have the war use of the cable in mind, she could easily put up the money on her own, to control the cable altogether without sharing it with the United States.

It could have gone either way in Congress. Field's persistence backfired. Seward wrote that:

> so vehement were the prejudices against Mr. Field, for what was then regarded as presumption and officiousness on his part, that the great bill was only saved by his withdrawing, at the request of Mr. Rusk and myself, from the Senate Chambers, its lobbies, and even from the Capitol Grounds, and remaining unobtrusive and unseen in his own lodging.

The bill passed the Senate by one vote on March 3, 1857, and was signed the following day by President Pierce. It was Pierce's last official act before yielding the White House to Buchanan, and it is needless to add that Field, who could not remain unobtrusive, was at his side to make sure Pierce's right hand did not falter. Almost immediately the measure was branded as unconstitutional—an insinuation that had crept into the earlier debate. Cyrus at once appealed to Caleb Cushing, a fellow Massachusetts man, who with equal promptness gave it his official sanction as Attorney General.

Nothing stood in the way now but the 1,834 statute miles between St. John's and Ireland. Berryman's soundings of that area of the Atlantic basin, taken the summer before, showed a general depth of about 2½ miles, shoaling on the Newfoundland side but rising more precipitously toward the Irish shore. The ocean bottom was found to be powdery detritus, "soft as a featherbed," offering no threat of damage to the cable. As Field expected, Maury disputed these findings. Privately he wrote to Cyrus: "All the documents, etc. are at the Observatory, come and see. They are worthless."

Maury had hoped that Field would concur in this opinion. But how *could* he? Being no expert, Field had to accept the facts given him.

Field stood high in the estimation of Maury who was too much of a scientist to let this off-side altercation come between them. He continued to cooperate with Cyrus by helping to obtain naval ships to lay the cable and by prescribing the route and the procedure to be followed. Late in March, after recommending a polygonal course, or series of straight lines, for the ships to follow (rather than the great-circle route which would be easier to steer), he added:

> You asked me also to state the best time for laying the cable. . . . The enterprise upon which you engage is an important one—good weather for it is very desirable, nay almost indispensable. . . . Perhaps it would be wise for the steamers not to join cables until after the 20th of July. I think that between that time and the 10th of August, the state of both sea and air is usually in the most favorable condition possible, and that is the time which my investigations indicate is the most favorable for laying down the wire.

To make sure of having the cable completed by this period, Field made plans to leave again for England. He had had little time to dispose of any of his stock in the Atlantic Telegraph Company. But even if more time had been available, it is doubtful that he could have done better. Though the press and the public were slowly awakening to the drama of the cable the investing public still seemed reluctant to back it. Altogether Field sold only twenty-one shares, some at a loss, leaving him still with $335,000 invested in the cable, plus more than $200,000 in the landlines.

He spent two weeks at home, pacing the floor in the last of these days while Mary had her baby. It turned out to be a son, who was indeed named Cyrus William, whereupon Cyrus senior sailed on March 18, 1857, for England, where he began at once to harry the cable manufacturers. Actually the manufacturers were proceeding at a dangerously rapid pace, drawing 335,000 miles of wire and spin-ning 300,000 miles of tarred hemp to be made into a cable 2,500 miles long—the extra mileage to allow for ocean depth and bottom contour, slack in paying out the line, and possible loss.

The cable presented many problems not encountered hitherto. It was more than five times as long as any previously manufactured; it would have to withstand the temperatures and pressures of extreme depths of two to three miles; it would have to be pliable, yet strong enough to support its own weight in suspension. In short, those responsible for its design—notably Dr. Whitehouse backed by Faraday and Morse—were forced to rely as much on theory as on experience, their theories differing markedly from those of Bright and Thomson.

The essential core or conducting center, made by the London Gutta Percha Company, consisted of seven strands of tightly interwoven copper wire. On the recommendation of Faraday and Morse, it was relatively small and light. Faraday argued that this would require less current to "fill it up" and emerge in full force at the other end. A parallel may be drawn with an ordinary garden hose. A smaller hose requires less volume and less pressure than a larger one, to produce a stream of water at the other end. The larger the central core, said Faraday, the greater the "retardation," or the time required for the current to match the core's capacity and pass through.

This later proved wrong in operation, as both Bright and Thomson had feared it would, Bright's theory being that "the resistance offered to an electric current by a wire *decreases* as the diameter of the wire increases."

The copper core was insulated with three coatings of gutta-percha and then surrounded with a protective wrapping of hemp soaked with linseed oil, tar, pitch and wax. Over all this went an armament of eighteen strands of iron wiring. The finished product, more than half an inch thick and containing enough metal wire to more than reach the moon, weighed a ton per nautical mile. For each end leading to the shore, much heavier strands of cable, twenty to thirty miles in length, were manufactured to resist sharp rocks, turbulent water, and ship's anchors. These ends would be spliced to the main cable after being laid ashore.

(For all its faults, it is remarkable that after more than 100 years of immersion, a section of the 1857 cable was accidentally retrieved from the bottom of the North Atlantic and found still capable of conducting electric current.)

To complete such an intricate job in the few months Field and the directors had allowed was a record scarcely equaled in that century. There was hazard in this haste. Professor Thomson examined the cable during its construction and found that different sections of its copper core varied greatly in quality. Since the specifications had been pushed through by "the dynamic energy of Cyrus Field," there was nothing he could do about it.

After two weeks in England, Field returned hurriedly to New York to arrange for ships to lay the cable. Because of its weight and length, it would require two vessels, each carrying half the cable, with a splice connecting the two sections. Maury had written that "we may be able to get the *Niagara* to lay the wire—so that it will be the best service ever yet rendered by a man of war steamer." It would also be the best steamer they could get to do the job. The *Niagara* was the largest steam frigate in the world. Also, conveniently, she was not yet fitted out with heavy armament, and Secretary Dobbin felt that laying the cable might offer a good test of her abilities. The U. S. frigate *Susquehanna,* a powerful paddle steamer, was assigned to be her escort.

To lay the other half of the cable, Charles Bright obtained the wooden-walled warship *Agamemnon,* veteran of Sevastopol. (Probably no one remembered that *King* Agamemnon had devised what was perhaps the first sea-bridging system of telegraphy some 1,000 years before Christ—a series of fire flares from mountaintop to mountaintop, skipjumping over the Aegean, to announce the fall of Troy to his palace in Mycenae and the waiting faithless Clytemnestra.) The *Agamemnon* would be convoyed by the frigates *Leopard* and *Cyclops.*

It was Bright's idea, as well as that of the other engineers, that the two ships, each carrying half the cable, should meet in mid-ocean. There the cable would be spliced, and the vessels would proceed in opposite directions to their separate terminals. This procedure would enable them to choose the weather for the ships to approach each other and make the splice and test it.

But they were again overruled by the technicians. Dr. Whitehouse, for one, argued that it was important to keep in constant contact with the shore throughout the operation. He advocated anchoring the line first at Valentia, Ireland, then proceeding to mid-ocean, splicing the second half of the cable to the first, and carrying it on to Newfoundland. At all times signals could pass back and forth to Ireland.

This was the plan that was adopted. As a gesture of international goodwill, the United States ship *Niagara* would start laying the first half out of Ireland; the British ship *Agamemnon* would go along beside her, splice the cable in mid-ocean, and proceed with laying the second section of the line to Newfoundland.

The holds of both ships had been gutted to make room for 1,250 tons of cable apiece, and the *Niagara* sailed from America to England late in April. Field followed on the steamer *Persia*. She was faster, and he used the extra time at home in getting the new President, Buchanan, to agree to exchange messages with Queen Victoria when the cable opened. When the telegraph fleet, both English and American, assembled in the Thames, the crews and company directors were generously feted at the Erith estate of Sir Culling Eardley. Two military bands provided music; the 850 guests played cricket, danced the polka, and dined sumptuously under an immense marquee pitched on the lawn.

Field took the opportunity to read to the gathering President Buchanan's letter. It gallantly suggested that Queen Victoria be first to send a message by the cable and that he, the President, "would endeavor to answer it in a spirit and manner becoming a great occasion."

All this discussion of initial greetings was a little premature. There followed a series of mishaps, one of which was that the *Niagara* was too long to dock at the Glass, Elliot wharf to take aboard her section of the cable. She exchanged roles with the *Agamemnon* and went on to Liverpool to pick up the *Agamemnon*'s half. Aside from the crew, only Field and Morse among the company directors would be with the fleet, aboard the *Niagara,* from now on, with John Mullaly, the reporter. Morse was even more seasick than Field when the vessel put to sea and remained so. Dr. Whitehouse had pleaded illness before the expedition started, and his place was taken, without pay, by Professor Thomson, assisted by the electrical engineer C. V. De Sauty, who had been a principal figure in the laying of the Black Sea cable, connecting Varna with Balaklava, during the Crimean War. Though unarmored, the line had operated long enough to prove decisive in the tide of battle. He had also helped lay the Cabot Strait connection after Canning's first attempt had failed. He was a quiet, practical, methodical technician who kept so much in the background of this long-sustained endeavor that his very existence was challenged as something of a myth.

Where precisely would the two ends of the cable come ashore? Samuel Canning had picked the site in Newfoundland. East of St. John's stretches Trinity Bay, eighty miles long and thirty miles wide, a beautiful evergreen-girded fjord. At its southwestern head lies the

Bay of Bull's Arm, terminating in a gentle sandy beach. Slightly in-land from this beach, a frame house for instruments and crew had been erected. It was connected by a spur of wire to the line from St. John's to New York. In the bay the company's steamer *Victoria,* along with Berryman's *Arctic,* occupied stations to await the landing of the western end of the cable.

On the southwestern shore of Ireland, sheltered from the great surf sweeping in from the Atlantic, lies Valentia Bay, which is also spelled Valencia by the olive-skinned descendants of the Spanish Armada who were wrecked here. On an island in this harbor the eastern end of the cable was to come ashore, and here the fleet was scheduled to assemble during the first week in August, 1857.

There was little doubt now about public enthusiasm for the project. Even before the ships arrived, Valentia came alive with joy. Festive crowds poured in from miles around. Small boats bedecked with bunt-ing jammed the harbor, and sightseers lined the shore. Peter Fitz-gerald, Knight of Kerry, and Queen Victoria's representative, the Earl of Carlisle, gave banquets and receptions and prolonged them with innumerable toasts and speeches. Lord Carlisle proved himself a seer, and a farsighted and compassionate one, in saying:

> . . . it behooves us to remember that the pathway to great achieve-ments has frequently to be hewn out amidst risks and difficulties, and that preliminary failure is even the law and condition of ultimate success. . . .
>
> However, upon this rocky frontlet of Ireland, at all events, today we will presume upon success. We are about, either by this sundown or to-morrow's dawn, to establish a new material link between the Old World and the New. Moral links there have been—links of race, links of commerce, links of friendship, links of literature, links of glory; but this, or new link, instead of superseding and supplanting the old ones, is to give a life and an intensity which they never had before.

Field rose to the occasion. When the end of the cable had been brought ashore and anchored—an operation in which everybody who could shoulder his way near enough, including Lord Carlisle, took part—he addressed the crowd by popular demand. In contrast with preceding speakers, he was brief:

> I have no words to express the feelings which fill my heart tonight —it beats with love and affection for every man, woman and child

who hears me. I may say, however, that, if ever at the other side of the waters now before us, any one of you shall present himself at my door and say that he took hand or part, even by an approving smile, in our work here to-day, he shall have a true American welcome. I cannot bind myself to more, and shall merely say: "What God has joined together, let no man put asunder."

If by that he meant the cable, it is true that it *had* been joined together. Steaming toward Valentia, the fleet had paused off Queenstown long enough to connect the two ends of the cable, from the *Niagara* to the *Agamemnon,* and to run an electric current through its entire length of 2,500 miles. The signals came through clearly; the cable was sound and ready to be laid.

When Cyrus finally returned to his stateroom in the officers' quarters of the *Niagara,* he found a basket of fruit from Peter Fitzgerald, along with a gracious note informing him that he had "stolen the hearts of my wife and children" and everyone who had met him, not to mention the "inroad you have made on the Lord Lieutenant's affection." Field had never had the inclination to cultivate or even think about popularity, but as an upstart "Colonial" from across the seas, he had scored an extraordinary victory over British reserve and coolness toward Americans.

It was too late to sail that evening. Field tried to sleep, gave up, and went on deck, where a chill wind blew across a cloudless sky. There was nothing for him to do but stare again at the ghostlike chain of drums that ran the whole length of the deck—from the spool of cable stacked above three others near the bow to the brake box and the giant wheel that dropped the wire from the stern.

At sunrise the *Niagara*'s engines throbbed, and imperceptibly the ships began to move. It took a moment to realize they were really under way; before that moment had passed, a crewman threw a wrong switch, and the cable parted from its shore connection. To splice the break took another day, and it was not till Saturday, August 8, a beautiful sunny morning, that the fleet bore confidently out to sea—slowly at first, as if the cable had to feel its way, and then increasing speed to five knots as the paying-out machinery began its monotonous rumble.

During the days which followed, Field scorned his cabin to remain on deck. He was, indeed, the unofficial commodore of that small fleet. Though Captain Hudson was in charge of the *Niagara,* he was deferential toward Cyrus, and the crew and officers observed a fond respect for him. It was because of this young, slender, sometimes distant figure that the finest ships of two great navies, with their warrior escorts, were embarked on a mission never before undertaken or considered.

All that day, the following night, and throughout Sunday the ships moved forward on a quiet sea. Messages passed steadily from the *Niagara* to the cable's terminal and Dr. Whitehouse in Valentia. On Monday afternoon, August 10, Whitehouse relayed the message that the fleet was now 300 miles from Ireland and all was proceeding "as satisfactorily as its best friends can desire." He went on:

> The depth of water into which the cable is now being submerged is about 1700 fathoms, or about two miles. The transition from the shallow to the greater depth was effected without difficulty. The signals are everything an electrician could desire. The ships are sailing with a moderate fair breeze, and paying out at the rate of five miles per hour. . . . All are well on board, in excellent spirits, and hourly becoming more and more confident of success.

As Henry Field described the mood (writing, as he must have, from what Cyrus told him):

> All through that night, and through the anxious days and nights that followed, there was a feeling in every soul on board, as if some dear friend were at the turning-point of life or death, and they were watching beside him. There was a strange unnatural silence in the ship. Men paced the deck with soft and muffled tread, speaking only in whispers, as if a loud voice or a heavy footfall might snap the vital cord. So much had they grown to feel for the enterprise, that the cable seemed to them like a human creature, on whose fate they hung, as if it were to decide their own destiny.

Early the next morning a more deadly silence struck the ship. The wire went dead; the signals stopped abruptly. Yet there was no break in the cable. Samuel Morse was routed out of his sickbed and hurried to the telegraph room. Not a sound or sign of current could be coaxed from the instruments. There was a break somewhere in the copper core, or perhaps, as Morse surmised, the insulation had given way or been damaged passing over the wheels and drums. As time slipped fatefully by, the engineers gloomily discussed either cutting the cable or turning back and somehow rewinding it as they returned home.

Then suddenly, inexplicably, the current came back; the instruments once more registered the signals from Valentia.

The cable had been dead for two and a half hours, and no one could explain it. Morse's hypothesis was that some gap in the insulation had been fortuitously closed. The return of the current was enough to satisfy most of the crew.

When Field climbed into his berth that night, he could not sleep. His mind demanded a reason. The incident "cast ominous conjecture on the whole success" and was a premonition of disaster. At a quarter to four, as dawn was breaking in the East, he was roused by shouts on deck that sounded like: "Stop her! Back her up!" Suddenly Charles Bright was standing in the doorway of his stateroom, saying "The cable's gone."

The ship had been sailing at four knots and the cable paying out at more than six knots, a differential accounted for at first by added depth or tricky currents. For safety's sake an engineer applied the brakes. Perhaps he applied them too suddenly; possibly a swell lifted the stern at that same moment and added to the strain. In any event, the cable snapped like a pistol shot and plunged 2,000 fathoms to the bottom. Half a million dollars in material and labor had been lost in a split second. Without an order being given, the flag of the *Niagara* was lowered to half-mast, and the other ships responded.

John Mullaly reported later:

> Mr. Field, who had more at stake than any member of the whole Company, and who might be supposed to feel the effects of the failure more than anyone aboard, proved himself equal to the emergency. Losing no time in vain regrets, he called a meeting at once on board the *Niagara,* at which Captain Hudson and the commanders of the other ships were present, and at which it was resolved to make a series of experiments in view of the resumption of the undertaking the following October, or in the summer of 1858.

There was no doubt in Field's mind that they would try again or that the directors would agree with him on this. He arranged to have the *Agamemnon,* the *Niagara,* and the *Susquehanna* stay where they were at sea and experiment together with the cable-laying operation. Was there something in the machinery, the weight of wire, or the handling of both that caused the accident? He instructed the *Cyclops* also to remain on station and take soundings to determine the precise depth. Meanwhile, he would board the *Leopard,* which was to take him as fast as possible to Southampton, from which point he could call an immediate meeting of the company directors.

He had substituted action for despair. There were lessons to be learned from this disaster. Men and ships had, for the most part, functioned smoothly; mechanical failures could, when determined, be corrected. This was not so much a failure as a temporary check. More than 300 miles of cable had been laid, some of it in the deepest waters of the North Atlantic, and with one interruption, it had performed superbly until now. There was no real cause to believe the project unsound or the final goal unobtainable.

Aboard the *Leopard* steaming to Southampton, he wrote the family in Stockbridge:

> My confidence was never so strong as at the present time, and I feel sure, that with God's blessing, we shall connect Europe and America with the electric cord. . . . Do not think that I feel discouraged, or am in low spirits, for I am not; and I think I can see how this accident will be of great advantage to the Atlantic Telegraph Company. All the officers and men on board of the Telegraph Fleet, seem to take the greatest interest in our enterprise, and are very desirous to go out in the ships the next time.

At the hastily summoned meeting of the London directors on August 15 he reiterated his confidence:

> Although this unfortunate accident will postpone the completion of this undertaking for a short time, the result of the experiment has been to convince all that took part in it of the entire practicality of it, for, with some slight alteration in the paying-out machinery, there appears to be no great difficulty in laying down the cable. . . . The experience now obtained must be of great value to the company, and it is understood that the directors of the company will decide whether it is best to have more cable made and try again immediately after the equinoctial gales are over, or wait until another summer.

He was supported as always by Bright, who, in his report as engineer, concluded:

> I do not perceive in our present position any reason for discouragement; but I have, on the contrary, a greater confidence than ever in the undertaking. It has been proved beyond a doubt that no obstacle exists to prevent our ultimate success; and I see clearly how every difficulty which has presented itself in this voyage can be effectually dealt with in the next.

The directors wholeheartedly endorsed these arguments, and it became only a question of whether or not another expedition should be sent that summer. It was decided that more time was needed: the equipment should be studied with an eye to possible improvements, and 700 miles more of new cable would be required to replace what they had lost and provide for further contingencies. For these purposes more capital was needed and subscribed.

The *Agamemnon* and *Niagara* stored their remaining lengths of cable in Plymouth and returned to their respective duties, and Cyrus left for home soon afterward. He took with him a parting note tinged with Irish optimism from Peter Fitzgerald, Knight of Kerry. Fitzgerald expressed gratitude at hearing "that you were, as indeed I might have judged from your character, plucky and well. It is a great comfort to think that the experience that has been obtained in this, the first attempt, must immensely improve the chances of success on the next occasion." To this Fitzgerald added the affectionate good wishes of his people.

12

Hope and Heartbreak, 1858

>>>>>><<<<<< Field returned home in September, 1857, to find the country in financial panic. Although the population of New York had grown to more than 750,000, its financial community was still a tight little circle, and its institutions collapsed like dominoes upended in a row.

It had seemed a remote catastrophe while he was overseas; there was too much else to think about. It edged into his consciousness as something real and ominous when he heard that Harper's was on the verge of bankruptcy, that Moses Taylor was in trouble, and that even Peter Cooper had been forced to liquidate some of his cable stock for precisely a quarter of its value. The final blow came when his partners wrote him that Field & Company was suspending payments with debts of more than $600,000, although a good half of that amount was owed to it by firms in comparable straits.

He immediately hurried to his office and was surprised to find it crowded with crisis-conscious men of Wall Street seeking priority on messages to Europe via the Newfoundland telegraph. Even the great Pierpont Morgan had come to "Mr. Field's" in person to keep in contact with London.

Calling his creditors together, as he had in taking over Root & Company, Field settled with them for notes carrying 7 percent interest. His reputation for discharging in full the debts of Root & Company served him well in this crisis. The notes were readily accepted. In addition, he disposed of stock whenever this might satisfy a creditor. He had no thought of giving up the business; he would need it to replenish his depleted capital.

The climate was hardly auspicious for reviving popular interest in

the cable project. Additional capital had been raised to cover the
£100,000 loss incurred in the first expedition, but it had come mostly
from the original shareholders in the Atlantic Telegraph Company.
They retained unqualified confidence in Field and, "recognizing the
need for unified leadership and for improvements in the apparatus,"
urged him to return at once to England to assume the role of general
manager. At the meeting of directors where this invitation was endorsed, "it was unanimously resolved to tender him, in respect to such
services, the sum of one thousand pounds over and above his travel-
ling and other expenses as remuneration."

Field accepted the responsibility but informed the directors he
would rather serve the company without pay. Thereupon the directors
formally expressed their gratitude "for his devotion to the interests of
the undertaking" and soon after passed resolutions confirming his
authority.

His first concern, along with everybody's, was: What had caused the
cable break? The fault did not seem to lie with the cable itself, although Matthew Maury still protested that it was too heavy, and there
were others who agreed with him. But in Morse's preliminary demonstration it had transmitted signals over the full 2,000 miles of wire.
And it had operated through 300 miles submerged. Besides, the bulk
of the cable remained; they could not afford to scrap it and start fresh.
They were stuck with what they had.

However, William Thomson was working on the problem of transmission, trying to overcome retardation and speed up the signals.
Field saw in Thomson a kindred spirit. Whitehouse, the company's
official electrician, had not even made the last voyage, pleading illness,
possibly to cover a reluctance to risk his reputation. In any event,
Field felt no sympathy toward him; Thomson was his man.

As for the accident to the cable, it seemed due to the paying-out
machinery. Even the general public seemed to think so. Field had
been deluged with letters suggesting other methods and improvements
—from both qualified engineers and amateur inventors. When the
shore cable parted from the deep-sea line, he had been impressed at
how William Everett, the chief engineer of the *Niagara,* was everywhere, supervising the handling of the cable while the splice was being
made, showing "a coolness and self-possession deserving of all praise."
Even before the third and final accident, Everett had told him straight-
forwardly that the apparatus was too cumbersome and that the brakes

gripped too tightly and might snap the wire. If the machinery needed fixing, Everett was the man to do it.

Early in December Cyrus went to Washington to consult with Secretary of the Navy Toucey. He wanted the same ships on the next expedition. Both Captain Hudson of the *Niagara* and Captain Sands of the *Susquehanna* had expressed an eagerness to try again, and the ships' crews seemed dedicated to the project. Field also requested Toucey to release Everett from his naval duties and assign him to the company as chief engineer. On December 30, 1857, Toucey called Field to his office and told him, "You've got everything you asked for."

The British government also was surprisingly cooperative. Field would again have the *Agamemnon* under a new captain, Preedy, with an escort steamer, the *Gorgon,* under the veteran Captain Dayman. A smaller steamer, *Porcupine,* would help the *Victoria* land the cable at Bull's Arm.

Soon after New Year's Day, 1858, Field was off again to England on the *Persia,* taking Everett with him. Everett spent the next six months at the Southwark mill which had built the paying-out machinery. He created a system that was lighter and simpler and took up much less room on deck. Among other things he substituted a new self-releasing jockey brake, adapted by an English inventor, J. G. Appold, from an apparatus used in English jails "to regulate the amount of labour in proportion to the prisoner's strength."

In April, Everett demonstrated his model to Field, Bright, and a group of experts that included Isambard Kingdom Brunel, who had never lost interest in the project. They were impressed with the refinements, especially with the new brake, which "seemed to have the intelligence of a human being, to know when to hold on, and when to let go."

In addition to this improvement in the paying-out machinery, the young electrical engineer Willoughby Smith had invented a more effective insulating and adhesive compound to replace the coal-tar naphtha used between the gutta-percha coverings of the cable. Smith had started his career in life by running growlers of beer from a nearby tavern to men working overtime at the Gutta-Percha plant. Someone sharp enough to recognize his potentialities brought him into the company as a fledgling engineer in 1848, about the time Faraday called attention to the insulating qualities of gutta-percha. Smith's rise was rapid. Within a year he was supervising both the manufacture and the laying of Brett's Channel cable.

Meanwhile, William Thomson had been going over the remaining 1857 cable inch by inch, as well as the new lengths being manufactured, eliminating all possibly defective sections, and testing the purity of the copper wire. His chief concern at this point was the matter of retardation. What was needed, Thomson felt, were instruments sensitive enough to detect the first slight trickle of electric current through the cable.

Now, standing at his laboratory window and absently twirling his monocle, he "noticed how swiftly the reflected light danced about the room." This simple observation led to his invention of the "mirror (or marine) galvanometer," in which a freely moving ray of light replaced the mechanical needle in detecting current variations. It consisted only of a tiny mirror on a lightweight magnet surrounded by a coil of wire and suspended on a filament of silk. A beam of light reflected from the mirror moved along a graduated scale as electric impulses through the wire moved the free-swinging magnet. It was extremely sensitive, supremely simple, since mechanical parts were eliminated.

The applause of Thomson's contemporaries inspired the brilliant scientist James Clerk Maxwell to compose a parody of Tennyson:

> The lamplight falls on blackened walls
> And streams through narrow perforations.
> The long beam trails o'er pasteboard scales
>   With slow, decaying oscillations.
> Flow, current, flow! Set the quick light-spot flying!
> Flow, current, answer light-spot, flashing, quivering, dying. . . .

Thomson's invention was to revolutionize submarine telegraphy. While Dr. Whitehouse had been advocating the use of a much stronger current to overcome retardation in the cable, one that would, he thought, force its way through the wire, here was a method of recording the most delicate of signals without endangering the line by overcharging it.

It was also to create one of those personal feuds, this time between Thomson and Whitehouse, that had plagued Field in his efforts to establish harmony and teamwork in the project. Again he was in the middle, but instinctively on Thomson's side. He had managed to buy out Whitehouse's interest in the company for $8,000, and was probably already agitating for Whitehouse's removal from the operation, though that, unfortunately, did not come till later. Whitehouse's indignation at the "sinister forces" working against him was directed, not only at his English associates, but at "the frantic fooleries of the Americans in the person of Mr. Cyrus Field."

But Cyrus had the solid backing of the Atlantic Telegraph Company. One of its directors, Samuel Gurney, took this occasion to commend him publicly and for good measure the Company passed another resolution in their next report:

> The directors cannot close their observations to the shareholders without bearing their warm and cordial testimony to the untiring zeal, talent, and energy that have been displayed on behalf of this enterprise by Mr. Cyrus W. Field, of New York, to whom mainly belongs the honor of having practically developed the possibility and of having brought together the material means for carrying out the great idea of connecting Europe and America by a submarine telegraph.

All this goodwill may not have materially advanced the cause, but it was reassuring to Field in the face of his realization that he had been far from the first to think of an Atlantic cable. Brett and Morse and Bright had had the idea earlier, and now in Canada the provincial governments were having second thoughts about the exclusive rights they had granted Cyrus. Tal Shaffner was urging them to launch a competing cable along lines he had suggested back in 1852. The latter proposal offered no real threat. The question was now admitted to be not who first thought of the cable, but who had made it a reality. By this criterion, Field's role remained unchallenged.

Hard on the heels of these displays of confidence came news that an epidemic of yellow fever had broken out aboard the *Susquehanna* and that the ship was quarantined. Field jumped into a cab and rode to the Admiralty to see Sir John Parkington, the First Lord. He was wise enough to adopt the attitude of a young man seeking fatherly advice. Acknowledging the great help that the Admiralty had so far given, he stated his problem and asked Lord Parkington the simple question: "Can you do anything for us?" Parkington could. He immediately made the warship *Valorous* available, to take the place of *Susquehanna*.

The four-ship squadron was complete, and it assembled at Plymouth to start loading the 3,000 miles of cable—a task which took all of April and part of May with a force of 160 men. Field had insisted on the extra length of cable, to be used in a rehearsal of the whole procedure before the expedition actually put to sea. He felt this might avert the failings of the earlier attempt. The rehearsal took place in the latter part of May in the Bay of Biscay, and involved "cable-splicing, issuing, retrieving, buoying and testing the newly designed and improved cable-braking machinery." The latter test was accompanied by a song the crew had adapted to the melody of "Pop Goes the Weasel"—no longer pertinent, it was hoped:

> Pay it out, oh! pay it out
> As long as you are able:
> For if you put the damned brakes on,
> Pop goes the cable!

"The paying-out machinery had worked smoothly, the various engineering operations had been successfully performed, and the electrical working through the whole cable was perfect." On June 3 the squadron reconvened at Plymouth for the final preparations. Cyrus' ubiquitous brother, the Reverend Henry Martyn Field, had arrived from New York to give the fleet his blessing. He conducted divine services on the *Niagara,* where an awning over the quarterdeck sheltered 500 officers and men, and summarized the mission as "an omen of the good time coming, when nations shall learn war no more."

Henry was at heart very much disturbed about Cyrus:

> The strain on the man was more than the strain on the cable, and we were in fear that both would break together. Often he had no sleep, except such as he caught flying on the railway. Indeed, when we remonstrated, he said he could rest better there than anywhere else, for then he was not tormented with the thought of anything undone. For the time being he could do no more; and putting his head in the cushioned corner of the carriage, he got an hour or two of broken sleep.
>
> Of this activity we had an instance while in Plymouth. The ships were then lying in the Sound, only waiting orders from the Admiralty to go to sea; but some business required one of the Directors to go to Paris, and as usual, it fell upon Mr. Field. He left on Sunday night and went to Bristol, and thence, by the first morning train, to London. Monday he was busy all day, and that night went to Paris. Tuesday, another busy day, and that night back to London. Wednesday, occupied every minute till the departure of the Great Western train. That night back to Plymouth. Thursday morning on board the *Niagara,* and immediately the squadron sailed.

Nor was there any rest for him on the *Niagara.* This time, even more than the previous year, the responsibility was wholly his. And the procedure would be different. Field had ruled in favor of Bright's original plan and decreed that the two ships would meet in mid-ocean, splice the ends of the cable, and then proceed in opposite directions to Valentia and Trinity Bay. He wrote:

> By this means, the period ordinarily required for traversing the distance between the two coasts will be lessened by one-half, each vessel having only to cover the eight hundred and twenty nautical miles in order to finish the task assigned to it. It is expected that the operation of laying the cable will be completed in about eight days from the time of its commencement.

Dr. Whitehouse once more excused himself from the expedition on the ground of illness, and Professor Thomson again took his place, without pay. Thus, Field had the same team with him, except for Samuel Morse, who remained in America by common agreement. Morse still felt that Field was pursuing a course hostile to his interests and had announced to friends, "I intend to withdraw altogether from the Atlantic Telegraph enterprise." When Field had written from London urging him to purchase the proffered shares of stock to secure his position as director, he replied, somewhat irrelevantly, that he thought the whole cable venture was aimed at "monopolizing and controlling all the telegraph lines of the United States." Then, with characteristic ambivalence, he sent Cyrus his best wishes for success.

They set sail on June 10, 1858, in the pleasantest of weather, under clear skies with a gentle breeze. Untroubled by any concern for the cable—since operations would not begin till they reached the point of rendezvous in mid-Atlantic—Field paced the deck with confidence. They were starting a month earlier this year, assured that June was the most favorable time for such an expedition.

The promise was a cruel deception. After three quiet days the breeze rose slowly to a gale. Field looked at the barometer; it was falling fast. Conserving coal for the time they would need steam for the cable laying, both the *Niagara* and the *Agamemnon* were proceeding under sail. Now they began to take in canvas, and Cyrus noted that the *Agamemnon,* more than a mile away, was pitching and rolling like a helpless toy.

As the sea grew angry and mountains of water walled them off from one another, the escorts *Valorous* and *Gorgon* vanished from sight.

Field told Captain Hudson to keep in sight of the *Agamemnon* at all costs. Both ships were overloaded with the deadweight of the cable, but the *Agamemnon* was smaller in tonnage, had less freeboard, and was far more vulnerable in a storm. That night Cyrus looked again at the barometer. Falling!

It was the same story on the fourteenth . . . and the fifteenth . . . and the sixteenth: "Barometer falling, strong gale, high seas; ship under very short sail." But always the notation: "*Agamemnon* in company." He watched the staggering ship, a mile away, with increasingly anxious eyes. On the seventeenth he noticed a lifeboat floating past them, bottom up, an ominous omen. Nicholas Wood, reporter from the London *Times,* unhappily assigned to the *Agamemnon,* noted that the wind was "getting worse and worse . . . ship straining dangerously."

A week of this seemed all that any ship could take. But on Monday, the twenty-first, when it seemed the sea had done its worst and must by now have spent its strength, the most violent storm in memory raged across the North Atlantic. Wind howled in the rigging, tearing at the battered canvas; the ship pitched and shuddered, rising on giant waves to drop sickeningly into the troughs. A spar snapped in the bow; another dropped from overhead, bringing down everything attached to it. The starboard wing of the gallant American eagle figurehead was swept off to sea. Worst of all, the *Agamemnon* had disappeared in that churning mass of wind and rain and fury. In the crew's opinion the ship had foundered.

Sick as he was from the violent motion, Cyrus had no need to remain on deck, where the driven spray was cold as sleet. But there was no escape below. With each rising sea the vessel creaked and shuddered in an almost human agony. Crockery shattered in the galley. Uprooted tables, chairs, and hardware smashed through the ship like living things in panic. Even the planks in his cabin gaped from the strain of the pitch and roll. And forward of all this, like a coiled snake trembling in its shaky prison, lay the giant cable—1,500 tons of mobile weight, threatening to break its bonds and smash the vessel's side out.

It was the cable Field was more concerned about than life itself, and he was also more concerned about the *Agamemnon* than about his own ship. For lack of room below, 250 miles of cable were resting on the *Agamemnon*'s forward deck. Could it possibly remain there in a sea like this? Was there a chance the *Agamemnon* could survive? If the British ship were lost, then with it would go every prospect of success. There could be no recovery from this catastrophe.

Aboard the *Agamemnon,* he later learned, conditions were even worse than he imagined—"desperate," wrote Nicholas Wood, before the storm had even reached its peak. As the top-heavy vessel rolled to a nearly fatal 45 degrees, almost everything seemed to give way. Tons of water thundered on the decks and crashed into the holds below. The wire shrouds were wrenched slack; the masts threatened to collapse. More than 100 tons of coal broke loose and carried everything ahead of it in an avalanche of black dust. The electrical equipment was a shambles; broken kegs of copper sulfate smothered everything in fumes; a pipe split, flooding the engine room with scalding steam. On the spar deck, sprawling sailors, cargo and coal, oil from overturned barrels, broken spars and loosened beams, and finally some fifty miles of cable ("resembling nothing so much as a cargo of live eels") pitched in a tangled mass from side to side. Wrote Nicholas Wood on the evening of that extraordinary day:

> The sun set upon as wild and wicked a night as ever taxed the courage and the coolness of a sailor. The night was thick and very dark, the low black clouds almost hemming the vessel in; now and then a fiercer blast than usual drove the great masses slowly aside, and showed the moon, a dim, greasy blotch upon the sky, with the ocean, white as driven snow, boiling and seething like a cauldron. But these were only glimpses, which were soon lost, and again it was all darkness, through which the waves, suddenly upheaving, rushed upon the ship as though they must overwhelm it, and, dealing it one staggering blow, went hissing and surging past into the darkness again. The grandeur of the scene was almost lost in its dangers and terrors, for of all the many forms in which death approaches man there is none so easy in fact, so terrific in appearance, as death by shipwreck.

The day following was no less fearful, as "gigantic waves were seen approaching the ship, coming slowly on through the mist nearer and nearer, with a crown of foam that seemed to double their height. The *Agamemnon* rose heavily to the first and then went lower quickly into the deep trough of the sea, falling over as she did so, so as to capsize almost completely." Waiting from second to second for the blow that might overturn his vessel, Captain Preedy decided to jettison the cable. It would lighten the ship and give the men a fighting chance. It was what Field had dreaded—although if he had been on board, he would have seen the wisdom of it. Preedy changed his mind; he would take that one chance and hold on.

On the morning of June 25, aboard the *Niagara,* after the first tolerable sleep in what seemed to have been weeks, Field woke to no more than a gentle rocking of the ship. The sky outside was bright and cloudless; there was not a breath of wind. They were, miraculously, at the point of rendezvous, where the sea was "as tranquil in the middle of the Atlantic as if in Plymouth Sound." More heartening still was the sight of the *Valorous* approaching from the south and the *Gorgon* from the east. Both had been badly battered but had suffered no disabling injury.

Field ordered a boat lowered to row over to the escorts, when he saw, with an overwhelming sense of relief, the *Agamemnon* limping over the horizon. He went to meet her and check with Captain Preedy. Coming aboard, he found the decks a shambles, black with coal dust, littered with wreckage from the storm. Preedy reported forty-five men in sick bay with fractures, cuts, and bruises; one man driven insane with fright; two others in a critical condition. Some hundred miles of cable lay strewn around the main deck. It would take incalculable hours to untangle it. Cyrus could not have been more elated or more grateful to divine Providence. The ship was afloat; the cable was intact.

By the following afternoon the *Agamemnon* and *Niagara* were brought stern to stern. The ends of the cable were spliced, with a bent sixpence inserted for good luck, and the worst storm in a century was forgotten as the two ships started on their way. This time, there would be no goodwill exchange of roles. The British ship would sail to Ireland; the American vessel to Trinity Bay. Five days, Field estimated, and the land ends of the cable would be anchored.

The ships had barely time to move apart when, according to Captain Hudson's log, "the cable, being hauled in the wrong direction, through the excitement and carelessness of one of the men, caught and parted in the *Niagara*'s machinery." It was exasperating, but no great amount of cable had been lost. The vessels put around, respliced the wire, and started off again. Things went beautifully from sundown until nearly dawn. They had payed out forty miles of wire, when the continuity went dead. Field and De Sauty came on deck and found the cable still intact; there were just no signals coming from the other ship. They assumed it had snapped aboard the *Agamemnon.*

As they came together for the third time, and Field was rowed to the British ship, he was hailed with the question "What happened to the cable?" It was intact aboard the *Agamemnon,* too!

With Cyrus beside him in the *Agamemnon's* telegraph cabin, Professor Thomson ran an electric current through the cable, as one might insert a wire in a stopped-up pipe to locate the obstruction. It was a simple process. Knowing by previous tests the resistance of each mile of cable, one could tell, by measuring the resistance, how far the current traveled—until it leaked away into the sea. Thomson estimated that the break was nowhere near the two ships, but about midway between them. They would never know what happened.

An accident was one thing, if you knew what caused it. But catastrophe without an explanation was another thing—and hard to take. Again they were haunted by some unknown abyssal force conspiring against them. The *Times* reporter somberly noted that:

> of all the many mishaps connected with the Atlantic telegraph, this was the worst and most disheartening, since it proved that after all human skill and science can effect to lay the wire down with safety has been accomplished, there may be some fatal obstacle to success at the bottom of the ocean which can never be guarded against. . . . Was the bottom covered with a soft coating of ooze, in which it had been said the cable might rest undisturbed for years as on a bed of down? Or were there, after all, sharp-pointed rocks lying on that supposed plateau of Maury, Berryman, and Dayman? These were the questions those on board were asking.

It had been agreed that they would continue until each ship had lost 250 miles of wire, at which point further effort would be useless. They still had adequate cable for another attempt. They were down to heavily salted meat that was old beyond edibility; their stocks of coal were running low. They reassembled once again, but this time Field called the nucleus of his team—Bright, Thomson, Canning, and Everett—to the *Niagara* for a consultation. He submitted this proposal for a third attempt: "Should any accident occur to part the cable before the ships have run a hundred miles from rendezvous . . . the ships shall return to rendezvous and wait eight days, when, if the other ships do not appear, then proceed to Queenstown." To make sure that this was understood by all, they signed it.

Once more the cable was spliced in mid-ocean, and the ships were on their way. It was hard to suppress a returning surge of hope as the distance spread between them. They safely laid 100 miles . . . 150 . . .

200. The sea was calm, and the vessels increased speed; the electricians reported "signals between ships eminently satisfactory. Scarcely a word was spoken; silence was commanded, and no conversation allowed. Nothing was heard but the strange rattling of the machine as the cable was running out."

Shortly after midnight on June 29, without warning or reason, the cable snapped from the *Agamemnon*'s stern. It was discovered later to have been due to damage inflicted by the storm. But this dreary explanation did not help the expedition now. The ship was in danger of running out of coal. Aboard the *Niagara,* hearing that contact had been broken, Field ordered the ship stopped. They were past the 100-mile limit agreed on, but waited briefly for the signals to resume. When they did not, he knew the fight was over.

13

Onward to Immortality

➤➤➤➤➤➤◄◄◄◄◄◄ The *Niagara* arrived at Queenstown on July 5, its entire crew despondent. Field expected to find the *Agamemnon* waiting for them. Since she was heading eastward, she had had a 200-mile head start. But there was no sign of the other vessel or her escort. He was the one harbinger of disastrous news, and while he regarded the misfortune as no more than an exasperating delay, he was reluctant to face the company directors without Bright and Thomson by his side. He needed some reassuring explanation to give them. He himself was in the dark.

He sent word to the chairman and vice-chairman of the board that he would wait in Queenstown for the *Agamemnon* and then go at once to London for a conference.

For Field, waiting was agony. There were reports of more bad weather on the North Atlantic, high winds and sea and dense fog, and he knew the *Agamemnon* would be low on coal. Accusations circulated behind his back: the *Niagara* had deserted her British partner and scurried home without waiting to make sure that all was well. Both ships had understood their orders to return home when 100 miles of cable had been spent. But was an extra 14 miles enough to quibble over or to warrant quitting?

When the *Agamemnon* returned one week later, it was learned that she had indeed considered 14 miles too close to constitute defeat. She had headed back to the rendezvous, beating upwind through gale and high seas, searching for the *Niagara* in a fog so thick that her principal worry had been that she might discover the *Niagara* by colliding with her. When the fog lifted in mid-ocean and there was no sign of the other ship, Preedy turned back for Queenstown, feeling somewhat as those on shore did, that they had been deserted by an over-cautious ally.

Field, Thomson, and Bright hurried to London to meet the directors in the same room where six weeks before they had been given such a vote of confidence. This time they faced sour, disillusioned stares. The news, of course, had preceded them, and rumors had already circulated that the cable enterprise had been abandoned. Chairman Sir William Brown had been unable to get down from Liverpool, but had sent a message: "We must all deeply regret our misfortune in not being able to lay the cable. I think there is nothing to be done but dispose of what is left on the best terms we can." Brown proposed dividing the proceeds equally among the shareholders; thereafter the company should be disbanded.

When Field, surprised and shocked, protested violently, and perhaps intemperately, he received another setback. Vice-chairman T. H. Brooking, who had previously been as dedicated to the enterprise as himself, "determined to take no further part in an undertaking which had proved hopeless, and to persist in which seemed mere rashness and folly." He walked out of the meeting and sent back his resignation.

Field looked around at those remaining and mustered all the sincerity at his command and all the salesmanship he had ever learned. He pointed out what he wholeheartedly believed: that this was simply a delay. They had lost 300 miles of cable, not a serious financial blow. Because of their foresight in obtaining more, originally, than required, they had plenty left for another try. The ships were assembled; they needed only supplies and fuel to set out again. Bright and Thomson were solidly with Field. They felt the cable could be laid; the repeated failures had been accidents from which they had gained experience and knowledge.

Resigned to the fact that they had nothing to lose, the directors gave their assent. Field hurried to the Admiralty and had an order dispatched to the ships to prepare immediately for departure. They were ready to sail on July 17, an earlier start than they had made the year before. This time there were no crowds to see them off, no words of encouragement and praise followed them. The squadron, Henry noted, seemed to slink away as if on some discreditable mission. "Many even of those on board felt that they were going on a fool's errand; that the Company was possessed of a kind of insanity, of which they would soon be cured by another bitter experience."

The ships headed separately for the same rendezvous, not bothering to keep in sight of one another. Wind and weather were quiet; smoke rose like pillars from the stacks, and the crew amused themselves by feeding scraps of pork to following gulls. To while away the time, Field offered a cash prize to the seaman who first caught sight of the *Agamemnon;* he was haunted by the past experience with that elusive ship. As a result, for the next two days, she was sighted as often and ubiquitously as the Loch Ness monster or the flying saucers of today. One week later Field and his shipmates spotted the escort *Valorous,* and Captain Hudson engaged Captain Dayman in one of those laconic semaphore conversations that pass between vessels in mid-ocean:

Hudson: I hope you are all well on board?
Dayman: All well, thank you. I hope you are the same?
Hudson: Thank you.
Both together: Have you seen the *Agamemnon?*
           (Pause: confusion)
Dayman: It is your turn. Repeat please.
Hudson: Have you seen the *Agamemnon?*
Dayman: No. Have you seen the *Gorgon?*
Hudson: No.

The two ships drifted listlessly for half a day, until the *Gorgon* hove in sight—and the ritualistic conversation was repeated. In this round the *Gorgon* added, "Have you any coal to spare?" Hudson replied: "No, none at all!" Both ships had been ordered to conserve coal and had been handicapped by the calm weather that forced them to use steam. Next to the cable itself, fuel was of paramount concern. It was futile to use sail to lay a cable.

On July 28 the *Agamemnon* met the group, and the following day at noon the cable was spliced. This time they did not bother with the sixpence for good luck, but tossed it over with a thirty-two pound shot for weight and little ceremony, "for those on board the ship had witnessed so many beginnings to the telegraphic line, that it was evident they despaired of there ever being an end to it." Field described the incident:

> I was standing on the deck of the *Niagara* in mid-ocean. The day was cold and cheerless, the air was misty, and the wind roughened the sea; and when I thought of all that we had passed through, of the hopes thus far disappointed, of the friends saddened by our reverses, of the few that remained to sustain us, I felt a load at my heart almost

too heavy to bear, though my confidence was firm and my determination fixed.

However, the crew felt that "Mr. Field was the only man on board who kept up his courage through it all." But his mind was anything but easy. To quiet his anxiety, he went to his cabin and, as he used to do in Stockbridge, made an inventory of the situation:

> Thursday, July twenty-ninth, latitude fifty-two degrees nine minutes north, longitude thirty-two degrees twenty-seven minutes west. Telegraph fleet all in sight; sea smooth; light wind from S.E. to S.S.E.; cloudy. Splice made at one P.M. Signals through the whole length of cable on board both ships perfect. Depth of water fifteen hundred fathoms; distance to the entrance of Valentia harbor eight hundred and thirteen nautical miles, and from there to the telegraph-house the shore end of the cable is laid. Distance to the entrance of Trinity Bay, Newfoundland, eight hundred and twenty-two nautical miles, and from there to the telegraph-house at the head of the bay at Bull's Arm, sixty miles, making in all eight hundred and eighty-two nautical miles. The *Niagara* has sixty-nine miles further to run than the *Agamemnon*. The *Niagara* and *Agamemnon* have each eleven hundred nautical miles of cable on board, about the same quantity as last year.

He kept this daily statistical journal throughout the voyage, noting the bare facts of wind, sea, depth, length of cable payed out, distance covered. His next entry noted a disturbing incident. As before, signals were passed between the ships at ten-mile intervals, informing one another of their progress and the cable's conductivity. But then, that night, signals from the *Agamemnon* ceased. Tests made by De Sauty indicated that the cable was still sound; the current simply was not coming through. Recalling the mysterious interruption of the signals on the previous year's voyage, Field ordered the engineers to keep on paying out the cable. The same thing happened as before. Within two hours the signals miraculously reappeared, the wire had seemed to heal itself; but that dread of unknown factors at the bottom of the ocean also reappeared to haunt them.

The next day brought another crisis. Comparing their sextant position with the mileage indicated on the log, they found they were paying out more cable than the distance warranted. At this rate there would not be enough to complete the line to Newfoundland. This time the explanation was simple. Their compass had been affected by the massive load of iron on the ship, and they had been sailing off course.

Had she been alone, the *Niagara* would have been helpless without knowing how to steer. But Field was able to have the *Gorgon* run ahead of her and assume the role of pilot fish. The escort now saved the expedition's life.

By Saturday, July 31, they had payed out 300 miles of cable, and according to her signals, so approximately had the *Agamemnon.* It was the point of no return. A break now would not leave them enough cable for another try. With great apprehension, Field continued to record their progress. He signaled the passing steamer *Puritan,* headed from Boston to Liverpool, that all was well. By Tuesday morning he had recorded nearly 800 miles of cable payed out by both ships.

That afternoon they sighted icebergs, which meant that they were near or on the Grand Banks. One spire floating toward them, topped with "a corona of fleecy white clouds," seemed to him an omen of approaching triumph. They took a sounding. Two hundred fathoms. They had reached the continental shelf! Next morning, confident that victory was in their hands, Cyrus noted in his journal:

> Wednesday, August fourth. Depth of water less than two hundred fathoms. Weather beautiful, perfectly calm. *Gorgon* in sight. Sixty-four miles from the telegraph-house. Received signal from *Agamemnon* at noon that they had paid out from her nine hundred and forty miles of cable. Passed this morning several icebergs. Made the land off entrance to Trinity Bay at eight A.M. Entered Trinity Bay at half-past twelve. At half-past two, we stopped sending signals to *Agamemnon* for fourteen minutes, for the purpose of making splice. At five P.M. saw Her Majesty's steamer *Porcupine* coming to us. At half-past seven, Captain Otter, of the *Porcupine,* came on board of the *Niagara,* to pilot us to the anchorage near the telegraph-house.

Sailing up Trinity Bay the forbidding shores of Newfoundland looked for once hospitable. The quiet harbor of Bull's Arm, with its encirclement of evergreens and sloping moors, seemed like a welcoming cradle. It would take awhile, until the next day probably, to bring the land extension of the cable onto shore. As usual, he could not wait.

It was two o'clock in the morning when they anchored. Field had a boat put overside and was rowed ashore to the landing beach. He set out for the telegraph house, not certain where it was but following the open stretch of sky that seemed to indicate a trail. He knew that the shack was less than a mile inland, but struggling through that overgrowth in darkness, wondering if he were lost, he felt it was twenty.

When he finally stumbled upon the gaunt frame structure, he was unable to find the door. He finally forced his way into a passage and, pausing to listen, heard someone breathing.

He shouted, a light came on, and he faced the startled sleepers in the dormitory. They rubbed their eyes and stared at this gaunt, hollow-eyed, windburned man, his clothing pricked with burrs and twigs. They were maintenance men; there was no operator who could send a message. The nearest station open on the line from St. John's to New York was fifteen miles away. Field asked for a volunteer to run there, and got two. He then dictated the first of a series of messages that were to burn their way across the wires of a continent and stun an unsuspecting world. The first, of course, was to Mary: "Arrived here yesterday. All well. The Atlantic telegraph cable successfully laid. Please telegraph me here immediately."

He sent a similar wire to his father in Stockbridge and a message to the Associated Press, which he knew would also reach the offices of the American Telegraph Company and Peter Cooper. Giving abbreviated details of their triumph, he conscientiously spread the credit, not forgetting the Almighty: "Captain Hudson, Messrs. Everett and Woodhouse, the engineers, the electricians, and in fact every man on board the telegraph fleet has exerted himself to the utmost to make the expedition successful. By the blessing of Divine Providence it has succeeded."

And finally, to President Buchanan at the White House, an announcement of their arrival and success, with an instructive paragraph: "As soon as the two ends are connected with the land lines Queen Victoria will send a message to you, and the cable will be kept free until after your reply has been transmitted."

The cable was connected shortly after sunrise. Later that day the *Agamemnon* reported landing her end at Valentia, after a voyage that made the *Niagara*'s look uneventful. The first day out a sportive whale had played around the stern and threatened momentarily to snap the cable. Time after time the men had discovered faults in the insulation, resulting evidently from the storm, and had to repair these while the cable was running out along the deck. Nearing Ireland, they had had to use their guns to drive off two American vessels that unwittingly approached too near their course. And they, of course, had suffered the same panic when the continuity of signals had stopped mysteriously in mid-ocean until it resumed.

Though the two continents were now connected, from the Missouri

Submit Dickinson Field, 1782–1861.

Courtesy, Captain Wells L. Field

Reverend David Dudley Field, 1781–1867.

Courtesy, Captain Wells L. Field

Portrait in relief of Cyrus Field
at seventeen.

Courtesy, Mrs. Reginald R. Belknap

The Parsonage as sketched in 1824.

At the Columbia Paper Mill in Lee, Massachusetts, operated by his brother Matthew, Cyrus Field got his start in the paper business in 1838.

Cyrus Field home on Gramercy Park, as sketched for *Leslie's Weekly,* 1879.

Advertisement of Cyrus W. Field & Company, printed around 1850.

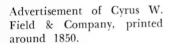

22 **CYRUS W. FIELD & CO.,**

WHOLESALE PAPER DEALERS,

No. 11 Cliff Street, New York,

PAPER WAREHOUSE, No. 11 CLIFF St., (Near John St.)

RAG WAREHOUSE, No. 58 CLIFF St., (Near Beekman.)

NOW OFFER

At the lowest wholesale prices, for cash, or satisfactory notes, by far the most extensive and desirable stock of all articles connected with the Paper Trade, or Manufacture, that can be found in this or any other country.

Our long experience and great facilities enable us to offer extraordinary inducements to large purchasers.

Orders accompanied with cash, or satisfactory references, will be executed with the same care and promptness as when given in person.

PAPER OF ANY SIZE AND WEIGHT MADE TO ORDER AT SHORT NOTICE.

Liberal Advances made on consignments of Paper and other Merchandise.

Cash paid for Rags, and all other Paper Manufacturers' Stock.

Mary Bryan Stone (Mrs. Cyrus West Field), 1840–1891.

This engraved portrait of Cyrus Field at his moment of triumph in 1858 was widely circulated.

(Left) Frederick E. Church, a leading painter of the Hudson River school, accompanied Field to South America in 1853. *(Right)* Lieutenant Matthew Fontaine Maury, founder of the science of oceanography, teamed with Samuel Morse in guiding Field's plans for the first Atlantic cable.

(Left) Peter Cooper's name, reputation, and dedication did much to aid Field in securing support for the Atlantic cable effort. *(Right)* Samuel F. B. Morse (1791–1872), promoter and self-styled inventor of the magnetic telegraph, was one of Field's original advisers.

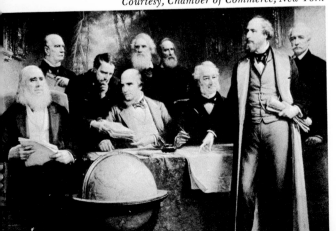

Daniel Huntington's masterful painting of the Atlantic cable projectors shows Cyrus Field (standing) as considerably older than he must have appeared at the time. Left to right are Peter Cooper, David Dudley Field, Chandler White, Marshall O. Roberts, Samuel Morse, the artist Huntington, Moses Taylor, Cyrus Field, and Wilson G. Hunt.

(Left) Charles Tilston Bright, holder of two dozen patents for inventions at the age of twenty, became chief engineer of the Atlantic Telegraph Company at twenty-six. *(Center)* John Watkins Brett (1805–1863) who laid the first Anglo-French cable in the English Channel joined with Field and Charles Bright to form the Atlantic Telegraph Company in 1856. *(Right)* Dr. William Thomson of Glasgow, later Lord Kelvin (1824–1907), contributed more valuable technical assistance to the Atlantic cable enterprise than any other of the many scientists involved.

After splicing the cable in mid-ocean, the *Agamemnon* and *Niagara* part for Valentia and Trinity Bay in the second temporarily successful expedition of 1858.

From Harper's Weekly, August 14, 1858

Robert Dudley's drawing shows a sportive whale jeopardizing the cable as it is payed out from *Agamemnon*'s stern during the second expedition of 1858.

The second telegraph fleet assembles in the Bay of Biscay in late May, 1858, for a rehearsal designed to avoid the errors of the previous year's expedition.

Fireworks set New York's City Hall ablaze in the two-week celebration of Field's fleeting triumph in late August, 1858.

New York, Aug. 21st 1858.

This is to certify that I have sold the balance of the Atlantic Telegraph Cable now on board of the U. S. S. S. "Niagara" to Messrs Tiffany & Co. Jewellers No. 550 Broadway of this city, and that the piece which accompanies this, is a genuine section thereof.

Cyrus W. Field —

Sections of the 1858 cable were sold as souvenirs by Tiffany & Co., each with an affidavit from Cyrus Field attesting to its authenticity.

The *Great Eastern* dwarfs her escorts as she heads out from Valentia, Ireland, on her first cable-laying expedition to America in 1865.

Robert Dudley's painting of the electrician's room on the *Great Eastern* shows William Thomson at the marine galvanometer and Cyrus Field, standing at left, in cloak.

Inspection of the damaged cable on the deck of the *Great Eastern,* during the expedition of 1865, led to the ugly (but later discredited) suspicion of sabotage.

Robert Dudley's sketch of Field on watch in the *Great Eastern's* cable tank, appearing in *The Atlantic Telegraph,* was captioned:

No useless sentry within the tank,
    Not in slumber or sleep we found him;
But he sat like a warrior stiff on his plank,
    With his Iverness cloak around him.

Front page story, with map, in the *New York Herald* appeared just when the first *Great Eastern* expedition was having trouble in mid-Atlantic.

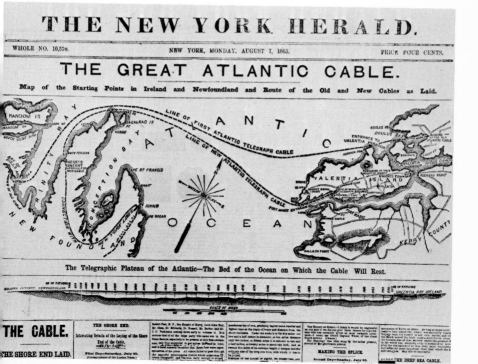

THE NEW YORK HERALD.

WHOLE NO. 10,570.   NEW YORK, MONDAY. AUGUST 7, 1865.   PRICE FOUR CENTS.

THE GREAT ATLANTIC CABLE.

Map of the Starting Points in Ireland and Newfoundland and Route of the Old and New Cables as Laid.

The Telegraphic Plateau of the Atlantic—The Bed of the Ocean on Which the Cable Will Rest.

THE CABLE.

THE SHORE END.

Interesting Details of the Laying of the Shore End of the Cable,

THE SHORE END LAID.

First Day—Saturday, July 22.

MAKING THE SPLICE.

Second Day—Monday, July 23.

THE DEEP SEA CABLE.

Cover of *The Atlantic Telegraph,* earliest shipboard newspaper to appear at sea, featured portraits of leading members of the first *Great Eastern* expedition.

Canadian artist Rex Woods painted this scene of the landing of the cable at Heart's Content in the summer of 1866. Field, with Captain Anderson, is shown at far right.

Courtesy, Burndy Library, Norwalk, Connecticut
Courtesy, Burndy Library, Norwalk, Connecticut

After landing the cable successfully at Heart's Content in 1866, Field and his associates were hoisted on the shoulders of an exuberant crew.

Front and back of gold medal awarded to Cyrus Field by Congress in March, 1867.

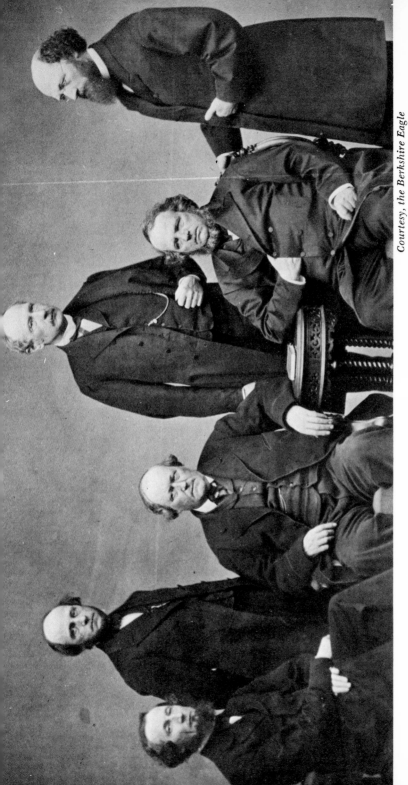

Matthew Brady's photo of the six Field brothers, taken in 1867, shows (standing left to right) Henry Martyn, 1822–1907; David Dudley, 1805–1894; Stephen Johnson, 1816–1899; (seated left to right) Cyrus West, 1819–1892; Matthew Dickinson, 1811–1870; Jonathan Edwards, 1813–1868.

England's liberal statesman John Bright (1811–1889) was Field's strongest supporter in the latter's effort to mend British-American relations in the Reconstruction years.

Courtesy, New York Public Library

William Gladstone (1809–1898), four times Prime Minister of England, was harshly critical of the Union in its war against the South until Field helped heal the breach.

Courtesy, New York Public Library

turn a position morally & incurably false, and will from the first enjoy & permanent gain in credit & character which such as will much more than compensate for its temporary material losses.

I am in short a follower of General Scott: with him I say "wayward sisters, go in peace: immortal fame to him for his wit and courageous advice, amounting to a prophecy. Finally, you have done what men could do. You have failed because you resolved to do what men could not do. Laws stronger than human will are on the side of current self-defence. And the aim to the impossible, which in other things may 'i folly only, when the path of search is

deals with misery and red with blood, is not folly only but guilt to boot.

I should not have used so largely in this letter the privilege of free utterance, had I not been conscious that I live with gladness in my admiration of the founders of your republic, and that I have no lurking sentiment either of hostility or of indifference to America; nor, I may add, even there had I not bilured that you are lovers of sincerity, and that you can bear even the rudeness of its tongue

I remain my dear Sir

Very faithfully yours

W E Gladstone

Cyrus Field Esq

2

Last two pages of letter to Cyrus Field from William Gladstone, dated November 27, 1862, declaring that the Union's war against the South "is not folly only but guilt to boot."

(Left) Samuel J. Tilden (1814–1886), disputed candidate for President in 1876, was accused by Field of betrayal for the wholesale dumping of his elevated railway stock in 1881. *(Center)* Jay Gould (1836–1892), the Wizard of Wall Street, was chief engineer of the "Manhattan Squeeze" that led to Field's financial ruin. *(Right)* Russell Sage (1816–1906) was Gould's partner in cornering the stock of Field's Manhattan elevated railways in the spring of 1887.

Steam locomotives pulled the elevated trains when the Sixth Avenue line was opened in 1878. Field later advocated, without success, the use of electric power, which was not introduced until the early 1900's.

From Leslie's Illustrated Weekly

A gift from his daughter Isabella, this portrait of Cyrus West Field, painted in his later years, hangs in the hall of the New York Chamber of Commerce.

Courtesy, Pach Bros., New York

Ardsley, overlooking the Hudson River, country home of the Cyrus Fields after 1869.

*Courtesy, Mr. and Mrs.
W. Wallace Ryan*

One of the last photographs of Cyrus Field and his wife, Mary, taken on the veranda of Ardsley around 1885.

River in America to the Volga in eastern Europe, Field wisely re-
frained from opening the cable for business. To reassure Peter Cooper,
the New York directors, and the Associated Press, he sent another
message:

> We landed here in the woods; until the telegraph instruments are
> all ready, and perfectly adjusted, communication cannot pass be-
> tween the two continents, but the electric currents are received freely.
> You shall have the earliest intimation when all is ready, but it may
> be some days before everything is perfected.

During the three days he spent at Trinity Bay, the wires hummed
ceaselessly with laudatory messages—from President Buchanan ("I
congratulate you with all my heart upon the success of the great enterprise with which your name is so honorably connected"), from the
governor-general of Canada, from Cabinet members, from governors
and mayors, from bishops and archbishops—and, most welcome, one
from brother Dudley:

> Your family is all at Stockbridge and well. The joyful news ar-
> rived here Thursday, and almost overwhelmed your wife. Father
> rejoiced like a boy. Mother was wild with delight. Brothers, sisters,
> all were overjoyed. Bells were rung, guns fired; children, let out of
> school, shouted, "The cable is laid! The cable is laid!" The village
> was in a tumult of joy. My dear brother, I congratulate you. God
> bless you.

Another message he may have prized as a reminder of the days
when he and Mary befriended the Indians at the Traverse treaty-sign-
ing ceremony, was wired to him via Utica:

> Beech Tree, chief of Oneida tribe, honors the white man whom the
> great spirit appoints to transmit his lightning through deep waters.

He replied with apparent gravity:

> The white chief beyond the salt licks, towards the rising sun, greets
> his red brother, and speaks with the tongue of lightning which is not
> forked. Let the words of the Great Spirit, who talks from the clouds
> with the voice of the thunder and who whispers through the deep
> waters with the swift lightning, sink deep into the Oneida Chief's
> heart. Let him avoid the fire-water which has ruined his mighty
> people, and when the singing birds open their bills, let him not close
> his ears to their song. Let him be honest and true and remember the
> traditions of his fathers, and the great Manitou will no longer veil his

face behind a cloud, but will permit the just Iroquois to journey on an open path from the happy hunting grounds of the red men to the great Heaven of the pale face.

On August 8 they sailed on the *Niagara* to St. John's to replenish their supply of coal, and Field was entertained by the governor, feted by the Chamber of Commerce, tendered an honorary dinner, and given a ball at the Colonial Hall. He was called upon for speeches and used these opportunities again to credit the work of his associates, even including praise for Brooking, who had walked out on the London meeting. He could not, however, resist saying, "We have had many difficulties to surmount, many discouragements to bear, and some enemies to overcome, whose very opposition has stimulated us to greater exertion."

Reports reached him from Valentia of a similar reception given to Bright, Thomson, and the *Agamemnon*'s crew. He found he missed his English partners now, as much as he was glad to be back home. Perhaps the most heartening letter reaching Field was from the company's secretary, George Saward:

> My dear Sir: At last the great work is successful! I rejoice at it for the sake of humanity at large. I rejoice at it for the sake of our common nationalities, and last but not least, for your personal sake. I most heartily and sincerely rejoice with you, and congratulate you upon this happy termination to the trouble and anxiety, the continuing and persevering labor, and never-ceasing and sleepless energy, which the successful accomplishment of this vast and noble enterprise has cost you. Never was man more devoted—never did man's energy better deserve success than yours has done. May you in the bosom of your family reap those rewards of repose and affection, which will be doubly sweet from the reflection, that you return to them after having been under Providence the main and leading principal in conferring a vast and enduring benefit on mankind. If the contemplation of fame has a charm for you, you may well indulge in the reflection; for the name of Cyrus W. Field will now go onward to immortality, as long as that of the Atlantic Telegraph shall be known to mankind.

The First Lord of the Admiralty sent his warm congratulations, as did the London directors and all British scientists and engineers connected with the venture. George Peabody, one of the directors, wrote: "Your reflections must be like those of Columbus after the discovery of America." Queen Victoria, in knighting Charles Bright for his part in the achievement, would have conferred the same honor, she confessed, on Cyrus Field but for his American allegiance.

As the *Niagara* rode in New York harbor, not yet assimilated into the city's boisterous welcome, he went to his cabin and wrote a letter to the directors in London, which closed with the paragraph:

> At your unanimous request, but at a very great personal sacrifice to myself, I accepted the office of General Manager of the Atlantic Telegraph Company, for the sole purpose of doing all in my power to aid you to make the enterprise successful; and as that object has been attained, you will please accept my resignation. It will always afford me pleasure to do anything in my power, consistent with my duties to my family and my own private affairs, to promote the interests of the Atlantic Telegraph Company.

He was closing the book on the second chapter of his life.

14

"The Columbus of America"

>>>>>><<<<<< When word reached New York of the simultaneous landing of the cable at Valentia and Trinity Bay, it took the city by complete surprise. Failures had conditioned New Yorkers to further failure. In this atmosphere of apathetic resignation the news broke and the city exploded. Guns thundered; fireworks lashed across the sky; whistles shrieked; bells pealed. People swarmed the streets with uninhibited enthusiasm. Bonfires broke out everywhere.

Newspapers ran banner headlines which proclaimed this the feat of the century, saluting "Cyrus the Great," "Gallant Cyrus," "The Columbus of America!" As with all public demonstrations, people clamored for a hero. His name was on 30,000,000 tongues across the land, and no matter what he did to spread the credit it returned to him. James Gordon Bennett in his morning *Herald* took to task those who had ever doubted and called on the nation to pay homage to its benefactor:

> Many terse and witty things have been said and written in all ages to show the difference with which the same enterprise is viewed when it results in success and when it results in failure. We have never had any better illustration of this than we have now in connection with the great enterprise of the age. After the first and second attempts to lay the Atlantic cable had failed, wiseacres shook their heads in sympathetic disapprobation of Mr. Field and said, "What a fool he was!" It was evident to them all along that the thing could never succeed, and they could not understand why a sensible, clearheaded man like Field would risk his whole fortune in such a railroad-to-the-moon undertaking. . . .
>
> Now all that is changed. Midnight has given place to noon. The sun shines brightly in the heavens and the shadows of the night have

passed away and are forgotten. Failures have been only the stepping-stones to success the most brilliant. The cable is laid; and now the most honored name in the world is that of Cyrus W. Field, although but yesterday there were "None so poor to do him reverence."

The wiseacres who shook their heads the other day and pitied while they condemned him are now among the foremost in his praise, and help to make his name a household word. Bells are rung and guns are fired and buildings are illuminated in his honor throughout the length and breadth of the land; and prominent among all devices and first on every tongue and uppermost in every heart is his name . . . [The] nation is proud of him, the world knows him, and all mankind is his debtor.

William Cullen Bryant, another friend of Field's and of the family's, took a more sober, global view of the achievement in his *Evening Post:*

Tomorrow the hearts of the civilized world will beat to a single pulse, and from that time forth forevermore the continental divisions of the earth will in a measure lose their conditions of time and distance which now mark their relations to one another. But such an event, like a dispensation of Providence, should first be contemplated in silence.

In London the *Times* told its readers:

Since the discovery of Columbus, nothing has been done in any degree comparable to the vast enlargement which has thus been given to the sphere of human activity. . . . The Atlantic Telegraph has half undone the declaration of 1776, and has gone far to make us once again, in spite of ourselves, one people.

The *British Workman* put it more lyrically, in one stanza of a poem reading:

> Henceforth the East and West are bound
> By a new link of love,
> And as to Noah's ark there came
> The olive-bearing dove,
> So doth this ocean telegraph,
> The marvel of our day,
> Give hopeful promise that the tide
> Of war shall ebb away.

As a whole, however, the British press belittled Yankee chauvinism, as it well might. It was hard to overlook the fact that, in terms of scientific enterprise and money, the greatest support had come from England. That Field deserved the lion's share of credit was not questioned.

Cooper was being offered £900 a share for the stock he was willing to let go, the year before, for a quarter of its value. Even the skeptical Abram Hewitt confessed that while he had "regarded the investment of so much money in a doubtful enterprise as a piece of folly, I am forced now to acknowledge the superior wisdom of Mr. Cooper." Field also found himself considerably better off. He had been obliged to hedge his losses by selling shares on the London market for £350, but he was now able to raise from £800 to £1,000 a share.

There was also a more spiritual reaction. To some it seemed like the millennium, bearing reverential overtones. Archbishop John J. Hughes had an inscription to Cyrus Field and to this scientific wonder buried in the cornerstone of St. Patrick's Cathedral, then rising on its foundations. Pastors across the land preached sermons on the cable in relation to the brotherhood of man. Never did the Twenty-eighth Psalm get such massive exposure, with the responsive reading of the lines "Their sound has gone out into all lands, and their words into the end of the world." Dr. Henry Ward Beecher was among the first to call a commemorative meeting, at which he spoke with mystic lyricism:

> I thought all the way in riding down here tonight how strange it will seem to have that silent cord lying in the sea, perfectly noiseless, perfectly undisturbed by war or by storm, by the paddles of steamers, by the thunders of navies above it, far down beyond all anchors' reach, beyond all plumbing interference. . . . To me the functions of that wire seem, in some sense, sublime: itself impassive, quiet, still, moving either hemisphere at its extremities by the tidings that are to issue out from it.

Field's pastor, Dr. Adams, unable to get the busy ear of Cyrus, for whom he had offered prayers during each day of the expedition, got in touch with Mary. It was a kindly gesture to include her in an achievement for which she had forgone companionship and normal married life for several years. But even Adams was at a loss for words.

> What shall I say to you? As your pastor I have known of your own private griefs and trials, and the sacrifices you have made for the success of your noble husband . . . [While] the *public* are rejoicing

over the national aspects of this great success, our joyful thoughts are most of all with those private delights which are playing through the hearts of your husband, his wife, and her children.

Mary's home became, by proxy, the western end of the Atlantic cable. Her doors were open wide to an increasing flood of well-wishers and to the eyes of the admiring and curious who thronged the park. Cyrus kept open house for Captain Hudson and the crew of the *Niagara,* for whom he gave a triumphant party at the Palace Gardens.

New York was on an all-time, uninhibited, freewheeling binge. But as the days went by, an undertone of restlessness crept in. If the cable was laid, why wasn't there evidence that it was working? Where was the message from the Queen? What was going on at Trinity Bay?

Field, though secretly concerned, told the persistent Associated Press:

> Before I left London, the Directors of the Atlantic Telegraph Company decided unanimously that, after the cable was laid, the line should be kept for several weeks for the sole use of Dr. White-house, Professor Thomson, and other electricians, to enable them to test thoroughly their several modes of telegraphing, so that the Directors might decide which was the most rapid method for future use. ... Due notice will be given when the line will be ready for business, and the tariff of prices.

Nonetheless he knew that the tests were not going smoothly. In the American Telegraph Office he spent much of his time checking with Trinity Bay, where De Sauty had remained as operator. Even after the cable had been linked up for a week, a full day's transcript of the messages between Valentia and Newfoundland read:

> Repeat, please.
> Please send slower for the present.
> How?
> How do you receive?
> Send slower.
> Please send slower.
> How do you receive?
> Please say if you can read this.
> Can you read this?
> Yes.
> How are signals?

Do you receive?
Please send something.
Please send V's and B's.
How are signals?

It seemed like two deaf people shouting at each other. Sometimes the signals were strong and sometimes weak, and sometimes they seemed blurred and indistinct. To De Sauty's admonition "Faster, send faster, send the word 'Atlantic,' " Valentia had trouble sending back the single word "Atlantic." In response to Field's impatient query about the confusion and delay, De Sauty, himself impatient by this time, replied: "Instruments require great care and adjustment. Doing fast as possible. You should not look on cable as on ordinary short line, as we encounter many little difficulties, but think all soon overcome."

On August 13, Field was elated to get the first official message from the London directors signaling that the line was open. It was appropriately lofty: "Europe and America are united by telegraphy. Glory to God in the highest, on earth peace, good-will to men." He was informed that the Queen's message would follow immediately, and in part it did: "The Queen desires to congratulate the President on the successful completion of the great international work, in which the Queen has taken the greatest interest." Then came the shocking interruption from Valentia: "Wait repairs to cable."

There was more to come—seventy words more, in which Her Majesty extolled the "link between the nations whose friendship is founded upon their common interest and reciprocal esteem." But because of the poor working of the cable, the words dribbled in over a period of fourteen hours (the first part of the message had taken two) and was not received in full until the following morning. Field could not wait. The truncated, terse-sounding sentence from the Queen was released as the whole message, to which President Buchanan replied in part: "May the Atlantic Telegraph, under the blessing of Heaven, prove to be a bond of perpetual peace and friendship between the kindred nations, and an instrument destined by Divine Providence to diffuse religion, civilization, liberty, and law throughout the world."

Wags joyfully parodied the messages between the Queen and President:

Dear Buchanan: I send this by my rope.
Dear Victoria: I send this by *Eur*ope.

Spontaneous rejoicing turned into mass pandemonium. A hundred guns boomed in City Hall Park. Flags fluttered from the rooftops; whistles blew; bells took up their clamorous pealing. Bonfires and fireworks exploded, lighting up the sky again and all but destroying City Hall when a chance spark turned its cupola into a flaming torch. Above the din one name was on all lips: "King Cyrus . . . Cyrus the Great . . . the Columbus of America!"

Workmen dropped their tools and organized extemporaneous processions, causing the public to wish they did their jobs with such enthusiasm. Spontaneous parades with blatant bands bore signs proclaiming: "Our Field Is the Field of the World" and "The Old Cyrus and the New—One Conquered the World for Himself—the Other the Ocean for the World." Blue silk ribbons with Field's portrait framed in a strand of cable were peddled on the street for female adornment and male hatbands. Under not unwelcome pressure, Cyrus sold the remainder of the cable to Tiffany & Company, jewelers, then on Broadway, who cut it up to sell to a public clamoring for souvenirs.

New York had never seen a celebration like it. Stores, hotels, and business houses displayed banners, placards, and transparencies illuminated from behind, with such legends as "S. F. B. Morse and Cyrus Field, Wire-Pullers of the Nineteenth Century" and "Married, August, 1858, by CYRUS W. FIELD, Old Ireland and Miss Young America." People danced to the "Atlantic Telegraph Polka," composed by A. Talexy and dedicated to Cyrus W. Field, Esq. Songs were written and ballads sung for the occasion. Arthur C. Clarke comments: "Inspiring poetry, almost as good as that which now can be produced by any self-respecting computer, was churned out by the yard to fit the occasion." It all echoed the same sentiments:

> 'Tis done! the angry sea consents,
>   The nations stand no more apart,
> With clasped hands the continents
>   Feel throbbings of each other's heart.
>
> Speed, speed the cable; let it run
>   A loving girdle round the earth,
> Till all the nations 'neath the sun
>   Shall be as brothers of one earth;
>
> As brothers pledging, hand in hand,
>   One freedom for the world abroad,

One commerce over every land,
One language and one God.

Among eminent scientists came a word from Joseph Henry, secretary of the Smithsonian Institution. Henry had greatly aided Morse in his development of the telegraph and had always been sympathetic toward the cable project. He now wrote: "This is a celebration such as the world has never before witnessed. It is not alone to commemorate the achievements of individuals, or even nations, but to mark an epoch in the advancement of our common humanity."

The carnival went on for two weeks, and as if that were not enough, Mayor Daniel F. Tiemann and the city council set aside two days, September 1 and 2, for the official "General Celebration of the Laying of the Atlantic Cable." Field had requested the delay so that his English partners might be represented at any ceremonies—especially the crew and captain of the *Gorgon,* for whom he had obtained a leave of absence from the Admiralty. "They were with us in our days of trial, and pray let them, if you can, share with us our triumph."

The interval gave Field a chance to visit Stockbridge during the last week in August; there he received the ovation that most deeply moved him. Following a testimonial dinner on August 26, given by companions of his boyhood years, a ceremony was held the next day on Laurel Hill beneath a floral arch depicting the Atlantic cable and clasped hands labeled "England" and "America." Called upon to address so many old, familiar friends, Field found that his feelings "got the mastery over him," so that his voice trembled as he spoke:

> Ladies and gentlemen, neighbors and friends of Stockbridge and old Berkshire: I could have said much to you, but here, in the presence of my father and my mother, my brothers and my sisters, my townsmen and my playmates, my friends, whose tears have watered the flowers that bloom upon the graves so dear to me, my heart is too full for words. All I can say, my friends, is thanks, thanks, thanks.

At the end, Samuel Sumner of Great Barrington, recited a poem, one verse of which is representative:

> Old Berkshire greets the nations all,
> The nations far away—
> Three cheers for Field, her gallant son!
> Hurray! Hurray! Hurray!

Not everyone hurrayed. In Manhattan Robert Balmanno, dealer in rare books and manuscripts, wrote to associate antiquarian George Livermore:

> What a to-do we are making about the submarine Cable, just as if it had not been done long ago. In the Black Sea—the Mediterranean, and various parts of the Channel between England and the Continent of Europe, it has been in successful operation for some years. To be sure the line is longer, but it is not new, and Mr. Cyrus Field is running away with the whole glory as if he was the inventor. I really am astonished at the fuss. Wall Street is covered with the flags of all nations.

Back in New York, Field continued to worry about the cable. The wire was still stuttering. Most of the trouble seemed to be at the Valentia end, and De Sauty found himself repeating: "We can't read . . . currents too weak to read," and then, "Very good currents but we can't read." It was an up-and-down affair, some days tolerable, some days hopeless.

Dr. Whitehouse had been experimenting at Valentia. Perhaps he could not be blamed entirely for the odd behavior of the signals, but he certainly contributed. In place of Thomson's delicate equipment, he had substituted his own, relying on a strong charge of electricity to get results—so strong that it burned the insulation. By the time he reverted to Professor Thomson's instruments, the damage had been done; there was some improvement, but it did not last.

The first public news message got through on August 17, sent to England by De Sauty: "Mr. Cunard wishes telegraph McIver *Europa* collision *Arabia* putting into St. John's no lives lost." But most of the time De Sauty and Thomson (who had relieved Whitehouse at Valentia) were struggling to read each other's signals, making suggestions for better transmission, and testing different methods and equipment. At times the current would come in strong, and along with business they indulged in personal exchanges. De Sauty informed Thomson: "Splendid aurora Bay of Bulls tonight, extending over eighty-five degrees of the horizon." He added a complaint: "Mosquitoes keep biting. This is a funny place to live in—fearfully swampy."

Thomson also had a problem: "Where are the keys to the glass cases and drawers in the apparatus room?" De Sauty could only reply: "Don't recollect."

Field was the only one among the directors acutely conscious of the difficulties. On behalf of Peter Cooper, the pessimistic Abram Hewitt wrote: "I hope the cable will get up speed enough to pay." It did pick up speed around August 27, when Field wired De Sauty: "Pray give us some news for New York, they are hungry for news." He shortly received the first comprehensive report to come from Europe by the cable. It announced, among other less significant events, "Chinese empire open to trade" and "Gwalior insurgent army broken up. All India becoming tranquil."

As a result of the last item, Thomson was able to relay two important messages to Halifax, canceling the planned departure of the Thirty-ninth and Sixty-second Regiments for England in connection with the Sepoy Mutiny. This quick communication, it was estimated, saved the British government some £60,000, one-seventh of the whole cost of the cable.

The first day of September broke mild and clear, ushering in a celebration which "surpassed anything the city had ever witnessed before." It began with services at Trinity Church, garlanded with flags of all nations, and continued with a mile-long parade from the Battery to the Crystal Palace, then at Bryant Park. Field rode with Mayor Tiemann in a carriage drawn by six white horses and was "wildly cheered" en route. Crowds were so dense that it took six hours for the marchers, with floats and bands, to reach their destination. There the mayor presented Field with an engraved gold coffer from the city and made a laudatory speech to which Cyrus replied.

Field's manner of public speaking, although sometimes pompous and stilted in keeping with the times, had a sincerity and simplicity of delivery that was winning and infectious. With indestructible naivete, he regarded every crowd and every audience as friendly, and they tended to become so. He thanked the mayor for his words of kindness, for the box that he would hand down to his children, and he thanked his fellow citizens for their generous reception. He then drew from his pocket a message that had been handed to him as he set out from the Battery from the London directors, announcing that they were "on their way to Valentia, to make arrangements for opening the line to the public."

The celebration wound up with a torchlight procession after nightfall, when "the illuminations, the fireworks, the many-colored lanterns, and the general gas and spermaceti demonstrations gave to

Broadway a carnivalesque appearance which it is almost impossible to describe."

The following evening an honorary banquet was given for Field, with 600 guests, at the Metropolitan Hotel. Forests of flowers lined the ballroom, along with coats of arms, flags, dioramas, statuettes, models of the cable ships, cornucopias and vases, ornamental temples, towers, pyramids, pagodas, and pavilions, many fashioned out of sweets and pastries. The seven-course bill of fare, including more than twenty entrees and forty choices of desserts, would have challenged the stomach of Lucullus. All was served with innumerable toasts, the first, of course, "To Cyrus W. Field: To his exertions, energy, courage and perseverance are we indebted for the Ocean Telegraph; we claim, but Immortality owns him."

Field rose to reply and an attending writer noted:

> In person, Mr. Field is slight and nervous. His weight is about one hundred and forty pounds. His features are sharp and prominent, the most striking peculiarity being the nose, which projects boldly. His body is lithe and his manner active; eyes grayish-blue and small; forehead large, and hair auburn and luxuriant. He does not appear as old as he is.

Old as he is, indeed! He was exactly thirty-eight. But he was old enough to see his own position in perspective. In his answer to the chairman's toast he said:

> To no one man is the world indebted for this achievement; one may have done more than another, this person may have had a prominent and that a secondary part, but there is a host of us who have been engaged in the work the completion of which you celebrate today.

The report in the *Herald* added a parenthetic comment: "(Loud, prolonged applause)."

A few weeks before he had been regarded as a crank, a visionary, even something of an idiot. At no time since he had undertaken the Atlantic cable had he found a great deal of encouragement, much less financial support, among his countrymen.

Ironically, Field alone now suffered doubts. As he sat listening to the repeated eulogies, he was haunted by the sound of faltering wires coming to a halt. Only that afternoon De Sauty had told him that the signals had grown so weak that they added up to no more than a blank; yet they had installed a sending and receiving instrument in the hotel for this occasion. Now it confirmed his worst suspicion. He was handed a message reading: "C. W. Field, New York: Please inform . . . government we are now in position to do best to forward—"

The rest was blank. The cable had fallen silent, dead. As he furtively shoved it into his pocket, he remembered that the final word was "forward."

15

Postmortems

De Sauty's interrupted message was the last of any consequence to be received. Signals continued to dribble into Trinity Bay, sometimes strong enough to give them hope, but never strong enough for real assurance.

For some time the public was unaware of the catastrophe, and Cyrus continued to wince under its adulation. There was no point in releasing information that might prove incorrect or premature. But on September 6, George Saward, the company's secretary, wrote the London *Times* a letter indicating that all was far from well:

> Sir,—I am instructed by the directors to inform you that owing to some cause not at present ascertained, but believed to arise from a fault existing in the cable at a point hitherto undiscovered, there have been no intelligible signals from Newfoundland since one o'clock on Friday, the 3d inst. The directors are now at Valentia, and, aided by various scientific and practical electricians, are investigating the cause of the stoppage, with a view to remedying the existing difficulty. Under these circumstances, no time can be named at present for opening the wire to the public.

At almost the same time, Field received a letter from George Peabody with a similar oblique suggestion of impending doom:

> I read the accounts in the New York papers in celebration of the great event of the year and age with great interest, and although I think in some respects that they are a little too enthusiastic, yet so far as it regards yourself they cannot be so, for if the cable should be lost tomorrow you would be fully entitled to the high honor you are daily receiving.

Field kept in constant touch with Newfoundland, and the messages passed between him and De Sauty make gloomy reading. A typical exchange took place on September 24 and 25:

> TO DE SAUTY, TRINITY BAY, N. F.:
> Despatches from you and Mackay are contradictory. Now please give me explicit answers to the following inquiries:
> First: Are you now, or have you been within three days, receiving distinct signals from Valentia?
> Second: Can you send a message, long or short, to the directors in London?
> Third: If you answer "no" to the above, please tell me if the electrical manifestations have varied essentially since the 1st of September.
>
> CYRUS W. FIELD

> C. W. FIELD, NEW YORK:
> We have received nothing intelligible from Valentia since the 1st of September, excepting feeling a few signals yesterday. I cannot send anything to Valentia. There has been very little variation in the electrical manifestations.
>
> DE SAUTY

By this time the accumulated silence spelled the message to the public. The cable was dead. Reaction was bitter and Field was the inevitable scapegoat. The cry of "Hoax!" was loud across the land. An eminent New York lawyer Charles O'Conor, a friend of Dudley Field's, proclaimed that this apparent sleight-of-hand stunt, a deception from start to finish, was a classic demonstration of how easily the public could be fooled.

Public outrage was well expressed in a three-column letter to the Boston *Courier* signed "Observer." Under the heading "Was the Atlantic Cable a Humbug?" the writer asserted that no intelligible message had ever passed over the cable, that the news reports had been faked, and that the exchange between the Queen and the President had been planted weeks before. Poor De Sauty, still laboring hopelessly with his instruments at Trinity Bay, was defined as "a sort of myth—not sufficiently identified to be yet known by a positive name, or his reality to be positively credited." To the delight of typographers who had struggled with that name, a newspaper humorist was moved to write:

Thou operator, silent, glum,
 Why wilt thou act so naughty?
Do tell us what your name is—come!
 De Santy or De Sauty?

Don't think to humbug any more,
 Shut up there in your shanty,
But solve the problem once for all—
 De Sauty or De Santy?

Even the venerable Henry Wadsworth Longfellow, writing at his Beverly Farms in Massachusetts, composed a poem beginning:

DE SAUTY
An electro-chemical dialogue

Tell me, O Provincial! Speak, Ceruleo—Nasal!
 Lives there one De Sauty extant among you,
Whispering Boanerges, son of silent thunder,
 Holding talk with nations?

Born of stream galvanic, with it he had perished!
 There is no De Sauty now there is no current—!

The nastiest dig of all was the *Courier*'s claim that the whole pretense of success had been promulgated so that Cyrus Field could dump $375,000 worth of stock on a gullible market. Overseas this slander was supported by an article in the London *Daily News* in which a British naval lieutenant offered to produce "evidence on oath, by eye witnesses" that the cable had broken in mid-ocean in July and had never been respliced.

The public as a whole was deeply troubled. Where was evidence that the Queen's and the President's cablegrams had been transmitted? Unfortunately, of the 400 messages that had passed across the cable, by far the majority had been technical communications, exchanged between the electricians. These would carry no weight with the public.

Henry Field went to great lengths to exonerate his brother of these charges but few would listen to him. There could have been no faking of the news reports from India and China on August 27, for these had appeared almost simultaneously in England and America. The almost immediate report of the collision between the *Europa* and *Arabia* could be verified by Samuel Cunard, who in fact had made a point of relating his experience before a meeting of the New York Chamber of Commerce. Moreover, Henry had been in London when word had come of the death of his friend James Eddy, superintendent of the American Telegraph Company. The notice had appeared in the London *Times* within forty-eight hours of the tragedy. Had it been a fake, Field observed, the report would have had to have been filed some two weeks in advance, and Eddy would have been obliged to commit suicide to confirm it.

What really hurt Cyrus were the charges that the whole thing was a stock manipulation. One financial commentator wrote: "Now that the great cable glorification is over, we should like to ask one question: How many shares of stock did Mr. Field sell during the month of August?" Again the answer was available, if anybody had investigated. Through George Peabody in London, Field had sold precisely one share at a loss of $500.

As Christmas approached, Archbishop Hughes sent Field a commiserating note adding, "But no matter, the glory of having laid it in the depths of the ocean is yours, and it is not the less whether the stockholders receive interest or not. At present you have no rival claimant for the glory of the project." Indeed all rival claimants had gladly stepped aside—leaving him the lone and ridiculed champion of a hapless cause. People crossed the street to avoid meeting him. Even his pioneer partners Moses Taylor and Marshall Roberts had all but openly deserted him. Only Peter Cooper stood solidly by, telling Cyrus simply, "We will go on." But how?

As public fury and lamentation began to subside countless theories were advanced for the cable's failure. Some attributed it to a severe thunderstorm in Newfoundland in late September. Others opined that some unknown peak or submarine sierra had hacked the line in two. Samuel Finley Morse, now happily withdrawing to the sidelines, declared that in its handling the cable had been improperly exposed to the sun, the heat of which had melted the gutta-percha and caused leaks.

Testing from the Irish end, Bright and Thomson decided that there was indeed a leakage of current about 300 miles from Valentia. This did not preclude the existence of other flaws throughout the line, some of which Thomson had discovered while it was being laid. But it did suggest that there might have been a sharper drop at this point than anticipated, in which case the cable might have slid too far too fast and broken of its own weight. Bright and Thomson recommended that fresh soundings be made, off both Valentia and Newfoundland, and the little steamer *Porcupine* was assigned to do the job.

The despair felt in America was not so prevalent in England, where cable laying, with its ups and downs, was familiar. Expert opinion called the cable "mechanically good, but electrically bad." Where had the electricians failed?

In one direction the question led to Dr. Whitehouse and his feud with Thomson. In spite of Thomson's invention of the mirror galvanometer, so delicate, so responsive that it required very little current to affect it, Whitehouse had insisted on hooking his batteries up with giant induction coils, five feet long, to send a stroke of lightning through the wires. The effect, remarked one critic, was as if "high pressure steam had been got up in a low-pressure boiler." Said Bright: "It is extremely doubtful whether any cable . . . would long stand a trial with currents so generated, and of such intensity."

Thomson, not a vindictive man, defended his colleague's industry and good intentions. But honesty compelled him to admit that when Whitehouse had used his own apparatus, only four intelligible words had been received, none longer than the word "be." The directors were more damning. Whitehouse, they declared, had been pigheaded, insubordinate, and rash, had violated their directions, and had uselessly wasted £12,000 of company funds on his experiments. They therewith fired him.

Whitehouse fought back, taking a sideswipe at Field, whom he accused of shortening the time he needed for experiments, rushing him on the installation of equipment, and complaining when miracles of speed were not performed. "The most exaggerated expectations are thus promulgated by Mr. Field, and fostered by bombastic articles in the American press known to be immediately under his influence." In a calmer vein he charged: "Mr. Field was the most active man in the enterprise, and he had so much steam that he could not wait so long as three months. He said, 'Pooh, nonsense, why, the whole thing will be stopped; the scheme will be put back a twelvemonth.' "

This was one of the fairest accusations one could make of Field. It was a fault deeply imbedded in his character but it was part of his drive, without which the cable enterprise would never have been undertaken.

Even his close friend and supporter Charles Bright reluctantly admitted that the cable manufacture had been hurried, something of which Glass, Elliot & Company complained. But there were other valid reasons for its mechanical failure. It was experimental to begin with, built without benefit of past experience; the longest previous cable had stretched a mere 300 miles. Between the expeditions of 1857 and 1858 it had been stored haphazardly, exposed to weather and corrosion and the heat of the sun. Worst of all, it had been stored dry, although it is essential for gutta-percha, if it is to keep its "nature," to be stored underwater.

Again, throughout those years the cable had been taken on and off ship, wound and unwound, until some of it had been coiled as many as ten times. The final reason was the 1857 storm and the damage it had inflicted on the *Agamemnon*'s cargo. Following that ordeal and again in 1858, Professor Thomson had detected and corrected numerous injuries suffered by the cable. All things considered, the question was not so much why the cable failed as how it had ever worked at all.

Of these, his "darkest days," Field noted in his journal: "When a thing is dead it is difficult to galvanize it to life. It is more difficult to revive an old enterprise than to start a new one. The freshness and novelty are gone, the feeling of disappointment discourages further effort." But it was imperative to his nature that he make that further effort. With almost the sole support of Wilson Hunt and Peter Cooper, he left for England in May, 1859. After the calumny heaped on him in America, it was like coming home again. England had taken the cable failure in stride.

On June 8 he met with the directors to decide what was to be done next. There was no talk of abandoning the project, only of reviving it with new capital and possibly new blood. Under Field's persuasion, the directors voted to raise £600,000 for another attempt. To vote the amount was easy; to raise it, something else again. Realistically they felt—and Cyrus was forced to agree—that the job had grown too big for a small group of promoters counting solely on public subscription and it was unlikely that private capital would be available without some guarantee. As a project of national interest, it fell rightfully in the domain of government, and the government should underwrite it.

Field accepted this conclusion reluctantly. Knowing the temper of the American people and of Washington, he had no choice. On behalf of the Atlantic Telegraph Company he applied to Palmerston's government, in which William Ewart Gladstone was Chancellor of the Exchequer, asking it to guarantee 8 percent interest on the capital amount for twenty-five years, regardless of success or failure. With such a guarantee, eliminating all risk to the investor, the sale of shares in England would be quick and painless.

It was a bold request. But the English tended to regard the cable as their own. They had put up most of the money and had provided most of the technical and scientific skill. America's principal contribution had been Cyrus Field, a favor they readily acknowledged, accepting him as a sort of honorary citizen. To England, an island in the center of a far-flung empire, contact with its possessions was important, and it had already established cables in a number of directions. Added to this state of mind was England's proverbial willingness to gamble on maritime ventures.

Field's timing was unfortunate. A cable to India had recently been projected by the Red Sea Telegraph Company. The government had guaranteed the interest on £800,000, considerably more than Field was asking. The first lap, from Suez to Aden, had been laid in sections at the bottom of the Red Sea and had failed, leaving the British Treasury liable for the payment of £35,000 a year for twenty years! The English were not inclined, just now, to favor any similar proposal.

However, they came back at Field with a sporting offer. Not only would they guarantee the interest on the capital but would also increase their subsidy from £14,000 to £20,000 a year—*provided that the cable worked.*

Under the circumstances this was fair, but it did not pave the way for any easy sale of stock. The whole question of submarine cables was now suspect. The government called for an exhaustive inquiry into the causes of cable failure and the methods of prevention, and put its weight behind this. It supported continued soundings off the coast of Ireland, to see what serious unknown hazards might exist along the ocean floor. It also established a scientific committee to investigate every phase of cable construction and operation, with four members from the Board of Trade and four appointed by the Atlantic Telegraph Company.

(At the same time a similar, although evidently less active group, was appointed to perform a parallel inquiry in the United States. Among Field's papers is the following: "Extract from the minutes of Proceedings of the Managing Committee of the Atlantic Telegraph Company, dated 1st of July 1859: 'Authority was granted to Mr. Cyrus W. Field to apply to Professor Morse, Professor Henry, Commander Maury, Mr. W. E. Everett, and Commander Berryman to act as an advisory committee in America.' " Field sent a copy to Alexander Bache of the U. S. Coast Survey in Washington, saying, "I hope that you will consent to assist them [the committee] with your advice in carrying out this great national work.")

The chairman of the British committee, which went quickly into action, was Captain Douglas Galton of the Royal Engineers, while George Saward was among those representing the Atlantic Telegraph Company. Among the panel members were several men whom Cyrus welcomed as new blood to refresh the cable group: George Parker Bidder, a mathematical prodigy; Cromwell F. Varley, an experienced telegraph mechanician; Professor Charles Wheatstone, an electricity expert who would replace the amateur-minded Whitehouse as an aide to Thomson; and Josiah Latimer Clark, an electrical engineer, who became a partner in the Atlantic Company the same year. The commission agreed to sit in conference until it found the answers, which took nearly fifteen months, and for the moment there was nothing Field could do but wait for the report. This was, as usual, a hard assignment.

From New York came a copy of the *Journal of Commerce* with an item of encouragement:

> We are pleased to learn that the house of Cyrus W. Field & Co., which suspended payments in the fall of 1857, during the absence of Mr. Field in England (on business connected with the Atlantic Telegraph Company) have recently taken up nearly all their extended paper, the payment of which is not due till October next, and have now notified the holders of the balance that they are prepared to cash the whole amount, less the legal interest, on presentation. This evidence of prosperity must be gratifying to their numerous friends.

It also must have pricked the consciences of those who had accused him of chicanery and financial double-dealing on the cable. His restitution and recovery after the 1857 panic had been far more rapid than expected. But he had barely returned to spend Christmas with his family at Gramercy Park when another catastrophe befell him. A fire which had broken out in the adjoining building spread to his offices, now at 57 Beekman Street, and swept through his warehouse. Racing down to inspect the damage, Cyrus found the buildings gutted and his entire stock consumed.

He took one look at the charred remains, then called on the offices of a friendly competitor, Seymour & Company in John Street, and arranged to make use of the Seymour facilities until he could find a new location. He then inserted an advertisement in the evening newspapers, to run beside the reports of the fire, announcing that "business will continue as usual" at the new address. The operation did not suffer from a day of idleness.

To reassure Zenas Crane, he wrote that he had been covered by $80,000 of insurance. What he did not mention was a loss of $40,000 in excess of this amount. He told Zenas: "As our stock of Merchandise was entirely destroyed in our late fire, we intend in future to confine ourselves strictly to a commission basis." In a sense he was pulling in his horns and limiting his operation; except for Zenas, his business from now on would be in cash. While the paper business was no longer his prime interest, he threw himself back into it and during the first half of 1860 was as deep in it as he had ever been.

This turn of events at least took his mind off his distress with the cable venture. He looked for more ways to stimulate business and turned to his continued faith in color as a merchandising catalyst, asking Zenas for more and varied shades and books of samples "with our name on the cover." He suggested that Zenas send some samples of "light purple," which proved so popular with the New York Central Railroad (it was still using the color in 1966) that he wrote to Dalton some weeks later: "Our customer for the Purple paper is constantly calling on us. The time you agreed to have it here has already gone by several days. Please forward this with the salmon without further delay."

By May, just four months after having been burned out, he was installed in new quarters of his own on Beekman Street. But it was an uneasy period. The anti-Northern sentiments of the South were growing hotter; business was haunted by uncertainty. At the convention of the new Republican Party in Chicago, Cyrus favored the nomination of William Seward, even though both Dudley Field and Peter Cooper put their weight behind Abraham Lincoln. Cooper had invited Lincoln to speak at his new Cooper Union. Field, of course, attended, and his normal sympathies went out to this ungainly candidate, who, like himself, had sprung from rural poverty and whose views were humanitarian and liberal. But Seward, under Buchanan, had helped immeasurably with the cable back in 1857, when he championed it before a hostile Senate. Seward was his man.

When Lincoln was elected, Field wrote to Seward expressing his personal regrets, and Seward responded with "a thousand thanks for your considerate letter," adding: "If the alternative were presented to a wise man, he might well seek rather to have his countrymen regret that he had not been president than to be president."

Concern for politics, impending war, and shaky business took a holiday in mid-July with the arrival from Southampton of the "Wonder of the Seas"—Isambard Kingdom Brunel's mammoth ship *Great Eastern.* The "Little Giant" had died the year before. Since then the iron ship's career had been, according to the New York *Times,* "one gigantic blunder." She was in New York to recoup her losses with sight-seeing passengers, and almost as many people as had heralded the abortive triumph of the cable swarmed the Battery and riverbanks to watch her slice off a section of the pier as the captain tried to berth her.

Field was curious to see the ship whose designer had said was destined to lay the Atlantic cable. He bought $10 tickets for his family and friends for a two-day excursion to Cape May. They found the ship in dreadful shape, as were the passengers two hours later. But by climbing around the ironwork stairs and ladders, inspecting the gargantuan engine room and hold, he got an idea of her tremendous size, stability, and power. Yes, she would do for the cable if the time ever came.

On this trip, however, the food was execrable, half the waiters were drunk, and the only potable beverage was champagne. The magnificent white and gold saloon was turned into a gambling casino. Brawls were frequent. At nightfall only 300 beds were available for 2,000 passengers. In short, as the New York *Times* reporter Alexander Holley noted: "I cannot now bethink me of a single means for annoying man, woman or child on a voyage of pleasure that these imperious gentlemen left untried." By the time they stood off Old Point Comfort, observed James Dugan, the *Great Eastern*'s chronicler, "Cyrus Field chartered a side-wheeler and seceded with his coterie."

This was a period of spectacles for New York's bursting population of 1,000,000 and the next one was the Prince of Wales. The nineteen-year-old son of Queen Victoria modestly presented himself to the city as Lord Renfrew. Edward M. Archibald was now British consul in New York and, owing to his previous services in Newfoundland, also an honorary director of the Atlantic Telegraph Company. Because of the high regard in which he was held in England, Field was one of the welcoming dignitaries. Just as the classic City Hall had all but burned down in the torch procession two years before, the floor of the Academy of Music caved in during a reception for the prince.

Despite this, Archibald assured Field that the prince had been "immensely gratified" with his reception and that the event "will, I am sure, create in England a profound feeling of admiration for and of gratitude towards this country, the effect of which I cannot but think will be very beneficial to the future of both countries."

The gloom that seemed to mar each Christmas holiday returned again. Business was bad and getting worse. Murray Crane wrote to his brother Zenas from New York that Field & Company's liabilities were $100,000 but "CWF & Co. are secure." This was prematurely optimistic. Field fought hard to stay afloat while his competitors went down in dozens, but late in December he knew that he was beaten. The firm suspended payments. For the third time in twenty years he was forced to face bankruptcy. His estimated losses from fire and financial panic exceeded $130,000. He handled the problem as he had done before, confronting his creditors with the facts and staking his future on his reputation.

To each of them he sent a letter summarizing the firm's record and position. He said in part:

> Such a series of misfortunes is not often experienced by a single firm, at least in such rapid succession, and is quite sufficient to explain the present position of my affairs. Against all these losses I have struggled, and until within a few weeks hoped confidently to be able to weather all difficulties. But you know how suddenly the late panic has come upon us. We found it impossible to make collections. The suspension of several houses, whose paper we held to a large amount, added to our embarrassment.

Explaining that he felt it unfair to incur further debt by trying to meet their claims immediately, he asked his creditors to prescribe the course they wanted him to take:

> My only wish is, so far as I am able, to pay you to the utmost farthing. I shall most cheerfully give up to you every dollar of property I have in the world; and I ask only to be released that I may feel free from a load of debt, and can go to work again to regain what I have lost.

His creditors agreed to accept twenty-five cents on the dollar and urged him to carry on, "rather than place all in the hands of a trustee or trustees." It was an honorable settlement, but it put him between the jaws of a vise. To meet even this demand and to keep up his subscribed payments in both the American and the English cable companies, he had to mortgage virtually everything he owned—all his stock in the two companies, his house, including furniture, on Gramercy Park (already heavily mortgaged), even the family portraits, and his pew in the Madison Avenue Presbyterian Church. It left him virtually a pauper, with everything staked on the future of the cable.

In this disastrous year there was one moderately bright spot: a healing of the breach between Finley Morse and Field. Perhaps Morse was getting mellow with advancing age. He had hailed the abortive success of the Atlantic cable with a warning against its possible misuse for the sole benefit of its promoters. Now he did an about-face and aligned his interests—all the Morse lines in the East—with Field's American Telegraph Company. He was therewith installed as a director, along with Cyrus, Wilson Hunt, and Abram Hewitt, who took over Peter Cooper's role as President.

This meant that the American Telegraph Company controlled all major lines on the eastern seaboard. It was the kind of monopoly that Morse had formerly complained of; only now he was part of it. But the company was under attack from the Associated Press, a client it depended on. The AP protested what it considered exorbitant rates charged by the American Telegraph and threatened to build rival lines. It was strong enough to do so. Field entertained everybody concerned at a party at Delmonico's and in that luxurious atmosphere used all his powers of persuasion to bring the two factions into harmony. As a result, they secured an operation that Gisborne had envisaged in the early stages of his Newfoundland adventure—a steamer and telegraph relay system for transmitting news between Europe and America. During 1860 thirty-one ships from Europe were met by Associated Press reporters off Cape Race, and their news was sent by wire to New York, saving two days in transmission.

In short, Field's domestic telegraph situation was good. But he never regarded this as more than the tail to the main enterprise, the still nonexistent transatlantic cable. And now there was a disturbing question. What would happen to both of these in the event of war between the states? On December 20, 1860, South Carolina seceded from the Union. The drums were sounding.

16

War Between the States

➤➤➤➤➤➤◄◄◄◄◄◄ The Peace Convention of February, 1861,
at which Dudley Field was an influential delegate, did all it could to
reverse the course of secession, but passions had grown too hot too
fast. By the time Lincoln took office on March 4, the war was a fore-
gone conclusion, and with the firing on Fort Sumter, as Samuel Eliot
Morison noted, "events now moved as swift as the telegraph."

The facilities of Field's American Telegraph Company were quickly
put at the disposal of the Union. Over its wires on April 15, Lincoln
flashed his call for troops to every quarter of the North. The response
was as electric as the medium. State after state delivered more men
than expected; bankers and financiers offered money to the cause;
manufacturers volunteered materials and services. Had the same appeal gone out by mail, desultorily reaching different cities at different
times, the Union would never have been galvanized to so compelling
an awareness of its destiny.

Five days after Lincoln's call went out, Cyrus sent a note to Dudley
concerning their nephew, Matthew's son, who had been with Field
& Company since its inception. "Heman has this moment informed
me that he has enlisted, and leaves at nine o'clock tomorrow morning
with his regiment for Washington. This is the first intimation that I
had of his desire to enlist." Another nephew, Henry Martyn, Jr., followed suit by joining the Thirty-fourth Massachusetts Volunteers.

Cyrus attached a second note to Dudley: "Please send me a check
on account for as much as you can conveniently spare, as I am paying
away a large amount for Rags." There would indeed be shortages,
and rising prices, but the paper trade was probably the least of his
concerns. What of the cable and its future in this crisis?

Almost immediately American Telegraph's facilities were cut in half by the division of the states. The firm had only recently acquired the powerful southwestern network covering the entire area south of the Ohio River to New Orleans. Now this was lost, along with some other of its wires, to the Confederacy. The unified system was dismembered, affording an opportunity for its rival, Western Union, to dominate the industry.

It was an economic blow, but to Field, economics were certainly not the issue. In reverse fashion, the disruption underscored the tremendous importance of telegraphy in times of crisis. Andrew Carnegie, who as a youngster had mastered Morse's instruments, was summoned to Washington to organize a military telegraphic system. He enlisted 1,800 boys to operate the keys. The telegraph became what Secretary of the Army Edwin McMasters Stanton called "the right arm of the army."

It was that indeed. During no previous major conflict had so many troops, spread over so vast an area, been kept in such close communication. Lincoln was an admirer of telegraphy and spent more time in the War Department's telegraph office than anywhere except the White House. One of his young operators, David Homer Bates, recalled well the "tall, homely form with a gray plaid shawl thrown carelessly over his shoulders," crossing the lawn from the White House to the Pennsylvania Avenue office morning, noon, and night, to check on the latest news from his armies at the front.

On May 14, England declared its neutrality, granting the Confederacy the belligerent rights of a sovereign nation. This strained Britain's relations with the North and Field's emotions were ambivalent. For the present he put aside the Atlantic cable and concentrated on the domestic crisis.

Early in June he met with President Lincoln, Secretary of State Seward, and other members of the Cabinet and suggested three important steps that should be taken. The first was to seize and review all messages that had passed over his and other wires during the preceding months, "as I feel confident they will on examination prove many persons not now suspected to have been acting as spies and traitors." The second was to connect all leading ports with Washington, by submarine cable where necessary, so that military traffic could be controlled from one source. Finally, he recommended the adoption of a code or cipher to keep communications secret, an obvious expedient that was quickly adopted. In a letter to Colonel Thomas Scott, Assistant Secretary of War, reiterating these suggestions he added:

> I consider it very important that the government should have the most reliable telegraph communication with its principal forts on the Atlantic coast.
>
> If there is any information that I possess that would be of service to you in carrying out the wishes of the government regarding telegraph matters it will afford me pleasure to give it.
>
> I presume you are aware that there are very few persons in this country who have had any experience in the manufacture, working, or laying of submarine cables of any great importance.

His ability to organize and complete an undertaking was invaluable to the Administration. He saw to it that the American Telegraph Company, whose lines already reached Washington from cities to the north, extended their wires to the War Department, the Navy Yard, the fortifications on the Potomac, and other points strategic to the capital's defense. The company bore the cost of poles, wires, instruments, and personnel, "a generous and patriotic act gratefully acknowledged by the President and Secretary." In another patriotic act he wrote to the Secretary of the Treasury recommending that the government "send at once a confidential agent to England, with a competent naval officer, to obtain from the British government by purchase, or otherwise, some of the improved steam gun-boats and other vessels to protect our commerce and to assist in blockading Southern ports."

Although his energies and thoughts were directed at whatever he could do in the immediate situation, he wrote to George Saward in London: "I never had more confidence in the ultimate success of the Atlantic Telegraph Company than I have today." Not an odd time to have confidence, for the nation, absorbed in a divisive war, was also being forced into a serious appraisal of its international position. Communication with Europe was becoming vital. Field was heartened by Saward's reply: "Vast improvements in everything relating to the structure of telegraph cables are constantly being made, and inquiry on the subject is very active. We are becoming much more hopeful of a good time for the Atlantic cable."

Cables had been laid successfully by the French—from Toulon to Corsica—and by the English between Alexandria and Malta. The latter was not yet completed, but "the event is certain," Saward wrote.

In midsummer Field was called to Stockbridge. There had been an epidemic of diphtheria in western Massachusetts that winter, and possibly some taint of the infection caused his mother's heart to stop in the eightieth year of a life spent in devotion to her family. Cyrus found his father bowed with grief and so old that he could only pace the paths around the parsonage as if he were looking for his wife. Four sons carried her to her grave, and of their solemn procession Dr. John Todd wrote: "Never did I see a grief more reverent or respect more profound. . . . They were all doubtless going back in memory to their early childhood, and to the loving care of this best of all earthly friends."

She had indeed been the best of all earthly friends to Cyrus. She never tried to hold or check him, never chided him for his impetuosity and its results, and always pitted her patience against his sometimes rash impatience. She gave him a great deal of her character, too. As Henry put it:

> When my brother Cyrus was wrestling for thirteen years with the difficulties, and what seemed the impossibilities, of the Atlantic Telegraph, I have seen him a hundred times in perplexities that would have driven him to despair, if he had not had in him that unconquerable hope, which he derived from his mother, and that indomitable resolution which rose up from defeat after defeat, and fought on to the final victory.

From Stockbridge, Field hurried back to the Willard Hotel in Washington, where he was spending more time now than at his house in Gramercy Park. In the middle of December, 1861, he sent to President Lincoln and General George McClellan a ten-point proposal for a military-oriented cable network, "trusting that this subject will at once receive the attention its importance demands." Characteristic of his correspondence with Lincoln was its frankness and lack of hyperbole. He said what he thought and signed himself simply, "Your friend, Cyrus W. Field." In this memorandum he proposed a girdle of submarine cables that would be an effective blockade of the South by keeping tight check on Confederate naval movements. The network would leapfrog from the mouth of Chesapeake Bay to Cape Hatteras and down to Fernandina on the east coast of Florida; from Ship Island, Mississippi, to Galveston, Texas; and from Cedar Key to Key West, Florida.

> With these lines established, and a despatch vessel running between Key West and Havana, the Government would be kept constantly

advised not only of the movement of its own forces, but also of those of the rebels, on the coast, and their vessels in the West Indies; and should the *Nashville,* the *Sumter,* or any other piratical craft appear in those waters, it would be at once known there. But it cannot be necessary for me to refer to individual instances to illustrate the advantages to the Government at all times of such means of communication, and especially during the existence of the war for the suppression of the present wicked rebellion, as its importance is too obvious. . . . A single message may be of more value to the Government than the entire cost of the line proposed.

Field offered to go to England and contract for the necessary length of cable, which would be made as quickly and cheaply as possible, bring it back to America, supervise its laying and being put in working order, for only his personal expenses. He also suggested, however, that he receive a commission on cost "as you yourself may designate." While this request for a commission might seem to dilute the high-mindedness of the offer, it is not out of character—Field's character and that of the times. There was a Christian virtue in profit—to such a degree that not to make a profit bordered on transgression. Reward was justice; to overlook reward was reprehensible.

General McClellan was quick to endorse Field's plan in writing: "I fully concur on the importance of the submarine telegraph proposed by Mr. Field, and earnestly urge that his plans may be adopted and he authorized to have the plans carried into execution." But Lincoln moved slowly. Few of the lines were executed, and not the one to Key West which McClellan strongly favored.

Meanwhile, another link in the domestic telegraph empire had been forged, and another Field came briefly on the scene. Since the passage of the Pacific Telegraph Act in 1860, efforts had been under way— by Hiram Sibley of Western Union and telegraph interests on the West Coast—to extend a wire from Omaha to San Francisco, despite expected troubles from rampant buffalo, hostile Indians, and defensive Mormons. The work had gone well. The buffalo had stayed away, the Indians had been friendly toward the white man's "wire rope express," and Brigham Young had cooperated in obtaining poles. In October, 1861, and in the absence of the governor, Stephen Field, now a chief justice of California, wired Lincoln that the line was open and his state was ready to stand by the Union.

This coast-to-coast connection opened up the entire northern continent to communication with Europe, but it also paved the way for a proposed competitive connection with Europe via Russia, across the Bering Strait. Sibley and an aggressive promoter named Perry Collins had already obtained a government grant to survey the route, and Samuel Morse, of all people, had privately endorsed the plan. The Atlantic cable failure of 1858 had given heart to rival speculators and spawned a rash of cable projects, including one from a triumvirate of financiers that would cross the Atlantic from France to the island of St. Pierre off Newfoundland and down to New England.

If Field was worried by these threats, he was too preoccupied with the war and the more immediate problems of the Atlantic cable to show it.

Fate was about to play into his hand, in the devious manner fate often adopts. In November, 1861, the Union warship *San Jacinto* under Captain Charles Wilkes intercepted the British steamer *Trent* en route to Europe and took prisoner two Southern emissaries on their way to London and Paris. It was a flagrant violation of the freedom of the seas, hailed by the North as a brilliant coup and by the South as a happy blunder that would bring the British to their side. A wave of indignation swept Great Britain. There was public outcry for war against the Union. Lord John Russell, Foreign Secretary, demanded an apology and the immediate release of the Confederate commissioners, and aboard the *Great Eastern,* 8,000 troops were dispatched to Canada to fortify the border.

Lincoln and Seward were taken by surprise. The latter drafted a letter to Lord Russell explaining that Wilkes had acted without orders. By the time these communications had crossed the ocean, taking almost a month to do so, war with England seemed nearly unavoidable. Seward was finally obliged to write Charles Francis Adams, Washington's minister in London, asking him to inform Lord Russell that the prisoners had been "happily released." Said Lincoln: "It was the bitterest pill I ever swallowed." It was also an ominous warning. Inadequate communication was at the heart of this misunderstanding. The London *Times* noted: "We nearly went to war with America because we had not a telegraph across the Atlantic."

There was another side to this coin. The delay in transmitting and replying to Great Britain's protest gave English anger a chance to abate. Field was quick to take advantage of the *Trent* misunderstanding and its implications. He wrote George Saward, "now is the time ... to act with energy and decision, and get whatever guarantee is necessary from the English government to raise the capital to manufacture and lay down without unnecessary delay between Newfoundland and Ireland a good cable." He cited the low rate of interest then prevailing in Great Britain as an added incentive for moving fast. But he realized that the bigger battle lay in Washington. On New Year's Day, 1862, he wrote to Secretary Seward:

> The importance of the early completion of the Atlantic telegraph can hardly be estimated. What would have been its value to the English and United States governments if it had been in operation on the 30th of November last, on which day Earl Russell was writing to Lord Lyons, and you at the same time to Mr. Adams, our minister in London?
>
> A few short messages between the two governments and all would have been satisfactorily explained. I have no doubt that the English government has expended more money during the last thirty days in preparation for war with this country than the whole cost of manufacturing and laying a good cable between Newfoundland and Ireland.

He went on to point out that Valentia was now connected with all the capitals of Europe, Algiers in Africa, Odessa on the Black Sea, Constantinople, and Omsk in Siberia, and that telegraph lines extended from St. John's to all British North American possessions and from New York to San Francisco. There remained only the Atlantic cable to create a network that would range almost around the world:

> Will you pardon me for suggesting to you the propriety of opening a correspondence with the English government upon the subject, and proposing that the Atlantic Telegraph Company should be aided and encouraged to complete their line, and that the two governments should enter into a treaty that in case of any war between them the cable should not be molested?

Seward replied that "it will afford me pleasure to confer with you on that subject at any time you may present yourself for that purpose." Before hurrying down to Washington, Field was able to determine that Field & Company had recovered with amazing rapidity from its near bankruptcy of the year before. All notes had been paid as fast as they had fallen due, and he informed his creditors: "You will see that we have reduced our liabilities to a very small amount, and we shall meet them all promptly at or before maturity."

Once again he had rallied from a sort of disaster, but his personal position was precarious. In spite of the firm's recovery, he was obliged to ask Crane's help in unloading forty shares of stock in the Western Massachusetts Insurance Company to bolster his family budget.

In Washington, he held long discussions with Lincoln and Seward. There must have been curious crosscurrents of political feeling at these meetings. Lincoln was notably aware of who had backed his nomination in 1860, and Cyrus alone, of all the Fields, had supported Seward. But Lincoln did not harbor grudges. Possibly the chief barrier between them was Field's impatience and the President's tendency to act with slow deliberation. In presenting his arguments for both extensive cable connections on the eastern coast and quick support for the Atlantic line, Field talked so fast that Lincoln could not follow him. The President suggested that he slow down. "Does *anybody* understand you?" Lincoln finally inquired. Yes, Field said; his telegraph operators generally did. "Then send me a telegram," said Lincoln, "and I'll read it."

Accordingly, David Bates was assigned to take down Field's proposals and, to judge from his diary, had much the same difficulty:

> ... being of an excitable nature, his words flowed from his lips in a rapid, intermittent stream, while his thoughts outran his spoken words ten to one, so that it was not long before I, not being a shorthand writer, was engulfed, and the result was, judging from my notes, that Field's memorial, like an ocean cable, was discernible only at its two ends, with here and there indications of a struggle and a splash. Several weary hours were spent in this way, and when at last some sort of order had been evolved out of seeming chaos and the memorial finally completed and signed, Field shot out of the door and rushed over to Stanton's room, waving the document as if it were a danger-signal, leaving me alone and in a semi-collapse.

The upshot of these deliberations, if they may be so called, was a letter from Seward to Adams dated January 14. It acknowledged concern over the *Trent* affair and instructed Adams to call on Lord Russell and press for action on the cable. Seward wrote:

> You may say to him that the President entertains the most favorable views of the great enterprise in question, and would be happy to cooperate with the British government in securing its successful execution and such arrangements as would guarantee both nations reciprocal benefits from the use of the telegraph, not only in times of peace, but even in times of war, if, contrary to our desire and

expectation, and to the great detriment of both nations, war should ever arise between them.

With considerable optimism, Field sailed for England on the *Arabia* late in January and, after having conferred with Adams, asked Lord Russell for an interview. Russell received him at the Foreign Office and listened attentively to Field's arguments, based not alone on the *Trent* affair but on the effectiveness of the cable, during its few weeks of operation in 1858, in enabling England to rescind its orders to the British regiments in Canada. Field pointed out the losses that his company had suffered, all to good purpose, and its willingness to carry the venture further if it only had some guarantee. Russell was polite but noncommittal, and shortly thereafter he sent Field a note that Her Majesty's government "have come to the conclusion that it would be more prudent for the present to defer entering into any fresh agreement on so difficult a subject."

A delegation headed by Field, Brett, and Saward promptly called on Lord Palmerston. They were equipped with samples of cable previously laid and specimens of the projected cable to illustrate the vast improvement. The Prime Minister asked some well-informed and searching questions: "Will not marine animalculae make an impression upon gutta percha? Will not the iron armament get corroded?" Satisfied with the answers, Palmerston then moved on to the questions of competition and commercial risk, in a dialogue recorded in the minutes of the meeting:

> LORD PALMERSTON— I heard the other day that the American Government had a notion of establishing telegraphic communication with Europe through Asia.
>
> MR. CYRUS FIELD— All that has been done is, I believe, that a Committee have reported to the Senate, advising the Government to allow an expedition to go and make soundings. . . .
>
> LORD PALMERSTON— My notion from what I heard was, that the Russian line was to be a long line, with a very short sea passage.
>
> MR. CYRUS FIELD— The sea passage would be about 4,000 miles if carried from island to island, and only about sixty if taken via Bering Straits [*sic*].
>
> LORD PALMERSTON— What is the distance by the Atlantic line?
>
> MR. CYRUS FIELD— 1,640 nautical miles.
>
> LORD PALMERSTON— The Russian land line was started, I thought, upon the notion that a submarine cable was precarious, but you would not gain much by it if that be so.

Palmerston was leading up to his point that "the answer to an application to the Government for a guarantee would be, under ordinary circumstances, that commercial speculations are not contributed to by Government; it is only in exceptional cases that that is done." Being told that this was an exceptional case and that "the Government would obtain enormous political advantages from the means of speedy communication with her own colonies," Lord Palmerston replied, "No doubt. I should like to have a written statement setting forth the proposal that is now made to the Government."

It was an inconclusive interview but Field was given a citation for his efforts. At the fifth meeting of the board that same month, he was elected an honorary director of the company—an opportune vote of confidence. He told the group that he believed Russell's and Palmerston's responses reflected only hesitancy, and "it is likely, if public opinion could be brought to bear upon them, the government might consent to render assistance in the undertaking."

Undoubtedly with this in mind there followed one of the most singular events of the 1862 London season. It consisted of a *"telegraphic soiree"* at Samuel Gurney's Victorian mansion at Prince's Gate, Hyde Park, on March 28 "to spread information on the subject among all classes but chiefly among educated and intelligent persons." Here distinguished bankers, financiers, business and social leaders, and earls, dukes and lords of the realm were shown various types of telegraphic apparatus and equipment, fully operative, along with "charts, maps, and specimens of telegraphic cables." The London *Evening Standard* reported:

> The company assembled had thus the opportunity afforded them of witnessing with their own eyes the actual manipulation of Morse's delicate and beautiful instruments by some of the expertest of operators, and the wonderful results developed by the prompt and ready obedience of the dainty spirit which, at the motion of a finger, as it were, "puts a girdle round the world in 40 minutes."

Through the associated lines of the Atlantic Company, Field had arranged for the installation of wires connecting Gurney's drawing room with every leading telegraph system in Europe. During the evening, according to a privately-published report,

> . . . messages were despatched and received from all parts of Europe, much to the amusement and astonishment of the guests. To illustrate the marvellous facility for transmitting thought by the aid of

lightning, the Earl of Shaftesbury sent a message to St. Petersburg through Berlin, enquiring after the health of the Emperor of Russia, and in four minutes he received word from the banks of the Neva, a distance of 2,000 miles, that he was in good health.

It is hard to measure the effects of such a public relations undertaking—especially since, in ironic counterpoint, signs of personal antagonism toward Field were developing in England. As they were anonymous they may have come from his own countrymen abroad. Most Americans living or visiting in Britain favored the Southern cause. Field's loyalty to the Union, his activities in military telegraphy, and his eagerness to keep Great Britain from supporting the Confederacy may have prompted the oblique attacks.

They were spearheaded by a triple-column weekly feature in the *Standard,* London's largest evening newspaper, headed simply "America" and signed "Manhattan." Typical was an assault on General "Napoleon" McClellan, who "at heart is not tainted, although people do not like his taking up that absurd but wretchedly impoverished Atlantic Cable Field, and quartering him upon the public treasury for a few millions to build a coast line Atlantic telegraph." And again, in a diatribe against the "notorious incompetency" of McClellan: "He has made the fortune of Cyrus Field, who is brother-in-law of McClellan's old patron (and perhaps his own), by giving him a contract to run telegraph wires along the coast."

There was, of course, no family relation with McClellan, no contract to run a coastline telegraph, no millions from the public treasury. But the *Standard,* supported shortly by the London *Daily Herald,* pressed the attack:

> The London people will be astonished to find that Atlantic-cable Cyrus W. Field has got a fat job from the United States. It will amount, I suppose, to a few millions, viz., to build a coast wire telegraph. The way it happened is this:—Cyrus is very poor. General McClellan and the brother of Cyrus were formerly partners in railroad contracts, or something of the sort. Hence the milk in that cocoanut. General McClellan recommends the coast telegraph. Certainly; why not?

Someone was out to get Field. Some sort of conspiracy was becoming obvious.

Certainly no credence was given to these calumnies. Field must have been aware that although British sentiment lay generally with the

South, his standing in Great Britain was secure. His championship of the Atlantic cable put him above wartime partisanship. George Saward made a point of praising him in a popular scientific journal, noting that he had never received a shilling for his work in England, and Professor Thomson wrote him: "If any degree of perseverance can be sufficient to deserve success, and any amount of value in any object can make it worth striving for, success ought to attend the efforts you and the directorate are making for a result of world-wide beneficence."

This encouragement was not confined to his circle of associates. Paul Julius von Reuter, who was creating one of the most powerful news services in the world, assured Field that even one cable might not be sufficient. He estimated that his agency could guarantee £5,000 worth of business annually. To Cyrus this was heady tonic. He wrote to Vermont-born Curtis Lampson, vice-chairman of the Atlantic Telegraph Company since Brooking's reproachful resignation in 1858, urging him to continue pressing Russell for a favorable answer. Meanwhile, grasping at straws, he approached Glass, Elliot & Company. Would the firm, as contractors, undertake to lay the cable at its own risk, providing the ships, the men, the wire itself?

Field did not wait for an answer. He caught the steamer *Asia* home and arrived in New York on April 11, spent two short hours with his family, determining that they were well, then raced down to Washington without unpacking.

The unkindest cut of all awaited him. A bill of indictment, charging him with treason—of conspiring with the public enemy (England) —had been brought to a grand jury in his absence. He tried to find out who had made the charges, but he was unable to do so; the grand jury had adjourned. According to the General Services Division of the National Archives, "Grand Jury proceedings are usually secret and a record of them is not kept."

He was being attacked on both sides of the Atlantic, for supporting the Union cause and for betraying it.

That he was pro-British there could hardly be a doubt. But this was a matter of interpretation and, in this instance, had been twisted by a vicious few. Considering the public temper in the North, which had expected an easy victory and was not getting it and which was critical of the conduct of the war, the time was ripe for wild and erratic charges.

They hurt and baffled Field. His desire to come to terms with England was due partly to his seeing both sides of a question and partly to his belief that should Britain join the South, the North was doomed. In view of England's naval might and her ability, with troops in Canada, to force a two-front war upon the Union, it was not an idle fear.

The mystery has never been altogether solved. The allegations, from an unidentified source, had been dismissed by the grand jury. They had then been sent anonymously to the New York press, which refused to publish them. But they found their way to England, where they were pounced on by the London *Daily Herald* and *Evening Standard* as authentic circulation-building news. Field was popular in England. He was one of them, and he was being maligned and disavowed in his own country, proving that the North was composed of "cowardly and irresponsible" rascals. Later—too late to matter—the *Herald* published an apology.

By taking his case directly to Seward and Attorney General Edward Bates, laying before them all his communications with the British government, Field was able to quash even a suspicion of suspicion. Actually, nobody in Washington had paid much attention to the allegations. Bates wrote him: "The affair looks rather like a stupid, practical joke. Could the scheme have been meant as a blow at your business in Europe?" Field continued to get poison-pen letters, all anonymous, which he forwarded to the Attorney General. That some may have threatened his life is suggested by a note to a supplier which appears among his papers at this time: "As we are all liable to be called away by death at any time, I should esteem it a favor if you would indorse the amount paid you by C. W. Field & Co., on the 5th instant, on my bond, and send the same to my office. . . ."

In general, though, he tried to forget the incident. He was more concerned with public acrimony toward Great Britain. He wrote to publisher-politician Thurlow Weed, who had interceded in the *Trent* affair and was then in London: "I regret exceedingly to find a most bitter feeling in this country against England. Mr. Seward is almost the only American I have heard speak kindly of England or Englishmen since I arrived." He was aware of equally hostile feelings in Great Britain. The English, he felt, had a misconception of the Union's cause and the progress of the war, due to inadequate information. He was so anxious to have favorable news reach London promptly that he arranged for important dispatches to be put aboard the first departing steamer.

Chafing for reports about the cable, he was disappointed to hear from Lampson that Palmerston "could not understand why it was necessary to go to Government for assistance in carrying out a project which, if successful, must necessarily be remunerative in the highest degree. . . ." Lampson urged Field to apply pressure circuitously, from Seward in Washington to Adams in London, then from Adams to Palmerston. Field did so and, at the same time, gave Lampson a trenchant account of his activities:

> Four weeks ago this evening I arrived from England, and almost every moment of my time since I landed has been occupied in working for the Atlantic Telegraph, either in seeing the President of the United States, or one of his Cabinet, or some member of the Senate or House of Representatives, or an editor of one of our papers, or writing to the British provinces, or doing something which I thought would hasten on the time when we should have a good submarine cable working successfully between Ireland and Newfoundland, and if *we do not get it laid in 1863 it will be our fault.*
>
> *Now, now,* is the golden moment, and I do beg of you and all the other friends of the Atlantic telegraph to act without a moment's unnecessary delay.
>
> I have written you and Mr. Saward so often since my arrival that I am afraid you will get tired of reading my letters; but from the abundance of the heart the mouth will speak, and I can hardly think of anything but a telegraph across the Atlantic.

He told Lampson that in spite of Palmerston's indifference, "we can succeed without further assistance from either government, as I believe that an appeal to the public will *now* get us all the money that we want, provided the business is pressed forward in the proper manner." At the same time, he notified Saward that he would arrive in England on October 20, and "I hope that we will . . . have *all* of the stock for a new cable subscribed within one month, and our other arrangements so perfect that I can at an early day return to my family and country."

Arriving in England, he received a final answer from Glass, Elliot. Yes, it would undertake to lay the cable—on the following conditions: it was to be paid weekly the cost of labor and material, and when the cable was laid and operating, it was to receive 20 percent of its cost in shares in the company. Meanwhile, "confident that this enterprise can be successfully carried out," it would subscribe £2,500 in advance to purchase stock. (In a parenthetical offer, Glass, Elliot agreed to provide and lay the cables which Field had proposed to Lincoln, connecting Union forts along the eastern coast.) It was a base to work from, but considering Glass, Elliot's estimated cost of £675,000, there was still much money to be raised.

Although Field had written that he thought only of the cable he spent these weeks in London working almost exclusively for better relations between England and America. In this effort he had two American allies. One was George Peabody, whose London home was a meeting ground for public figures of both nationalities and whose Fourth of July dinners were an institution. The other was Peabody's partner, Junius Morgan, "one of the chief links in the financial relationship between Great Britain and the United States."

On the other side of the fence was the journalist John Louis O'Sullivan, Irish-American champion of lost causes, whose writings on Manifest Destiny had fired Field's imagination a decade before. Like Field, O'Sullivan was in London as a self-appointed diplomat and was urging the British government to recognize the Confederacy. Both were playing for high stakes.

Field had adopted as his headquarters the Buckingham Palace Hotel at Buckingham Gate ("Quiet and genteel, kept by Mr. Beach for families and gentlemen"), a handsome Victorian edifice overlooking the Royal Gardens and only a step or two from Whitehall. From it he went out each morning, armed with pamphlets and books from America explaining the nature of the issues in the war. These he placed where he thought they would do most good. He aimed first at Gladstone, the "Grand Old Man" of British politics, whose pro-Southern views were well known, asking Stuart-Wortley, chairman of the Atlantic Telegraph Company, to arrange a meeting with the Chancellor. Stuart-Wortley did, and there began an exchange of views, by visit and letter, between Field and Gladstone that continued for some time.

Gladstone expressed the prevalent English attitude in writing to Field of "the heavy responsibility you incur in persevering with this destructive and hopeless war at the cost of such dangers and evils to yourselves, to say nothing of your adversaries, or of an amount of misery inflicted upon Europe such as no other civil war in the history of man has ever brought upon those beyond its immediate range." But he admitted the war could be seen from many different angles, and later he thanked Field for tolerantly receiving his somewhat harsh opinions.

John Bright, the liberal-minded statesman (unrelated to Charles Tilston Bright), was more considerate of Field's views, as was Lord

Shaftesbury, with each of whom Field left what he considered enlightening documents on the rebellion. Bright, in fact, was wholly on his side; he was not only for the Union, but also for a mightier Union that would stretch from the North Pole to the Gulf of Mexico, affording "at least some hope that man is not forsaken of Heaven, and that the future of our race may be better than the past."

Consciously or not, Field was acting as an ambassador without portfolio. Philip McDonald, in his *Saga of the Seas,* was well within limits to write:

> From his knowledge of the powerful resources of the British at that time, he realized what a calamity it would be if they should align themselves with the Confederacy, as their upper classes were inclined to do. Since England did not officially espouse the cause of the South, thanks are certainly due to men like Field who used their special knowledge to explain conditions, and their influence to dissuade the British leaders from rash action. The course of American history might have been decisively changed had England been swayed by her dominant statesmen to render official aid to the Southern States.

Field was well adapted to this role of intermediary. He had a combination of humility and native pride, deference without servility, good manners, and great warmth. Beyond that, his boyish enthusiasm, even when it reached extremes, could hardly make him anything but likable. It was infectious, breaking down stiff British barriers. Even his soft Massachusetts accent seemed to blend with British cadences.

The great English houses were open to him as they had been open to few Americans before. He spent several weekends in Cliveden at the Dowager Duchess of Sutherland's, evenings with Lord and Lady Shaftesbury, Sir Culling Eardley, Lady Franklin, Captain Galton, the John Brights, and Charles Francis Adams. The servants at the Palace Hotel complained he never slept.

By the time he was ready to leave in late December it was obvious that he would again miss Christmas with his family. It had been years since he had spent a holiday at home. Perhaps troubled by conscience or anxious to know just where his hours went, he compiled a detailed list of his engagements from the time of writing to the time of leaving and mailed it jointly to his daughters, Alice, Isabella, Mary Grace, and Fanny. He noted that "almost every meeting I am engaged until a very late hour" and that "several times since I arrived I have had three invitations for the same evening, and I *decline* all that I can without injury to the object of my visit to England."

Of a dinner he was giving at his hotel for a dozen dignitaries, he observed: "How much I wish that I could have this dinner-party in our own home! . . . I have very often regretted that your mother or some of you were not with me. . . . I have purchased *all* the things that you gave me a memorandum of, or have written me about."

17

Swing of the Pendulum

➤➤➤➤➤➤➤◄◄◄◄◄◄◄ Four days after Lincoln's Emancipation Proclamation in January, 1863, Field returned to find New York's confidence restored by the previous September's victory at Antietam. This time he stayed with Mary and the children for five days before going down to Washington. In the capital he called at the War and Navy Departments to submit Glass, Elliot's proposal for laying submarine cables to strategic Union forts. After urging acceptance of the offer, he returned home, only to receive a telegram from Secretary of the Navy Gideon Welles asking him back for further consultation.

Trips between New York and Washington were almost as arduous as ocean voyages, involving an hour's plodding across Philadelphia to make train connections. But Washington's optimism was encouraging. With Lee's retreat into Virginia, the threat of invasion from the South had been removed; there was talk of ultimate victory and peace. In England, belief that the Confederacy was invincible subsided, and John Bright wrote to Field: "Opinion here has changed greatly. In almost every town great meetings are being held to pass resolutions in favor of the North, and the advocates of the South are pretty much put down."

Now indeed was the golden moment to press for subscriptions to his cable. He dropped all other pursuits and through the spring months canvassed the Eastern cities tirelessly working from before eight in the morning until after ten at night. "I have never worked so hard in all my life," he wrote. He traveled some 1,500 miles to visit, among other cities, Philadelphia, Albany, Buffalo, Providence, and Boston, noting afterward: "I have promises of subscriptions from all these places."

But promises were often all he got. Conservative Boston, for example, applauded him as a speaker, as a native son of Massachusetts, as the promoter of "one of the greatest enterprises ever undertaken by man," and then passed a resolution commending his effort to the attention of the American public. "But," as Henry Field noted, *"not one man subscribed a dollar!"*

New York was little more receptive. He addressed gatherings at the Corn Exchange, the Board of Brokers, and the Chamber of Commerce, of which he had been elected an honorary member in 1858. To the produce brokers he emphasized that potential markets like England and France were in immediate telegraphic communication with the European grain-producing countries whereas they had to wait weeks for price quotations from the United States.

To the New York Chamber of Commerce—which had just passed a resolution condemning Great Britain's tacit assistance to the South and open hostility to the North—he explained Glass, Elliot's cost-plus proposal and also cited its offer to help the military efforts of the Union:

> This same company ... have also addressed a letter to me relative to laying down a submarine cable from Fortress Monroe [Fort Monroe, Virginia] to Galveston, Texas. They will manufacture it in England, bring it out in their own ship, lay it down, and only ask payment when it is in perfect working order. If it is not a success, they are willing to lose the whole part of it; a risk sufficient to show their confidence in laying it successfully.

Summarizing his case for the Atlantic cable, he said:

> *But from our own interest,* here in the United States, it is greatly to be desired that a larger proportion of the stock should be held this side of the Atlantic. ... This is a work which concerns us *far more* than it concerns England. England it connects with the United States and the British Provinces, but America it connects, not only with England, but with the continent of Europe and the East, in fact with the whole civilized world.

In short, he was appealing to the Chamber *not* to let Great Britain get too tight a hold on an instrument that might affect the country's international position. Commenting on the cable undertaking, the Chamber's president, Abiel A. Low replied:

Anyone listening to Mr. Field . . . could not long entertain a doubt as to the success of the cable effort. He has studied it in all its bearings, and with the aid of the science and intelligence so readily at command on the other side of the ocean, where he has had the benefit of an experience far exceeding that of this country with regard to ocean telegraphs.

Low warned that if Americans ignored the cable out of hatred or mistrust of England, Britain could do the job alone and block American participation in the end result.

In a sense, Field was talking to himself or to his counterparts when he addressed such groups, even when he toured the city from house to house, ignoring those who dodged into doorways to avoid him. People like Low, Cooper, Hunt, and the other financiers he knew were already committed to the cable and were underwriting what they had lost. Those who came in for the first time did so, his brother Henry wrote, "more from sympathy and admiration of his indomitable spirit than from confidence in the success of the enterprise."

By the end of May he had received subscriptions totaling £66,615, barely one-tenth of the capital required. He admitted: "One feeling, I am aware, may embarrass the effort to raise money for this enterprise at the present time. It is the feeling toward England on account of her course towards the United States since the commencement of the present war." Beyond that, the dollar had sunk in value in relation to the pound; money was tight. All things considered, he wrote to London that he thought he had "done well." He might have pointed out, but did not, that £66,000 was somewhat better than he had done in 1856, when American support had amounted to only a pittance.

The pendulum of war was swinging back from the costly triumph at Antietam. Jackson and Lee were on the march again; Union optimism faded. Before leaving once more for England, Field warned his associates at Field & Company: "During my absence in Europe you will please not sell any rags or paper manufacturer's stock except for cash, as in these times we had much better keep our goods than to sell them even on a few days credit. . . . I would only purchase such papers as I wanted for immediate sales and could sell at a good profit." Partly because of his long absences and the cautious policy that these imposed, volume and profits were decreasing.

Arriving in England in early June, he learned that George Saward had not had any better luck in selling stock to his countrymen than he had had. Saward reported to the Atlantic Telegraph Company directors:

> I myself have personally waited upon nearly every capitalist and mercantile house of standing in Glasgow and in Liverpool, and some of the directors have gone round with me in London for the same purpose. We have no doubt induced a great many persons to subscribe, but they do so as they would to a charity, and in sums of corresponding amount.

The important development in their venture at this time was the final report from the committee of inquiry appointed by the British government in 1859. Published in July, 1863, the study filled a volume larger than the Bible and in its secular field was almost as absolute. The conclusions, signed by the eight-man panel, culminated in:

> We, the undersigned . . . do hereby state, as a result of our deliberations, that a well-insulated cable properly protected, of suitable specific gravity, made with care, and tested under water throughout its progress with the best known apparatus, and payed into the ocean with the most improved machinery, possesses every prospect of not only being successfully laid in the first instance, but may reasonably be relied upon to continue for many years in an efficient state for the transmission of signals.

Behind these broad generalities lay days, weeks, and months of meticulous investigation, demonstration, and analysis. The committee had listened to anyone who had an idea or experience—business executives, engineers, scientists, admirals, contractors—had taken down hundreds of thousands of words of testimony; had barred no angle of approach.

Once and for all the committee of inquiry settled the debate between Thomson and Whitehouse, with the latter protesting from the sidelines. There was no need, it proved conclusively, for an extensive voltage to send a signal through 2,000 miles of wire. As Henry Field poetically expressed it: "God was not in the whirlwind, but in the still, small voice. A soft touch could send a thrill along that iron nerve."

The committee's chief concern was with the type of cable to be manufactured. It had the benefit of past experience in the success of the Mediterranean and Red Sea cables, which were operating under a combined distance of nearly 4,000 miles. Its conclusions led to standards that were never radically improved upon.

Field felt his company could accept the committee's report without reserve. A consulting committee was formed, largely from members of the committee of inquiry—among them Galton, Wheatstone, and Thomson—to choose the type of cable they would use next. Although the company still lacked the money to make a positive commitment, the group invited bids and samples from seventeen different firms. These were subjected to countless tests, after which the committee settled, as might have been expected, on Glass, Elliot & Company. Apart from past association and familiarity with the problem, the firm had by now laid 90 percent of the submarine cables functioning in Europe.

There was still no money, and there was still disturbing news from overseas. Hard upon his victory at Chancellorsville, Lee was marching north, and General George Meade was set back severely. On July 1, 1863, Field & Company wrote to Cyrus: "Business has been almost entirely suspended for the last week on account of the great excitement arising from the rebel invasion of Pennsylvania. . . . Harrisburg, Baltimore, and Philadelphia are threatened by Lee."

Reports were reaching London via Queenstown two weeks after the event. Field found himself more than ever unable to sleep from the anxiety. He haunted the offices of Reuter's for the latest news. When a clerk refused to let him in, he stuck his foot in the door until he gained admittance. When an operator refused to give him information, because it might cost him his job, Field offered to hire him at twice the salary. By such means he learned of Lee's defeat at Gettysburg, and like a triumphant Paul Revere, he rode through London and its suburbs, telling his pro-Southern friends of the great Union victory and gleefully taunting them with the parting cry: "Oh, you rebels! Oh, you rebels!"

It is fortunate for his peace of mind that no Atlantic cable could bring him news of the draft riots, taking place the same month, which swarmed around his house, terrifying Mary and the children. No harm came to them, although they "were threatened by incendiaries who warned them to leave the premises." His sister-in-law reported: "As the rioters approached our house they were met by a company of soldiers that Dudley had just sent for; their glittering bayonets and steady march soon sent them back before they had time to effect their demoniacal purpose." This armed detachment killed thirteen of the rioters almost on his doorstep and wounded eighteen more, but proved to be a nuisance afterward, making the house a sort of open bivouac.

Field, knowing none of this at the time, stayed for the rest of July and August, battling to raise funds for the cable and still working for a rapprochement between England and America. There was a general feeling that the South would lose, but there remained the question of how Northern statesmanship might bring about a stable peace. Only Gladstone remained adamant, declaring that Jefferson Davis had "made a nation" and that the advocates of the North "have not yet drunk of the cup which the rest of the world sees they nevertheless must drink."

Salmon P. Chase, Secretary of the Treasury, wrote Field late in August:

> The war moves too slowly and costs too much; but it moves steadily, and rebellion falls before it. . . . I trust you are succeeding well in your great scheme of the inter-continental telegraph. It is an enterprise worthy of this day of great things. If I had the wealth of an Astor you should not lack the means of construction.

Little hope remained for raising capital that year in England. To Field's £66,615 raised in America, Saward and the London directors had sold or themselves subscribed to £220,000 in shares. But the total of £286,000 was still less than half the capital they needed.

Field started home the first week in September (it was his thirtieth Atlantic crossing), spending most days in his cabin catching up on sleep and reaching a decision. It was almost ten years since he had first projected the Atlantic cable in his mind, as long as he had spent in building up his paper business in the decade from 1842 to 1852, and there were still no positive results. It was time to let Field & Company go and to focus on the cable.

During his absence another brother had achieved unique distinction. Stephen Field, chief justice of the State of California since 1859, had been appointed by Lincoln Associate Justice of the United States Supreme Court, an office he was to hold for the longest term (more than thirty-four years) in the history of the Court. He was the first judge from the Pacific coast ever to be seated in the Court, and when his nomination was presented to the President, Lincoln had only one question: "Does David want his brother to have it?" Being assured

that David Dudley would be more than pleased, Lincoln was quick
to decide: "Then he shall have it." Confirmation by the Senate was
unanimous.

The Fields, especially Cyrus, Dudley, and Stephen (although Jonathan had made his mark as state senator in Massachusetts), were recognized as national figures now, and immediately on arriving in New
York, Cyrus was given the task—probably at the request of E. M.
Archibald, the British consul—of welcoming a British naval unit to
New York. It was a ticklish assignment. Nobody wanted English ships
around. Two Confederate privateers, the *Florida* and *Alabama,* had
been allowed to slip from Liverpool to prey on Union shipping, and
in addition, there were reports of two more ironclads being built in
Britain to use against the North. Vice Admiral Sir Alexander Milne,
who led his squadron into New York harbor on the flagship *Nile,* was
warned in advance that his "reception would probably be unsatis-
factory."

As with the visit from the Prince of Wales, things went off smoothly,
thanks immeasurably to Field's tact and hospitality. He and Mary
held a formal reception for Sir Alexander and Lady Milne in their
Gramercy Park home. In the course of it, a letter came from Secretary
Chase suggesting that Field could best cement relations by clearing the
air on the question of "full reparation for the injuries inflicted on
American commerce by unneutral acts of British subjects, known to
and not prevented by the responsible authorities."

Almost certainly he never brought up so delicate a subject. But he
did reply to Chase regarding the matter of cementing relations:

> I fully concur in every word you say in regard to the conduct of
> the British government towards us, and hope, with you, that they
> will see it is for our mutual interest, as well as for that of all man-
> kind, that friendly feelings should always exist between "the two
> great branches of the Anglo-Saxon family." Vice-Admiral Milne left
> for Washington this morning.

With the admiral off his hands, Field wrote to the Cranes in Dalton
that he was closing down the firm. His stock would be distributed
equally between L. T. Valentine & Company and Messrs. Wood &
Wood, both of New York and both of which he recommended as his
successors. In his more formal announcement to the trade, he added
a little human touch. He had his young nephew Heman Field, on

leave from the fighting in Virginia, append his signature under his. Heman had been only a clerk, but he had been with Cyrus until his enlistment in the Army. He deserved some recognition in this closing document.

Field was now free to devote all his time and effort to the cable. The company directors urged him to return at once to England, to put his own broad shoulder to the wheel. For once, however, he let nothing interfere with his spending Christmas with his family, and it was not till the third week in January, 1864, that he arrived again in England, where a London business journal took occasion to observe: "Mr. Cyrus W. Field, one of the leading spirits of the undertaking, is again amongst us, full of hope and ready to embark once more on the gigantic enterprise."

If he was full of hope, the directors were not; they depended increasingly on Field's presence to give them any kind of lift or confidence.

There was need for a new and magic element—some signal transcending all communication barriers, which would set the wheels in motion to run smoothly and harmoniously toward the goal. By a stroke of good luck, Field stumbled on it. He was sent, probably by John Bright, to the home of Thomas Brassey, a London financier and a man of wide interests. Brassey had things going for him all around the world. "His ruling passion," wrote his biographer Arthur Helps, "was the execution of great works of the highest utility with punctuality and thoroughness." He had only one defect: "a difficulty in saying no, which led to involvement in some disastrous undertakings."

The interview, as described by Field, was something of an inquisition:

> In attempting to enlist him in our cause, he put me through such a cross-examination as I had never before experienced. I thought I was in the witness-box. He inquired of me the practicability of the scheme—what it would pay, and everything else connected with it; but before I left him, I had the pleasure of hearing him say that it was a great national enterprise that ought to be carried out, and, he added, "I will be one of ten to find the money required for it."

Here was new blood and a powerful ally. Just as he had had Peter Cooper's name to rally New Yorkers to his side in 1854, Field had someone now to build on.

I then went to work to find nine other Thomas Brasseys (I did not know whether he was an Englishman, a Scotchman, or an Irishman; but I made up my mind that he combined all the good qualities of every one of them), and after considerable search I met with a rich friend from Manchester, Mr. John Pender, and I asked him if he would second Mr. Brassey, and walked with him from 28 Pall Mall to the House of Commons, of which he is a member. Before we reached the House, he expressed his willingness to do so to an equal amount.

Field's success began to snowball. As a millionaire industrialist and director of both Brett's Magnetic Telegraph Company and the Atlantic Telegraph Company, Pender not only understood all aspects of the cable business, but also had an important stake in Field's endeavor. He now used his influence to effect a consolidation of Glass, Elliot & Company with the London Gutta Percha Company. Up to now the latter had been manufacturing the vital inner core, turning it over to Glass, Elliot to build into the finished cable.

Their merger, early in April, 1864, into the Telegraph Construction & Maintenance Company brought the entire operation under one efficient roof. It also brought new talent to the team, among them Gutta Percha's electrician, Willoughby Smith, and a young engineer, named Henry Clifford, who would work with Samuel Canning. Richard Atwood Glass was managing director, and other directors included Thomas Brassey and Daniel Gooch—the latter an engineering genius who, as locomotive superintendent of the Great Western Railway at the age of twenty-one, had given Queen Victoria her first ride on the steam cars. Gooch had risen to be chairman of the railway and now also owned a large share of the Brobdingnagian *Great Eastern.*

With this powerful combine, another problem was settled at a stroke. The new company agreed to subscribe the entire remaining amount of capital, £315,000, giving Field's group the £600,000 they needed. Beyond that, they took an additional £100,000 in bonds, still further strengthening the financial structure.

It had been like prying the first olive from the bottle; the rest came easily. The cable prescribed by the consulting committee was in every way better and stronger than that used in previous expeditions. But it was twice as heavy as the 1858 cable that had loaded two ships to capacity. Where could they get a single ship to carry this tremendous cargo? Again the answer came like magic: the *Great Eastern.*

Not only was it easy for Field to arrange a deal with Daniel Gooch, since the ship was now idle and unwanted, but because of Gooch's personal interest in the enterprise, the deal was also eminently sporting. For Gooch had a sentimental streak. "They seem to have been made for one another," he said fondly. The *Great Eastern* would lay the cable for nothing, and if the undertaking were successful, the owners would be rewarded with £50,000 worth of cable stock. Field told his associates, "In all my business experience I have never known an offer more honorable."

She was a fabulous, legendary ship, this "Wonder of the Seas." Every superlative in the dictionary would apply to her. She was five times as large as any ship afloat. Built of iron, with five funnels and six masts, she was longer than three city blocks, displaced 32,000 tons, and could carry 6,000 passengers (many more than any modern ocean liner) and 16,000 tons of coal—enough to take her practically around the world without refueling. No ship was to match her size until the *Lusitania* was built. But size was her undoing. No pier was large enough to berth her; no normal quota of passengers or freight could fill her. Her history was one of ludicrous failure. She lost $5,-000,000 for her various owners, and the ghosts of a score of men who had died in the course of her creation, including that of her designer Isambard K. Brunel, rode with her into bankruptcy.

Now the *Great Eastern* was dispatched to Medway to have giant tanks built in her hold to house the cable; the cable itself—2,600 miles of it—was ordered. An enterprise that had seemed doomed only eight weeks before was now viable and again full of promise.

All this had happened with such speed and incredible good fortune that a celebration seemed to be in order, and Field invited all concerned to a dinner at the Buckingham Palace Hotel. It took place on April 15, 1864, precisely the date on which the New York, Newfoundland and London Telegraph Company had received its charter ten years earlier. Gathered at the table, according to Stuart-Wortley, who was present:

> was a company of distinguished men—members of Parliament, great capitalists, distinguished merchants and manufacturers, engineers and men of science, such as is rarely found together even in the highest houses in this great metropolis. It was very agreeable to see an American citizen so surrounded. It was still more gratifying, inasmuch as we were there to celebrate the approaching accomplishment of the Atlantic Telegraph.

Field had intended this "inauguration banquet" to be largely a tribute to the newcomers who had helped revive the project—Pender, Brassey, and the directors of the amalgamated company. But, as usual, the honor was turned back upon himself. John Pender remarked:

> No living man knew better than Mr. Field the years of toil and anxiety it had taken to bring this great international undertaking to its present stage, and no man could estimate better than he the advantages which the combination now formed would confer, not alone upon this country and America, but upon every nation in the world whom it is desirable to bring into intimate and friendly alliance.

Even George Bidder, the mathematical genius, who was generally silent even when tempted by figures, addressed Field on a personal note: "I have lately been brought much into contact with you, and there is one fixed opinion I have formed of your character, and it is this, that when you make up your mind to effect a great object you will never abandon it." He told the group that while his computations had predicted failure for the 1857–58 attempts, his current calculations based on new conditions pointed to "a great and triumphant success."

For Field, this was to have been something of a farewell party. It troubled him to be away from home during this period of crisis in America, and he let it be known that he felt it was his duty to return as soon as possible. He told the assembled guests:

> My stay in England is now drawing to a close, and never before, when about to embark for America, did I feel more satisfied and rejoiced at the position of our great undertaking; but, with all this, a feeling of sadness at times steals over me. It seems to me very doubtful whether any of us will ever meet again. What little I can do has been done, and the enterprise is now in the hands of the contractors, who, I am sure, will carry it to a triumphant success. It will do much to bind together England and America; and base, indeed, will be that man, to whatever country he may belong, that may dare, with an unhallowed tongue or venomous pen, to sow discord among those who speak the same language and profess the same religion, and who ought to be on terms of the completest friendship.

The announcement that he was leaving London, even temporarily, brought alarm to some of the directors. His presence seemed to give them confidence; his spirit was the catalytic agent that kept things moving. George Saward hurried home to write him a lengthy, pleading letter urging him to stay and ending:

> On the present occasion the undertaking has benefited very greatly by your presence, and the contracts now about to be entered into are in their present position mainly on account of your exertions ... and I feel that if you remain I shall have security for getting them into proper position. I therefore on every ground ask you not to leave us until you have seen with your own eyes the cable actually commenced and everything organized for its due continuance.
>
> I know how hard all this is for Mrs. Field, and you, who know how much I love my own home, will, I am sure, believe me when I say how much I sympathize with you and her in the sacrifices involved in these continual separations; but it must be borne in mind that you have been marked out by the Ruler of all things as the apostle of this great movement, and this is a high mission and a noble distinction, in which I am sure Mrs. Field herself would deeply regret that you should come short of success. . . .

Two thousand miles from Gramercy Park, deeply missing his family and pricked by conscience for his absence, Field was evidently moved by this appeal to Mary's interests. He stayed on in London for almost another two months.

There was not much, actually, for him to do. Everything was in the hands of the contractors, the Telegraph Construction & Maintenance Company. It would take six to eight months to manufacture the cable, and he had promised not to hurry them. The manufacturing process would be supervised by the same experts who had debated how the cable should be made and had settled on "the one most calculated to insure success in the present state of our experimental knowledge concerning deep-sea cables." It would have the same type of seven-stranded copper core with gutta-percha insulation as the earlier cable, but the steel wires of its outer armor would be stouter and stronger and wrapped with hemp. This would make it bulkier but lighter in the water and more than twice as strong as the preceding cable.

Only two points remained to be settled. The *Great Eastern* was without a crew. More important, she was without a captain to select a crew. In his many Atlantic crossings, always on Cunarders after their western terminus had been moved from Boston to New York, Field had become acquainted with Captain James Anderson, veteran skipper of the *China* and knew him as a rare combination of imagination, discipline, and brains. He decided to see if Samuel Cunard would release the captain and if Anderson would take the job.

The second unsettled question was the landing point in Newfoundland. Bull's Arm was too far up the bay to handle the thirty-four foot draft of the *Great Eastern*. Shortly after he had arrived at New York in May and had met with the American directors to receive their thanks for having so successfully arranged affairs in England ("to him is due the credit, and to him this company and the world will be indebted"), Field set out again for Newfoundland. At St. John's he was met by the British survey steamer *Margaretta Stevenson* and, with Captain Orlebar of that ship, cruised up and down Trinity Bay, going ashore from time to time to reconnoiter.

Field had come to love this northern land—the rugged coastline and the barren tideflats, the sea wind sighing through the pointed evergreens and rustling the grasses on the moors. It had an elemental lonely peace, which was something he had missed in his drive toward achievement. On the beach he stooped from time to time to gather up shells and seaweeds and bedraggled birds that had been battered down by storms. These he carefully packed and shipped to Louis Agassiz for his new zoological museum in Washington.

The landing place he finally selected had the soothing name of Heart's Content. It was twenty miles closer to the open sea than Bull's Arm, and the water leading up to it was deep and sheltered. There was nothing there but a soft beach sloping up to dense pine forests and a scattering of fishing shacks. Nobody had ever heard of Heart's Content before. Field gave it his blessing and put it on the map.

The next few months were spent traveling around the Maritime Provinces and the northern states, strengthening and consolidating the network of lines connecting with the New York, Newfoundland and London Telegraph Company. With his penchant for making lists, he sent George Saward in October his complete itinerary, noting that in sixteen major cities visited. . . .

> I have seen almost all of the persons who control the principal telegraph lines in America . . . and have traveled over sixty-three hundred miles, viz:
> By railway, over 3,280 miles.
> By steamers, over 2,400 miles.
> By open wagon, over 500 miles.

By stage-coach, over 150 miles.
By fishing-boats, about 100 miles.

Cyrus Field did almost as much to advance telegraphy in the United States as he did to promote the Atlantic cable. The international importance of the latter overshadowed his domestic work, but one played counterpoint to the other. Especially during the decade from 1855 to 1865 he was instrumental in establishing the American Telegraph Company and then the broader-based North American Telegraph Association, and he finally helped bring together the "Titan of the East" and Western Union, the "Colossus of the West." Now, once the new cable had been safely landed at Heart's Content, every major city on the continent would be in telegraphic touch with Europe.

But, as always, it was the Atlantic cable which took first place, and returning to New York in late October, he confessed as much in a letter to Saward: "I can hardly keep the business of the Atlantic Telegraph Company out of my mind for a single moment." On his return, too, he found waiting for him a letter from Captain Anderson, who accepted, with restrained enthusiasm, the command of the *Great Eastern.*

Field was ready now. He had the money, the cable, the ship, and the commander. He could relax—if only he did not find relaxation so exasperating. Instead, he threw himself into social life with Mary. In a round of dinner parties in December, they entertained General John A. Dix, commander of a New England military district, and the British minister, Lord Richard Lyons. This encounter coincided with what Samuel Eliot Morison calls "the most explosive incident in our Canadian relations."

Dix was sitting by Lord Lyons when he, Dix, received a telegraph message from St. Albans, Vermont. It informed him that an anti-Union force had crossed the border, taken possession of the village, robbed the local banks, and imposed a reign of terror. Excusing himself from the table, Dix wired the commanding officer in Burlington to relieve the town, capture the invaders, pursue them into Canada if necessary, "and destroy them."

Rejoining the group, the general told Field what had happened and what he had done about it. It promised to be another *Trent* affair, with American forces trespassing on British territory; it also looked like what it was—a Confederate plot to spark war between Great Britain and the Union. Field took Lyons and Dix into another room, and forced them to discuss the crisis openly and frankly. As a consequence, Dix rescinded his order and wired Burlington that no American troops should cross the border, that the matter should be left to the Canadian authorities. The evening ended amicably, and in another small corner of history, Field's role as intermediary had helped save Anglo-American relations.

18

The *Great Eastern* Disappears

⟫⟫⟫⟫⟫⟪⟪⟪⟪⟪ The year 1865 dawned bright for Field and for the country as a whole. Lincoln's reelection followed victory after victory. The Union was all but saved.

It had been, and still was, something of a telegraph war, in which communication was vital to the fluency of armies. Statistics are scarce, but there were from 12 to 15,000 miles of wires in the field, of which less than 1,000 were working behind Southern lines. General Grant, now commander in chief of all the Union armies, had Lee pinned down at Petersburg, and Field visited Grant at his field headquarters in Virginia.

Having promised to supply whatever might be needed, Field returned to Washington and called on President Lincoln. With him he had a petition he and Peter Cooper had drawn up, signed by the directors of the Atlantic Telegraph Company. It requested government ships to aid in the cable-laying expedition. The British were supplying two warships, the *Terrible* and *Sphinx,* as escorts. Surely the United States could do as much. The petition had also gone to Gideon Welles as Secretary of the Navy. Lincoln left it up to Welles and discussed with Field only his hopes for ending the war, with a just peace for the South.

The request for escorts was denied. There were sad, but understandable, reasons. Palmerston's and Gladstone's attitude had alienated most of Washington. The British government had lent £2,000,-000 to the Confederacy on yet to be delivered cotton. The privateering *Alabama* had slipped from a British harbor to prey on Union merchant vessels (cause of the later, so-called *Alabama* claims). On top of all was the Twenty-four Hours Rule, denying effective use of English ports to Union warships. Acting Secretary of the Navy Gustavus Fox wired Field in early June:

> No official information has been received at the State Department modifying the "twenty-four hour rule" proclaimed by the English Government concerning vessels of war of the United States. Consequently it is impossible for this Department to send a naval force to the west coast of Ireland to accompany you in this important undertaking.

However, help *was* being given to the plodding progress of another line being laid overland by Perry Collins, to Russia via the Bering Strait.

There was nothing much else to be done at home, and when the *China* sailed for Liverpool on March 8, 1865, Field was aboard her. He wanted to talk to Captain Anderson who had been given leave from Cunard to captain the *Great Eastern*. On this voyage he and Field discussed every detail of the undertaking. It was plain that Anderson would figure largely in this venture, being a man, as Henry Field noted, "of much general intelligence and of no small scientific attainments."

He was also insistent on thoroughness and careful preparation. Once his ship had been berthed and Field had gone to the Buckingham Palace Hotel in London, Anderson followed their conversation with a long letter detailing his planned procedure:

> I do not apprehend or fear any difficulty to your great enterprise, but as little as possible should be left to chance or inspiration.
>
> The essentials, as far as I am concerned, would be to *see for myself all* the ground tackling *clear* and efficient;
>
> The steering gear and prevention ditto in good order;
>
> The sails necessary to steady the ship in a chance breeze;
>
> The *compasses* and their *adjustment* and all the means that are available of freeing the ship from water.
>
> I should like to get around me such a staff of men that I might hope to rely on at least a portion of them.

Among many other stipulations, he wanted to go over every inch of the ship, talk with every man on the staff, visit the harbor at Valentia, and in short be sure of the tools he had to work with. He followed Field to London and had breakfast with him to make sure that they understood each other. His meticulousness was a check to Field's impetuosity. If anything went wrong, it would not be from reckless haste.

As soon as he could, Field went down to Morden Wharf at Greenwich to see how the cable was coming along. Its manufacture had been started in September, 1864, and the cable was already feeding from the huge machinery into eight large water-filled tanks, each holding 140 miles of line. The *Great Eastern* was at Sheerness, 20 miles below the works. Drawing 34 feet of water, she was too large by far to come up to the wharf. Two scows, with the poetic names of *Amethyst* and *Iris,* were to take the cable down to her, in sections, as completed.

Before boarding the *China,* Field had received a letter from Abiel Low:

> I have the pleasure to inform you that you have been selected to represent this Chamber at the Conference of representatives of Chambers of Commerce invited to meet at Alexandria, Egypt, on the 6th day of April next sent by the Universal Company of the Suez Canal to survey and report on the works undertaken by them to connect the Mediterranean and Red Seas and the great advantages to commerce which this new line of water navigation promises.

Field arrived at Alexandria on April 5, 1865, as the sole American emissary among eighty-five delegates representing fourteen nations, was welcomed cordially at De Lesseps' home, and wrote Low afterward: "From Mr. De Lesseps, and all the Delegates, I received the greatest kindness."

After the convocation had passed by camel-drawn boats through the canal (navigable, but not yet officially opened), from the Mediterranean to the Red Sea, Field was asked by De Lesseps to address the gathering of scientists and delegates. It is only natural that he should have drawn a parallel between De Lesseps' undertaking and his own:

> You, Mr. President, are engaged in the great work of dividing two continents for the benefit of every commercial nation in the world. . . . Within the next three months I hope to have the pleasure of seeing two hemispheres connected by a submarine cable, and when that is done you will be able to telegraph from this place in the Great Desert of Africa, through a part of Asia, across the Continent of Europe, under the deep Atlantic, and over America to the shores of the Pacific; and your message will arrive there several hours ahead of the sun.

Before leaving Cairo, he sent Abiel Low:

> a Report which I drew up at the request of many Delegates, after
> our arrival at Suez, and which was signed, and handed to Mr.
> De Lesseps. I include eight charts which will give much valuable
> information in regard to the Suez Canal, and I hope soon to be able
> to forward you several books, pamphlets, and reports of Engineers
> on this most interesting subject.

He also invited all the delegates, including De Lesseps, to visit him
whenever they came to the United States.

Back in England on May 1, 1865, Field was greeted by news both
good and bad. With Lee's surrender at Appomattox on April 9, the
shooting war was over, and Field had had some small part in the
Union victory. Veteran Major General Richard Delafield recorded:

> The battlefields of Petersburg, Richmond, Atlanta, and many other
> localities . . . have shown that over the land and under the water, as
> armies advanced, the orders of the commanders were disseminated
> with lightning speed. It may be confidently asserted that electro-
> magnetism thus introduced by Field . . . was a powerful auxiliary in
> hastening the success of our armies in overthrowing rebellion.

Hard on the heels of this came word of Lincoln's assassination and
the near death of Field's friendly supporter William Seward. At a
London gathering presided over by Charles Francis Adams, Cyrus
told of his talks with Lincoln before leaving the United States, of the
President's great desire that peace prevail not only between North and
South, but also between England and the United States. "If Mr. Lincoln could speak today he would urge upon every one to do all he
could to allay the passions which have been excited in America; and
I hope all will comply with what I believe would be his wish."

There was brighter news awaiting him when he went down to
Greenwich. The cable was all but completed. The two scows had been
shuttling back and forth for nine weeks, carrying 140-mile sections to
the side of the *Great Eastern,* where a small steam engine drew it yard
by yard into the mammoth hull. But there was no sign of the cable
when he mounted to the 700-foot deck of the giant ship—a strange
ghost of the ship that he had known in her day of fleeting glory—nothing in sight but the paying-out machinery on the afterdeck. This was,
in principle, the same as the apparatus used before; but it was larger,
with more built-in safety factors, especially in the way of self-releasing

brakes. In the bow was the only innovation: tackle and machinery for recovering lost sections of the cable if it broke.

The cable was stowed in giant tanks below—three of them, to distribute the 9,000 tons of weight, and each filled with water to keep the line from drying out. The cable was already working. As each section was spliced and periodically, day and night, signals coursed around and around the coils to assure the engineers and electricians that the line remained in sound condition. Not for a minute, from now until the cable was laid, would the wires be allowed to rest.

Captain Anderson had preceded Field aboard the ship, climbed to the top of one of the paddle boxes and, in his own words:

> tried to look into the future, to see what I had undertaken and realize if possible what this new step would develop. I cannot say I believed much in cables; I rather think I did not; but I did believe Mr. Field was an earnest man, of great force of character, and working under a strong conviction that what he was attempting was thoroughly practicable; and I knew enough of the names with which he had associated himself in the enterprise to feel that it was a real, true, honest effort, worthy of all the energy and application of one's manhood; and come what might in the future, I resolved to do my very utmost, and to do nothing else until it was over.

The *Great Eastern* attracted other visitors, swarming around her in every type of small boat and excursion steamer, to most of whom the drama lay in the new career of the great ship, already carrying in her vast interior the link which was about to initiate a new era in human communications. This time there was no ridicule or skepticism. The sheer size of the adventure evoked awe and admiration.

Only the *Illustrated London News* had some doubts about the target of this public approbation:

> ... let us hope that, as English money has made the cable, and an English ship has taken it out; as it has been made upon English ground, designed by an English firm, and has owed its construction to English inventors, our Transatlantic friends will let us have a little more credit in the matter than they did some years ago, when the junction was made complete for one moment and then failed. How many ardent English souls felt bitter disappointment then! Mr. Thackeray was one who lost a thousand pounds in that adventure for the partial success and incipient boldness of which Mr. Cyrus W. Field and the Americans took all the credit, and gave the blame of non-success to the elements. ...

To this Cromwell Varley replied at great length, reviewing Field's intricate work and energetic promotion: "On the contrary he seems to have given a fair share, indeed I may say the lion's share of the credit to his English associates. . . . As an Englishman I am especially grieved that my countrymen appear to give less credit to Mr. Field than is undoubtedly his due." William Thomson added his amen.

On May 30, 1865, a bell sounded in the Telegraph Construction & Maintenance Company's works, signaling the completion of the last mile of cable. Field and Pender led everybody present to the nearby Ship Tavern, to be fueled wth food and wine, and Field again was toasted by his directors.

It took six weeks to coil the completed cable yard by yard, all laid by hand, in the three great tanks of the *Great Eastern,* after which Albert Edward, the Prince of Wales, came down with his entourage to inspect the work. Field took him below to see the cable and invited His Royal Highness to send a message through its 2,700-mile length, and the seven words "I wish success to the Atlantic cable" were sent and received within a minute. A few days later, members of the scientific committee appointed in 1859 made a more professional inspection. Chairman Stuart-Wortley, apparently still thinking of Ship Tavern banqueting, dictated a message for Varley to send to Thomson through the cable: "We are all ready for dinner." Again, it took barely a minute to send and receive this message through the cable, but their report read that "it was a disputed point whether the word *the* was included in the message before *dinner.* Varley said it was, Wortley said he did not give the word *the.*"

Meanwhile, Captain Sherard Osborn, who had laid the Red Sea cable and knew the logistics involved, was supervising the equipping and supplying of the cable ship. The upper deck was turned into a barnyard, where sheep and cattle munched on straw, with pens for pigs and housing for the poultry. "Such a freight had not been seen before since Noah's Ark was stranded on Mount Ararat." What could not walk was stowed in hundreds of barrels, mostly containing beef and pork. Altogether, the *Great Eastern* took on enough provisions to feed 500 men for weeks, and its overall cargo, including cable and machinery, weighed 21,000 tons—more than was carried by Nelson's entire fleet at Trafalgar.

Field followed his compulsion to make lists of everything accumulated:

Live Stock	Dead
10 Bullocks	28 Bullocks
1 Milch Cow	4 Calves
114 Sheep	22 Sheep
20 Pigs	4 Pigs
29 Geese	300 Fowls
14 Turkeys	
500 Fowls	*18,000 Eggs*

The human cargo was handpicked and no one, regardless of influence or importance, was allowed on board unless he related specifically to the purpose of the expedition. Strict battle stations were assigned. Thomson and Varley, representing the Atlantic Telegraph Company, were under De Sauty, the chief electrician. They could give advice but were otherwise to stay out of the way. Willoughby Smith was the assistant electrician. Samuel Canning was in charge of the engineers, including Henry Clifford. Captain Anderson was field commander. He imposed strict discipline: if you haven't anything to do, stay below.

There was only one American aboard the vessel—one American accompanying an expedition which was carried out exclusively by British ships and British crews—and that, of course, was Cyrus Field. Field represented Atlantic Telegraph, while Daniel Gooch went along as representative of the contractors. Every major newspaper in England and America had applied for permission to send along a correspondent, but the Telegraph Construction & Maintenance Company, official managers of the expedition, accepted only one. He was William Howard Russell of the London *Times,* first of the great war correspondents, who had been in the Crimea, reported the Franco-Prussian conflict, and had covered both sides of the Civil War. Lincoln had dubbed him "Bull Run" Russell. Because of his unbiased version of that engagement, he had been banned from the United States and was free to take on this assignment.

Russell brought with him the London artist Robert Dudley whose lithographs illustrate Russell's book on the expedition. In Dudley's pictures Field appears clean-shaven but with unfamiliar spectacles, in the dress he wore on these expeditions: doeskin trousers, a long Inverness cape, and deerstalker cap.

On July 15, 1865, to the salute of her escorts' cannon, 200 men hauled the *Great Eastern*'s seven-ton anchor aboard, and the ship moved majestically down the channel, preceded by the little *Porcu-pine,* which had led the *Niagara* into Trinity Bay in 1858. Off Falmouth they took in tow the steamer *Caroline* carrying the heavy shore end of the cable, and proceeded to Bantry Bay, where the *Caroline* detached herself from the mother ship and took the shore line to Valentia.

Here again, a different landing place had been selected—rocky, sheltered Foilhummerum Bay on Valentia Island, under the ramparts of Oliver Cromwell's ruined castle. As the *Caroline* approached, half of Ireland appeared to have flocked to that remote shore, and once again Peter Fitzgerald, Knight of Kerry, reigned as king of the carnival. In tents and booths the crowd was provided with whiskey, games of chance and fortune-telling. Pipers and fiddlers played Irish jigs for dancing couples. Barefooted women and children perched among the rocks, and the small bay was alive with coracles, dories, and pleasure yachts. Flags were everywhere: the Union Jack, the Stars and Stripes, and the white flags of the temperance societies.

There was vast disappointment when the *Great Eastern* failed to appear. She drew too much water for Valentia Bay and stayed at Bantry, leaving the *Caroline* to bring the shore end of the cable to Valentia Island.

A trench had been dug to receive it, leading across cliff and meadow to the instrument house. Volunteer boats were lined up like a pontoon bridge to pass the line ashore from hand to hand. All might have gone well but for the exuberance of the crowd, which wanted to participate, flocked to the water, grabbed the line, and started pulling it ashore. John Mullaly quoted an eyewitness as to the chaos that followed:

> Not being aware that it was necessary to bring in and lodge a certain quantity of cable in excess of the distance from ship to shore, in order that it might be passed up the cliff and across a couple of fields to the Telegraph House, these Irishmen, as soon as they got hold of the future line of communication with America, threw it upon the ground, and raised a wild "Hurroo!" This was caught and repeated by the crews of the boats, who, concluding that their work was well done, at once proceeded to heave the massive rope into the sea. From boat to boat the first bad example was followed by all, until, to the dismay of the cablemen, who could not gain a hearing amid the continued cheers, every fathom up to the stern of the *Caroline* was thrown overboard. The result of this touching enthusiasm

was that every foot had to be underrun, preparatory to the whole operation beginning *de novo.* It took some time to effect this, during which the Irish were silent enough.

When the land line was properly installed, the Knight of Kerry repeated to the crowds the sentiments which had launched the 1857 expedition; Sir Robert Peel, father of the London bobbies, called on divine Providence to give His blessing to the venture; and the crowd joined in singing the doxology. After the ceremonies the *Caroline* stood out to sea, carrying the thirty miles of connecting line to its rendezvous with the *Great Eastern.* The splice was made, and on Sunday, July 23, 1865, the iron ship swung slowly around and headed toward Heart's Content.

Just before the departure Field mailed two letters. One to his brother Henry reflected his perennial confidence, "You may expect us at Heart's Content about the 5th of August. I am in good health and spirits, and all is going well." The other reflected his instinctive thoughtfulness and his enduring loyalty to friendships past. He wrote to Captain Preedy of the *Agamemnon,* recalling Preedy's pioneer service and dedication and enclosing clippings covering the present expedition. Preedy, a lonely and forgotten man, had retired to a seaside home in Portland, Dorset, England. His reply, which Cyrus kept among his papers, was pathetically grateful: "You are the only gentleman connected with the Atlantic Telegraph Company that I have heard from since our return on the *Agamemnon* in 1857. *No one* more heartily wishes you success."

In writing, "Happy is the cable laying that has no history," correspondent Russell was expressing the hopes of everyone aboard the iron ship that Sunday. The auspices promised well for an uneventful expedition. Flanked by her escorts, the *Great Eastern* picked up a speed of six knots:

> and as the sun set a broad stream of golden light was thrown across the smooth billows towards their bows as if to indicate and illumine the path marked out by the hand of Heaven. The brake was eased, and as the *Great Eastern* moved ahead the machinery of the paying-out apparatus began to work, drums rolled, wheels whirled, and out spun the black line of the cable, and dropped in a graceful curve into the sea over the stern wheel. The cable came up with ease from the after tank, and was payed out with the utmost regularity from the apparatus. The system of signals to and from the ship was at once in play between the electricians on board and those at Foilhummerum.

Field alone had free run of the ship. With no specific duties he spent part of his time on the bridge with Captain Anderson, who was becoming more and more absorbed in his assignment so that, as he later wrote, "I had no mind, no soul, no sleep, that was not tinged with cable." At other times Field would simply pace the main deck, called "Oxford Street" by the cable crew because of its twin rows of night lights. Or he would hover outside the test room sandwiched between the captain's cabin and the grand saloon, listening, watching, waiting for any significant word or sound.

Here, with blackout curtains on its doors, was the nerve center of the expedition. Here Varley, Thomson, and De Sauty were virtually captives of their instruments, which connected by wire with the cable in the tanks. Second by second they kept in touch with Ireland by a prearranged schedule of tests and signals. James Dugan wrote:

> On both ends, however, the electricians minded one small thing, a pinpoint of light in the dark, which showed if the cable was alive. The speck was reflected on a graduated mirror attached to a magnet at the end of the conducting wires. It was the key test instrument, Professor William Thomson's astatic mirror galvanometer, the talisman of ocean telegraphy. It read the ohm resistance of the cable in little jiggling flickers. If the dot bounced off the index it meant a fault in the wrapping allowing the current to escape to the sea, or a cable break. If that happened the watch electrician ducked through the curtain and struck a bronze alarm gong hanging outside the door.

As long as all was dark and quiet in that critical compartment, all was well. But shortly after midnight the gong sounded, followed by the warning boom of the *Great Eastern*'s cannon, and the great ship drifted to a stop. The spot of light had flickered out of range. It was not a complete break, Field was assured. Current still faltered through. But somewhere in the eighty-four miles of cable they had payed out there was a leak.

Since they knew the resistance of each mile of cable, it was possible to trace by formula approximately where the fault lay—in this case roughly ten miles from the ship. It meant rewinding the cable until they found it. In anticipation of such a mishap, pickup machinery had been installed in the ship's bow. But the bow was an eighth of a mile away—down the full length of "Oxford Street." It meant cutting the cable, shackling the sea end to a wire rope, and hauling it from stern to stem—over davits and lifeboats, around the halyards, across the

giant housing of the paddle wheels—in an acrobatic drill that strained
both agility and patience.

It took ten hours to recover the ten miles of line, and it would have
taken longer except for the relatively shallow depth. Wrote Russell:

> All during the night the process of picking up was carefully carried
> on, the Big Ship behaving beautifully, and hanging lightly over the
> cable, as if fearful of breaking the slender cord which swayed up
> and down in the ocean. Indeed, so delicately did she answer her helm,
> and coil in the film of thread-like cable over her bows, that she put
> one in mind of an elephant taking up a straw in its proboscis.

When the cable was finally brought aboard and the fault discovered, a disturbing cause was found. A small piece of wire, like a
needle, had been driven through the cable and had penetrated the vital
core, allowing the current to escape. "Flagrant evidence of mischief,"
Russell suggested in his notes, while Daniel Gooch observed in his
diary: "If our difficulty is known in London it will have a very important effect on Atlantic cable shares."

No one chose to dwell for long on this sinister discovery; it could
have been an accident. The damaged section was cut out, the sea end
was hauled back to the stern and spliced to the cable in the tank, and
the ship was on her way again, having lost a full day and a half. Within
half a mile the current stopped again, and Russell wrote feelingly:

> Such a Penelope's web in twenty-four hours, all out of this single
> thread, was surely disheartening. . . . Even the gentle equanimity and
> confidence of Mr. Field were shaken in that supreme hour, and in
> his heart he may have sheltered the thought that the dream of his life
> was indeed but a chimaera.

Miraculously, as in the first attempt in 1857, the current returned
of its own accord; the wire had somehow healed itself, or some mal-
functioning of the equipment at Valentia had possibly been corrected.
In any event, "the index light suddenly reappeared on its path in the
testing room, and the wearied watchers were gladdened by the lighting
of the beacon of hope once more."

Hope grew into serene confidence as day by day passed unevent-
fully. A heavy sea began to make things rough for the escorts *Sphinx*
and *Terrible,* but the *Great Eastern* rode as steadily as an island in
a quiet lake, and Field for the first time on an ocean crossing escaped
being seasick. Gradually the *Sphinx* began to slip behind, and even-

tually she dropped out of sight completely and for good, leaving the *Terrible* to reconnoiter and clear the path ahead.

By mid-Atlantic, life aboard the ship assumed the aspect of a happy holiday cruise. Field's confidence was high:

> There was a wonderful sense of power in the Great Ship and in her work; it was gratifying to feel that man was mastering space, and triumphing over the wind and waves; that from his hands down into the eternal night of waters there was trailing a slender channel through which obedient lightning would flash for ever instinct with the sympathies, passions and interests of two mighty nations.

In this relaxed atmosphere, there appeared the first ship's newspaper in history, a journal which, according to Willoughby Smith, "certainly touched a chord of humor that would otherwise have remained mute amid the cares and anxieties felt by all." The first edition announced that: *"The Atlantic Telegraph* will be published till further notice. The price will be, for the series, five shillings, including the cover, and the proceeds will be devoted to such purposes as Captain Anderson shall appoint." It printed news from England as received by cable from Valentia, stock quotations, and a schedule of the day's amusements and activities, including: "From daylight till dusk— Looking out for the *Sphinx.* (Through the kindness and liberality of the admiralty, this amusement will be open to the public free of charge.)"

"Bull Run" Russell and Robert Dudley were principal contributors to this now rare journal, which was neatly transcribed in longhand. Dudley fashioned covers, now in the British Museum. Russell contributed topical verse, including a ballad to De Sauty. One verse and chorus ran:

> Under the sea! under the sea! Here's what de Sauty is saying to me,
> Such testing as this is the perfectest bliss! Insulation is holding up strong,
> So we'll test! test! test! with coils and rheometers, keys and galvanometers!
> Test! test! test! test each minute all night and day long.

> *Chorus*
> Copper and zinc! acid and stink! tink-a-tank-tink-a-tank-tink-a-tank-tink.
> Copper and zinc! acid and stink! success to continuity.

Field and Gooch were good-natured targets for a large part of this spoofing. They were credited with having invented "an ingenious and elegant mode of lighting" consisting of a candle in a bottle (illustrated), by which "Mr. Field has just finished his 700th letter." Under "Quotations (Literal and Otherwise) from Shakespeare" appeared the lines "C. W. Field: Age cannot wither, nor custom stale his infinite prospectuses."

For the first time Field, Gooch, and many of the ship's community had a chance to explore the mighty iron ship, of which "poets, engineers, and kings had stood in awe." Most of the magnificent saloons and cabins had been gutted or removed to make room for the cable, "but they discovered crypts under the tanks, and meandered and crept about the shafts and boilers of the tremendous gloominess—vast and dark as the Halls of Eblis." None of them, noted Russell:

> found the hiding-place of the ghost on board the *Great Eastern,* which is believed to be the disembodied essence of a poor plate-riveter, who disappeared in some aperture of the nascent ship, never to be seen of mortal eye again. He is heard at all hours, with ghostly hammer, tap-tap-tapping on the iron wall of his prison, even through the clangor of donkey-engines and the crash of matter.

As the days passed sunnily and the cable unwound smoothly from the tanks, *The Atlantic Telegraph* joyfully observed: "The *Great Eastern* speeds nobly on her mission of towing the islands of Great Britain and Ireland to America. In less than ten days it is expected that a splice will be effected between the two countries, and long, long may it last."

On the seventh day, with 800 miles of cable laid, the bronze gong sounded from the test room and the *Great Eastern*'s cannon boomed again. This time tests indicated that the fault lay not far from the ship. But instead of 400 fathoms as before, the depth was more than 2 miles! Even as the tests were being made and the ship drifted in its tracks, there was a sense of peril, for:

> to the inexperienced eye it looked as if the *Great Eastern* were bent on snapping the thin black thread which cut the waves like a knife-blade as she rose and fell on the swell. When the strain increased, the Cable ran with an edge of seething foam frittering before it backwards and forwards in the track of the ship, taut as a bar of steel.

It was a relief to see the cable cut and secured by wire rope again for the long, laborious trip from stern to stem. Russell reported:

> The men under the command of Mr. Canning were skillful in their work, but as they clamoured and clambered along the sides, and over the boats, and round the paddle-boxes, hauling at hawsers, and slipping bights, and holding on and letting go stoppers, the sense of risk and fear for the Cable could not be got out of one's head. . . . Thousands of fathoms down we knew the end of the cable was dragging along the bottom fiercely tugged at by the *Great Eastern* through its iron line. If line or Cable parted, down sank the Cable forever.

In due, but weary, time they started reeling in the damaged cable, but night fell early on the operation, bringing with it a dense and ghostly fog. The forward deck was turned into a massive iron foundry "Bull Run" Russell described as a "wondrous and unearthly sight":

> The forge fires glared on her decks, and there out in the midst of the Atlantic, anvils rang and sparks flew. . . . As the blaze shot up, ruddy, mellow, and strong, and flung arms of light aloft and along the glistening decks and then died into a red centre, masts, spars and ropes were for the instant touched with a golden gleaming, and strange figures and faces were called out from the darkness—vanished—glinted out again . . . and one might well pardon the passing mariner whose bark drifted him in the night across the track of the great ship, if, crossing himself and praying with shuddering lips, he fancied he beheld a phantom ship freighted with an evil crew, and ever after told how he had seen the workshops of the Inferno floating on the bosom of the ocean.

After nineteen tedious hours the faulty section of the cable was brought on deck, detached from the rest, and the line respliced for paying out. It was midnight then, and no one knew or troubled to find out what caused the accident. Wrote Russell: "Mr. Field, to whom such accidents are never discouraging, remarked pleasantly during the crisis of picking-up, 'I have often known Cables to stop working for two hours, no one knew why, and then begin again. Most likely it's some mistake on shore.' What can discourage a believer?"

On Sunday, July 30, 1865, they examined the defective portion of the cable, untwisting the hemp and iron-wire covering, "and before a foot of it was uncovered an exclamation literally of horror escaped our lips! There, driven right through the centre of the coil so as to touch the inner wires, was a piece of iron wire, bright as if cut with nippers at one end and broken off short at the other." It was precisely the same length as the other needle that had pierced the cable, and observers noted that the same crew had been handling the cable at the time the fault occurred.

It seemed apparent that the line had been sabotaged. Veteran cablemen recalled a similar incident during the laying of the England-Holland line in 1858, when a workman had been hired by a rival company to drive a nail into the cable.

Field and Canning, the chief engineer, decided to take the crew into their confidence, showed them the damage, and told them that from now on watchmen would be posted in the tanks to catch any future acts of vandalism. The crew wholeheartedly agreed and offered to lynch any man among them who was proved guilty.

It was an unpleasant duty to stand guard, but Field, having more free time than anybody, was frequently posted in the tanks, two hours at a stretch. For the next two days things went smoothly. As they approached the Grand Banks, the shore line for Newfoundland was brought out and made ready for the landing. The cable was working perfectly. Tests indicated that the pressure and probably the temperature on the ocean bottom improved the insulation, and the signals grew clearer with increasing distance. The operators at Valentia reported that they could tell, from the sensitivity of the signals, each time the *Great Eastern* rolled.

Only minutes later, however, the same operators were struck dumb when the signals disappeared completely. As fast as an electric spark could travel, news of the break in continuity reached London. The steady flow of messages from the *Great Eastern* had raised high enthusiasm in the British Isles, which now reacted with alarm. What conceivable disaster could have happened? Previous interruptions had been warned of in advance, or tests had shown the cable was intact. But this time—nothing. The British press, including the staid London *Times,* was calmest in its explanation. It reported "a magnetic storm of singular violence" spreading all across the North Atlantic which undoubtedly had affected the insulation of the cable just as it damaged telegraph communication throughout Europe.

But the storm had by now surely ended! As the hours grew into days and weeks, people recalled the experts who had said the vessel was top-heavy; she had capsized in a swell. Others muttered of icebergs in the area capable of shattering the double hull and sinking her. Even the seawise Herman Melville had called the *Great Eastern* a "vast toy of perishable structure." Whatever the cause, the fact was ugly: the cable ships "had vanished from human knowledge as completely as if the ocean had swallowed them up."

19

"This Thing Is to Be Done"

>>>>>><<<<< Early on Wednesday morning, August 2, Field dressed in his customary battle uniform of cap and cape and spectacles and went below to stand watch in the tank.

The crew on duty were the same men who had attended the cable when it had been damaged twice before. Perhaps for that reason he kept a tighter watch than ever on the great coil snaking up toward the canvas funneling, eyes and ears sharpened for any irregular sight or sound. There were only 600 miles of line to go, much less before they cleared the deep and dangerous waters of Maury's "Telegraph Plateau." These critical hours were all that stood between them and the blessed safety of the Grand Banks.

There was a grating sound. A wicked flash of silver pricked the rising thread of cable. A workman shouted, "There goes a piece of wire!" The alarm was relayed to the watchmen on the top deck. But the warning never got there. By the time Field had climbed the ladder and reached the paying-out machinery, the faulty stretch of cable had started its plunge into the sea. At the same time, at Valentia and in the test room aboard ship, the phantom spot of light began to flicker out of range. Field looked at his pocket watch—just eight o'clock.

This time they were uncertain what to do. De Sauty reported continuing contact with Valentia, although there undoubtedly was a leak. But the decision was not up to Field or to Thomson, by far the most knowledgeable electrician aboard. The cable was being laid by the Telegraph Construction & Maintenance Company of which Samuel Canning was chief engineer. The contract called for a flawless cable operation and Canning would be responsible for any failure or shortcoming arising from the fault. So they would turn around, reel in the cable, cut out the damaged section, and resplice again.

Slowly the *Great Eastern* swung about. The cable was cut, without warning to Valentia, and carried along the outside of the ship to the pickup machinery in the bow. From Field's notation of the time the cable had gone overboard, no more than six miles could have been released. It should not have taken them long to rewind, but everything went wrong. The erratic donkey engine brayed and balked. First the steam gave out, and then the water in the boiler. A man with a piece of elastic on a marlinspike somehow managed to keep the mechanism going. But it was taking twice as long, and all that time the *Great Eastern* drifted with the tide, the cable chafing on the iron hawsers of the prow. Anderson tried his best to keep the bow clear of the grating wire. But a ship without power is hard to maneuver against wind and current.

Field felt the *Great Eastern*'s stern rise slightly, adding strain to the taut line, heard the gunshot report as the cable snapped and plunged into the ocean. "The shock of that instant was as sharp as the snapping of the Cable itself," wrote "Bull Run" Russell. "I fear," said the staff commander, "we will not be much interested now in knowing how far we are from Heart's Content."

Years later Russell wrote to the London *Times:*

> Captain Anderson, Mr. Thomson, Mr. Varley . . . all on board the great ship in fact, were so elated by success and so confident of the acomplishment of the work that the sudden cessation of the strain on the indicator and the cry that followed, "The Cable is gone!" produced an effect not short of consternation on every one save one man—Cyrus Field. He rushed upon deck when the fatal announcement reached his ears, made his way through the silent despairing group astern who were gazing into the sea in which thousands of fathoms deep their hopes were buried, satisfied himself that the Cable was broken beyond remedy, and then, calmly surveying his associates without a trace of agitation on his face, said, "Well, it's so. I must go down and prepare a new prospectus immediately. This thing is to be done," and stalked quietly back to his cabin where he set to work to write out the proposal for a new cable ere the end of the other had well settled down in the Atlantic.

The editor of *The Atlantic Telegraph* noted that Field went to his cabin "with composure admirable under the circumstances, though his lips quivered and his cheeks were blanched."

It was a mishap which they were ill equipped to overcome. But there were grappling irons and five miles of buoy rope aboard. Canning and his associates had had experience in raising cables from the bottom of the Mediterranean, the difference being that the inland sea was only 700 fathoms deep. No one knew how deep the water was here. The little *Sphinx* had been gone for six weeks with all the sounding gear aboard her.

Canning, like Field, did not give up easily. They decided on a reckless gamble, one that wiser heads regarded as a harebrained act of desperation. In an unestablished depth of two to three miles, with a makeshift line pieced together with swivels, they would fish for a wire one inch in diameter whose exact location was unknown. It was a chance in a million, but $5,000,000 worth of cable and possibly the future of communication among nations were at stake.

Both Field and Captain Anderson had noted the position when the cable parted. The *Great Eastern* steamed to windward of that point. A five-pronged anchor was fastened to the iron rope and lowered overboard. It took two hours to sink to the bottom, with two and a half miles of rope payed out. The ship's engines were shut down, and she was allowed to drift across the cable's path. It was like trawling for some deep-sea fish. But at each tug on the line, detected by the dynamometer which registered excessive strain, there was no knowing what they had hooked—whether the grapnel had caught a rock, was mired in ooze, or was simply resisting with its own weight.

Back and forth, all night long, they steamed to windward, drifted back. At dawn they had what seemed to be a strike. It was about where the cable ought to be. Not only did the strain show on the dynamometer, but the ship's bow was also being turned into the wind. As the men started winding in the line, the strain grew greater. Whatever they had caught, it was not a loose or drifting object. As the strain increased, a sign of some substantial object on the other end, they knew they had hooked the cable.

Three-quarters of a mile of rope had been reeled in when a swivel connecting a section of the line broke. The sprung fiber whipped across the forward deck, lashing at everyone in its path. Two men with bleeding arms and gashed cheeks watched it disappear—two miles of precious fishing tackle.

They had hooked the lost cable once; they could hook it again. As the *Great Eastern* steamed upwind, a second grapnel was readied. But dense fog settled in, preventing any action for the next three days.

The *Great Eastern*'s cannon boomed at intervals to warn the *Terrible* of her position. The men used the time to patch the grapnel line, check the swivels which were obviously the weakest points, and get the pickup machinery in running order.

On August 7, 1865, the weather was auspicious for another try. The grapnel was lowered in late afternoon and promptly hooked the cable. Throughout a beautiful moonlit night the machinery clanked smoothly, reeling in fathom after fathom of the swivel-jointed rope. At seven the next morning it was estimated that the cable had been hoisted at least a full mile from the bottom—almost halfway up—when another swivel broke. Russell wrote:

> The rope flew around the capstan, over the drum, through the stops. The end of the rope flourished its iron fist in the air, and struck out right and left with it, as though it were animated by a desire to destroy those who might arrest its progress. It passed through the line of cablemen with an impatient sweep, dashed at one man's head, was only balked by his sudden stoop, and menacing from side to side the men at the bow, splashed overboard.

Down went more precious line to join the tangle of wire rope and cable on the ocean floor. The little *Terrible,* waiting on the sidelines ran up its signal flags: "So sorry!"

They dropped another buoy as a second marker and headed back in a high wind for a third and last attempt—"last," because they were running out of tackle. The only line they could put together was "a thing of patches and shreds." When the wind died, Canning had the forges brought on deck. Throughout the night the ship again glowed like some Dantesque Inferno floating in the middle of the ocean, while the anvils forged new sheathing for the capstan.

On the night of the tenth the men fished again but crossed the path of the cable without hooking anything. The grapnel was hauled up, and one prong was found tangled in the rope. The line was becoming chafed, unstranded, and badly worn. So were the nerves of everyone on board. No dynamometer could have measured the increasing strain on their emotions.

The *Great Eastern* signaled the *Terrible:* "We are going to make a final effort. We are sorry you have had such uncomfortable waiting." The tangled grapnel had given them a reprieve; now they tossed it over for a fourth attempt, having used up every scrap of rope aboard.

It was raw and rainy. Field was one of the few who had the heart to stay on deck. "It was too much," wrote Russell, "to stand by and witness the terrible struggle between the hawser, which was coming in fast, the relentless iron-clad capstan, and the fierce resolute power of the black sea . . . none liked to go forward, where every jar of the machinery made their hearts leap into their mouths."

It was almost a relief to hear the cries "Look out!" and "Stop it!" The silence that followed told Field all he needed to know. The cable had gone, and so had their hopes—for 1865.

As the *Terrible* steamed toward them for a final rendezvous, Field went below to formulate his plans. Wrote William Thomson: "Cyrus Field's last prospectus was completed in the grand saloon of the *Great Eastern* on the day when we gave up all hope for 1865."

Before Field drafted the prospectus, he wrote a message to his family and gave it to Captain Napier of the *Terrible:*

> *Great Eastern* left mouth of the Thames July 15th. Shore end landed in Ireland on 22d. Parted on August 2d in latitude 51°25' north, longitude 39°6' west, 1062.4 miles from Valentia Bay, 606.6 miles from Heart's Content. Spent nine days in grappling; used up all wire, rope; nothing left, so obliged to return to England. Three times cable was caught, and hauled up for more than three-quarters of a mile from the bed of the ocean.

The escort was running low on coal and would go directly to St. John's, Newfoundland, and send the wire from there. The *Great Eastern* would head for Ireland. The parting was solemn. William Howard Russell ended his chronicle:

> There was profound silence aboard the Big Ship. She struggled against the helm for a moment as though she still yearned to pursue her course to the west, then bowed to the angry sea in admission of defeat, and moved slowly to meet the rising sun. The signal lanterns flashed from the *Terrible,* "Farewell!" The lights from our paddle-box pierced the night, "Goodbye! Thank you," in sad acknowledgment. Then each sped on her way in solitude and darkness.

While the cable ship steamed eastward, the company tried to keep its spirits up. *The Atlantic Telegraph* noted that "the lazy brute" of a cable was probably feeding on sea animals and therefore would not respond to any less appealing bait. It was announced that Captain Anderson would hold a public auction in the grand saloon of the *Great Eastern,* offering the ship for sale along with "the good will of the Atlantic Telegraph Company. (This invisible property is in Mr. Field's possession.)" Also on the block would be Russell's free pass on the Cunard Line from America back to England, which he would not need.

Of the buoy which Canning had left behind to mark the cable's resting place, Russell contributed another ballad, "Sung by Mr. Canning to the tune, *The Girl I Left Behind Me*. It went:

> Twas not that I was void of heart,
>   As some kind critics have defined me,
> That I was forced by fate to part
>   And leave my darling buoy behind me.
>
> When dozing in my easy-chair
>   Whilst softest chains of slumber bind me,
> Still shall my fancy wander where
>   I left my dearest buoy behind me.

Field laughed appropriately but spent the next five days in the saloon with Canning, Glass, and Thomson, polishing his prospectus for the following summer. Anticipating defeatism in London, he marshalled his defenses. These boiled down to twelve main points, all based on experience. The more important were:

> That the expedition of 1858 proved, beyond a doubt, that messages could be sent by submarine cable from Ireland to Newfoundland;
> That transmission actually improved with distance, as the pressure and colder temperature of ocean depths improved the insulation;
> That a cable accidentally lost in the deepest parts of the North Atlantic could be retrieved by grappling with the proper equipment;
> That the *Great Eastern* was a veritable gift from heaven when it came to cable laying and had proved able to do the job in any kind of weather.

Granted, some improvements would be needed—in the paying-out and pickup machinery, in the grappling tackle, possibly in the cable, though the cable had in general functioned beautifully. But the men knew precisely what alterations were required and none was difficult to make.

They reached Brookhaven, on the southwestern tip of Ireland, early in the morning of August 17, to be greeted with the cry "We thought you'd gone to the bottom!" Field went ashore to wire the directors to be ready for a general meeting. To his surprise, he found himself greeted as a conquering hero. In fact, all over the British Isles, as soon as the return was known, the reaction was one of joyous celebration. This was not just relief that the men were safe, but admiration for their near success. And there was a new feeling for the *Great Eastern,* which had been such a thorn in the side of the British maritime pride. As James Dugan wrote: "In the hour of her deepest failure, the big ship was a heroine. And Cyrus Field was the hero. He had eclipsed the biblical Job, who had endured only seven years of misery. Field had survived eight years of knockouts, and still had some time to go."

In London, Field faced a very different reception from that which confronted him after the failure of 1858. There was scarcely need to present the arguments that he had prepared. James Stuart-Wortley, now chairman of the company, had come to the same favorable conclusions. So had the directors. They would most certainly try again. Field pressed his luck and suggested that they not only lay a new cable the following summer, but also try to retrieve the one they had lost, thus getting, in a sense, two cables for the price of one. This, too, was agreed on.

The Telegraph Construction & Maintenance Company offered him the same terms as before. On a cost-per-week basis, it would manufacture and lay another cable at its own risk, taking 20 percent in company shares as profit *if* the cable was successful. In addition, it would undertake to raise and repair the broken cable, manufacturing whatever wire was needed to supplement that left aboard the *Great Eastern.* The directors voted in late 1865 to raise another £600,000 of capital, with the new preferred stock paying an attractive 12 percent. This was a heavy load on top of the 8 percent preferred stock they had sold to underwrite their recent failure. But nobody doubted it was sound. The prevailing faith in Field's judgment was well expressed in a letter from John Bright:

> When the news came that your great attempt, for this season, was a failure, I thought of your anxiety & bitter disappointment, & I asked myself how would even your buoyant spirit bear so great a misfortune—and I hear that you have borne it with the fortitude which has been shewn in all times by men who have accomplished great deeds. I have often wished that my circumstances were such that I could have been one of your helpers in your noble work— I have not been able to render pecuniary aid to the undertaking, for I have given too much, in fact, nearly all my life to the public and to public affairs—but I have given all I could give, my good

wishes, & my hearty admiration to those, & to yourself in particular, who have so laboriously & so nobly sought to connect your new world & our old one by the Electric Cable.

With things well settled, Field was able to return home in September. He had been gone six months. On the return voyage one of his fellow passengers observed: "We felt the deepest sympathy for him, and to our surprise he was the life of the ship and the most cheerful one on board. He told us: 'We've learned a great deal, and next summer we'll lay the cable without a doubt.' "

This was the man who, when Charles Fox, an engineer, warned him that there were difficulties in the way of laying the Atlantic Telegraph, turned round with some disdain and said, "My dear sir, there is no difficulty, we shall get rid of all difficulty."

Only one thing bothered him on his return: the Newfoundland cable to Nova Scotia. The line across the Gulf of St. Lawrence had now been submerged for ten years. Field's prospectus, prepared on the *Great Eastern,* noted that the cable of 1865 was a hundred times better insulated than that of 1858. He suggested to Peter Cooper and the rest at the New York, Newfoundland and London Telegraph Company that they test the line for flaws and consider ordering another cable to replace it. They agreed; it could be sandwiched in with the order for the transatlantic cable. As for repairing the existing line, they would take a chance on its holding out until the new one came along.

Field had not been home a week before a letter from Captain Anderson arrived: "I am sorry you are not here. Somehow no one seems to push when you are absent." His daughter Isabella was being married the last week in October to William Francis Judson of Philadelphia, a good reason for Cyrus to refuse to leave the country. But provoked by Anderson's reports that they were losing time and would end up with last-minute compromises, he sailed back to England on the *Scotia* in the middle of December, 1865. He arrived in London on the twenty-fourth and noted sadly that "the next day was not a 'Merry Christmas' to me." In his absence the Attorney General of England had decreed that the Atlantic Telegraph Company had no legal right to raise additional capital with 12 percent preferred stock in addition to the earlier stock. Such a move required an Act of Parliament, since the company had been organized with parliamentary consent. But Parliament had recessed for the Christmas holidays. Consequently, everything was at a standstill, and what stock they had sold had been redeemed.

Field knew now who his staunchest friends were. He went first to Daniel Gooch, who had promised him the use of the *Great Eastern* once again. Gooch suggested that the only solution to the dilemma was to organize another company capable of acting independently. To such a company he would subscribe £20,000, his first investment in the undertaking. Field went next to Thomas Brassey, who had been his stout right arm before. Brassey told him, "Go ahead—and count on me for a tenth of the capital you need." Ten other directors, as well as Field himself, pledged subscriptions of £10,000 apiece.

With such a nucleus the Anglo-American Telegraph Company was born on March 1, 1866, capitalized at £600,000. Even before its books were opened to the public £230,500 was privately subscribed, with the Telegraph Construction & Maintenance Company putting up £100,000. The officials of these two companies were generally the same, overlapping as well with the Atlantic Telegraph Company. Their operations were further bound together by contracts which included the New York, Newfoundland and London Telegraph Company. In short, all four groups constituted an operational community.

Again they had been pulled from a morass by Field's refusal to be beaten. Anderson wrote him gleefully: "I feel as if our watch had got its mainspring replaced, and had been trying to go without it for the last three months. At all events, I know nothing will be left undone that human energy can accomplish." Nothing, indeed, was left undone. In just fourteen days the entire amount of £600,000 had been raised, the order was placed with the Telegraph Construction & Maintenance Company, and by the middle of March the cable was rolling from the factory at the rate of twenty miles a day.

Only one major improvement was required. The iron wires binding the outer cover were galvanized, to make them stronger and less brittle. There would be less chance of splinters breaking off to pierce the insulation. It was figured that with what remained on the *Great Eastern,* 1,660 nautical miles would be more than adequate both to lay a new line and to extend the old one, with 90 miles for a new cable for the Gulf of St. Lawrence.

On April 5, 1866, at the Buckingham Palace Hotel Field gave his annual dinner for his associates and friends, at which he spoke (reported the London *Morning Star*) "with almost inspired fervor of the certainty with which it would soon be possible to speak between England and America in a minute of time." He was still immensely concerned about Anglo-American relations and continued to exchange communications with John Bright, who wrote him: "I am anxious about what is doing in Washington, but I have lost faith in the President, and think Mr. Seward is allowing himself to be dragged into the mud of his southern propensities. . . . But if I despair of the President, I shall have faith in the people."

Restless for action again, Field sailed back to America almost as soon as his dinner was over. While home he had just time to check with his directors, who were more concerned with the consolidation of the American Telegraph Company with Western Union, which by June of that year brought all major lines in the United States together, than with the failing cable in the Gulf. He spent a few days with his family at Gramercy Park and then set off again for England on the steamship *Java*.

On his arrival Thomson wrote from Glasgow: "I am very glad to learn that you are again in this country. You are not come too soon as the A.T.C. seems to require an impulse, and I am sure will be much the better for your presence." There seems to have been some question raised either by Field or the directors, about whether or not he should absent himself from London by participation in the expeditions. Captain Anderson may have had the final word to say about it. During the debate he wrote to Field: "I weary to hear that all is settled . . . without you I would do what I could to decline going. I told Mr. Lampson this much and as plainly the other night." It was decided: Field would go.

At Sheerness the cable was being coiled into the *Great Eastern*'s tanks, and he found attention focused on the ship. Lovingly, Captain Anderson was giving her the grooming of her life, shearing acres of barnacles and marine growth off the hull. The machinery on deck was overhauled, with more powerful engines installed for paying out and hauling in. The telegraph cabin included new and marvelous instruments perfected by Varley and Thomson. These enabled them to check constantly on conductivity and insulation and to detect the slightest flaw in any section of the cable long before it had a chance of slipping overside. Also aboard were twenty miles of iron rope and several kinds of grapnels to raise a broken cable from the bottom.

The telegraph fleet would be larger this time. In addition to the *Great Eastern* under Captain Anderson, the British warship *Terrible* would be along again, with two new escorts chartered by the company, the *Albany* and *Medway*. A 2,000-ton vessel, *William Corey*, affectionately known as "Dirty Billy," was commissioned to land the heavy shore end at Valentia. At Heart's Content there would be another British warship waiting to assist them.

The personnel aboard was a familiar, reassuring group. Field again was the sole American. ("He could no more be absent than the cable itself," wrote artist Robert Dudley, who was also on the expedition.) With him were Daniel Gooch, the faithful Thomson, Varley, Glass, Canning, and Willoughby Smith. A few ghosts haunted their memories. John Brett had died, as had Berryman and Hudson. Charles Tilston Bright was now too occupied in Parliament to make the expedition. Those who were there were all veteran comrades-in-arms, sure of one another and of ultimate success. Only Daniel Gooch appears to have had some doubts, as the first entry in his diary indicates:

> Yes, I am again seated in this familiar cabin. What is my present hope? Is it the same as last year? Do I feel the same confidence? No. The hope is as strong, but not the confidence; the experience of last year showed me by what a slender thread our success hung, how little might destroy all our hopes ... we must hope for the blessing of God upon our endeavours.

But Gooch quickly switched to a practical note: "This large party makes beds scarce."

When they steamed away from Sheerness, there was no crowd to see them off, no ceremony, only one salute to the *Great Eastern*. As the big ship passed The Nore, there was a breathless moment when her overloaded hull just barely cleared the sandbar. Once free and clear and sailing proudly toward Margate, an impromptu band aboard the lightship broke out with the strains of "Good-bye Sweetheart, Good-bye!"

Five days out from Sheerness, headed for Valentia, the *Great Eastern* found itself off Fastnet Rock on the southern coast of Ireland, and Willoughby Smith noted in his record of the expedition: "This being the anniversary of the American Declaration of Independence, the American flag was hoisted, and speeches made in compliment to Mr. Field." More than speeches marked the celebration. In a makeshift amphitheater, christened the "Great Atlantic Haul," the company presented a satirical revue, again lampooning the favorite targets,

Field and Gooch. It was entitled "A Cableistic and Eastern Extravaganza." A little of the dialogue is an ample sample:

> (*Enter* Gooch *and* Field, Field *with his pockets full of shares*)
>
> *Gooch.*   Tell me, dear Cyrus, are not the banks around Newfoundland those on which the wild thyme blows?
>
> *Field.*   My wildest time was in the tank, (See Dudley's sketch) tho' not on any bank.
>
> (*Turning to Gooch who retires and sits and gradually falls asleep*)
>
> Oh! That I could shuffle off this mortal coil!
> (*A la Hamlet*) I've furrowed the Atlantic many times,
> And 'mid such toil have held convivial dinners.
> For me the sparkling wine cup nightly flowed,
> And often flowed in vain;
> While others to the joys of music clung,
> I plied the bottle, but 'twas then of ink.
> Prospectuses I drew; percentage showed,
> And e'en through worse times on 'change
> Could lead grave, bearded men
> To wander forth and muse
> On the triumphant joys I promised them.

Precisely fifty miles away by sea, a more expectant audience was gathering for a more enthralling drama; the lights were beginning to glow around the rocky amphitheater. People from all over County Kerry were converging on Valentia. They had no band to play an overture; they made their own music, sat by their fires and cooked their meals, and kept their eyes turned toward the south where the great ship would shortly make its appearance.

20

Double Triumph

>>>>>><<<<<< On Friday, June 13, the shore end of the cable was landed from the "Dirty Billy" over a floating bridge of forty fishing boats. In contrast with the carnival atmosphere of the year before, in place of flags and bunting there were the gaudy shawls of old crones smoking clay pipes and the bright red dresses of the Irish colleens gathered on the cliffs of Foilhummerum. The gravity of the occasion prompted the company to hold religious services on shore with the Reverend Henry Field officiating.

The *Great Eastern* hovered 30 miles from shore to receive the land section of the cable. Once it was spliced to the line on board, signals were sent through the 2,500-mile length to Valentia. Varley and Glass, who would stay with the instruments in Ireland, signaled back that all was well, and the four-ship squadron sailed toward America—the *Terrible* running ahead, the *Albany* and *Medway* flanking the *Great Eastern*. They were right on schedule; the sea was calm and the weather clear. If ever Field felt justified in hoping for success, it was on this sunny Friday, when all the auspices were promising.

Every precaution had been taken against past mistakes. The cable crew were encased from head to toe in canvas. "They certainly look like convicts," Gooch wrote. The costume "covers their whole person and fastens in the back, and is without pockets, so that no one can take anything into the tanks without its being seen." On the bridge stood the Job-like Captain Anderson, "modest and grave, of few words, but seeing everything, watching everything, and ruling everything with a quiet power." The cable appeared to respond to this human discipline, paying out evenly at six knots. The polished hull of the *Great Eastern* slid so smoothly through the water that her stern propeller was disengaged to reduce speed. Interrupting the silence of the ship, hens cackled, geese honked, pigs grunted and cattle lowed.

Three days out, Cyrus used the fast-extending cable to send a message to Valentia: "Field to Glass.—Please write Mrs. Field today at Newburg, New York, and tell her, 'All in good health and spirits on board of this ship, and confident of success.' Machinery works perfectly, and the cable pays out splendidly."

That night John Deane, secretary of the Anglo-American Company and historian of the expedition, wrote in his ledger of a day "so calm that the masts of our convoy were reflected in the ocean," of porpoises that had played around the ship for half an hour, of "a glorious sunset and later a full moon." He had barely finished when the cable snarled in the paying-out machinery, and before it could be checked, 500 feet was hopelessly entangled. The ship was stopped, and Captain Anderson had the delicate job of holding the *Great Eastern* in position, keeping the cable from straining or twisting at the stern, while the crew worked for two exasperating hours to straighten out the mess.

Once under way again, things went as smoothly as before. But Field returned to anxious days of watching in the tank, eyes peeled for any telltale flash of silver in the cable's somber armor, and to sleepless nights, when he listened to the rumble of the paying-out machinery. Any irregularity of sound or movement made him come to from a momentary doze to feel that the ship had stopped. This would send him to his cabin porthole for a quick check on the giant paddle wheels. They would be turning—but too fast? Too slow?

Daniel Gooch, who, like Field, had much time to worry helplessly, recorded the tension in his diary:

> I now hear the rumble of the cable over my head in my cabin, and am constantly listening to it. This stretch of the nerves day after day is hard work, and the mind has no change; morning, noon, and night it is all the same—cable, cable, cable.

Their course lay thirty miles south of where the previous cable rested, to avoid snagging the new line when they came to grappling for the old. By Sunday they had passed the point where the 1865 cable had been lost, but the buoy which Canning had left to mark its precise location had disappeared. Things were so uneventful aboard ship that for once the company was more concerned with news from Valentia and Europe than with what was going on around them. Austria was bitterly engaged in a two-front war with Italy and Prussia, and they learned now that the Austrian armies were trapped between the advancing Prussians and Vienna. The news was flashed to the escorting ships.

One event not reported, of which probably only Field was aware, was threatening their future from the other side of the world. Collins and Sibley were pressing their overland route to Europe in a grim race with Field's expedition. The cable was at the Bering Strait waiting to be laid; 300 miles of wire had been strung in Alaska, 350 in Siberia; and the Russians were pushing a 7,000-mile line eastward from St. Petersburg. The multimillion-dollar Western Union enterprise was predicated on Field's failure.

However, Field's confidence that they would reach Heart's Content is reflected in the next two entries in his diary:

Monday, July 23rd

At 8.54 A.M. I sent the following telegram:

Field to Glass.—Please obtain the latest news from Egypt, China, India, and distant places for us to forward to the United States on our arrival at Heart's Content.

At 7.05 P.M. I sent the following telegram:

Field to Glass.—Please send us Thursday afternoon the price that day for cotton in Liverpool and the London quotations for consols, United States five-twenty bonds, and also bank rate of interest. The above we shall send to New York on our arrival, and I will obtain the latest news from the States and send to you in return.

Tuesday, July 24th

At 9.05 A.M. I sent the following telegram:

Field to Glass.—We are within four hundred miles of Heart's Content, and expect to be there on Friday. When shall the Atlantic cable be open for public business?

At 10.25 A.M. I received the following:

Glass to Field.—If you land the cable on Friday, I see no reason why it should not be open on Saturday.

By Thursday they had reached the Grand Banks. The sea had the salty tang that somehow seems much stronger close to land; gulls swooped above the ships and dived for scraps thrown overboard; schools of Atlantic salmon ruffled the untroubled waters in their path —and an iceberg told them they were nearing northern shores.

John Deane wrote happily in his diary: "May we have three days more of such delightful monotony!" But the monotony was accompanied by dense fog. "Oxford Street" was like its namesake on a soupy London evening; Field could barely see beyond the visor of his deer-stalker cap. The four ships, dangerously close but unseen, shrieked at one another with their whistles. Anderson looked for the full moon he had counted on to light them into Heart's Content. It remained an occasional ghost in the overhanging vapor.

With the escorting ships taking repeated soundings, the *Great Eastern* groped her way down Trinity Bay. At eight on the morning of July 27, the fog lifted like a magic curtain. There suddenly was Heart's Content! The pine-girt bay was crowded with boats anticipating their arrival, two British ships, the *Niger* and the *Margaretta Stevenson,* were on hand to greet them, and from almost every house on shore waved the Stars and Stripes and Union Jack. The *Great Eastern* "dressed ship, fired a salute, and three cheers were given." Field made a next-to-last notation in his diary: "We sent the end of the cable to the *Medway* to be spliced. I left the *Great Eastern* in a small boat at 8:15 A.M., and landed at Heart's Content at 9 o'clock."

The *Great Eastern* log preserved in the Greenwich offices of Submarine Cables Ltd., successor to the Telegraph Construction & Maintenance Company, reads: "Friday, July 27, 2:30. *S. S. Medway* passed in with shore end. 4:00. Shore end landed successfully, fired a Royal salute; *H.M.S. Terrible, Niger* and *Lilly* following example. Ships dressed with flags." Daniel Gooch's diary is more colorful. As the cable end was brought ashore, "there was the wildest excitement I have ever witnessed. All seemed mad with joy, jumping into the water and shouting as though they wished the sound to be heard in Washington."

When the cable end was dragged to the wooden telegraph house constructed to receive it,

> . . . another wild scene of excitement took place. The old cable hands seemed as though they could eat the end; one man actually put it into his mouth and sucked it. They held it up and danced around it, cheering at the top of their voices. It was a strange sight—nay, a sight that filled our eyes with tears. Yes, I felt not less than they did. I did cheer, but I could better have silently cried.

Connecting the line to the instruments was mere and melancholy ritual, for Field's elation at reaching Heart's Content had been immediately deflated. The superintendent who rowed out to meet him announced that the line from Newfoundland to Cape Breton had ceased to function; no messages could be relayed from the cable. Time and again Field had begged for an early replacement, for the cable that had lain for ten years in the Gulf was now obsolete in the light of subsequent manufacturing improvements. Although he had ninety miles of brand-new cable on the *Great Eastern,* to be laid across Cabot Strait as soon as possible, this was no help at the moment. He was forced to make what quick amends he could.

He sent out a call for ships to help in this crisis and found two available at St. John's. The steamer *Bloodhound* was sent around to the Gulf to fish up and repair the defective cable. How long this would take, it was impossible to tell. To bridge the interval, another ship, the *Dauntless,* was chartered to shuttle back and forth across the Gulf, carrying messages to the terminus in Nova Scotia, which still remained in contact with New York. There would be a delay in transmitting cablegrams from Europe, but it was the best that he could do. Public blame, as Field anticipated, was directed at his lack of foresight.

It was not till Sunday, August 29, that Mary received the first news of the expedition from her husband: "All Well. Thank God the cable has been successfully laid and is in perfect working order. I am sure that no one will be as thankful to God as you and our dear children. Now we shall be a united family. We leave in about a week to recover the cable of last year. . . ."

Driving home from church that Sunday morning, Mary saw the Hudson River steamer coming to its pier with all flags flying. The sight prompted her to stop at the local telegraph office, where she found Cyrus' message. There was public rejoicing when the ship docked with the news. There was rejoicing in her heart as well, but it was clouded by the sentences, "Now we shall be a united family. We leave in about a week to recover the cable of last year." In those lines was a capsule of their marriage.

Mary received some consolation and support throughout these trying times from Dr. Adams and from Edward M. Archibald, the British consul in New York, who had been close to the cable operation since he first secured the landing rights for Field in Newfoundland. On August 6 he wrote her:

> I congratulate you most heartily and sincerely—and upon the prospect of having Mr. Field henceforth more to yourself and your family, and less of a *Mother Carey's Chicken* than he has been for the last ten years. I suppose he has returned in the *Great Eastern* to the

spot where the end of last year's cable is supposed to lie in the bottom of the ocean, upon the principle that as he has been hard at work all summer, he ought now to have his holiday and his *fishing excursion!*

As soon as the Cabot Strait cable was repaired (surprisingly this took only forty-eight hours), messages poured into Heart's Content from every quarter of the globe. Gooch wrote in his diary on their second day in port: "Yesterday we had fifty messages, paying us, I suppose not less than twelve thousand pounds." (The rate then was $1.25 a word—a bargain compared with later rates.) Queen Victoria and President Johnson exchanged the traditional greetings. And there was a flow of laudatory messages to Field, although after his 1858 experience these sounded somewhat repetitious. Seward and the President sent congratulations, as did the London and New York directors. Bishop Mullock exhorted his congregation "to have the example of Mr. Cyrus W. Field before your eyes." John Greenleaf Whittier composed his "Cable Hymn," with its hopefully prophetic verse:

> What saith the herald of the Lord?
> "The world's long strife is done;
> Close wedded by that mystic cord,
> Its continents are one."

As if to confirm this oneness, Field received two wires simultaneously—one from California via Western Union; the other from Ferdinand de Lesseps in Alexandria, Egypt, expressing *"félicitations pour persévérance et grand succès."*

Field must have got his greatest satisfaction from a letter of William Gladstone's. The Chancellor of The Exchequer, who now branded his remark that Jefferson Davis had "made a nation" as a mistake of "incredible grossness," had obviously softened in his attitude toward America. He wrote to Field: "I offer you my cordial congratulations, and I trust that the electric line may powerfully contribute to binding our two countries together in perfect harmony."

For Field, however, the job would not be over as long as there was still a loose end in the North Atlantic. The *Great Eastern*'s departure was delayed because she had to take on coal, 8,000 tons of it, which had been ferried from England on six barges, one of them lost at sea. Two of the escorts, the *Terrible* and *Albany,* went on ahead to pinpoint the area where the cable had been lost twelve months before and

where the richest trawl in history would now commence. Both were
equipped with grappling tackle and planned to make a few casts of
their own. If they caught the cable, they could hold it up with buoys
till the big ship came along.

While waiting in the harbor, the *Great Eastern* entertained visitors.
"Over the hills they came on foot and on horseback, and in wagons
and carts of every description; and from along the shore in boats and
fishing-smacks, and sloops and schooners."

Captain Anderson who had been a guest at the Field house at Gramercy Park wrote Mary. After warning her that they might be all of
a fortnight on the task ahead, he said in part:

> Then what next? God knows. But Mr. Field is not one bit quieter
> than he was in London. He wants a third cable laid, and two complete
> lines from here to New York, before he will be satisfied. The success
> of this one will make the others comparatively easy, but I am not
> sure if he will even then take the repose both he and you deserve.
> He is very well; but how he stands the endless excitement I do not
> know. One thing I may give you now as a sound opinion: he would
> not stand many more London campaigns without you or one of your
> daughters with him. He takes absolutely no repose in London, and it
> is only because he cannot help himself that he gets it at sea.

There was little repose awaiting him at sea now. With the remainder
of the 1865 cable in her hold, the *Great Eastern* sailed from Heart's
Content at noon on August 29, 1866, accompanied by the *Medway*.
By Sunday they had joined the *Albany* and *Terrible* 600 miles from
Newfoundland. A seaman's uncanny intuition had led the preceding
ships directly to the spot where the lost cable lay, for these were men,
Field said subsequently, "who knew the ocean as a hunter knows
every trail in the forest." In fact, they had caught the cable once, then
lost it, and had since staked out its position with a row of buoys. Now,
like an armada in attack formation, the four ships were to space out
to windward of the buoys and drift down on the line with grappling
irons.

"I often went to the bow," wrote Field in his diary, "and sat on the
rope, and could tell by the quiver that the grapnel was dragging on
the bottom two miles under us."

It was a long, frustrating process, groping blindly in two miles or
more of water for an inch-thick cable somewhere at the bottom.
("Cable? Thread!" said Captain Anderson.) Two hours to drop the

tackle; hours more to reel it in, often finding nothing more than mud or loose rocks caught between the iron teeth or the points of the grapnels bent by rocks. "At first it was a little awkward to fish in such deep water," Cyrus later remarked, "but our men got used to it, and soon could cast a grapnel almost as straight as an old whaler throws a harpoon."

It was not till Thursday evening that they snagged the cable firmly. It took fourteen hours of tense, anxious reeling in to bring it to the surface. "We had it in full sight for five minutes," Field noted, "a long, slimy monster, fresh from the ooze of the ocean's bed—but our men began to cheer so wildly that it seemed to be frightened, and suddenly broke away and went down into the sea." It had evidently parted of its own weight. Over and over this disappointment was to be repeated as the weather worsened and the ships could maneuver as a unit only with the use of foghorns. They could snag the cable but could not bring it to the surface. Apparently weakened by submersion, it would snap before they got it several hundred fathoms from the bottom. Wrote Henry Field in the subjunctive: "It were idle to relate all the attempts of those two weeks." Yet he went on to relate:

> Every day brought its excitement. Whenever the grapnel caught, there was a suspense of many hours till it was brought on board. Several times they seemed on the point of success. Two days after that fatal Friday, on Sunday, August 19th, they caught the cable again, and brought it up within a thousand fathoms of the ship, and buoyed it. But Monday and Tuesday were too rough for work, and all their labor was in vain. Sometimes the wind blew fiercely and drove them off their course. Sometimes the buoys broke adrift and had to be pursued and taken.

And sometimes, Field noticed, when the sun occasionally shone, the wind dropped altogether. The ships, which were using sail as much as possible to save on coal, stood motionless on a glassy sea, and "like giant sea-birds with folded wings, sat watching their prey."

There were false alarms to add to their frustration. At one point the *Albany,* off fishing on her own, sounded her guns in exultation. She had hooked the cable and was reeling in! By midnight she signaled that she had brought the cable to the surface and would hold it there by buoy. When daylight came, the mother ship could pick it up. But when the *Great Eastern* brought the line on deck, it was found to be only a loose section broken off in grappling. The men stowed it below as an ironic mocking souvenir.

It was at such a time as this that Field told Willoughby Smith, "When this is over, I'm going to retire to my own farm in the Berkshires, with plenty of cows and chickens, and receive my dividends in eggs and fresh milk." They were running low on provisions, for by then it was the end of August. The men were exhausted; the grappling had gone on day and night without a letup. They had made twenty-seven, twenty-eight, then twenty-nine attempts—and failed. Captain Temple of the *Albany* had collapsed from sheer fatigue and was brought aboard the *Great Eastern*. Captain Commerill, who had replaced Captain Napier on the *Terrible,* reported he was running out of fuel, his men were on half rations and were falling ill; he asked permission to return to Newfoundland for fresh supplies. His ship had barely enough coal to get to St. John's. They watched the vessel limp away, the first serious casualty of this strange ocean war. While they were watching, John Deane, groggy from sleeplessness, fell from the *Great Eastern*'s bridge, fracturing his arm.

Field, Canning, and Anderson decided to try for "better luck in other waters," and the three remaining ships moved farther east along the cable's estimated path. On August 31 the sea was calm, the weather clear. For the thirtieth time they lowered the grapnel from the bow—and hooked the cable. Repeated failures had conditioned them against hope. But as the dynamometer registered increasing pressure and hour after hour brought the cable closer to the surface, excitement rose. The higher the cable got, the greater its suspended weight and the greater the chance of its breaking. "What was the anxiety of those twenty-six hours?" Field asked in retrospect. "The strain on every man's life was like the strain on the cable itself."

This time Canning took no chances. He buoyed the recovered end a short way from the surface, and the ship moved farther up the line to get a fresh hold. The *Medway* also gripped the suspended cable at a third point two miles farther east. With the weight thus distributed, the *Great Eastern* moved back to the cable's end and inched it to the surface. Two veteran seamen were lashed with rope and lowered from the bow. Tenderly they freed the cable from the sharp grip of the grapnel and secured it to a five-inch halyard. Gently they lifted it aboard.

"Men are sometimes stunned by sudden success, and hardly know if it be not all a dream," wrote Henry. "There the monster lay, its neck firmly in their grip, and its black head lying on deck. But even then there was no cheering." There was instead a sense of disbelief and awe. Sailors touched it warily, as if to make sure it was real. Some dared to take it in their hands and study it. It was indeed the cable they had lost the year before.

Then came the next surge of anxiety. Here it was, but *did it work?* Its 1,100 miles had been submerged for thirteen months, exposed to God knew what attacks from sea, rocks, creatures of the depths. As the cable was passed along the deck and gently carried to the test room, there was more electric tension on that ship than any instrument could measure. Field, Canning, Smith, and Thomson were sketched by artist Robert Dudley as they hovered over the electricians who ran a wire from the cable to the testing apparatus. Dudley wrote:

> Nearly a quarter of an hour has passed, and still no sign! Suddenly Willoughby Smith's hat is off, and the British hurrah bursts from his lips, echoed by all on board with a volley of cheers, evidently none the worse for having been "bottled up" during the last three hours. Along the deck outside, over the ship, throughout the ship, the pent-up enthusiasm overflowed; and even before the testroom was cleared, the roaring bravos of our guns drowned the huzzahs of the crew, and the whiz of rockets was heard rushing high into the clear morning sky to greet our consort-ships with the glad intelligence.

Field described that stroke of time:

> Never shall I forget that eventful moment when, in answer to our question to Valentia, whether the cable of 1866, which we had a few weeks previously laid, was in good working order, and the cable across the Gulf of St. Lawrence had been repaired, in an instant came back those six memorable letters, "Both O.K." I left the room, I went to my cabin, I locked the door; I could no longer restrain my tears—crying like a child, and full of gratitude to God that I had been permitted to witness the recovery of the cable we had lost from the *Great Eastern* just thirteen months previous.

He recovered long enough to send a message farther than any telegram had previously traveled—from the *Great Eastern* to Valentia, and from Valentia to Newfoundland and New York (a distance of roughly 5,500 miles):

Mrs. Cyrus W. Field, Newburgh, New York

The cable of 1865 was recovered early this morning, and we are now in perfect telegraphic communication with Valentia, and on our way back to Heart's Content, where we expect to arrive next Saturday. God be praised. Please telegraph me in full at Heart's Content. I am in good health and spirits. Captain Anderson wishes to be kindly remembered to you.

Cyrus W. Field

There remained now only to splice the recovered cable and carry the remaining length 600 miles or so to Heart's Content. The *Albany* gathered up the marking buoys and set out for England; the *Great Eastern* and the *Medway* headed west to Newfoundland. As if to exact toll for their good fortune, the weather became vicious. For thirty-six hours they battled storms and high seas. Even the *Great Eastern* rocked and pitched, albeit with some dignity. In his diary Field wrote:

> In the very height and fury of the gale, as I sat in the electrician's room, a flash of light came up from the deep, which having crossed to Ireland, came back to me in midocean, telling that those so dear to me, whom I had left on the banks of the Hudson, were well, and following us with their wishes and their prayers. This was like a whisper of God from the sea, bidding me keep heart and hope. The *Great Eastern* bore herself proudly through the storm, as if she knew that the vital cord which was to join two hemispheres, hung at her stern; and so on Saturday, the seventh of September, we brought our second cable safely to the shore.

To the crowd awaiting them at Heart's Content, this unique triumph had a special glory. Word of the success had flashed via Valentia to North America, and everyone for miles around flocked to the small fishing village. Henry Field described the scene:

> As the ships came up the harbor it was covered with boats, and all were wild with excitement; and when the big shore-end was got out of the *Medway*, and dragged to land, the sailors hugged it and almost kissed it in their extravagance of joy; and no sooner was it safely landed than they seized Mr. Field, Mr. Canning and Mr. Clifford in their arms, and raised them over their heads, while the crowd cheered with tumultuous enthusiasm.

When it came time to leave the ship and the men with whom Field had endured so much and been associated for so long, it was a moment of sincere grief. Captain Anderson was the last to shake his hand and then called to his crew, "Give him three cheers!" This they did, and Anderson, a very human being, called again, "Now three more for his family!" The cheering followed Field as he rowed away and echoed in his mind on shore as he watched the *Great Eastern* curve around and steam through the gates of Trinity Bay for England. It was not much later that he was able to collect his thoughts and put his emotions into words:

> It has been a long, hard struggle. Nearly thirteen years of anxious watching and ceaseless toil. Often my heart has been ready to sink. Many times, when wandering in the forests of Newfoundland, in the pelting rain, or on the deck of ships, on dark, stormy nights—alone, far from home—I have almost accused myself of madness and folly to sacrifice the peace of my family, and all the hopes of life, for what might prove after all but a dream. I have seen my companions one and another falling by my side, and feared that I too might not live to see the end. And yet one hope has led me on, and I have prayed that I might not taste of death till this work was accomplished. That prayer is answered; and now, beyond all acknowledgments to men, is the feeling of gratitude to Almighty God.

By now the reaction overseas had been reported—even more jubilant than the American response. In the small shack at Valentia a pair of lonely electricians, May and Crocker, had been hovering for more than a year over the instruments connected with the broken cable. Night and day, month after month, they had been sending signals into that 1,200 miles of empty length. Sometimes the returning echoes took the form of eerie gibberish, garbled words and sentences that suggested some deep-ocean creatures trying to communicate with man above. It was like an electric shock to see the flashes turn to clear words: "Ship to shore: I have much pleasure in speaking to you through the 1865 cable." It must have seemed, said the *Spectator,* "like the first rational word uttered by a high-fevered patient, when the ravings have ceased and his consciousness returns."

Especially in Great Britain, where naval triumphs and defeats were vital matters, there was a deep sense of gratification in this revenge for the previous year's failure. On September 8, *The Great Eastern Telegraph* published a compendium of all messages received over the 1865 cable since its recovery on September 2, 1866. These included a dispatch from Valentia: "Picking up of old cable excites even greater interest than laying new one, and is general topic of conversation."

The London *Times* observed: "There is extreme satisfaction in finding any lost treasure, especially when it has cost labour, skill, knowledge, talent, perseverance, and all the valuable and priceless expenditure of mind. The Atlantic Telegraph is triumphant out of all its trouble."

On the other side of the world, reaction to the news had seriocomic aspects. In British Columbia, where work on the Russo-American overland route had been pushing ahead, word of Field's success came via Western Union. The work crews dropped their tools and quit. A 16,000-mile land wire could never compete with a 1,600-mile cable. It took longer for the news to reach Siberia, where half a dozen separate armies were erecting 20,000 poles to carry the line from the Amur River to the coast. George Kennan, one of those directing the work, was the first to hear of Field's triumph. "You mean the cable works?" he asked the ship's captain who brought the message. "Works like a snatch tackle," he was told.

Kennan and his associates closed up shop, but first they turned their corner of Siberia into a bazaar to get rid of their miles of wire and surplus products. As R. L. Thompson reported it:

> They glutted the market with pickaxes and long-handled shovels which they assured the natives would be useful in burying their dead, and threw in a lot of frozen cucumber pickles and other anti-scorbutics which they warranted to fortify the health of the living. They sold glass insulators by the hundred as patent American tea cups, and brackets by the thousand as prepared American kindling wood. They offered soap and candles as premiums to anybody who would buy their salt pork and dried apples, and taught the natives how to make cooling drinks and hot biscuits, in order to create a demand for their redundant lime juice and baking powder. They directed all their energies to the creation of artificial wants in that previously happy and contented community, and flooded the whole adjacent country with articles that were of no more use to the poor natives than iceboats and mouse-traps would be to the Quaregs of the Sahara desert!

In short, recorded Kennan, "they dispensed the blessings of civilization with a free hand."

Field was still not in a position to return to Mary and his family. Before her departure, the *Great Eastern* had transferred her ninety miles of cable for the Gulf to the *Medway,* and Cyrus boarded the latter ship to supervise its installation from Cape Ray to Aspy Bay, on the northern tip of Nova Scotia. The trouble in communications from New York to Newfoundland had worried the New York directors —as well it might have, since it was due largely to their neglect—and Field wired his brother Dudley to assure them that the old line was now repaired, and a new one being laid. The operation would take the balance of September.

Aboard the *Great Eastern* on her leisurely return to England, Field's absence did not detract from the attention he received. In the middle of both September and the North Atlantic, the thespian members of the company presented another "Great Atlantic Haul" extravaganza, this one entitled "CONTENTINA, the Instructive Story of Cyrus in Search of His Love." Robert Dudley played the part of Cyrus Field ("The Original Yankee") who, having recovered the lost cable, feels entitled to the hand of Neptune's daughter. He woos her, wins her heart, but in the final scene confronts an angry Neptune intent on foiling the marriage, even if it means destroying Field. All comes to a triumphant climax:

NEPTUNE: Cyrus, of all men else I have avoided thee,
          But Neptune, ruling god of azure sea,
          Disdains to turn his scaly back on thee.
CYRUS: As English Shakespeare says, Lay on, my duffer,
          You'll soon find that you have had enuffer.
          For if I can I'll prod you in the duffer.
          (He does so. *Neptune* is mortally wounded)
NEPTUNE: Your buffer thrust doth quite o'ercome my spirit,
          Why did you push your sword so fiercely in it?
          Lift me (groans). I'll speak as long as I am able,
          My daughter splice, and also splice the cable. (He dies)

Although Field had courted no daughter of Neptune, he had brought that sea-god to his knees. Never again would the depths of the Atlantic, hitherto impenetrable, be a barrier of silence between nations.

21

"Lord Cable"

➤➤➤➤➤➤◄◄◄◄◄◄ Cyrus Field had battled throughout half his adult life to bring about the seemingly impossible, had risen to certain wealth and popular acclaim, and had contributed soundly to the cause which Matthew Maury had defined for him as international cooperation between nations.

Although he was still only forty-five, still at the peak of his capacities, much of his youth and its reserves had gone into that undertaking. "It had been a long hard struggle, nearly thirteen years of anxious waiting and ceaseless toil," he wrote and although the editor of the *Atlantic Monthly* had called that stormy period "one of the noblest in American enterprise," only Cyrus and possibly Mary knew what it had cost in overtaxed health, anxiety, and money. And not he alone. Richard Glass, managing director of the Telegraph Construction & Maintenance Company, had collapsed and now lay "dangerously ill from over-taxed mind and body." His office had been filled by Sherard Osborn.

The Field family's existence at Gramercy Park was not spartan, but the heavily mortgaged house, the servants, and the education of the children had been precariously maintained. Even Mary was probably unaware of the extent to which her husband had jeopardized his fortune and security for the laying of the cable. Wrote his daughter Isabella: "All waited for that day, but not always patiently, for one or another was often heard to exclaim, 'Oh, if that old cable was only at the bottom of the ocean!' and to this he would invariably answer, 'That is just where I wish it to be!'"

The success of the Atlantic cable made, as his brother Henry wrote:

a profound impression throughout the civilized world. Yet it was a singular illustration of the changes in public interest, that, whereas in 1858 a temporary success had kindled the wildest enthusiasm in the United States, while in England it was regarded almost with indifference, now the state of feeling in the two countries was completely reversed. In Great Britain it was the theme of boundless congratulations, while in America the public mind—dulled perhaps by the excitement of four years of war—received the news with composure.

There was a more direct reason for this contrast than the war's excitement. In its inception the Atlantic cable had been purely an American adventure, and that prideful feeling had prevailed till 1858. As it developed, it had been absorbed by England—English capital, English scientists, English ships, materials, and men. It was, in the eyes of Britishers, an exclusive triumph for Great Britain. Yet there was a singular generosity in their recognition of Field's part in the triumph.

Scarcely had the *Great Eastern* steamed into the Mersey than plans were advanced to honor those aboard. Professor Wheatstone, because of his preeminent position as a scientist, was asked by Lord Derby, then Prime Minister, to recommend those in the expedition who should be honored by the Queen. He did so, in a memorandum starting:

> The person to whose indomitable perseverance we are indebted for the commencement, carrying on, and completion of the enterprise is undoubtedly Mr. Cyrus Field. Through good and through evil report he has pursued his single object undaunted by repeated failures, keeping up the flagging interest of the public and the desponding hope of capitalists, and employing his energies to combine all the means which might lead towards a successful issue. This gentleman is a citizen of the United States, and there would perhaps be a difficulty in conferring on him any honorary distinction.

This difficulty was acknowledged at a banquet held in Liverpool, presided over by Sir Stafford Northcote at which it was announced that Anderson, Thomson, Canning, and Glass would be knighted; baronetcies would be conferred on the directors, Gooch and Lampson. To this list, Lord Derby added a significant amendment:

> If among the names thus submitted to and approved by Her Majesty, that of Mr. Cyrus Field does not appear, the omission must not be attributed to any disregard of the eminent services which,

from the first, he has rendered to the cause of transatlantic telegraphy, and the zeal and resolution with which he has adhered to the prosecution of his object, but to an apprehension lest it might appear to encroach on the province of his own Government. . . .

Field had no concern for titles. In his affiliated companies he had preferred to operate somewhat anonymously, thereby more freely. So keen were his English associates to grant him recognition that Charles Bright had a telegraph wire run into the banquet hall, by which they could flash to Field the sentiments expressed that night.

It was undoubtedly the personal tributes he received from England, where his reputation was attacked in 1862, that Cyrus treasured most. John Bright was lyric in his praise, publicly acclaiming "my friend, Cyrus Field" to be (in a phrase that had already become trite) the "Columbus of the age." In a confidential moment he remarked of Cyrus according to Field's brother Henry, "He makes me feel uncomfortable, for he is always successful, and I am not."

Professor Thomson wrote him feelingly, as did Cromwell Varley. And the man in the street, aware of Field's absence from the list of the Queen's honors, gave him the spontaneous title of "Lord Cable" —a nickname that spread fast through press and populace.

In America Field's popularity was riding high, with all previous disillusionments forgotten. William Maxwell Evarts, whose father had roomed with Dr. David Dudley Field at Yale and who was shortly to become Secretary of State, paraphrased the legend on Genoa's statue of Columbus: *"There was one world;* he said, *'Let there be two,' and there were two."* Relating this inscription to Cyrus Field, Evarts remarked, "Let us now, then, say of the Atlantic Cable and its author: 'There were two worlds; *he* said, "let there be one again," and they were one.' "

On his return to New York from Newfoundland in late September, with the new Cabot Strait cable successfully laid, he was greeted by a repetition of the accolades that reached him from abroad. Resolutions were passed and showered on him like confetti.

When a magazine writer asked Peter Cooper who he thought was the greatest living American, "He [Cooper] went along the wall and laid his finger on a portrait of Cyrus W. Field. 'If any other of the foremost men of our time had died, their places would have been filled,' he said; 'but Field did what no other man could do; he saved the scheme and brought victory out of despair.' "

Of all this ovation, Field said, "Were I to consult my own feelings I would avoid any public demonstration, and leave the Cable to speak for itself." However, he never hesitated to mount a platform at the slightest courteous urging, albeit often to redirect attention to his less acclaimed associates. He was at ease on his feet before crowds, and if his speeches often had an oldtime Gospel flavor, that was only natural. In fact, if one wanted to relieve him of responsibility for this, it would be possible, though not completely sound, to credit Henriette Field's remark about her husband, the Reverend Henry Martyn Field. When asked where the preacher was during a cable celebration, she replied, "Oh, probably at home writing one of Cyrus' speeches."

In mid-November the New York Chamber of Commerce held a banquet in Field's honor, at which his staunch supporter Abiel Low presided. Three hundred distinguished guests from every walk of life attended, some of them veterans of other struggles: Admiral Farragut, warrior of Mobile Bay, and General Meade, "who was loudly called for as 'the hero of Gettysburg,' to which he replied that there was but one hero on this occasion, and he had traveled a hundred miles to be there that night and do him honor." Abiel Low pronounced the opening toast: "To Cyrus W. Field, the projector and mainspring of the Atlantic telegraph; while the British government justly honors those who have taken part with him in this great work of the age, his fame belongs to us, and will be cherished and guarded by his countrymen."

Wealthy financier and yachtsman Edwin Morgan (unrelated to the House of Morgan) footnoted his encomium with the most practical suggestion yet made for saluting Field's achievement:

> And now, gentlemen, let us use this cable, use it often and freely, by day and by night, in our public affairs, in our social relations, and for commercial purposes. None can estimate or anticipate how largely our interests will be promoted by doing so. Besides, in no other way can we so practically and sufficiently compliment and remunerate its originator for the untold benefit he has conferred upon mankind.

Field's reply to all this was his own appraisal of the cable's significance, expressed with feeling toward that country which had given him so much encouragement:

> As the Atlantic Telegraph brings us into closer relations with England, it may produce a better understanding between the two countries. Let who will speak against England—words of censure must come from other lips than mine. I have received too much

kindness from Englishmen to join in this language. I have eaten of
their bread and drunk of their cup, and I have received from them,
in the darkest hours of this enterprise, words of cheer which I shall
never forget; and if any words of mine can tend to peace and goodwill, they shall not be wanting. . . . America with all her greatness
has come out of the loins of England, and though there have sometimes been family quarrels, still in our hearts there is a yearning for
our old home, the land of our fathers: and he is an enemy of his
country and of the human race, who would stir up strife between
two nations that are one in race, in language and in religion.

This basic purpose of the cable as an instrument of better international relations never left his mind. His immediate reaction to success, however, was typical. He looked to what was left undone. Top
priority was his indebtedness to the creditors of Field & Company, resulting from the 1860 panic. As in 1853, there was no legal obligation to clear up these debts.

Before six weeks had passed, he sold enough of his company stock,
some $200,000 worth, to pay off those notes, adding 7 percent in-
terest covering the intervening years. Commented the New York *Evening Post:* "Such a fact, however he may wish to keep it a secret,
ought to be known, to his honor and to the honor of the merchants of
New York." George Peabody, when he heard about it, sent Field a
silver table service which became a family heirloom, later to find its
way to the Smithsonian Institution.

The impact of the cable on finance, trade, and business was immediate. Field was able to go to his telegraph office on Liberty Street at
nine o'clock and review the noon quotations on the London Stock
Exchange. The rash of shady speculation that had plagued American
finance, much of it based on lack of knowledge or facts known only
to a few, was halted. Trading was based on sound and public information; much of the business instability of past years was corrected.

Curiously, in its first few months the cable, far from promoting international cooperation, was a source of friction. Transmission started
slowly at 8 words a minute, compared with 400 or more a minute over
modern lines. As operators and equipment improved, the rate increased to 15 words a minute, sometimes more. But the rate had now
advanced to $10 a word, close to exorbitant. In addition, there were
flaws in both the management and the mechanical efficiency of the
landlines operating between Newfoundland and the United States.
The 400-mile two-wire line had had to be operated with manual relays

installed every 100 miles, a cumbersome business now outdated. At the commemorative dinner in Liverpool, the otherwise amenable Sir Stafford Northcote had remarked that the expansion in transatlantic telegraphy would come "when the land lines on the American side are improved" (a remark greeted with "hear, hear!"). John Deane, too, was obliged to explain to a questioning British press that interruptions in the cable service were due to breakdowns in the Canadian provinces. Gisborne's wires had seen better days, as had Canning's original cable in the Gulf of St. Lawrence.

There was obviously some fence mending to do, and Cyrus wired to his brother Dudley, then in London, that he was leaving for England on December 12, 1866, again skipping Christmas with his family. He was obliged to follow this up with a letter to Dudley regarding his (Cyrus') older son:

> Yesterday afternoon Eddie was thrown from his horse on his way to the Central Park, and very much injured. We have had Dr. Paine, Dr. Van Buren and Dr. Watson with him three times; the latter not leaving him all night. His consciousness has returned—all think him better but it would not do for me to leave home at present, but I do hope to be able to sail within the next fortnight and shall telegraph the Anglo American Company before I leave.

The injury to Edward much later had grave consequences, and it is merciful that these, which were unavoidable, could not have been foreseen.

Field was able to leave for England the first week in February, 1867. His mission was twofold: to patch up the differences between the New York and London directors over the sloppy lines in Canada, and to contract with the Telegraph Construction & Maintenance Company for yet another cable to be laid that summer between Placentia, Newfoundland, and Sydney, Nova Scotia, to bypass Gisborne's obsolete landline between St. John's and Cape Ray. With these tasks disposed of, he had time to attend a banquet given for him by the Liverpool Chamber of Commerce, where he received another medal for his collection. Almost simultaneously, in America, President Andrew Johnson signed the congressional request for a gold medal to be struck in Field's honor in behalf of the United States, and the King of Italy conferred on him the cross of the Order of St. Mauritius, or Order of Knightly Commanders of Italy, from the country with whose Columbus he was being frequently compared. Later would come the Grand Prix, to him and his associates, awarded at the Paris Exposition.

He made a point of sailing home on the *Great Eastern* twelve days later, with Captain Anderson still at the helm. The ship was bizarrely changed from its cable-laying days, decked now in a showman's dream of gilt and silver with lemon-colored paneling and with accommodations for 3,000 luxury-addicted passengers. Once again the mercurially fated ship had changed hands. Napoleon III of France had formed a company that acquired her to ferry transatlantic visitors to his Paris Exposition. Daniel Gooch's aides had raised the price by circulating rumors that the Sultan of Turkey was about to buy the vessel for his harem. Napoleon corralled some $500,000 to obtain her charter and convert her to a floating palace. Gooch, perhaps from sentiment, then put up £20,000 of this investment.

Performing the past role of William Howard Russell as seagoing correspondent was a young French science-fiction writer named Jules Verne. The departure was ominous. Four men were killed in trying to hoist anchor, and subsequently there was a storm, in which another man was killed as hundreds of tons of water crashed over the deck and down the companionways. Among the macabre details Verne observed were the shattered corpses of 30,000 papier-mâché dolls, part of the cargo that was scattered by the raging water, inside and outside. Captain Anderson confided brokenheartedly, "My vessel is disgraced!"

Anderson ran with the storm till it subsided; but the ship was delayed for nearly a week, and Field arrived home to learn of his father's death in Stockbridge on April 15, 1867. The good doctor's departure had been gentle. He had been riding through his cherished Berkshire hills that sunny April afternoon, and returning home, as a friend described it, "he walked into the house with his old quick step, and sat down in the large armchair in the quiet parlor, just beneath the picture of that beloved daughter Mary, who had died some years before. A few minutes after, someone going into the room saw him sitting there, and going towards him, discovered on the instant that the imprisoned soul had fled."

The death of his father, following that of his mother, broke for Cyrus the silver cord that had bound him emotionally to his native Stockbridge. He returned only fleetingly thereafter, although both Dudley and Henry had homes in the surrounding hills. Instead, Cyrus bought a piece of property in the Hudson River Valley belonging to the brother of his first employer, A. T. Stewart. It was time, he felt, to assume the type of life becoming to his station, with a country estate, as well as a city home, at which to entertain his friends. The house, a three-story mansard-roofed affair, would require alterations and additions, and he would have to have a telephone installed, a cumbersome wiring operation at the time. (His grandson later complained that "neighbors came down at all hours to use it" and turned the house into an information center.) But he had already settled on a name. He would call it Ardsley after the English birthplace of John Field, the sixteenth-century astronomer.

That summer he spent largely in the Maritime Provinces where he directed his attention to laying the cable from Placentia to Sydney and to improving the operation and maintenance of the landlines running to New York.

He was faced, to his dismay, with a plethora of problems. The Atlantic cable, far from fulfilling the high hopes Field had had for it, was in a managerial and operational mess. The complaint against rates was growing louder. The line had not fully opened for commercial business until July 9, 1867, at which time the charge for messages was nearly $100 for a minimum of ten words. Even at this rate the company handled 2,772 messages between July 28 and October 31, resulting in a daily revenue of $2,500.

It was a fair return, but the company needed far more customers. To get them, the rate was cut by more than half—to $48.60 for ten words. This encouraged business and increased the daily take to $2,800. Even so, the two cables were operating at only 5 percent of capacity.

In addition to the matter of rates was the question of messages sent by code. Should they or should they not be allowed? Obviously the use of ciphers was a sensible way of reducing the number of required words. But a code suggested subterfuge and possible misuse of the cable for secret, sinister purposes. In England the code was banned. But was this being realistic? A government communicating with its emissaries overseas was certainly not going to use the cable for a confidential message unless the message could be coded. And a sender could, even by using intelligible words spelled out in full, transmit a message meaning something altogether different by a preestablished key.

Field appealed to Deane, as secretary of the Anglo-American Company, to urge cooperation in reducing rates and lowering the ban on ciphers:

There are people who can make messages apparently in plain text but which are actually cipher, and in the various attempts to get much into little there lies the germ of many disputes between customers and receiving clerks. The truth is, we make nothing and lose much. Many who were our best customers now use the line only in cases of emergency, whereas they would use it daily if our terms were liberal. The U. S. government and the representatives at Washington of all the foreign governments are determined to use us as little as possible. We are reviled on every side. The government, the press, and all the people will do all in their power to encourage a competing line. Something must be done to arrest this feeling.

Public complaints were compounded by errors in transmission. Messages were being badly garbled. Delays and corrections were extremely costly. Typical was a message sent as: "Letter thirteen received; you better travel," which came out as: "Letter thirteen received; son pretty well." A more serious matter was a message supposed to read: "Protect our drafts," but transmitted as "Protest our drafts."

Ironically, these mistakes were due in part to new, improved equipment and increased speed of transmission. Both took getting used to, on the part of management and operators; and presented a serious threat to the cable's usefulness and purpose. Shortly after the turn of the year Field wrote again to London:

> I think there can be no doubt if the several telegraph lines between London and New York were under an efficient management the business could be done much better and enormously increased, and I would work energetically with you, Mr. Morgan, and others to secure this object if it can be done in a satisfactory manner.

There existed an odd confusion of purposes between the Atlantic Telegraph Company and the New York, Newfoundland and London Telegraph Company. Theoretically they were a unit; both had originally been spawned by Cyrus Field, but one was predominantly English, and the other principally American. While some directors of each held shares in both, they represented different points of view, based largely on different national conditions.

One could hardly blame this internecine friction on the distrust that then existed between England and America, growing out of the Civil War. For the next five years Field would dedicate a large part of his time and effort to healing the breach which the war had opened between the two nations. With this principally in mind, he sailed for

England in February, 1868, taking with him his youngest daughter, Fanny, and Jeanie Lucinda, a niece, to keep her company.

They arrived on the twenty-ninth, were met by Junius Morgan, and swept into a dizzy whirl of social engagements and activities. Four entries from his diary are typical:

Tuesday, March 3. Went to Mr. Littons at Norwood to lunch, and afterwards visited the Crystal Palace. Rode through the underground Railway. In the evening Capt. Sir James Anderson, Lady Anderson, and Mr. Saward dined with us.

Wednesday, " 4. The Revd. Newman Hall and Lloyd breakfasted with us. Dined with Mr. and Mrs. Lloyd in the evening where we met Mrs. Napier & others.

Thursday, " 5. Lieut. Mitchell and others breakfasted with us. Visited the House of Commons. In the afternoon Mr. Edwin Field dined with us, and in the evening went with him and his daughters to see a collection of Water Colors where we met Miss Sullivan, Mr. Litton, and other friends.

Friday, " 6. Breakfasted with Capt. Galton. After, returned to Hotel and had Mr. Collett and others to breakfast with us. Lunched with Lord and Lady Russell at 2. Visited the House of Commons in the evening and heard Shaw Lefevre, Lord Stanley, W. E. Forster and others speak on the *Alabama* Claims.

The debate he heard that night was generally conciliatory and recognized some justice in the *Alabama* claims. Actually, in England there were many influential friends of the North both during and after the Civil War, many of them friends and backers of Field's. John Bright was outstanding among them, along with the Duke of Argyll, the Earl de Grey, Sir Stafford Northcote, and Lord Frederick Cavendish. At the evening's conclusion Field sent a private cablegram to Washington: "When you see the President, Mr. Seward, and Mr. Sumner, please say to them that I am perfectly convinced that the English government and people are very desirous of settling all questions in dispute between the United States and this country, and that with a little conciliation on both sides this desirable object can be accomplished."

Four days later he sponsored a dinner which had become a tradition. The invitation read: "In commemoration of the signature of the agreement for the establishment of a telegraph across the Atlantic on the 10th of March, 1854." Sixty guests crowded the banquet hall of the Buckingham Palace Hotel. Most were friends and directors of the Atlantic cable, but Field had also invited members of the press. He expected that this time much of the speechmaking would concern the *Alabama* claims, and he wanted to set the record straight. He established the tone of the evening in his welcoming address. Citing, as he generally made a point of doing, the work of his British associates in making the cable a success, he went on to say that:

> the paramount recollection that should gratify those gentlemen above and beyond all is the satisfaction that the enterprise we have completed binds together two nations that are absolutely brothers. Your fathers were my fathers. My venerable father, at seventy years of age, came to England, and spent six months in tracing out the genealogy of our family. Gentlemen, I say accursed be the man—I care not whether he be an Englishman or an American—that would sow discord between these two kindred nations.

In a speech that followed, Stuart-Wortley aimed those sentiments directly at the issue that divided England and America. Referring to the cable, he observed: "One of its greatest feats has been lately accomplished under the auspices of our worthy chairman by his sending the conciliatory debate on the *Alabama* Claims to America. I am very glad this has been done, as it is far more likely to create good feeling between the two countries than anything else."

A telegraph wire with receiving instruments had been installed in the banquet room, and messages were exchanged between Field and President Andrew Johnson, to be read to the assembly. Cyrus also took this opportunity to send a telegram to Mary. Its cool lack of imagination may be attributed to the fact that it was sent in public circumstances: "To Mrs. Cyrus Field, Gramercy Park, New York. We are now at dinner and all in excellent spirits, and hope that you and all that are with you in the same happy condition. . . . Please reply saying what time you receive this. Cyrus W. Field."

Mary dutifully replied that all were well and that she would be glad to entertain her husband's English guests at Gramercy Park someday. She neglected the critical query—how long it took her husband's telegram to reach her.

During the evening Field received a note from Gladstone. The

Chancellor was being kept by business at the House of Commons and explained:

> We shall be here until midnight but not without thoughts of your festival and of the greatness of the country with which it is connected. You are called upon to encounter difficulties and to sustain struggles which some years ago I should have said were beyond human strength. But I have learned to be more cautious in taking the measure of American possibilities; and, looking to your past, there is nothing which we may not hope of your future.

Field wound up the evening with a sly look to the future. In a toast to the memory of Richard Cobden, who had urged the British government to put up half the money for the Atlantic cable, he remarked: "If the government had followed his advice they would today be receiving half the dividends on the Anglo-American and Atlantic telegraph stocks. I hope this consideration may lead them to pursue a liberal policy in regard to the extension of the telegraph to India, China, and Australia."

It was the first time he had publicly expressed an interest, on prescribed lines, in the future of telegraphy. Was he now looking toward other seas to conquer?

22

Man of Two Worlds

➤➤➤➤➤➤◄◄◄◄◄◄ In the early spring of 1868 Field was riding the crest of popular recognition, as both hero of the Atlantic cable and international ambassador of goodwill. The matter of the Placentia-Nova Scotia cable had been arranged; there was no urgent business to attend to; he could relax, as much as his nature allowed, to the enjoyment of good food, good wine, and stimulating conversation with knowledgeable, active people like himself. Equally at home in England and America, he had become a man of two worlds and enjoyed the best of each.

He took a house on Clarges Street in London and there he gave elaborate breakfasts, prolonged luncheons running till midafternoon, beefsteak and Burgundy dinners that continued until midnight. Among his guests were the elite of aristocracy and politics: William Gladstone, Lord and Lady Russell, Sir James Shuttleworth, John Bright, the Earl de Grey, Lord and Lady Airlie, the Charles Francis Adamses, Sir Frederick Halliday, the Dowager Duchess of Somerset, and others who made the pages of his calendar read like *Burke's Peerage* blended with the *Social Register*.

The exclusive precincts of several St. James's clubs were open to him. He lunched and dined with Sir Henry Holland, First Lord of the Admiralty Sir Alexander Milne and Lady Milne, Lord Morley, Sir Austen Layard ("the Nineveh explorer"), Lord John Hay, the Marquis of Lime, Sir William Fenwick Williams, and, of course, his friends of longer standing—Junius Morgan, Charles Bright, Pender, Anderson, Gooch, and Varley. During the day he and the girls visited the Crystal Palace, whose American section had been arranged by George Peabody, and went to art exhibitions, afternoon receptions,

concerts, and, of course, to church on Sundays, especially to Westminster Abbey to hear Dean Arthur Penrhyn Stanley preach. Field
warmed quickly to the eminent divine, and they became close friends.

The Atlantic telegraph was on its feet financially, but the going
had been rough. On March 19, 1868, Field's diary noted: "Evening:
—The practical business men connected with the Atlantic Cable dined
with us." On that occasion he told his guests:

> It is within the last six months only that we have received the first
> return from the money we had put at the bottom of the Atlantic.
> I do not believe that any enterprise has ever been undertaken that
> has had such a fortune, that has been so low, and one might also say,
> so high. I have known the time when a thousand pounds of Atlantic
> telegraph stock sold in London at a high premium. I have known the
> time when a thousand pounds of the same stock was purchased by my
> worthy friend, Mr. Wortley [sic] for thirty guineas.

He also recalled:

> At one time when I was in London to raise money . . . a certificate
> for ten thousand dollars in the New York, Newfoundland and Lon-
> don Telegraph Company sold at the Merchants' Exchange in New
> York for a ten dollar bill.

The bewildered owner had asked Field on the latter's return to New
York what he ought to do with it.

> I told him, "Lock it up in your safe. Do not even think about or
> look at it until you receive a notice to collect your dividends." The
> holder now receives a dividend of eight-hundred dollars per annum
> in gold for his investment. If any gentleman here has ever possessed
> a more fluctuating investment I should like to hear it.

On July 1, there was to be another banquet in his honor, in Willis's Rooms, on King Street. Even for that starched period, it was an
extravagant event. It was attended by close to 300 guests, epitomizing,
reported the *Daily Telegraph,* "the rank, fortune, talent, and energy
which compose the world of London." Ferdinand de Lesseps came
from Suez to be present, and even the irascible Charles Dickens found
something American he could honor.

The Duke of Argyll presided. Being a scientist, he put the cable in
a new perspective—as a product of basic research, "of the pure desire
and love of knowledge." It sprang, he said, from the laboratory work

of men like Thomson, Faraday, Wheatstone, and Varley, who were pursuing nothing more than their own curiosity. Without this selfless dedication little could have been accomplished. But to bring their diverse skills together and lead their findings to fruition, it took the perception and energy of one like Field. One could not overlook the commercial motive, but "of all commercial enterprises which have ever been undertaken, this one on the part of Mr. Cyrus Field represents the noblest and purist motives by which commercial enterprise can ever be inspired."

He concluded: "On these grounds, ladies and gentlemen, I ask you to drink his health. But on one other ground also I ask you to drink it, that he is personally one of the most genial and kindly-hearted of men."

Field took note of Argyll's reference to commercial motives, observing that "on this very day the holders of every description of Atlantic Telegraph stock have received a dividend," a comment which drew laughter and applause. He also revealed again his thinking for the future: "Do not, my friends, be content with having connected Europe and America together by the electric cord, but remember that India, Australia, China and Japan, South America, and the isles of the sea, both in the east and in the west, have yet to be brought into instant communication with England and America."

An abortive aftermath of this affair was instigated by John L. O'Sullivan, one of the many characters who popped in and out of Field's life, sometimes from one angle, sometimes from another. O'Sullivan had helped guide Field toward the Manifest Destiny concept in the forties, had opposed him on the Southern question in the early sixties, and now rose to champion his compatriot in a letter to Lord Edward Henry Stanley. Stanley was the son of Lord Derby, who as Queen Victoria's Prime Minister had conferred extraordinary honors on the English members of the cable enterprise. Now, what could be done for Cyrus Field? Listing Field's hardships and contributions in connection with the cable, O'Sullivan noted: "He was to it what Peter the hermit was to the first Crusade. He was the very *steam* of it. . . . When his thread would break he was no more disheartened than Bruce's spider. Without him there would have been no Atlantic Cable." O'Sullivan contended that England "ought to do something more than a dinner at Willis's Rooms!" Aware that Lord Stanley was one of the sponsors of a statue to George Peabody, the American-born philanthropist, he concluded: "One to Field would be a still finer act of cosmopolitan recognition of service to the whole world, & of oneness of nations in sentiment towards great cosmopolitan benefactors."

No statue to Field was ever erected, and he was most likely unaware of the proposal. But when he returned to America that fall in time to vote for General Grant, he was summoned to Washington to receive the medal which Congress had voted him two years before. It was as evanescent as the statue. Arriving at the capital, he was told apologetically that the medal had disappeared. After having been cast in gold and approved by the Cabinet, a bewildered clerk had for some reason sent it to the mint in Philadelphia. The mint had been equally confused. Not knowing of anything better to do, they had drilled a hole through the middle. A duplicate was being ordered, and Field was asked to keep the embarrassing matter quiet.

Storm clouds were meanwhile gathering. The success of the Atlantic cable led inevitably to the projection of competing lines. Toward the close of 1868 both Field and Peter Cooper were dismayed to learn that a new European company, the Société du Câble Trans-Atlantique Français, had been organized in Paris to lay a cable from Brest to the tiny French island of St. Pierre, just south of Newfoundland, and on to Duxbury, Massachusetts. The distance—over 3,300 miles—was more than twice as long as the first Atlantic line. Submarine telegraphy now enjoyed such public favor that the entire capital of $6,000,000 was subscribed in only eight days. Especially galling was the fact that much of the money came from England, some of it from Field's past supporters.

The Anglo-American and the New York, Newfoundland and London companies bitterly opposed the new line, but had no legal grounds to stand on. Their exclusive landing rights, extending from Maine to Labrador did not cover St. Pierre and Massachusetts. The directors had relied on the great distance, from those points to Europe, to protect them. Now, with improvements in cable manufacture, distance had ceased to be a factor. Cooper persuaded Charles Sumner, then chairman of the Senate Committee on Foreign Relations, to introduce a bill in Congress extending the company's landing rights to Massachusetts—a move branded by the New York *Herald* as "about the meanest swindle ever before Congress."

There was too much opposition to the "telegraph monopoly ring" to check this threatening competition, and Congress ruled in favor of the new line. The Telegraph Construction & Maintenance Company agreed to make the cable, the *Great Eastern* was secured to lay it. The fact that all the experience, all the manufacturing facilities, and all the public investor confidence created by Field's companies were now appropriated by the competition was a source of consternation and, of course, of bitter controversy.

Among Field's companies on both sides of the ocean a certain reaction seemed to set in. As often happens with a war won, the allies were at odds about the peace and the administration of the captured territory.

So alarmed was Cromwell Varley, since, like many of them, he held shares in all three companies concerned with the Atlantic cable, that, during a visit to New York, he told Peter Cooper:

> It seems as if they were re-enacting just the same farces that were performed when we were endeavoring to raise funds both for the 1865 and 1866 cables. I venture unhesitatingly to assert that we should not have succeeded but for the indomitable energy and the excellent judgment of Mr. Cyrus Field.

He went on to say:

> I do not believe the present attempt at an adjustment will end in any useful results unless someone like Mr. Cyrus Field, enjoying the confidence and personal regard of those interested on this side, as well as such men as Brassey, Hawkshaw, Fairbairn, Fowler, Gladstone, Bright, Whitworth, and others in Europe, go to England empowered to act on behalf of your company.

It sounded like old times, the call for Field's reassuring presence. He agreed to return to London as soon as possible, but meanwhile suggested that Varley take time to acquaint himself with the American telegraph operation. This Varley did and concluded that the industry needed some sort of czar, and Field was obviously the man. Mergers and consolidation tended to force together hostile factions with opposing points of view.

Field had no intention of being czar of anything. Right now he was concerned with a banquet that he, Abiel Low, and the portrait painter Daniel Huntington were planning for Samuel Finley Morse. Morse and Field were back in each other's favor, and Cyrus headed the invitation committee. The dinner took place at Delmonico's, Fifth Avenue and Fourteenth Street, on December 29. Coats of arms of all nations using the Morse patents decorated the banquet hall and the 200 guests represented, according to the press, "practically every man of prominence in New York at that time."

Field installed what had now become a feature of most ceremonial events, a telegraph set. By it, he was able to read to the assembly congratulatory messages to Morse from President Johnson, President-elect Grant, Speaker Schuyler Colfax, Admiral Farragut, and others. Not unexpectedly, Morse again used the occasion to mount the dais in defense of his invention, which had been for so long in dispute: "I have claimed for America the origination of the modern telegraph system of the world. Impartial history, I think, will support the claim." Morse, however, shared that history with the Almighty, declaring that the final message was "not what hath man, but 'what hath God wrought.' "

A week later, in early January, 1869, Field sailed for Europe accompanied by William Orton. Rather than accept czarship over the Atlantic and domestic lines, he felt the answer lay in still further consolidation, a merger between the Anglo-American and Atlantic telegraph companies. One was the successor to the other anyway, and their purposes overlapped. His larger goal was to absorb the Société du Câble Trans-Atlantique Français, so that all Atlantic cables would be under one coordinated management.

For a change, on an Atlantic crossing, Field was not concerned with business. He was joining his wife and daughters, who had sailed ahead of him, in Paris, where Fanny was marrying James Bruyn Andrews, a young New Yorker in the Foreign Service. After the wedding on March 17, Cyrus took Mary and Isabella down to Pau in southern France. At the expensive Hôtel de l'Univers, they dined well on the region's famous *jambons de Bayonne,* drank the white wine of Jurançon, attended the Protestant church built by the Duchess of Gordon ("It is unfortunate that it should be so very ugly a building"), and admired the startling view of the saw-toothed Pyrenees.

Characteristically Field could not long abide a life of cultivated indolence. Leaving his wife and daughter to enjoy the sun, he went back to England in the late spring, where the so-called *Alabama* claims were reaching a disturbing crisis, as they were in the United States.

Originally these claims had referred chiefly to damages inflicted by Confederate raiders operating out of British ports. A settlement had been attempted with the signing of the Johnson-Clarendon Convention earlier that year. But with Grant as President and Sumner active in the Senate, this was thrown out. Sumner had made an impassioned speech accusing England of incalculable damages through its recognition of Southern belligerency. He raised the total claim to $2,125,-000,000, with the implication that it could be met only by ceding Canada to the United States, a preposterous idea. In England it was widely thought that this meant war.

Field felt there was justice in the claims but agreed with Secretary of State Hamilton Fish, by far the strongest member of Grant's Cabinet, that they could be settled by further arbitration. He was in a unique position to be useful. With Gladstone's return to power, he had four friends high in the British government: the Prime Minister and three members of his Cabinet, Lord Clarendon, the Duke of Argyll, and John Bright. In America, he had the ear of Grant and was friendly with Vice-President Colfax, Secretary Fish, Charles Sumner, and William Seward. With the last two, who advocated an unyielding attitude toward England, he was in disagreement. But they would listen to him; that was something. At any other time in history Field might have been acceptable as a representative of the United States. But with distrust of England widespread in America, he could only work for his country in an unofficial, personal capacity. This he did, with somewhat the same dedication he devoted to the cable.

Much as he disagreed with Sumner, he called on the Senator several times in Washington, after his return from London in mid-June. In a follow-up letter, he wrote: "I do most sincerely hope that we shall soon have a better feeling between this country and England, and I know of no one that can do more to bring about this desirable result than yourself. You may be sure that I shall do all I can." He urged Sumner to write John Bright "frankly" and get that liberal Englishman's opinions or even to invite Bright to America for consultation.

Sumner rejected the latter idea, but Field continued to pin much faith on John Bright as an intermediary in this dispute. Bright had a shrewd understanding of the American nature, tolerance for its faults, and appreciation of its virtues. If he could visit the country, his very presence would do much to calm resentment and suspicion. Ignoring Sumner's attitude, Field drew up an invitation signed by himself and such men of influence as William Cullen Bryant, Peter Cooper, Abiel Low, and Hamilton Fish: "Your presence at this time would tend to strengthen the ties between your country and ours, and we beg leave to suggest a visit during the ensuing Spring." Bright replied: "I am deeply indebted for your kind invitation. . . . I need not tell you how many are my engagements here, and how uncertain is the prospect of my being able to see the many kind friends I have in the States."

Alone, Field could get nowhere in his persistent talks with Sumner, and perhaps in the hope of getting rid of Cyrus at least for a while, the Foreign Relations Committee chairman put forward a wholly unrelated proposition. He wrote to the Secretary of State recommending that Field represent the United States at the formal opening of the Suez Canal since he had been present at the preview several years before. "He would like to do so," assumed Sumner conveniently, "but will not make any application ... is personally well acquainted with Mr. de Lesseps, who came a long way to be at the banquet in London given for Mr. Field. ... I do not think of any person who would be more truly a 'representative man' for this post."

Field declined to go. He was busy settling the family at Ardsley, their new country house in Irvington. It was a massive Victorian house of brick and slate, square and somewhat tasteless, but comfortable and roomy. A wide veranda along the back looked out across the Hudson to the Palisades, a view similar to those enjoyed by Finley Morse and Hamilton Fish from farther up the river. Some fifty acres of parkland, with groves of pines and chestnut trees, surrounded the house and sloped down to the Hudson, and Field planned to expand this to a sort of family compound of several hundred acres, providing homes for his children and grandchildren. Meanwhile, they would keep the Gramercy Park house for city living.

Ardsley all but adjoined Lyndhurst, the Irvington estate of Jay Gould, and it was inevitable that this proximity should breed acquaintance, if not friendship. Gould commuted to Wall Street on his private steam launch, and occasionally Field joined him. There was also a connection in that Dudley Field was attorney for the Erie Railroad. When it was announced that President Grant would attend the Peace Jubilee in Boston in mid-June, 1869, Gould and James Fisk included Field. Fisk had just bought the Narragansett Steamship Company. He and Gould invited the President to sail to Fall River, Massachusetts, on one of their two new luxury steamers, the *Providence*. Field was invited to join the party and naturally accepted: Grant was his friend, and Gould his neighbor. Along with Secretary of the Treasury George Boutwell, they boarded the *Providence* at Chambers Street to be greeted by a brass band, 250 singing canaries, and "Admiral" Jim Fisk "in full uniform and lavender kid gloves."

On the surface it was an innocent enough excursion. But its hidden purpose was to sound Grant out on Gould's plan to manipulate the price of gold, and undoubtedly Field had been asked along, not only as a friend of Grant, but also to lend an aura of propriety to the occasion. Nothing came of this jubilee voyage for Gould; nothing for Fisk, except the nickname Jubilee Jim. But for Field it was an unfortunate association. Black Friday and the financial pandemonium that Gould created were only thirteen weeks away.

It was the beginning of several unfortunate associations. It was Field's Achilles' heel to see the best in people and refuse to recognize the worst. It was also natural that as a wealthy man, he was often thrown with other wealthy men, some in the robber baron class. He was sometimes assigned to this group, but he had got where he was by overcoming obstacles, not people.

He never hesitated, however, to use friendship to promote a worthy cause. During that summer he bombarded President Grant, Fish, Colfax, and Sumner with letters advocating moderation on the *Alabama* claims. He circulated the view of Yale's president, Theodore D. Woolsey, on the subject, which coincided with his. Nor did he overlook his English friends. He pinned much faith on John Bright, and wrote to him on August 9:

> I am more than ever convinced that if the English government would send to Washington yourself, the Duke of Argyll, and Earl Granville as special ambassadors to act with the British minister, the whole controversy between England and America could be settled in a few months. Please give the matter your careful consideration.

Bright replied from Rochdale, qualifying his comments with the note:

> I write all this privately to you. It is not from a Cabinet minister, but from an old friend of yours, who is . . . in no degree expressing any opinion but my own.

The British government, Bright felt, had done all that it could, had signed the Johnson-Clarendon Convention in good faith, only to see the agreement torn to shreds in Washington. Who could say that any future agreement would not be similarly treated? Bright went on:

> If you have an envoy who has no power to negotiate, and an executive government which cannot ratify a treaty, where is the security for further negotiation? . . . I could easily suggest a mode of settlement which all mankind, outside the two countries, would approve of; but how do I know what your government will do? If there is passion enough for Mr. Sumner to appeal to, or believers in his wild

theories of international obligation, how can any settlement be looked for?

Field replied: "I regret Mr. Sumner's speech and his course of action about the *Alabama* claims more than I can express and shall do all I can to counteract the effects of his action. . . . I am anxious to do all in my power to keep good feeling between England and America."

It was partly to make good these words that Field sailed for England in December, 1869. There were also other matters on his mind. In the North Atlantic zone alone the question of cable competition versus unity (often branded as monopoly) was reaching a state of confusion like that which had existed in domestic telegraphy in the 1850's, when assorted companies were out to cut one another's throats. There were cries for government control and even government ownership of domestic lines, which would in turn affect the usefulness of the Atlantic cable. Success had spawned a whole new set of problems.

23

Eyes on the Pacific

➤➤➤➤➤➤◄◄◄◄◄◄ In the decade beginning with 1870 cables proliferated around the world, spreading under the seas in all directions. The *Great Eastern* had completed the cable from Brest to Massachusetts. Britain and India were finally successfully linked, and a further extension was projected from Singapore to Australia. Virtually no country or even major city in the Northern Hemisphere was inaccessible to telegraphic communication.

"Few things are duller," Arthur Clarke wrote, "than a record of steady and uninterrupted progress; when the telegraph fleet first anchored in Heart's Content on July 27, 1866, the adventurous, pioneering days were over, and with them the excitement they engendered."

From this time on Field seemed motivated more by obligation than by inspiration; some of the fire of enthusiasm disappeared.

His immediate goal on arriving in England in January was to get the Atlantic cable and its auxiliary lines operating smoothly and to be free to look toward other theaters of expansion. The Anglo-American and Atlantic telegraph companies were consolidated, with the former absorbing the latter under its name. On January 15, an agreement was signed between this combine, the French Société, and the New York, Newfoundland and London Telegraph Company, making them all partners, with a "common purse," in the control and management of the North Atlantic cable business.

There was a significant clause in the agreement that would come up later—namely, that the New York, Newfoundland and London Telegraph Company was "the sole representative in America of the cable combination of which said company is a member." This pinned on the New York company the responsibility for its end of the operation that in Europe was still somewhat scattered.

With this consolidation established, Field thought he could leave the North Atlantic cable business to its own momentum. Sailing for home in April, Field spread a map of the world across his table and inked in the major telegraph lines and submarine cables he knew existed or were being built in Europe, Asia, and America.

The resultant calligraphy showed, of course, one great gap, the Pacific Ocean, along with a small section of Siberia, where a line was under contract for construction. Except for the latter (and he inked that in with a row of dots), communication was complete from San Francisco running east toward the rising sun to Shanghai, for practical purposes around the world. But the white expanse of ocean was a challenge to Field's dream.

It was time, this March, 1870, for another meeting of his 1854 associates. Except for Chandler White, he was able to gather in his study essentially the same group as before: Cooper, Morse, Taylor, Roberts, Hunt, and Dudley Field. They were noticeably aging and grown a little portly; Field, too, filled out with the good years of success, appeared less wiry and tense, a little more the bearded patriarch. To this gathering he invited fresh blood in the persons of William Webb and Darius Ogden Mills.

Both were in the Gilded Age tradition of self-made giants. The stocky, bullet-headed Webb had rivaled Donald McKay in building the greatest aggregate tonnage of ships produced in America, including the famous *Golden Gate* for the Pacific Mail Steamship Company and clippers for the China trade. He knew the routes and islands of the North Pacific. Ogden Mills, a Californian, who had made his money in the Sierra gold mines, had come East to establish himself in a Fifth Avenue mansion "of which a Shah of Persia might have been proud." More important, both men were as well known financially in San Francisco and throughout the West as in the East.

Field spread out his map and traced the alternate routes of his proposed Pacific cable. Both went from San Francisco to Tokyo and then to Shanghai; but one rode via the Aleutians, the other traversed the Hawaiian Islands. The group unanimously voted to present to Congress a bill entitled "An act to incorporate the Pacific Submarine Telegraph Company, and to facilitate telegraphic communication between America and Asia."

The bill authorized the organization of the company with a capital of $10,000,000, with authority to lay a cable "from the shores of the State of California to Japan and the Empire of China, either direct or by the way of the Hawaiian Islands, or other island or islands of the Pacific Ocean, by the most practicable or eligible route." It provided for ships of the United States Navy to survey the route and help lay the cable within three to five years after the company was founded. No government subsidy or other special privileges were considered.

Although Field wrote a memorandum to accompany the proposal, he was shrewd enough to get John Ward, former minister to China, to present the bill to Congress. Ward first tackled the Foreign Relations Committee and did a masterful job. He noted the 400,000,000 people of China "sometimes starving for want of food" and the billions of wheat-growing acres in America. Clipper ships were not enough to bridge this gap; equally important was communication on market needs and prices. He also cited a letter to Field from Admiral David Dixon Porter confirming the need for better naval communication in the Pacific, by which "four vessels would be as useful to him as six are now." He also waved the red flag of British competition:

> Let us refuse to assume its control, and from British Columbia, instead of San Francisco, the cable will soon be laid by the Government, or people of Great Britain, to her own colony at the mouth of the Canton River.... This immortal discovery, due to the genius of one of our own people. Its greatest development accomplished by the restless energy and patriotism of another, is thus disgracefully abandoned to our rivals.

Of the nine promoters, Ward observed that they:

> are neither speculators nor adventurers, but are men known throughout the civilized world, and honored wherever commercial integrity is recognized as a virtue. They are asking no alms from Congress, but offer in exchange vastly more than they receive ... ask nothing from the nation until success has been achieved.

He concluded:

> A grand foundation has been laid and a noble superstructure erected. Leave not the work unfinished and incomplete. Crown its summit with this electric capstone, and "put a girdle round about the earth in forty minutes."

With this strong support, Field got the backing of Abiel Low and the New York Chamber of Commerce, which urged Congress to approve the bill. The Chamber's resolution did, however, note the missing link across Siberia, referring to it as "soon to be laid." Actually, its future was in the hands of Alexander II of Russia, whom Field thought of approaching next. Meanwhile, he had an alternative, as he wrote on April 23:

> If I obtain (as I hope) my telegraph bill, I propose that the Pacific Submarine Telegraph Company make an agreement, offensive and defensive, with the submarine lines from England to China *via* India. Our cable would give an alternate route from China to England, and I would suggest that we have a joint office in China, and that parties there have the option of either line; and in case one line should be down, messages should be immediately forwarded by the other.

Congress could hardly ignore the project. It had done much to approve and subsidize the ships of the Pacific Mail Steamship Company and the railroads now running from coast to coast which advertised: "Passengers to China this way!" A cable connection with the Orient seemed a logical concomitant of this development. Field had submitted figures obtained from Captain Sherard Osborn, now managing director of the Telegraph Construction & Maintenance Company, for a Pacific cable 7,843 nautical miles long, costing altogether nearly $15,000,000, or almost $2,000 a mile. Possibly because of this high estimate, he revised his route, and wrote on August 20:

> At the request of prominent members of the United States government we have decided to adopt the following route for the Pacific cable:
>
> | | | |
> |---|---:|---|
> | San Francisco to Sandwich [Hawaiian] Islands .... | 2,080 | miles |
> | Sandwich Islands to Medway [Midway] Island .... | 1,140 | " |
> | Medway Island to Yokohama .... | 2,260 | " |
> | Yokohama to Shang-Hai .... | 1,035 | " |
> | | 6,515 | " |

Field had experienced much frustration at the hands of a reluctant Congress, but nothing could have prepared him for the incredible delay and sidestepping that this proposition met. Perhaps fortunately, however, his impatience was diverted by another problem: the question of government control or ownership of domestic lines.

From C. C. Washburn, chairman of the Postal Telegraph Committee in the House of Representatives, Field received a letter:

Dear Sir: The Special Committee on the Postal Telegraph, well knowing your familiarity with the subject of Telegraphy, and the interest you have taken in the extension of the blessings of the Telegraph throughout the world, has instructed me to solicit your opinion in regard to the measure now before Congress, which proposes to combine in the hands of the Government the Telegraph with the Postal Service. Is it reasonable to expect that the great boon of cheap communication by Telegraph will be reached by competition between private lines, or the voluntary reduction of tariffs, so long as the Telegraph is managed by private Companies? What would be the effect of the assumption of the Lines by the Government? . . . Could the Government manage the business as cheaply and efficiently as now managed? What knowledge have you in regard to the operation of the Telegraph in other countries in connection with the Post Office?

Would a Government system in this country at such rates as to bring the Telegraph into use with the masses of people be self-sustaining, or would it be a charge in the Government?

Field replied that he would look into the matter, and promptly wrote to Thomas H. Dudley, the United States consul in Liverpool, with whom he had been in touch before: "My only desire is that the Government & people of the United States shall have the best and cheapest telegraph system in the world; and then I believe that it would be used much more extensively in this country than in any other." Since the United Kingdom had already imposed government control, he asked Dudley for "your opinion on this subject, and also the tariff on telegraph messages in Great Britain & Ireland, and whether the business is well done by the Government."

Strangely enough, considering New England's penchant for free enterprise, Field was in favor of government ownership of domestic lines. Using the figures and facts from Dudley that supported this view, he wrote to Washburn: ". . . I am firmly convinced it would be wise on the part of the Government to purchase all the telegraph lines in this country at a fair valuation, and combine them with the Post Office Department, and that this can be done with advantage to the Government and great benefit to the people." He went on to say, "I think every post office in America should be a telegraph office, and that in the large cities letter boxes in the street should be used to receive telegrams. . . . The rates could, in my opinion, even be reduced to twenty-five cents to any part of the country."

Field knew that government ownership would end the wrangling between domestic companies, unify and probably reduce rates between American cities, and make the use of the Atlantic cable cheaper and more universal. There was a degree of self-interest in this attitude, certainly, but it was an enlightened self-interest.

In his reply to Washburn he could not resist taking a swipe at a small-time competitor, the International Ocean Telegraph Company, with cable and landlines from Florida to Cuba. The company charged $4 per ten word message between the two points, with a $2 surcharge if the message was destined for Europe via the Atlantic line—from Havana to London, for example. This was a direct penalty placed on the use of Field's cable. "Such an unjust discrimination as this would not be allowed by the government for a day," he wrote. By way of contrast, he cited his own company's operation:

> The lowest price for a telegraph message between New York and England was, when the line was opened for business (less than four years since), one-hundred dollars in gold. This has been reduced from time to time, until it is now $7.50 between the same points for a message of ten words, and only $3.75 for a message of the same length containing political and general news for the press, and I hope that the business will increase so that we can continue to reduce the tariff from time to time until a message can be sent from any part of the United States to any part of Europe for one dollar.

Agitation for government control or ownership was to continue for the next thirty years until, by 1900, domestic telegraphy had corrected its own faults largely through the discipline of healthy competition. In the meantime Field turned his attention back to the Pacific cable. Six months after submitting his proposal to the legislature, he was writing with (for him) extraordinary self-restraint: "It is uncertain what Congress will do with regard to the Pacific Telegraph." He might have come closer to exploding with impatience, except for an opportunity arising from association with his longtime pastor Dr. William Adams.

Adams was a staunch pillar of the Evangelical Alliance, an organization formed in Britain in 1846 to promote spiritual union among Protestants. The Alliance had strongly supported international arbitration on the *Alabama* claims, resolving "that between the different branches of the Anglo-Saxon race the sword can never be called in as arbiter." Field not only had contributed generously to the movement, but also had worked with Adams and Dr. Philip Schaff of the

Alliance in their campaign for conciliation. Now Adams and Schaff were concerned with another objective: relief for the religiously oppressed in Russia. The Lutheran Church especially had suffered persecution in the former German provinces of Russia, and delegates from eight European countries and America were gathering to wait upon the Czar and urge reforms.

There had been intimations from abroad that "between the absolutism of Russia and the Republic of America there exists a certain kind of sympathy," so that the United States delegation had high standing in the group. Field was one of nine Americans to make the journey, via London, to St. Petersburg. They were rerouted and ended up in Friedrichshafen, where Field became acquainted with the artful diplomacy of the Russians.

Alexander II apparently had no intention of receiving what he regarded as a group of meddlers. He ducked from place to place avoiding them and finally referred the delegation, first to Prince Gortschakoff as his representative, then to the Grand Duke Constantine. The grand duke cautiously acknowledged the just protests of the group, but warned that "the goodwill of the Emperor is an uncertain guarantee." He reminded them of how, when Alexander I was told by Mme. de Staël, "Sire, you are the constitution of the Russian empire," he had replied, "Madame, I am not a constitution; I am only an accident." As the interview progressed, the grand duke showed no reaction other than mild irritation, although he did promise to lay the delegation's views before his master.

Field stopped in London on the way back and, the night before sailing for America, sent a memorial to be delivered to the emperor from "Cyrus West Field, a citizen of the United States of America."

It was long and skillfully worded, its facts tempered with flattery. He pointed to past achievements in submarine telegraphy and the 40,000 miles of cables then in operation. He stressed the great interest in America for a Pacific cable as a means of promoting Russo-American commerce and relations, noting:

> From communications which memorialist has had with the government of the United States and with many leading members of Congress, he is able to say with confidence that both the government and the legislature takes a deep interest in the subject, and that, as memorialist believes, they will readily join with your Majesty in making such arrangements as may be found necessary to carry out the enterprise.

The cable would be 6,000 miles in length, made in at least two sections and meeting at "one or more islands in the Pacific Ocean." The cost was left as something that "cannot be ascertained until the route is definitely settled." What he expected from the Emperor was that, among lesser provisions, both Russia and the United States should guarantee, for twenty-five years, an interest of 3 percent per year on the cost of the line; that all profits above 6 percent annually should be split between the stockholders and respective governments; and that at the end of the twenty-five years of guarantee the company should own the cable. "Memorialist believes that with such assistance . . . the cables could be made and laid within three years."

He received no answer. With rumbles of a revolutionary movement in his empire—and throughout Europe, for that matter—it is doubtful that Alexander looked on a free exchange of international information as an asset. Field persisted with a follow-up letter to the Grand Duke five weeks later, adding, as a bait, a few provisions "which I think will commend themselves to your good judgment." The first of these were:

1. The proposed guarantee of three percent *not* to commence until the day the cable is completed and in successful working order.
2. The amount of capital guaranteed *not* to exceed £3,000,000.
3. The company to bind itself not to kill seals, nor to deal in furs in any portion of Russian territory.

"It is important," he appended, "that I should know the views of His Imperial Majesty's government at the earliest moment, as the Congress of the United States meets on the first Monday in December." Neither he nor Congress pressed hard on the matter. Field had other worries.

On November 30, 1870, both Atlantic cables ceased to work. Their functioning had been erratic from the start. During the previous year the cable of 1866 had operated only 99 days out of the 365. Oddly enough, the older, recovered cable had done somewhat better. But the simultaneous stoppage in each threw a heavy strain on the remaining French cable between Brest and Massachusetts, which also began to be hopelessly blocked with long press messages from Europe. As a remedial measure, rates were temporarily doubled, and a fifty-word limit was imposed.

There was no immediate protest. The restrictive move seemed justified, but serious trouble was set off by two messages sent at the turn of the year, each giving in code the Liverpool weekly quotations on cotton. One read: "Wright, New York. Choral absolute assign bridal migrate longitude lispingly romance ointment melodious MacIntosh liturgy. Bates."

The other, containing similar camouflaged information, was sent by the Associated Press as part of its news service. Both were filed in Liverpool at precisely the same time. But the first was dispatched and received in New York *seventeen hours* ahead of the A.P. message.

J. W. Simonton, general agent of the New York Associated Press, protested to Field, reminding him that responsibility for delivering messages in America rested with the New York, Newfoundland and London Telegraph Company. He charged that nine previous A.P. messages had been similarly delayed, whereas other cablegrams filed in England had been promptly relayed. Obviously, noted Simonton, favoritism of a sinister sort was operating. When these time discrepancies were applied to stock quotations, they took on a double and shady significance.

Field's secretary reported he had left his office; later he was said to be ill, then that he was about to leave for England and preoccupied with other matters. Simonton persisted and Field wrote that he was looking into the matter. "All messages must, by law and agreement between the companies, be forwarded in the exact order in which they are received," he announced, and sent a somewhat ambiguous letter, written on behalf of his directors, pointing to the blockage in the cable system and the general confusion it had caused.

Field was apparently trying to protect his English colleagues. The delay had been in sending, not receiving, so the responsibility fell on Henry Weaver, general cable manager in London. Unwilling to lay the blame to Weaver, Field wanted to avoid the issue. Simonton would not let him. After four exasperating months with no good explanation, Simonton turned his correspondence over to the press. The *Journal of Commerce* felt the matter was serious enough to comment on editorially. On May 13 the paper observed:

> We regret that Mr. Cyrus W. Field should so far compromise himself, as to allow his character and reputation to serve in any way as a shield for the wrongdoers; but we are frank to say, that since the cable first went into operation, his conduct in this respect has justified the censure of all right-minded men. We do not go as far as some in attributing directly to his counsel and influence the tricky, illicit, and disreputable course pursued by these monopolies.

But, said the writer, he owed to all concerned a frank explanation of "his own connection with evident abuses of official power."

Field would not offer an explanation that incriminated someone else. He pointed instead and again to the clogged condition of the cables and the inevitable confusion therefrom. The New York *World* responded simply, "Humbug!" and the *Times* reported: "It would almost seem that Mr. Cyrus W. Field desired to rival the reputation of his brother of 'pettyfogging.' " This must have stung, for Dudley Field, as attorney for the Erie Railroad, had done a questionable job of whitewashing when he could and defending when he could not, the culpable performances of Jay Gould and Boss Tweed.

The accusations were fortunately short-lived, and left Cyrus Field more or less unscathed. His reputation was too solid. Nonetheless, it was unwise to fight the Associated Press. Rumors began spreading that he was about to finance a newspaper empire and, with the aid of Jay Gould, was planning to take over the New York *Times*.

Field was busy with other matters, notably the claims dispute with England. On his return from London he called on Charles Sumner in Washington and laid before the Foreign Relations Committee chairman what he believed, from talks with Gladstone and the Earl de Grey, would be an acceptable approach. It was that the United States name three heads of government, from whom Great Britain would pick one as final arbiter, or that, vice versa, England designate three likely rulers, and America select one.

Sumner did not favor the idea. The New York *Herald* reported: "With all his respect for royalty, he does not think the United States will get a fair show from any of the crowned heads of Europe. He is opposed to all sorts of arbitration in this matter, because he considers it beneath the dignity of our government to submit to anything of the kind."

Though nothing came of the talks the principle advanced was sound. It is worth noting that the British commission which met with Hamilton Fish and his associates in Washington in February, 1871, was composed of several of Field's closest British friends: Sir Edward Thornton, the Earl de Grey, Sir Stafford Northcote, and the Marquis of Ripon. From this meeting evolved the Treaty of Washington, which did, in fact, submit the dispute to a tribunal named by the crowned heads of Europe and the American President.

In early June, 1871, a statue of Finley Morse was unveiled in Central Park. Field had been one of the sponsoring group that had financed the monument and had also solicited $1 contributions from "Morse's children," the telegraph operators of America. Morse, out of modesty or failing health (he had just passed his eightieth birthday), did not attend; but present were Theodore Roosevelt with Morse's daughter, Leila, Governors John T. Hoffman and William Claflin of New York and Massachusetts, and William Cullen Bryant, who with customary florid oratory set the keynote of the dedication:

> Every telegraph station is a memorial. . . . Every telegraph wire strung from post to post, as it hums in the wind, murmurs his eulogy. Every sheaf of wires laid down in the deep sea, occupying the bottom of soundless abysses to which human sight has never penetrated, is a testimonial to his greatness. . . . The whole world itself has become his monument.

Morse appeared at the evening gathering in his honor at the Academy of Music and thanked those who had befriended him throughout a turbulent, inventive life, particularly Cyrus Field, Joseph Henry, Ezra Cornell, and Alfred Vail. In closing, he sent his valedictory to the countries of the New World and the Old, manipulating the telegraph key to sign his name in the dots and dashes of the Morse code: "Greetings and Glory to God in the highest, on earth peace, goodwill to men." As the replies poured back from every continent, the white-haired master dropped his head in his arthritic hands and wept.

Field spent a peaceful summer with his family at Ardsley. The green lawns carpeting the sloping hills were growing richer and more settled. The cows and chickens he had dreamed of, during his deep-sea battles with the cable, were producing at sufficient speed to satisfy him. The view of a placid Hudson in its heyday of palatial river steamers was a restful contrast with the stormy North Atlantic that had been his arena for so many years. Mary had her greenhouse, one of the largest in the county, and bunches of fresh-cut flowers were delivered almost daily to their house on Gramercy Park. Wherever they lived or moved, they dwelt in greenery.

Two sons and three daughters were now at home. Fanny was with her husband at Menton in southern France. Isabella's husband had died, and she had returned with her two young sons to live with her parents at Ardsley; both Alice and Mary were at home, and Edward and Cyrus junior were being groomed for college. It fitted Cyrus senior's nature to have two homes in operation. He shuttled between Ardsley and New York with restless frequency, and the city house was always open to his host of friends. He never asked that these be cosily congenial, only that they be stimulating. To mix Jay Gould with Horace Greeley, Hamilton Fish with Samuel Tilden, provided high-pressure conversation.

In October, 1871, the great fire which devastated Chicago moved him to action, as disaster always did. Field contributed to and sought aid for the stricken thousands of that city and looked for help as much in England as among his neighbors. He used the cable to urge wealthy British friends like Peabody and Morgan to solicit funds in their financial circles. The response from London was so generous that Mayor Roswell B. Mason wired him: "Receive our warmest blessing for your most noble response to our stricken city. It was received by our committee in tears."

As a representative of American cable and telegraph interests, Field was invited by the Italian government to attend the Triennial Telegraphic Convention at Rome in December, 1871. Twenty-one countries sent delegates, and twenty-six languages were spoken—a potpourri of national attitudes and differences that emphasized the needs and problems of telegraphy. Morse wrote him before he left:

> The telegraph has now assumed such a marvellous position in human affairs throughout the world, its influences are so great and important in all the varied concerns of nations, that its efficient protection from injury has become a necessity. It is a powerful advocate for universal peace. Not that, of itself, it can command a "Peace, be still" to the angry waves of human passions, but that, by its rapid interchange of thought and opinion, it gives the opportunity of explanations to acts and to laws which, in their ordinary wording, often create doubt and suspicion.

Field agreed implicitly with Morse that the convention should pass "some resolution to the effect that, in whatever condition, whether of peace or war between nations, the telegraph should be deemed a sacred thing, to be by common consent effectually protected both on land and beneath the waters." Arriving on December 20, almost three weeks late, he found that a similar resolution had been proposed and all but smothered by opposition. It made the road ahead look difficult. He reported later to the directors of the New York, Newfoundland and London Telegraph Company:

As soon as I got all the facts, I determined my course. It was to get personally acquainted with every delegate and urge my views upon him before bringing them before the conference. Finally, on Thursday, the 21st ultimo, I presented my views in a carefully prepared argument to the conference. Every single member was in his seat, and finally, after a long discussion, in which there were forty-nine separate speeches, my propositions were carried without a dissenting voice. . . .

To revive an already defeated proposition and obtain its unanimous acceptance was a remarkable personal victory. Field was also able to have inserted in this proposal the recommendation "that no government should grant any right to connect its country with another without the joint consent of the countries to be connected." Although this provision looked and actually was innocent enough, it nevertheless placed a certain control over future cables in the hands of countries now connected by them, notably England, the United States, and their possessions.

Although he wrote of returning home in January, Field got as far as London and fell ill from sheer exhaustion. His intense nervous energy was waning. He was in and out of bed for almost three months; months of vigorous debate in Parliament on the *Alabama* claims, and this gave him a cause to turn to—always his most effective tonic.

24

Ambassador of Goodwill

➤➤➤➤➤◄◄◄◄◄◄ In early March, 1872, Field received a note from Thomas Hughes, author of *Tom Brown's School Days* and an M.P. with pro-American leanings. He wrote: "I take the liberty, as an old acquaintance, of asking whether you cannot do something in your compulsory leisure to help our countries in this untoward business. . . ."

The business was the *Alabama* claims. While the international tribunal was already in session at Geneva, the American demands as presented to the five arbitrators, went far beyond what England had expected or considered reasonable. In addition to reparations for damage wrought by Southern privateers, it included such items as the cost of pursuing and destroying the marauders, insurance losses, transfers of shipping to British vessels, and—most objectionable of all—England's "prolongation of the war, and the addition of a large sum to the cost of the war and the suppression of the rebellion."

Being in London, Field got the full reaction. British parliamentarians were stunned, some regarding the claims as so preposterous as to throw doubts on the whole American case; others thinking them some political maneuver connected with the imminent Presidential elections. Almost all agreed with the Manchester *Guardian* that "such unjustifiable tactics as the United States was employing would discredit the whole principle of arbitration."

Thomas Hughes suggested:

> If you, who are so well known here, believe your government to be in the right, and that they never did waive or meant to waive, the claim for indirect damages, and if you will make this statement publicly here, in any manner you please, it would certainly go far to

induce me, and I think most of the other public men who were strong
Unionists during your civil war, to advocate the submission of the
whole case as it stands to the Geneva board. On the other hand, if
you cannot do this, I really think we may ask for your testimony
on the other side.

Field felt his country's stand was intransigent, but he had no wish
to undermine it. He wrote to Vice-President Schuyler Colfax, whom
he considered the obstructionist, that he thought the dispute and
England's outburst of hostility hinged on a misinterpretation of the
treaty:

> It is desirable that Americans should remember this fact—that
> until the publication of the American Case, nobody on this side of the
> water had the remotest idea that the Washington Treaty contem-
> plated more than arbitration with reference to the direct losses in-
> flicted by the *Alabama* and other Confederate cruisers which escaped
> from British ports during our civil war. . . . I therefore contend that,
> whether the public sentiment of England be well founded or not, its
> existence is so natural that, even if we Americans are wholly in the
> right, we ought to make every allowance for it—in fact, treat it with
> every forbearance.

He documented carefully his reasons for believing as he did, quoting from Members of Parliament and British statesmen who had
hailed the Washington Treaty as acceptable and had defined it as they
saw it. Their statements had been well publicized. If General Robert
Schenck, the American minister to London, had thought they represented a misunderstanding why had he not spoken out? Why had
Schenck congratulated the British government on its signing of the
document "if he knew all the while that their construction of the
Treaty . . . fatally differed from the construction put upon it by the
Government at Washington?" Field went on:

> I have not given my own, but the English view of this matter.
> When such momentous issues are at stake—when a false move on
> the diplomatic board may endanger the peace of two kindred nations
> —it is absolutely necessary that our people should know what is the
> English side in this controversy. The first duty of a loyal American
> citizen is to ascertain the whole truth, and not by ignorance or ob-
> stinacy to commit himself to a wrong course.

He underestimated the weight of his words, for although he was a
private citizen his views were often accepted as American opinion. He

sent a copy to Thomas Hughes suggesting: "You are at liberty to make what use you think of my letter, feeling as I do that at so serious a crisis it is the duty of every man to speak out his mind frankly, and with an eye only to the interests of truth and justice." Hughes promptly relayed the copy to the London *Times,* as representing the views "shared, to my knowledge, by other Americans of high standing," and the *Times* reprinted it in full.

The letter became something of a *cause célèbre.* Bancroft Davis, who had drafted America's side of the case, referred to it as "Cyrus Field's little piece of self-glorification" and told Hamilton Fish it had "misfired." General Schenck bridled at the insinuation that he had failed to correct British false impressions of the treaty. He wrote to the Secretary of State:

> One great and increasing difficulty I have to contend with is a growing and pretty general impression here, shared by this government, that there is a large portion of the people of the United States sympathizing with the English view, and opposed to having the indirect damages insisted on. This may come in a good degree from the officious scribbling and intermeddling, in that vein, of certain amateur diplomats, such as Cyrus Field and others, who have written to the English papers.

Field had not written to the English papers but he doubtless did not object to the wide circulation given to his views, and he knew that they had support on both sides of the ocean.

The situation was still cloudy when he arrived home the end of March. He reported to Bright on April 2:

> Since my return I have devoted much of my time to ascertain the real sentiment of the people of this country in regard to the Washington Treaty, and as far as I can judge, after seeing many persons of different political parties, it appears to be almost unanimous that our government has made a great mistake in including these indirect claims in the "case!"

Largely through the efforts of two friends he admired most for statesmanship, Charles Francis Adams and Hamilton Fish, the Geneva tribunal was kept on the track that spring and summer and worked toward an agreement that eventually allowed the United States a gross sum of $15,500,000 as indemnity for damage suffered from the Southern privateers. It also provided for the future handling of such disputes.

Samuel Finley Morse died in early May. One of his last acts was to urge Field to continue and extend his work in submarine cables:

> No one better than yourself can lead in this Pacific Cable enter-prise, and as in the case of the Atlantic Cable project I never doubted, but, on the contrary, uniformly predicted its success, so now I have entire confidence not only that you will be able to accomplish it, but that you will have and will deserve the honor of *completing* the "fairy girdle that encircles the world."

Field was a pallbearer at the funeral and arranged to bring the family to Washington for a memorial service in the hall of the House of Representatives where he installed telegraph wires over which they received messages of condolence from all over the world. Finley's daughter, Leila Morse, enclosed in her letter of thanks "a small lock of Papa's hair which Mamma sends to his namesake Edward Morse Field."

That summer Field was torn politically between Grant's candidacy for a second term and Horace Greeley's nomination for the Presidency by the liberal wing of the Republican Party. Tending to look upon domestic politics in international terms, he inclined to overlook Grant's ineptitude at home and focus on the more enlightened foreign policy of his administration. Field voted for Grant but felt some sympathy for Greeley, who had supported him during his troubles with the cable.

He returned to England in the fall, partly to keep alive his tradi-tional Thanksgiving Day dinner for cable associates and friends, a typical New England feast of roast turkey, sweet potatoes, and as-sorted pies. With the Geneva conference over, there was more cause than usual for thanksgiving. Friction between the two countries had been largely eliminated, and the presence of Prime Minister Glad-stone, who sat at Field's right during dinner, was something of a rec-ognition of Field's role in this accomplishment. Gladstone referred to his host as "the most efficient promoter of the settlement of the *Ala-bama* question," comparing Cyrus to "a telegraph wire, so often has he crossed the Atlantic, and always charged with messages of peace and good will from nation to nation." The remark prompted a press cor-respondent to observe: "We all knew Mr. Field was a *wiry* man, but were not prepared to have the adjective transformed into the noun."

Shortly after the Thanksgiving dinner he met, through Junius Morgan, General Luigi Palma di Cesnola, an Italian-American who was representing the United States as consul in Cyprus. Cesnola had been soldier, statesman, and something of an amateur archeologist. During his ten years in Cyprus he had been alarmed at the plundering of its ancient wealth by grave robbers and souvenir merchants. He had "transformed 'digging' from a mischievous pastime into a weapon of historical science." As a result, he had amassed the largest collection of Cypriot antiquities in the world and, by a cloak-and-dagger routine that outwitted Turkish customs agents, had smuggled it for safety into London.

Cesnola had already sold some items to meet expenses, and one consignment had been lost at sea; but 35,000 pieces still remained. Field arranged with the consul to have them cleaned, photographed, and properly exhibited. While they were being viewed by museum representatives from London, Paris, Athens, Perugia, Constantinople, and even Boston, Field was negotiating with Morgan to have them purchased for the Metropolitan Museum in New York.

After an exhibition arranged by Field in New York, Cesnola wrote to Isabella Field Judson: "your father asked me to drive back with him to Mr. Morgan's office, and suggested to Mr. Morgan that he close the purchase of the collection with me *verbally at once,* and a payment was made on account without delay, and without waiting for the papers to be drawn up."

January, 1873, found Field home again at Gramercy Park, where a chapter was closing in his life. Early that year the New York, Newfoundland and London Telegraph Company was absorbed by the Anglo-American Telegraph Company and passed out of existence. Field now had only his dream of a Pacific cable, and he returned briefly to London in the early spring to discuss its prospects with Sherard Osborn, managing director of the Telegraph Construction & Maintenance Company. He appears to have given up hope of conducting negotiations with the evasive Russian emperor and set his sights on landing the cable from Japan in China. He had also failed to obtain landing rights in Hawaii and decided to investigate the Aleutian Islands route.

Lacking a Matthew Maury to advise them on the oceanography of the North Pacific, he and Osborn would rely on the findings of H.M.S. *Challenger,* which had set out the year before on a research cruise around the world. In addition, they would require, Osborn told him: (1) soundings along the coasts of California, the Aleutian Islands, and Japan and (2) detailed charts of the best landing places in those areas. Next came the question of landing rights in Japan. At Osborn's suggestion it was decided to send A. B. Freeman-Mitford, former secretary to the British legation in Japan, to Tokyo to see what he could do.

Freeman-Mitford left from San Francisco the following month, but there is no record of his having accomplished anything substantial. Perhaps at this juncture his failure was of little consequence, for Field was waiting for Congress to approve his bill, and he was unable to make any further progress until it had done so. Any move he might have made, even concerning the Pacific cable, was blocked by the financial panic of that autumn, 1873.

He had been through such storms before, but none like this. Field suffered financially, of course, but mostly on paper and never to the extent he had suffered from preceding panics when he had his own firm and was simultaneously promoting the Atlantic cable. In fact, he felt sufficiently secure to sail for London on January 13, 1874, with no apparent reason other than to dine with Lord and Lady Frederick Cavendish, breakfast with Gladstone, and play host to old friends on Clarges Street.

He returned home in mid-February on the *Cuba*—making, he noted, his fifty-sixth Atlantic crossing—in time for the marriage of his eldest daughter Mary Grace to Daniel Allen Lindley, Jr., on March 5. It was the first of two marriages between the Field and Lindley families, and the affinity was natural. Daniel Allen Lindley, Sr., was a Presbyterian missionary of the old-time Gospel-preaching school, very much in the character of the Reverend David Dudley Field. His numerous children had been brought up in the same strict Puritan codes of duty and responsibility as had the second-generation Fields. "My boys behave like gentlemen and Christians," Dr. Lindley boasted.

"One of the most magnificent private weddings of the season," one newspaper reported. "Nearly 1,500 cards of invitation were issued and yesterday all the hairdressers in town had more orders than they could fill. . . . The latest Paris fashions and styles were illustrated to perfection."

Shortly after the wedding Dan Lindley wrote to his family: "Mr. Field gave to Grace as a wedding present a very pretty cottage at Irvington-on-Hudson, near his own & on the 1st May we took possession." It was Field's first move to keep his family together in the Ardsley compound. He had placed Daniel in the banking firm of Jesup, Paton & Company and in the interest of his son-in-law had agreed to perform commissions for them when abroad, a fact to which Daniel was referring when he wrote enthusiastically, "We expect to get a great deal of European business."

For the moment, however, Field was concerned with developments at home. To relieve the depression, Congress had approved a bill for expansion of the currency, which meant the dilution of savings and investments, and was a step toward national repudiation, shaking faith in the dollar abroad and disrupting trade in Europe and at home. Meetings of protest were held throughout the country, the most significant at Field's home on April 15, 1874. Those present comprised a blue-ribbon panel of financial experts, among them John Jacob Astor, August Belmont, William Aspinwall, A. T. Stewart, Abiel Low, Marshall Roberts, Moses Taylor, W. M. Evarts, and, always by Field's side in time of crisis, Dr. William Adams.

A committee from this convocation, headed by Field, went to Washington to petition Grant for his veto. The President not only listened but also acquiesced, thereby ending the potential threat.

Field next decided to combine his investigation of a cable landing site near San Francisco with a pleasure trip to California and entrained for the West Coast by private car with Mary. A few miles south of San Francisco he noted: "There is an excellent sandy beach, and the cable could be easily connected with the existing telegraph lines across the continent." On the return trip they stopped at Cincinnati, where at a reception Field met Murat Halstead. To him he revealed a forthcoming venture, saying, "Why not join me on a trip to Iceland? It's the millennial year of the island's settlement; the King of Denmark will be there; and the whole affair should be extraordinary."

He wasted no time in getting under way and, reaching New York, sailed immediately for England. By sheer chance Bayard Taylor, who had chronicled the trip aboard the *James Adger* in 1854, had been assigned to cover Iceland's Millennial Jubilee for the New York *Tribune*. Already fatigued from overwork, Taylor was endeavoring to obtain a release from this assignment, but when he heard of Field's plans he promptly joined him in London for the expedition. Halstead met them at the Buckingham Palace Hotel, and found that the group had grown to include Dr. I. I. Hayes, the Arctic explorer; Gladstone's son William Henry; and Professor Eiríkur Magnússon of Cambridge University, an Icelander by birth.

They proceeded to Edinburgh, where Field chartered the eighty-five-ton *Albion* from the Edinburgh & London Shipping Company, along with her Captain Howling, a "mariner and gentleman." Since the *Albion* was not licensed as a passenger steamer, they could board her only as members of the crew. Each was accordingly registered as a regular seaman—Field signing on as electrician for a shilling's pay —and was pledged to obey the captain's orders and refrain from mutiny. The vessel was to take on coal at Aberdeen, and since this promised to be an unexciting run, Field persuaded Halstead to join him on the harder trek by land. They coached and hiked across the Grampian Mountains, via Braemar and Balmoral, and arrived at Aberdeen "soaked with Highland rain, and bearing bunches of heather."

Sailing past the Shetland Islands, the ship picked up the Danish king's flotilla and raced his fleet to Reykjavik, arriving almost simultaneously on July 30, 1874. With Field's sporting instincts aroused, it was now a question of who would reach shore first. He had never competed with a king before—and this was the monarch who had encouraged a rival to beat him with an Iceland-Greenland cable to America! He posted a watch on deck to alert him the moment the king put out for land, and Bayard Taylor recorded the ensuing action:

> We had scarcely been helped to a superb Iceland salmon, when there were signs that the royal landing was about to come off. The boats were made ready in all haste; we rushed from the table and pushed for the shore, but His Majesty was already under way. His boat and our two were nearly abreast. He had eight oars, and we but three apiece. . . . The Danish flag on one side, and the American and the English on the other seemed to be running a desperate race; the Icelanders must have enjoyed the spectacle. . . . Urged by words and promises of reward, our sailors did their best, and just as the King stepped upon the scarlet cloth of his landing place, we sprang upon the nearest jetty.

At the official ceremonies Field and Taylor introduced themselves to the king, but "there was no more than was necessary for politeness, on either side." Even the populace seemed somewhat unresponsive to the royal visitor. They "opened their mouths as they took off their hats, made the beginning of a shout, then timidly gave it up." One barrier between king and subjects may have been that the monarch talked so softly that nobody could hear him.

There followed two days of dancing, feasting, and "great flying fires," the wind sometimes reaching such velocities that Field's group sought refuge on the steamer. The only untoward incident occurred, Bayard Taylor wrote, when:

> Captain Howling, proposing to take stones from the nearest harbor island as ballast, was quite taken aback by the refusal of the proprietor to allow any portion of his volcanic real estate to be carried away. The reason was that the island would be gradually diminished in size, and furnish so much less breeding-ground for eider duck!

After the ceremonies, the visitors and most of the Reykjavik populace embarked on a pilgrimage inland to the Great and Little Geysers. They formed two teams—Field and his band on ponies with Icelandic guides to lead them, the king's caravan made up of carriages with scarlet-coated lackeys.

It was neck and neck over fields of lava, ice streams, and tundra, shunning the shelter of farms that might, the guides warned them, be afflicted by the native plagues of rinderpest and epizooty. Bayard Taylor, in spite of his normal hardiness, was miserable and quickly tired of the competition. "Messrs. Field and Halstead pushed on at a gallop," he reported; "I preferred keeping with the baggage." They camped at night beside the royal bivouac, dined on a plover stew ad libbed by Field and Halstead, and turned in early. Wrote Taylor: "I gave myself up to untroubled rest, trusting to Mr. Field, who is never more in his element than when a start is to be made."

At 3 A.M. Field exhorted the group to be on their way again, getting a head start on the breakfasting king, who, as they passed, "replied to our salutations with a piece of bread and meat in one hand." They reached the vicinity of Hekla, site of the Great and Little Geysers, a good half hour ahead of their opponents. On the king's arrival the geysers failed to spout. Handfuls of sod were thrown into the bubbling caldrons to provoke eruption, only to be messily discharged like foul emetics. For a whole day, they plied the craters with tossed turf. Taylor reported:

> The King, who had turned aside to salute our company, was in the act of expressing to me his admiration of the scene, when the Little Geyser gave sudden signs of action. There was a rush of the whole party; His Majesty turned and ran like a boy, jumping over the gullies

and stones with an agility which must have bewildered the heavy officials, who were compelled to follow as best they could. It was a false alarm. The Little Geyser let off a few discharges of steam, as if merely to test the pressure, and then, as if satisfied, resumed its indolent, smoky habit.

The king settled for carving his initials in the soft volcanic rock.

Field's troupe had an easy victory in the race back, although he accused the king of letting his ponies ahead to clear a path through the tangled tundra. By the end of the week they were on the way to Scotland. Too impatient to wait for the vessel to reach Edinburgh, Field disembarked at Thurso, the first likely landfall, and entrained to Liverpool to catch a ship for home. Taylor was with him and filed his report with Whitelaw Reid of the *Tribune*. When it appeared, the article was headed "Waiting for the Great Geyser."

25

The Elevated Railway

>>>>>><<<<<< Field's trip to Iceland was essentially a means of marking time, an outlet for his restlessness. He had reached a peak in his career, but peaks to him were no more than plateaus. They raised the question: Where next?

The depression which lasted from 1873 to 1878 was a period of stocktaking, not only for Cyrus Field but also for the country as a whole. And New York, as the commercial capital, needed re-appraising. The city had been practically rebuilt since Field arrived in 1835. Gramercy Park was the only spot of greenery in the middle of the city, and tall buildings blocked the river views. Brownstone fronts were spreading north in a chocolate-colored grille. In the previous two decades the population had more than doubled to reach 1,500,000, pushing up along the rivers in a clamorous stampede for living space.

New York City was desperately in need of an adequate transportation system. Horsecars and omnibuses vied with horse-drawn vehicles of every sort to clog the streets and reduce the city's commerce to confusion. A pedestrian was barely safe on Broadway. In short, New York was suffering from the national disease of uncontrolled growth, which was making millionaires of men like Gould, Fisk, Vanderbilt, and Sage, while confounding the welfare of the ordinary citizen.

Still, there was cause for pride in many phases of American expansion. This found expression in the Philadelphia Centennial Exposition of 1876. Crowds were so great in Fairmount Park (estimated as "the largest ever seen upon this continent") and the celebrities so numerous that many went unrecognized, although, wrote Dee Brown, "the crowd gave out occasional shouts for such well-known figures as Cyrus Field and J. Pierpont Morgan."

Undoubtedly part of Field's interest in the Philadelphia Exposition focused on the "talking telegraph," Alexander Graham Bell's invention which transmitted human voices over wires. Bell's telephone was meeting the same apathy and ridicule that Morse's telegraph and the Atlantic cable had experienced. Far from scorning the new instrument, Field would be among the first to have one privately installed.

In the same general area of communication was the exhibit of a so-called dummy locomotive being used on New York's elevated railroads. Light and ornate, it was "built to eliminate cinders, noises, and the scaring of horses." The New York elevated railways at that period were nonetheless having legal and financial difficulties, and in their planning and construction were a fragmented mess. Field's sometime Gramercy Park neighbor Samuel Tilden, now governor of the state, had become involved in their promotion and, by granting a disputed franchise to the pioneer New York Elevated Railroad Company, had brought charges of bribery and political chicanery on his head. After Tilden lost the 1876 Presidential election, he retired for a while to Sea Girt, New Jersey, and Field visited him there.

Tilden may well have directed Field's interest to the elevated system, now almost at Cyrus' doorstep. A new Third Avenue line had been projected that would pass his home, linking Wall Street with Grand Central Station. Plainly the overhead rails had come to stay. And if they were going to stay, they would have to grow and would need Field's personal investment in the venture. Field and Tilden agreed to purchase a substantial block of stock at the then highly favorable price of $14 a share.

Now, at fifty-six, Field wanted money and success, but he also wanted to feel involved in a humanitarian crusade. His friend Murat Halstead, who knew him perhaps as well as anybody, wrote of this decision:

> He saw earlier than others the enormous requirements of rapid transit systems in our great cities, and the adaptation of the elevated roads to the needs of New York, and believed the intuition of discovery in this enterprise was greater as a matter of business than Atlantic Cable leadership. He had no shadow of doubt in his mind that the achievement of rapid transit by elevated railroads would be of enormous public value and personal emolument. . . . The influence of the roads would be to expand the city and augment the demand for property at both ends of the line.

The transportation problem in Manhattan was unique. Confined between its rivers to a long and narrow island, its business district was at the southern end and its residential areas to the north. As the former expanded, the latter was pushed farther away, becoming constantly more remote. It was easier for Field to get to and from his country house in Ardsley than to travel from Gramercy Park to Harlem or the Battery.

The most sensible proposal was to build a subway from the Battery to Thirty-fourth Street, with a second line to Central Park. This was arbitrarily rejected by the New York legislature for no apparent reason, unless it was that of elderly ladies who protested that "it would be cold down there," or on the ground of Russell Sage's later comment: "Subways? Imagine! What if the trains got stuck in a hole twenty feet under the ground? People would suffocate, they'd swelter to death."

The projectors of the subway then raised their sights aboveground, and the Tilden-sponsored New York Elevated Railroad Company, or El, began construction of a one-legged, single-track line on Greenwich and Ninth Avenues to run eventually as far as Harlem. A competitor, the Metropolitan Railway Company, or Metro, started lines from the Battery up Sixth and Second Avenues. Traction was provided by stationary engines placed at intervals of 1,500 feet to pull the cars along by cable.

As long as Boss Tweed was in power, neither of these projects had much chance. The New York *Herald* of June 5, 1877, noted:

> The corruptionists went so far as to try to indict the Greenwich Street elevated railroad as a nuisance; they boasted that they would not only tear down the road, but would fine and imprison the enterprising citizens who advanced money to try this important and now entirely successful experiment. Engineers and newspapers were hired to assert that the road would not stand; that it was dangerous to the lives of passengers; that it would cause constant runaways of horses; that it would destroy business; and attempts were even made at one time to incite mob violence against it.

The introduction of steam locomotives to the elevated railways gave them a temporary lease on life but gained them little more acceptance. Newspaper cartoons showed the engines setting fire to adjoining buildings, showering sparks on those below, panicking horses, dropping unwary travelers into space. Property owners complained of falling values; horsecar lines and omnibuses bitterly attacked the overhead competition on their routes. The railroads pushed stubbornly upward but evolved as ugly, isolated scaffolds, beclouding certain sections of the streets and covering only minor distances.

Such was the state of the lines when Cyrus Field took over, and as J. B. Walker wrote: "It was under the stimulating influence of his genius and capital that they were completed and made into a really important transportation system." Allan Nevins later added: "The progress of the elevated roads was due largely to Cyrus W. Field, who late in the seventies had used most of his fortune to purchase control of the system, and whose talents and energy gave a marked stimulus to the whole undertaking."

On May 14, 1877, he wrote John H. Hall and David Dows, leading stockholders in the New York Elevated Railroad Company, that he would buy a majority interest in the debt-ridden corporation and serve without salary as its president, but with certain provisions. He wanted it free of debt and, to this end, asked the stockholders to accept bonds at 60 cents on the dollar for what was owed them. Also, all future purchases were to be made in cash, and the most rigorous economy was to be practiced. The construction cost of elevated railways was ten times that of surface lines, and the average passenger fare much lower. As a step in the direction of economy, he canceled contracts for building the Third Avenue line at a cost of $1,200,000 per mile as being excessive and suggestive of improper dealings. The whole affair was renegotiated, and the line completed in precisely fourteen months.

In June there took place a seemingly unrelated event, that obliquely played a part in these developments. Field's elder son, Edward Morse Field, married Clara Louise Lindley, his sister-in-law by virtue of Dan Lindley's marriage to Mary Grace Field. As with his daughter and Daniel, Cyrus helped the young couple acquire a home—this time, at their request, in town. He went a step further, advancing funds to both his son and Daniel to start their own brokerage firm. Daniel had had some experience with Jesup, Paton & Company, but Edward had had none at all. Cyrus had himself incorporated as a special partner.

Shortly after the wedding Field organized a meeting in Chickering Hall of the friends and supporters of the elevated railways. Oddly Charles O'Conor, who had called the 1858 Atlantic cable a humbug and a fraud and heaped invectives on Cyrus Field, now came out publicly in favor of his railways:

It is said, and doubtless with truth, that the great cities have hitherto been destroyers of the human race. A single American contrivance promises to correct the mischief. The cheap and rapid transportation on the elevated rail . . . will give healthful and pleasant homes in rural territory to the toiling millions of our commercial and manufacturing centres. It will snatch their wives and children from tenement-house horrors, and, by promoting domesticity, greatly diminish the habits of intemperance and vice so liable to be forced upon . . . them by the present concomitants of their city life.

Public investment in the elevated railways was still cautious—Field and Tilden alone were heavily committed—and as with the cable, Field looked to England for a measure of support. English capital had poured into American railroads. Murat Halstead noted:

Mr. Field held the opinion that Manhattan stock could be very largely disposed of on the London market at rates far above any that had been reached. The property was so famous, so much in evidence, so easily inspected under the eye, and obviously of enormous earning capacity; it was the best thing in the world for England. What Mr. Field could not permanently hold, he might easily and at an advance part with, and British gold would have been far better bestowed in Manhattan than in South America where such a flood of it was poured out to evaporate.

Still recuperating at Sea Girt, Samuel Tilden had decided on a trip to Europe. He wrote Field, as the most experienced transatlantic voyager he knew, asking him to arrange for reservations. Cyrus replied, "I have secured for you on the *S. S. Bothenia,* sailing July 4, the two staterooms marked on the enclosed plan—the best on the ship. I sail on July 18 on the *Scythia.* The Cunard Co. will transfer you if you desire." Tilden chose to sail with Field, and they were accompanied by Tilden's lifelong friend John Bigelow. Cyrus left them in Ireland, while he traveled to London to promote his railway stock; when Tilden later reached that city, Field arranged for his accommodations at the Buckingham Palace Hotel, introduced him to Curtis Lampson, Junius Morgan, and Dean Arthur Stanley (John Bright proving inaccessible), and arranged for his acceptance at the Cosmopolitan and Athenaeum clubs.

There is no record of how much elevated railway stock he placed in England. But there was another, more melancholy purpose to his visit. His second daughter, Alice, had been failing mentally for some years. No doctor in America had been able to help her, and she was now with friends in London, under the care of an English neurologist. Fanny, her sister, was with her, and there was little that Field could do. Just before sailing home, in a noticeably shaky hand, he wrote: "My dear, dear Alice—one word before I leave. Do be careful of yourself, and come home strong and well." He never saw her strong and well again.

Back home, he further cemented relations with Tilden and other New York financiers who might support his plans for the elevated railways. Tilden had ruled out public appearances for the time being, but he accepted Field's invitation to preside at a dinner for Junius Morgan at Delmonico's that autumn. Further, he made a "felicitous speech" that must have touched Field deeply. He told the assembled guests, all men of appreciable wealth, that "there is something better than money, and that is the merited esteem of one's fellows; and there is something better than merited esteem of one's fellows, which is a consciousness that human society is better because we have existed."

Field endorsed these sentiments wholeheartedly. He wrote to Tilden for permission to publish the speech in pamphlet form for selective distribution and was surprised when permission was granted to publish a *corrected* copy. Tilden had had some second thoughts.

In fact, Tilden was proving a little slippery. He had pledged his support, and the following May, 1878, Field wrote in gentle protest: "There is not a share of N. Y. Elevated R. R. stock standing in your name on the books of the Company." He suggested that if Tilden's shares were held in somebody else's name (David Dows would be a likely suspect), "I would advise you as a friend to have them transferred at once." Field was anxious to keep everything aboveboard and to know just who his partners were.

By now he had so identified himself with the job he was known as the "locomotive in trousers." Before the year was up, the Third Avenue line reached One Hundred and Twenty-ninth Street, and the Ninth Avenue track ran to Sixty-first Street. Expansion was not all he strove for. He tried to improve the comfort and appearance of the railroads, ugly and obnoxious as they were, and was successful to the extent that *Leslie's Illustrated Weekly* paid homage to his efforts:

> The general style of the exterior of the buildings, with their many gables, ventilators, finials, etc., might be properly classed as a modification of the Renaissance and Gothic styles of architecture, present-

ing somewhat the appearance of a Swiss villa. The glass ventilators are to be in variegated colors, and the ornamental bay windows in the waiting-rooms are to afford a view of the street below. The heating apparatus will be arranged in an artistic manner, so as to mar as little as possible the appearance of the place. . . .

Of the passenger accommodations, the magazine observed:

> Each car has seating capacity for sixty-four people. The woodwork of the doors, seats and sides of the car is of mahogany, and the ceiling is paneled with oak and mahogany. The seats are furnished with flexible backs of maroon morocco, and spring bottoms with cushions of morocco for Winter use, and in Summer are to be covered with woven rattan. The floors are to be covered with heavy Axminster rugs and carpets.

Field reported to the directors on November 1, 1878:

> It is not eighteen months since I purchased from some of your then directors a majority of the stock of your company at such a price that today it sells for more than five times as much as it cost me; and at the same time I bought from the same parties a very large amount of bonds, and today they sell for more than double what they cost me, including seven percent interest to date.

During his visit to Alice in England, Field had pressed his friend Dean Stanley of Westminster Abbey to pay a visit to Ardsley, an invitation the dean accepted the ensuing autumn. Cyrus was surprised to find that his visitor knew more about the history of his region of the Hudson than the residents did. The dean pointed out that the British spy during the Revolutionary War, Major John André, had been captured and executed in the neighborhood, and he and Field spent a day determining precisely where the major had been hung. Having established the spot, Field suggested that Stanley write a fitting inscription, and he, Cyrus, would erect a monument to André.

When the monument was erected and became known, Field was castigated in letters to the press for his "attempt to please the English nobility by erecting a monument on American soil to an English spy." The tall concrete column was destroyed by dynamite. Field had the monument restored. When it was blasted a second time, a correspondent suggested that the spot was now well marked with rubble; it would not be readily forgotten. Field followed the writer's suggestion to erect a monument to the American hero Nathan Hale near the Seventh Regiment Armory, where the patriot had died.

This seemed to silence public doubts about his sentiments, but the destruction of the André plaque had ominous overtones. As in 1862, when Field had been charged with treason, it signified that he had enemies, irrational and not opposed to violence. He would hear from them again.

A more propitious monument was dedicated in the same month, October, 1878. Since Dr. Field's death his sons had discussed a fitting memorial to their parents. It was finally decided to purchase the Meeting House Green in Haddam, Connecticut, where the minister and Submit had spent so many years, and convert it to a public park. This was done (Cyrus' share coming to $9,000), and a leading landscape designer was hired to plant trees and shrubs and lay out roadways. Among Field's papers for this month are bills for thirty hemlocks, thirty Norway spruces, twenty Austrian pines, and ten each of white pines, oaks, elms, poplars, larches, beeches, and spruces, along with items of construction that include a surrounding fence to keep out "cattle and hogs."

October 31 was the day of dedication, and Cyrus, Dudley, Stephen, and Henry—the four surviving sons (Jonathan had died in 1868 and Matthew two years later)—arrived in Haddam at noon, to be welcomed by escorting country wagons, "upholstered for the occasion with horse blankets," and a red-coated brass band playing "Home, Sweet Home." The procession moved down the flag-draped main street of the village to the fifteen-acre park, where 400 dinners were served on board-and-sawhorse tables. The ceremonies were untraditionally brief. Dudley Field made a short speech of presentation, with a reference to the surrounding "shaded walks, green lanes and spreading trees," concluding: "Reverently we dedicate these memorials of our parents to the enjoyment forever hereafter of those and the descendants of those whom they loved and among whom they dwelt."

The Fields could not overlook their native Stockbridge. Cyrus conveyed to the town a plot of land in the center of the village for a park, and close by, Dudley erected the Children's Chimes as a memorial to his descendants, the bells in the tower to be rung at every sunset "from apple-blossom time till early frost."

The first months of 1879 saw Field's Elevated Railroad Company more than fulfilling its promise. According to Julius Grodinsky: "Within less than two years after he acquired control, both the gross and net showed excellent increases; the financial condition was improved, the standard of service was raised, and the price of the stock increased ninefold." In terms of service to the public there were equally impressive figures. When Field took over the twin lines, before either reached Harlem, the total number of passengers carried was slightly over 9,000,000. By 1879, when the Ninth Avenue line had been extended to One Hundred and Twenty-fifth Street, the number had jumped to 46,000,000. By the time it reached Harlem and the Third Avenue line had gone to Sixty-seventh Street, the passenger total had leaped to nearly 61,000,000. The city at last had an efficient rapid transit system.

There had been some problems and not a few complaints. When the Third Avenue El was built past Cooper Union, "the noise was so appalling that a dozen recitation rooms had to be transferred to the Fifth Avenue side." His friend and neighbor Abram Hewitt, secretary of the union, sent Field a bill for $540 to cover the cost of the move, protesting that "it was unfair of the railroad to cut down, for its own profit, the facilities available for educating the poor boys and girls of the Union." Field was glad to pay the penalty.

26

Enter Gould and Sage

>>>>>><<<<< With his penchant for pursuing more than one activity at a time, Field kept alive the project of a submarine cable across the Pacific. His childhood vow to throw a chain around the world had become a mild obsession—actually, telegraphic continuity around the world had been established. There were 60,000 miles of cable in every sea but the Pacific. New York could wire Hong Kong via Europe almost as readily as it could have via California had a Pacific link existed.

The stumbling block was still the Hawaiian (also called the Sandwich) Islands, whose reactionary king, Kalakaua, had failed to confirm his offer of landing rights with an official guarantee.

Field had waited for a guarantee until his patience wore thin. In July, 1878, he told his friends, with a note of resignation: "When the Hawaiian government fulfill their promise to me in regard to landing cables on their shores, the question of a Pacific submarine cable may be entertained by me. Until then I certainly shall do nothing towards the accomplishment of the enterprise via the Sandwich Islands."

However, on the twenty-fifth anniversary of the founding of the New York, Newfoundland and London Telegraph Company, during a banquet Field gave, he told this distinguished assembly:

> I have received this very day a concession from King Kalakaua, by his minister, who is here tonight, for the laying of a cable from San Francisco to the Sandwich Islands, and from thence to Japan, by which the island groups of the Pacific may be brought into communication with the continents on either side—Asia and America— thus completing the circuit of the globe.

Field shortly wrote to Elisha Allen, a former New England attorney, serving as Kalakaua's minister plenipotentiary, that he was sailing for Europe to "confer with my friends in regard to the Pacific cable, and I am willing to head a subscription list with my own subscription of one hundred thousand dollars. . . . I have had a bill introduced into Congress granting permission to land and operate cables in the United States, which I hope will pass during this session."

It was a quick trip, and he took Alice with him. She had returned not appreciably better from her previous stay in England, and he was anxious now not to let her out of his sight. The voyage on the *Bothenia* was uncomfortable and Alice was so ill when they reached Liverpool that she had to be carried on a stretcher from the boat. Field arranged for a special train to take them both to London.

His daughter Fanny Andrews came over from Menton to look after Alice, while Field went about his cable business. Besides sounding out potential British investors in the venture, he wanted to get estimates from Sherard Osborn of the Telegraph Construction & Maintenance Company on the cost of making and laying the required wire. What he proposed now was a three-way network, "one cable from San Francisco to the Hawaiian Islands; one cable from the Hawaiian Islands to Japan; one cable from the Hawaiian Islands to Australia, touching at the Fiji Islands and New Caledonia." The company was so anxious for the business that Osborn offered him a personal commission of $150,000 on the deal if it went through. This Field declined.

He spent less than a fortnight in London and, on his return in late May, 1879, mentioned none of his troubles with Alice, telling a greeting reporter, "I was in London thirteen days and had a delightful frolic." He returned to grim developments. Samuel Tilden, whom he had regarded as a trusted partner in the elevated railways venture, had disposed of his shares in the company, and the stock had responded by dropping thirty-six points. Tilden's only excuse was that he suspected Field was going to dump *his* stock in London, and he wanted to get out while the price was still right.

Field was outraged: "I don't want any man with his lack of faith in any enterprise of which I am a part," he told reporters at the dock. The more he thought about it, the more angry he became. On August 21 he told a New York *World* reporter that he would not even discuss the matter. "You may say, however, that my feeling for Mr. Tilden is one of intense disgust; that nothing, nothing, *nothing* would induce me to have anything more to do with him whatever, socially or in business."

Said the reporter: "We know of course that he disposed of his elevated railroad stock. But he had a right to do so, didn't he?"

Said Field: "He was free to do as he pleased. He has made a million dollars, and has the money in his pocket. I am heartily glad for the business that he is out of it."

He was briefly diverted by a happier event. His son and namesake, Cyrus, had graduated from Williams College and almost immediately married Susan Andrews of New York. Field presented his son with a seat on the New York Stock Exchange and gave the couple a house on East Fifty-sixth Street.

Tilden's betrayal had a strange, indirect effect: it forced Field into the camp of two equally unconscionable financiers, Jay Gould and Russell Sage. Field's New York Elevated Railroad Company was still solid, but the Metropolitan Railway Company was decidedly shaky— even though Metro had more than forty-four miles of track to the El's thirty-seven. Better management accounted for the difference. This makes Field's next move hard to understand—except that both Sage and Gould were interested in the elevated railways, both were stockholders, and both had long since taken Field's measure—honest, gullible, and subject to persuasion. They suggested a merger: the nearly defunct Metro with the profitable El. This, they argued, would eliminate the competition! That Field agreed can only be attributed to his desire for a coordinated, single transportation system. The goal was worthy, but the method was disastrous. Moreover, Field was now throwing in his lot with men whom he was ill equipped to handle. Sage and Gould, to an even greater degree than Tilden, were experienced speculators, ruthless, prevaricating, close to the thin edge of the law.

The merger was accomplished through the Manhattan Railway Company, which had been organized by the legislature in 1875 to police the elevated railroad industry. Russell Sage suggested that rather than have one company acquire the other, both lease their facilities to the Manhattan as a holding corporation. Each would receive $6,400,000 worth of stock in the parent organization. While the Manhattan would own no stock in either of the leasing companies, it would in effect become the operator of the entire system—responsible, too, for badly needed new construction.

On the surface it looked well enough. Brokers and the public rushed to buy Manhattan stock, and before the year was up, the price had doubled. Field and Gould were now partners of a sort, and Gould had no trouble in turning Field's interest to another venture—the Wabash Railroad he had acquired earlier that year. He had great plans for expansion of the Wabash, justified by its strategic linking of the East and West, and he would need to market stock abroad, as well as in America.

Field, of course, had had no experience in railroad management. He had dabbled in railroad stocks, and that was all. Neither had he had experience in paper merchandising, cable laying, or elevated railways when he plunged so deeply into these interests. It had never made him hesitate before. It still did not. That the Wabash grew and flourished during his brief tenure as president was more a matter of circumstance than intervention on his part.

Field spent the fall and winter of 1879 and 1880 with Fanny and her husband, James Bruyn Andrews, at their home in Menton in the south of France. Returning home in March, he renewed his campaign in behalf of the Pacific cable. Congress had taken no action—would it ever?—but he found he had a stalwart ally now at Washington in Secretary Evarts. Evarts had been counsel to the United States in the *Alabama* arbitration and also a member of Field's committee which had petitioned Grant to veto the currency expansion bill, and he and Field had been in close touch ever since.

Now Evarts wrote to ask what progress Field was making on the cable. Had he any estimates on cost? Field replied:

> I have received from London an estimate of the probable cost of a line from San Francisco to the Sandwich Islands, and from thence, by separate cables, to Japan & Australia. Such a line could be laid, & the cables, with instruments, stations, etc., complete, be handed over in good working order to the Company, at a cost of from fifteen to twenty million dollars cash.
>
> If the United States Government would give an unconditional guarantee of 4% to make up any deficiency in the earnings required to pay that amount of dividend on the capital expended I could, I feel sure, raise the money & have the cables in operation within two years. Without that, or a large subsidy in place of it, it would be useless to attempt to do so.

When Evarts balked at the 4 percent government guarantee, Field quickly revised his proposition:

I am of the opinion that I could raise the capital required for these cables, *on an unconditional guarantee of three percent by the United States Government;* but I suppose the Government would prefer not to give a guarantee for a longer period than 25 years. If the guarantee was for the *principal and interest at 3%,* or whatever lesser rate might be needed to make up a 3% dividend, I think the amount required for the manufacturing & laying of the cables would be raised without very much difficulty.

He urged Evarts to sound out the English government "through Sir Edward Thornton or our Minister in London" on the possibility of their collaborating on the guarantee with the United States; "and it is also possible that the Australian Government might join with England in its guarantee." Later he asked, "Have you ever written to the American Ministers in Japan & China on the subject? If the United States Government desires it, & took the proper steps, I think that England, Russia, France, Japan & China would each do something towards encouraging the enterprise."

Late in the summer he made his final pitch. He suggested that the government:

obtain from some eminent electrician specifications for the best description of cable suitable for the great depths and the great lengths required to connect the western with the eastern coasts of the Pacific.

He suggested further:

That the government advertise for tenders to manufacture and lay such description of cable, one-fourth the amount to be paid when the cables are all manufactured, one-fourth when they are on board the steamers and the steamers are ready to sail, one-fourth when the cables have been successfully laid, and the remaining fourth when they have been worked successfully and without interruption for thirty days.

He went on to state:

By adopting this course, I think you would obtain a good cable at the lowest price. The government could pay for such a cable by selling its four percent bonds, having a long time to run, at a considerable premium; and the revenue from such a cable would, in my opinion, steadily increase from year to year, and at no distant day be a source of revenue to the country.

With all his experience in cable laying, Field must have known that the government at this particular time was unprepared for such an undertaking. There were no cable manufacturers in the country; except for the *Niagara,* no American vessel had ever laid an ocean cable; there were no scientists or engineers or crew with the least experience in such an area.

Meanwhile, never having crossed the Pacific or seen the countries he had proposed as landing places for the cable, he decided to take a trip around the world. On March 15 he resigned his presidency of the Wabash, reminding all concerned that he had volunteered to serve, without pay, only until the time arrived when his supervision was no longer needed. Under his year's administration, the common stock had increased from $7 or $8 to $44 a share. He also resigned as president of the New York Elevated Railroad Company, though he maintained his stock interest in the company.

Field's trip was postponed. That spring of 1880 he and Dudley made the family's first strong bid for political distinction. Justice Stephen Field had been proposed as a possible Democratic nominee for President. As a Californian, he was believed to represent the West, and he was popular in the South for his support of states' rights. Cyrus and Dudley chartered special cars to take Field advocates to the convention in Ohio and, with the help of Murat Halstead and his Cincinnati *Commercial,* launched a strong campaign for Stephen—bolstered by street displays and brass bands, full-page advertisements in the *Commercial,* and more spectacular support than any other candidate enjoyed.

While the sights and sounds of triumph could be bought, the results were disappointing. California turned against Field for his defense of the rights of Chinese immigrants, Cyrus' and Dudley's support backlashed as representing Eastern capital, and one Washington magazine observed that "Judge Field . . . has worse relatives than Grant."

On the convention floor Stephen received only 65 of 728 votes; on the second ballot his margin remained the same, but a landslide toward Winfield Scott Hancock shortly siphoned off his votes. Field switched his allegiance to the Republican nominee, James Garfield.

Instead of setting out on his voyage, Field wrote to Evarts on September 15, 1880:

> After mature reflection, I have determined to remain until after the election and do all I possibly can to secure the success of the

Republican ticket by working until the polls close on the evening
of November 2d, and then leave on the morning of the 3d for San
Francisco, and sail from thence on the *Oceanic* on the 18th. . . . By
remaining and working I hope to induce others to vote for our
mutual friend, James A. Garfield.

Late in October Field's friends and neighbors invited him to a farewell dinner "to extend him greetings and God-speed."

As he sailed across the Pacific that November, Field saw at last the
vast world which he proposed to conquer. Sherard Osborn had estimated the depth in certain areas at 4,000 fathoms, or more than 4½
miles—double the depths that Field had encountered in the Atlantic.
The tremendous distances between the islands, even as covered by the
relatively speedy *Oceanic,* tried his patience and credulity. His faith
in a Pacific cable—as something to be accomplished in his lifetime—
seems to have waned from this point on.

India was the only country where he lingered. The Marquis of
Ripon, his old friend from the *Alabama* controversy days, was governor-general, and in this British colony he was more at home than
elsewhere in Asia. His thoughts, however, were directed at his concerns at home—above all, the elevated railways—and he was anxious
to get back. As soon as he reached Europe, he booked passage for
New York, having compressed his trip to less than six months.

On his arrival in May, 1881, the Manhattan bubble burst. At the
time of Tilden's sellout, Field had remarked: "I wish he would sell
the remainder of his stock in the elevated railroads; I'd gladly buy it."
Now Tilden obliged. On April 22, 1881, he wrote to David Dows,
a fellow investor in the elevated system, that he had studied the situation carefully and deemed it "prudent" to reduce his holdings still
further or dispose of them altogether, concluding: "I have substan-
tially done the latter." Dows replied: "I think you have acted judi-
ciously, not that I think the bonds unsafe, but I think the chances are
they will decline in price."

Decline in price they did, and rapidly during the first half of 1881.
At no point was there anything unethical in Tilden's actions. But two
things made them reprehensible. First was the fact that his name and
strong support had rallied investors to the company; the least he could
do was not depress the value of the stock. Second, of course, was his
understood partnership with Field, to whom a man's word was always
dependable. Cyrus was bitterly disillusioned—in Tilden, in his Man-

hattan Railway Company associates, and in the public's lack of loyalty. On all sides the structure he had nurtured was crumbling.

What hurt most in this debacle was the finger of accusation now pointed at him. Paul Sarnoff recorded:

> There was widespread suspicion throughout the financial district that Tilden, Field and Sage not only had sold out at high levels, but they also stood in the breach at the $20 level to cover their vast short position! Having been accused of gulling millions on the rise, the manipulators were now accused of reaping further millions on the stock's decline.

Actually, Field had held onto his stock, and so had Sage—Field being an optimist and Sage an opportunist. It was no coincidence that at this point Jay Gould came into the picture.

For some time Gould had been watching the development of the elevated railroads, wondering about their potential for a financial coup. In recent years he had acquired control of the Western Union Telegraph Company and also—by "mere accident," he insisted—of the New York *World*. He thus could be sure of a supporting press in almost anything he undertook.

Gould was a "man of disaster," whose technique was based on destruction. You undermined faith in a corporation to depress the stock; and if this was not enough, you wrecked the company and bought it as distress merchandise. At a hint from its proprietor the New York *World* obediently published stories denigrating the Manhattan Railway Company: "The elevated railroad properties may be very valuable, but the business of these roads is not valuable enough to warrant the present prices of the stock." Down further went the market value.

Gould and Sage were now ready for the master stroke. They attempted to persuade the attorney general of New York to declare Manhattan Railway insolvent, sue for revocation of its charter, and place it in the hands of receivers—the receivers to be all but selected by Jay Gould. Simultaneously, two separate suits were brought against the company by irate stockholders charging that they had been swindled. These, too, were instigated by associates or friends of Gould's.

In his usual trusting manner, Cyrus Field saw nothing strange in what was happening. He distrusted Gould and resented his appearance on the scene but failed to see the method behind the man. The Manhattan Railway Company was plainly in bad trouble—that was all. Finally, in July, he sued to have his New York Elevated Railroad Company separated from its dying parent.

On July 9 Manhattan Railway stock closed at twenty-three, and by the end of the month it had dropped to fifteen and a half. This was Gould's cue to move in and start buying—secretly. While the stock firmed with his purchase orders, puzzling everybody, Gould continued in public to do all he could to depreciate the standing of the company. Field endorsed Gould's written and sworn statement that "the Manhattan Railway Company is hopelessly and irretrievably insolvent" and in all good faith supported putting it into the hands of receivers.

By October Gould had purchased all the stock he needed for control, 48,000 shares. He promptly sued Field's New York Elevated Railroad Company, as well as the Metropolitan Railway Company, for the $6,400,000 of stock awarded each in return for operating rights. This, too, seemed not to be unfair to Field—especially when Gould offered to forget the matter provided that he, Sage, and Field formed a triumvirate to operate the railroads. Field would remain as president of the El, Russell Sage would be president of the Metro, and Gould would be head of the Manhattan. With that snug arrangement, satisfactory to the district court, the company was released from the threat of receivership, and all was precisely as before. Only the parties in control—excepting, temporarily, Cyrus Field—were different.

The financial editor of the *World* promptly reversed his previous stand and gave the development his blessing:

> Manhattan opened today [October 18, 1881] at forty-five, sold down to thirty-seven, and closed at forty-three, the recovery following the announcement of an agreement among the three elevated companies. As I said long ago, the elevated railroad franchise is too big a thing to give away, and I never believed but that Manhattan would be rescued by men who have the brains and means to make the most of it.

But the independent New York *Times* took a markedly different view, commenting editorially: "There is no more disgraceful chapter in the history of stock jobbing than that which records the operations of Jay Gould, Russell Sage, Cyrus W. Field and their associates in securing the system of elevated railroads in New York City. . . ."

This was familiar music to the ears of Sage and Gould but Cyrus Field, mindful of his reputation and fearful for his family's social standing, was appalled and stirred up such feeling that the El fare was cut back to five cents.

Field saw the elevated railway system as a public service institution, which was not exactly Gould's idea. Gould was anxious to keep the fare at 10 cents for all hours of the day; how else were he and Sage to get a quick return on their investment? They had already authorized the issue of $26,000,000 worth of new Manhattan stock on the basis of this augmented revenue. But Field had forced their hands, and the fare came down for all lines in the system. Cyrus did not know it, but he had sealed his fate. He had antagonized the Wizard of Wall Street, and "Gould, aided by Russell Sage, ate his revenge cold and waited almost six years to teach Cyrus Field a lesson in loyalty among thimbleriggers."

On the surface everything was amicable. Gould even made it possible for Field to purchase a large share of his Western Union stock and supported his election as a director. And however much Field may have disapproved of Gould, he could not deny that the Manhattan Railway Company had been saved from ruin and that the elevated railways, at least temporarily, were on a solid footing. Nor could he overlook the fact that he was better off—worth, it was estimated at this time, about $6,000,000 (small, however, compared with Sage's $50,000,000, and double that for Gould). The future, both for himself and the railroads, looked rosy.

27

Squire of Ardsley Park

➤➤➤➤➤➤◀◀◀◀◀◀ The first week in July, 1881, Field invited President Garfield to visit him at Ardsley on his way to Williamstown for the commencement ceremonies (Garfield was a Williams graduate). Field was working with Major J. M. Bundy of the New York *Daily Mail* to publish a biography of the new President in serial form. Garfield's last act on leaving the White House for Ardsley on the morning of July 2 was to hand his wife a book, saying: "I have promised to return this book to Mr. Field. Put it in your trunk and do not let me forget to give it to him when we are at his house." Field noted tersely in his diary: "... It was as Mr. Garfield was leaving Washington that he was shot in the Pennsylvania depot."

Garfield's assailant, a member of the Stalwarts who had rabidly advocated a third term for Grant, had wounded him mortally, but the President lingered on for ten agonizing weeks. On the day that he would have been Field's guest at Ardsley, Cyrus sent identical cablegrams and telegrams to many of his wealthy friends in Europe and America:

> If President Garfield should die from the wounds received on 2d instant he would leave for his wife and five children about $20,000. I shall tomorrow, Thursday, morning exert myself to the utmost to raise a sum of money to be presented to him at once, as I feel confident it would help his recovery if he knew that in the event of his death his family would be provided for. I shall cheerfully subscribe $5,000 towards the sum to be raised. If you or any of your friends would like to join, please telegraph to me early tomorrow, for what amount I may put your name, and oblige.

His name was sufficient magic on both continents to draw a flood of contributions, from the pennies of office boys to $5,000 checks to match his own, the total amounting to more than $362,000. He acknowledged each, and to one young girl who had sent an early silver dime, he wrote: "I showed your letter to a gentleman who came to see me at my office, and he kindly said he would give one hundred times the value of the coin, and handed me twenty dollars for it." His Garfield fund was the basis of a bill, later introduced in Congress, providing for $5,000 pensions to widows of former Presidents.

The money was deposited with the United States Trust Company, which at Field's suggestion waived all administrative charges, and Lucretia Garfield later wrote to Field: "We trust you may not doubt that you are held in highest esteem, by my children and myself, as a friend whom General Garfield loved and honored, and to whom we are deeply indebted." Field also wrote to Dr. Mark Hopkins in Williamstown: "I am obtaining designs for the Memorial Window to General Garfield to be placed in the chapel of Williams College, and am desirous that it should be the most beautiful window in this country." The $3,500 window was designed by John La Farge, the New York artist who had created similar stained-glass memorials for some of the principal churches of the country.

Field, too, was not immune from acts of violence. In April of the following year a package wrapped in an old German newspaper was mailed to him. Providentially, it never arrived. Hurled from a train in the process of delivery, it exploded and was found on analysis to have contained canisters of guncotton, which, the police observed, was four times as deadly as gunpowder. Investigation revealed that a similar "infernal machine" had been mailed to William Vanderbilt, a protest, it seemed, against the country's leading capitalists. It was a period of rising violence, later to explode in dynamite attacks on Wall Street figures, such as Russell Sage. Even Jay Gould was ambushed on the sidewalk in broad daylight and hurled ignominiously down a stairwell by an irate victim of his methods.

Field, according to his daughter Isabella, "took the matter very calmly, only afterwards telling the butler that no package brought to the house must be delivered until it had first been plunged in a bucket of water. This order spread consternation among some members of the family, who trembled for their new spring clothes." Whereas Gould hired bodyguards for protection, the only decisive step Field took was to have a Holmes electric telegraph alarm installed on all floors of his Gramercy Park house and in the Ardsley mansion. He disliked doing even that.

It was at this period in Field's life that Alexander Patten of the New York *Sunday Journal* wrote of him:

> A tall, thin man, with a small, but very expressive face, may be seen hastening along the streets of New York. His steps are always rapid, and he always seems full of thought and business. Nevertheless his quick, penetrating eyes seem to observe every passer-by and every object as he goes along. Though you may not know him, you are ready to say, "What an intelligent-looking and observing man!"

Patten described Field's appearance at the moment of his cable heyday as:

> a tall nervous-looking gentleman, with light-brown hair and beard, a Roman nose, bluish-gray eyes, and the sanguine face of a born Yankee. As he was then, so Mr. Field is now—a trifle stouter perhaps, and with a tinge of silver in his auburn hair. The years since his great triumph have touched him lightly.

They had also blessed him with abundance. At Ardsley Park (the name had been expanded) he had become something of an early Dutch patroon, lord of a manorial estate that had grown from its original 20 acres to nearly 200 acres, with a half mile frontage on Broadway between Dobbs Ferry and Irvington. Around him his family was grouped in villas, said the Tarrytown *Argus*, "each distinct and separate, making together a beautiful picture on the landscape." North of his own centrally located manor on the summit was the home he had built for Cyrus junior, and on the south were the houses of his son-in-law Dan Lindley and his nephew Frederick Stone, the only son of his sister Mary. On the slope below was the house of his elder son, Edward Morse Field. His two daughters, the unmarried Alice and the widowed Isabella, were living in the main house. All his children and grandchildren were around him now, except for Fanny's family, still at Menton.

In addition he owned the 98-foot steam cruiser *Inanada,* which he shared with his sons. He had had enough of seagoing in his time, and his stomach was no more immune to heavy weather than it had been in his cable-laying days. When Edward and Cyrus junior were otherwise engaged, he used the vessel for entertaining visitors and sometimes for commuting to Manhattan.

Almost next to Gould's estate and Russell Sage's manor—fortresses of security in an often hostile world—Ardsley was one of the show spots of the Hudson, pointed out by hawkers on the river steamers in its proud location. The editor of the *Argus* wrote:

> The view from Mr. Field's residence is very fine, taking in the Palisades with the river in front, and delightful inland vistas. In the rear the land rolls down to a meadow valley in which is a small lake of fresh spring water from which the reservoir on the summit is supplied. . . . The carriage road . . . winds about the margin of the lake through the meadow, and then by a wilder way to the house of the farmer, Mr. Francis Clarke, adjoining which are the greenhouse and grapery, which at present give promise of abundant fruit.
>
> The woodland embraces thirty or forty acres of timber, including chestnut, oak, hickory, white wood, and other deciduous trees. At the very summit in the rear is a rustic arbor, from which a number of beautiful vistas are plainly seen, also the Palisades, a view of Long Island, and near by the Neperan Valley and the Hartsdale Depot. It is a wildly beautiful spot in the very heart of the woods, and is reached by good carriage roads in different directions. It is said that on a clear day four States can be seen from that outlook.

With so substantial a community, Field decided that Ardsley Park deserved to be a railway stop, and when he suggested this to R. M. Gallaway, vice-president of the New York City & Northern Railroad, received the reply: "This seems to be all right. As soon as the weather gets a little pleasant I will willingly go up with you to locate the depot." The station was duly erected, and six trains every weekday stopped at Ardsley.

On the basis of this convenience, Field decided to enlarge the Hudson River community. He purchased 500 additional acres in the Neperan Valley, on which stood a number of houses, for $500,000, and the residents became his tenants. His idea, unique in that period and ahead of his time as always, was for a low-cost housing development. He would build a number of "small but comfortable" houses for workmen, each with its own plot of land, renting for from $10 to $20 monthly. As Peter Cooper had done with Cooper Union, Field was beginning to think in terms of social welfare as an outlet for his wealth.

He was sixty-three years old now, but there were still worlds to conquer. He had done battle with the press and had cooperated with it.

In either case here was an extension of his dream of furthering communications. He had helped Charles Dana buy the New York *Sun*, and he had envied, if not always agreed with, men like Horace Greeley and William Cullen Bryant, who had made themselves instruments of power through the printed word. Impulsively he decided to be one of them.

Through his connections with Major J. M. Bundy of the *Daily Mail*, in which he had earlier invested $40,000, and W. T. Clark of the *Express*, he began negotiations for the purchase of those papers. Both were in financial straits, with a combined daily circulation of less than 15,000. In December, 1881, he acquired control of them for $228,000 and, before the new year started, merged them into a single two-cent daily, the New York *Mail and Express*.

The first edition of the merged papers appeared on December 5, 1881, its editorial page announcing that "with the advantages of membership in the Associated Press, the MAIL AND EXPRESS will spare no effort to become the best evening newspaper in the country, and that means the best in the world."

The *Mail and Express* had a more difficult future than he imagined, even with its exclusive advantage, among evening papers, of membership in the Associated Press. Field left its operation to his $75-a-week senior editor, Major Bundy. For now that he had a mouthpiece there were other enterprises to pursue.

He next purchased what was then perhaps the most desirable business site on the island of Manhattan, a tract of land between the lower tips of Greenwich Street and Broadway on the Battery. Here stood the Washington Hotel, on what was erroneously considered the location of George Washington's former headquarters, and here he began construction of the Washington Building, to be hailed by *Leslie's Illustrated Weekly* as "the finest office structure in the city." It might rightfully be claimed to be Manhattan's earliest skyscraper. Six of New York's foremost architects submitted plans in competition; the winner was Edward Kendall, whose drawing was described as "a reminder of the old Colonial days." It was not an inspired concept, a square building 150 feet in height, but in an era when New York's profile was distinguished by church steeples and ships' masts, it dominated the skyline.

Field had originally planned a structure of eight stories above cellar and basement but later added several more stories and an observation tower rising 300 feet from the curbstone, not only overshadowing all neighbors but also providing, said the New York *Times,* the finest panorama in the city. "When Henry Irving was here, after arriving at his hotel from his voyage he took the first opportunity to climb to the top of Cyrus W. Field's building to enjoy the view from it, which he had heard of in England." Housing on the roof contained a kitchen, so that visitors could be entertained alfresco, perhaps the first taste of outdoor dining that the city enjoyed.

Into the building he moved the staff of the *Mail and Express,* installing the presses and equipment in the basement. Dudley Field took space for his law firm in what soon became known as the Field Building, and to the same address came Cyrus Field, Jr., with his brokerage business, and Edward's commodity firm of Field & Lindley. Field estimated that the building, fully rented, would bring in an income of $280,000 a year, and he formed a company to manage it, headed by John Lindley, Daniel's younger brother, thus providing a future for another Lindley son.

Field's empire, if he ever thought of it as such, was now complete —or at least at the peak of its maturity. A page from his personal ledger for April 21, 1882, brings the picture of his situation up-to-date. He owned some $3,000,000 worth of railway stock in nine different companies, his principal holdings being in Vanderbilt's New York Central and, somewhat surprisingly, in the New York & New England Railroad, a potential Vanderbilt competitor. He also owned stocks in coal, steel, Western mining ventures, and utilities, including £5,000 worth of shares in Edison's new Electric Light Company in London.

He was a principal shareholder in the Newfoundland Land Company, which had been organized to develop the territorial grants of 1853 to Frederick Gisborne's company; he owned 3,244 shares, a majority of which he distributed to members of his family, keeping 1,500 for himself; and had a one-fifth ownership of the Acadia Coal Company in Nova Scotia. He owned four blocks of real estate in Manhattan, including lots in Harlem; appraised the Washington Building at $1,600,000; and listed his Gramercy Park house and "½ stable" (the other half being Dudley's) as worth $75,000 and his country estate at Ardsley at a modest $500,000.

His personal income was listed as $74,642. His brother Henry estimated it as $300,000 a year at this time, but Cyrus may have been thinking in net terms. For against this income was an extraordinary number of personal loans—mostly to his family, one to Henry of $3,460. Cyrus listed $52,500 in bad debts, the penalty of his blind faith in his fellowmen, and $120,000 worth of "doubtful stock" (one section of his files was packed with worthless stock certificates and bonds with unclipped coupons). In this compilation of his worldly possessions, there was some concern for his unworldly soul. Among his assets he listed the $500 value of his pew in Dr. Adams' Madison Avenue Presbyterian Church and a similar amount, with $1 a year for upkeep, for a plot in the Stockbridge Cemetery.

If it seems that by reason of capital wealth he cast his lot with the robber barons of the era—Sage, Gould, Drew, and Vanderbilt—it was no deliberate affiliation. This appears evident from the fact that he continued to pursue his own uncompromising, generally public-minded course, fighting, for example, all attempts to raise the revenue of the elevated lines by raising fares. He owned 10,000 shares in the Manhattan Railway Company, compared with the 50,000 owned by Jay Gould. But this minority holding did not prevent his censoring Gould's actions or demanding an accounting when he felt that one was warranted.

The year 1882 had already proved to be a rough one for Gould, and what was bad for Gould was bad for Field and Manhattan Railway. With the issue of $26,000,000 worth of new Manhattan shares, there were charges that the stock was being diluted, and in addition, there were rumors that Gould was overextended, that his heavy loans were being called. Field, along with Russell Sage, demanded that Gould show his hand.

Gould admitted them to his office and sent his secretary to the private vault. Back and forth the man trudged, bearing armfuls of papers, which Gould spread before his visitors. They represented perhaps the most extraordinary display of one-man wealth in Wall Street history: $23,000,000 worth of shares in Western Union; $12,000,000 in Missouri Pacific; and $18,000,000 in Manhattan Elevated and other railroads—$53,000,000 in unencumbered stock.

"Does that satisfy you about rumors of insolvency?" demanded Gould, assuring them this was only a portion of his holdings.

Field was satisfied. He was, unfortunately, more than satisfied and continued to regard Gould as a shrewd man who knew his business. Unlike Gould, Field never overlooked what he regarded as his moral obligation to society. He was, for example, enlarging his low-cost housing operation on the Hudson to 800 acres. And although he associated, more by circumstance than choice, with strategists like Sage and Gould, he consciously cultivated as his close friends men like Dr. Adams, Henry Ward Beecher, Dean Stanley, and more recently Frederic W. Farrar, Archdeacon of Westminster. He entertained Dean Farrar at Ardsley Park on the latter's many visits to America and arranged his lecturing and preaching schedules, which the dean acknowledged in his *Great Americans*. He wrote, in part, of Cyrus Field:

> I was his guest in New York, and he was mine more than once in England. He was a genial, hearty, hopeful man, and a man, as it seemed to me, of very sincere and simple piety. Some writer has said that many a man would do one a kindness, yet would not on any account get up at seven in the morning to make himself of use. I can only say that, when I arrived by steamer at *three* in the morning at New York, the streets of that great city were empty and deserted, but Mr. Cyrus Field was there in person to meet me with his carriage! . . .
> Mr. Field loaded me with kindness, both in New York and at his splendid house on the Hudson; and he asked many of his most distinguished Americans—including one ex-President—to meet me at dinner. . . . I went with Mr. Field to tea at Mr. Beecher's house, and had some interesting conversation with him. It was at Mr. Field's house that the clergy of New York of all denominations presented me with a very kind and cordial address of welcome—their spokesman being the eloquent and highly respected Rev. Dr. [Richard Salter] Storrs.

Perhaps the person who influenced Field most throughout his life, apart from members of his family, was Peter Cooper. Cooper's death in the spring of 1883 left Field not only with sorrow for a vanished friend, but also with a sense of lost support. A rock—in fact, the cornerstone—was gone from the human structure of his world. He had confided in Cooper in his times of deepest trouble; Cooper was the only man who had ever seen him break down utterly, if temporarily, with the cable break of 1857. Now there would be no one he could turn to for advice and reassurance.

The city mourned Cooper's passing as it had mourned the passing of few other great men in its time. Flags from the Battery to Harlem hung at half-mast, tens of thousands filed by the coffin in the nave of All Souls' Church, and the pallbearers at the funeral, one of whom was Cyrus Field, constituted a roster of the nation's leading citizens. At the service were read the lines of Richard Watson Gilder, in which Cooper would surely have taken pride:

Mourn for his death, but for his life rejoice,
Who was the city's heart, the city's voice.

Before his death Cooper made a strange prediction: "There may at some future day be a whirlwind precipitated on the moneyed men of this country." That whirlwind was already in the making. During the remainder of 1883 had come "a steady stream of business failures," followed by a faltering stock market in the early months of 1884. In April prices dropped sharply, and by May the break was real.

While the Rich Man's Panic of 1884 did not damage Field financially—at the time he held no stocks on margin—it brought him concern for his associates. Scandalous irregularities wrecked the firm of Grant & Ward, and General Grant was forced into retirement to write his memoirs in a valiant effort to recoup his losses. Sage was reported to have lost $7,000,000 in three catastrophic days, a figure perhaps to be discounted since it was his own. Gould suffered heavily. By ingenious bluffing he managed to escape a fatal trap; but he shortly announced that he was through for good with market speculation, and for once he nearly spoke the truth.

What bothered Field most, apart from the questionable tactics of investors which had brought about the panic, was the vulnerability of the railways in a nation rich in railroads and dependent on them. Something was wrong somewhere, and he was heavily involved in railway stock, especially Gould's Oregon Transcontinental Railroad. He decided on a tour of the roads from coast to coast, and received an invitation from Sir Donald Smith of Montreal, director and promoter of the Canadian Pacific, to return by his nearly completed transcontinental railway. Once it was linked to the United States by a trunk line to St. Paul, the new Canadian Pacific might greatly affect rail transportation on the continent.

With his numerous directorships and former position as president of the Wabash, Field was able to make more than adequate arrangements. He chartered a Pullman car named appropriately Railway Age, a private palace of red plush and mahogany, for "$45 a day (with servants) plus 3¢ per mile," according to notations on the car plan in his files. The plan shows a layout typical of luxury travel at the time: a rear observation lounge, a master stateroom with adjoining bath, a mahogany-paneled parlor in the center, two compartments for the servants, a fully equipped kitchen with a refrigerator, and an adjoining heating unit for the car.

With Mary and his daughter Isabella he left Tarrytown on August 25, 1884, and in the next six weeks traveled more than 11,000 miles by rail, stopping first at Cleveland to visit Lucretia Garfield and her children. From there they rode to San Francisco, up to Portland, Oregon (the only state, he told the group, that he had never visited), and on to Tacoma where they boarded a steamer for the voyage up Puget Sound. From this heart of the lumber country, he learned with some nostalgia, the masts of the *Great Eastern* had been cut and shipped around the Cape to England. At Vancouver their car was attached to Sir Donald's special train for the four-day trip across the Rockies to the railroad's western terminus at Winnipeg.

In the heart of the Rockies, not far from Banff, the train was halted and a tent erected to give the company some respite from their constant travels. Before moving on, Sir Donald decreed that the place should hereafter be a regular Canadian Pacific depot, to be known as Field. At the same time he looked around the neighboring peaks and picked out one which he also christened Field. Told that the mountain had a name, Sir Donald settled that with quick authority: "It's Field now." At telegraph offices along the line, as Field stopped to send or collect news from his office, "Are you the original Cyrus?" the operators asked.

He arrived home as the fall (1884) political campaigns were starting. Stephen Field had again been suggested as a possible Democratic candidate for the Presidency; but the hostile factors that had routed him in 1880 were still rife, and his name was never voted on at the convention. With Cleveland the Democratic nominee, there was no question of Cyrus Field's support for his close friend James G. Blaine. He, Jay Gould, and other well-to-do Republicans arranged a lavish dinner at Delmonico's for the Senator from Maine. The gesture backfired in a hostile press. Gould had sold his *World* to Joseph Pulitzer, and Field's *Mail and Express* was "not the kind of paper apt to influence the voters."

The *World* called the dinner the "Feast of Belshazzar and the Money Kings," and ran a cartoon on its front page showing Blaine, Field, Gould, and Sage dining off "Monopoly Soup," while a starving

family in rags looked through the window. Across the page was bla-
zoned the headline:

MILLIONAIRES AND MONOPOLISTS
SEAL ALLEGIANCE
A List of the Men Gathered by
Cyrus Field and Jay Gould

"Delmonico's was filled with millionaires last night," the feature
story read. It went on: "The object of the banquet was twofold—
nominally to honor James G. Blaine, but really to raise a corruption
fund of $500,000 with which to attempt to defeat the will of the
people." The evening assumed dire proportions in the subsequent
election battle and may well have contributed to Blaine's defeat.

Field's Republican loyalties were undiminished by the outcome. He
shifted his concern to General Grant, for whom he had always had a
warm affection. It was not an unlikely bond between them. Grant's
tendency to trust those whom he liked and found congenial had led
to his downfall at the hands of his associates at Grant & Ward. In
many ways lovable and in all ways unaffected, he lacked, to the same
degree as Field, the ruthlessness that might have saved him. Now
racked by cancer of the throat, he was struggling to complete his
memoirs to ensure his family of funds after his death. Field wanted to
help by raising money for the family's support, as he had done for
Garfield. At the turn of the year he sent letters of solicitation to half
a dozen wealthy friends he knew were sympathetic.

Through rumors in the press, Grant heard about the proposal and
wrote to Field on January 6, 1885: "I appreciate the motive and the
friendship which have dictated this course on your part, but, on ma-
ture reflection, I regard it as due to myself and family to decline this
proffered generosity." With a ready understanding of the general's
pride, Field wrote immediately that he was canceling all appeals for
funds, adding, "I have for several days been anxious to call and see
you, but have been prevented by press of business and a severe cold."
As it turned out, Grant's autobiography, completed just before he
died, netted his family about $500,000.

28

Lamb Among Lions

>>>>>><<<<<< With Cleveland in the White House in 1885 and a new Secretary of State replacing Evarts, Field despaired of any rapid action on his Pacific cable bill. The landing rights granted in 1879 had been voided by failure to exercise the option. There had been, his daughter wrote, "no enthusiasm shown, and no company formed"; and the project was only jokingly kept alive in a favorite toast of Dudley Field, who, after every family dinner, would remind his brother: "And now, Cyrus, we mustn't forget to drink to the world encircling." Even his first two cables had long since ceased to function; Gould's Western Union had replaced them with a pair of new ones.

Field kept in touch with those who had shared in the original adventure, and in the early summer of 1885 he sailed to England to refresh those friendships. Since George Peabody's death, there had been no one to sponsor the annual Fourth of July dinner in London, and Field assumed that role. He took the opportunity to cable General Grant, through Western Union's manager at Saratoga, that the group was joining in a toast to the former President.

In less than three weeks Grant was dead, and Cyrus, still in London, arranged with Dean Farrar and the American minister, Edward Phelps, for memorial services in Westminster Abbey to which Queen Victoria sent her personal representatives.

The main event of his London visit, however, was the dinner he gave at the Star and Garter Hotel in Richmond, commemorating the twenty-seventh anniversary of the first Atlantic cable. Field hired a special train to take the 200 guests from Waterloo Station and back, arranged for an eight-course dinner with seven kinds of wine, and provided background music for the evening.

He was among battle-tested friends now—cable veterans like Captain Anderson, Daniel Gooch, William Thomson, George Elliot, all knighted now, while he remained "Lord Cable" in name only. He was the sole survivor of the group that in 1854 had formed the nucleus of the cable undertaking in his Gramercy Park house. He could not resist appropriating much of the evening for his personal sentiments and recollections and quoted the lines of Whittier:

> Weave on, swift shuttle of the Lord,
> Beneath the deep so far,
> The bridal robe of earth's accord,
> The funeral shroud of war.

The London *Evening Standard* reported:

> Need he say more to enforce the higher view of the mission of oceanic telegraphy? He thought not; but nevertheless, in presence of the fact that within the last fortnight their great General had passed away, he could not help reminding them that before the sun on the day of his death had ceased to shine upon the cottage in which all that was mortal of him lay, the tidings of the sad event had thrilled through the "magic thread" of the cable, and within a few hours had caused the American flag to be lowered half-mast high in every great commercial port of the world.

Except for his brief appearance at a formal dinner at the Liberal Club the following July, for the distinguished London journalist F. W. Chesson, it was his last meeting with his friends in London.

At no period in its brief lifetime was Field's *Mail and Express* a truly paying proposition. During its first year it lost $31,000, and it continued to lose about $2,000 a month, with no increase in circulation. There are indications that he began to think of disposing of it as early as 1883, barely one year after its purchase and merger.

He received offers for the paper throughout 1883 and 1884—from publishers in Washington, Wilmington, Cleveland, and Albany and from individuals without portfolio—and although none met his asking price of $250,000, he was serious enough at least to talk with each of them.

It was his $45-a-week managing editor, James Foster Choate, who put the paper on its feet—at least to the point where it stopped losing money. Choate attacked the policy of featuring financial news since the gist of such news, for those who were interested, came over the ticker tape hours before it could appear in print. Wisely he insisted, "The news, instead of following the financial on the fourth page, should precede it."

He advocated eliminating all reporting that duplicated the services of the Associated Press, brightening the editorial page with "crisp and gossipy" writing, and devoting the columns to more universal subjects than "The Perils of Drinking Chloral Hydrate." As a result, circulation increased by 150 percent during 1885, with only a fractional increase in cost, and in the following year the paper produced its first profit of $461.22. It was still paying no dividends but it was a stable property.

Choate's revisions did not affect Field's painting a favorable and generally accurate picture of enterprises in which he had a financial interest; this in turn led the critical and captious New York *Times* to refer, whenever applicable, to "Field's afternoon stockjobbing sheet," and to Field himself as "that friend of British lords and deacons."

When it came to the Manhattan Railway Company, his partiality and aims were obvious. At their most recent meeting he had told the Manhattan stockholders:

> One step yet remains to be taken.... Already in Europe short lines of railway are run by electricity; and we have the highest authority in the world—that of Sir William Thomson, the great electrician of England, who has recently made a visit to America—for saying that nothing could be better fitted for the application of electricity as motive power, than an iron track raised in the air, whose "elevation" furnishes the best possible facility for "insulation." The use of electricity in place of steam ... would bring this system of rapid transit as near to perfection as we are likely to attain in our day.

This solo promotion was prompted by a family as well as business interest. For his nephew Stephen (Jonathan's son) had returned from the Coast after working as an electrical engineer for seventeen years, during which time he had helped develop one of the first electric traction motors in the country. Cyrus, Dudley, and Henry equipped Stephen with his own workshop in Stockbridge and paid him a salary of $200 a month to continue his experiments, while Cyrus—with a characteristic leap toward a half-formed but exciting idea—talked up electric power to the officers of Manhattan Railway.

An interview with an "anonymous director," published predictably in the New York *Times,* implied that Field was out of his mind in suggesting such a thing. "We haven't all got nephews who are scientific inventors," it concluded, "but a majority of us are determined to keep the elevated railroad system free of doubtful experiments. There won't be any electric motors on the elevated railroads . . . you can put that down in black and white."

Indignantly Field wrote to each director demanding to know if he was the author of the interview. All denied responsibility. He then made a typical decision. If no existing company would support him, he would create an organization that would. He formed the United States Electric Railway Company, with offices at 65 Fifth Avenue, and drew up a contract for the trial use of the New York Elevated Railroad's tracks, a section along Second Avenue, "for one year at our own expense and risk." While young Stephen later did create and test an electric locomotive, the unsigned contract remained among his uncle's papers, a reminder that Field was a generation ahead of his time. The elevated railroads were not electrified till the early 1900's.

He still could have no complaint about their operation. Manhattan stock had fluctuated, but not the patronage of its lines. The growth in number of passengers carried since he took over in 1877 makes (in round numbers) a shining record:

1877	3,000,000
1878	9,000,000
1879	46,000,000
1880	60,800,000
1881	75,600,000
1882	86,400,000
1883	92,000,000
1884	96,700,000
1885	103,300,000

Gross earnings over the same period had increased from $303,200 in 1877 to more than $7,000,000 in 1885. While Field had been president only in the early years, it was he who organized the lines and charted their future, and remained a major shareholder in the company with a substantial interest in its management.

He was now looking beyond the city's boundaries, in the only direction befitting a son of Stockbridge—to New England. As a large stockholder in the New York & New England Railroad, he now evolved a plan to bring a trunk line via Danbury, Connecticut, to connect with the New York elevated system at a terminal he would build on Second Avenue at Twenty-third Street. Thus, one would be able to travel from Boston to any point in Manhattan without getting one's feet wet on a rainy day.

He formed a pool with Russell Sage to corner New England stock. Seeing in Field's scheme a chance to get the better of Vanderbilt by diverting traffic from the New York Central, Sage readily joined in buying up New England stock to the extent of $1,850,000. The second largest single block of $450,000 was held by a Boston syndicate.

Complete control was all but in their hands when the State of Massachusetts put on auction $7,000,000 worth of New York & New England mortgage bonds. Control was arbitrarily snatched from them when their bid was rejected in favor of one, presented by the Boston syndicate, which was $94,000 lower. The argument advanced by Governor George Robinson and his council was that the award was "in the best interests of the state." But it was believed that the governor feared that Gould was backing the New York offer; this meant to him the calculated ruin of the road. Robinson was right. Unable to resist a fight, Gould had come from his declared retirement to throw his financial weight into the battle.

Field was so disgusted that he sold his New York & New England Railroad shares at a $100,000 loss, declaring, "I would not go back in that directors' room if they gave me the whole State of Massachusetts." He was later able to force an oblique apology from Robinson for implying that he was involved in a scheme to wreck the railroad in order to take it over at rock-bottom prices.

At this time he began, uncharacteristically, to plunge into the market deeply, speculating in commodities and joining Gould in a pool to trade in Western Union stock. The fever spread to members of his family. Edward was speculating heavily, and Cyrus junior wrote in behalf of his small brokerage firm: "Dear Papa—We will be willing and glad to buy 25,000 shares of Western Union at any time on 10% margin. We will give the numbers to the pool and promise not to loan to anyone for use." A million and a half dollars' worth of stock on 10 percent margin—quite an order for a young man six years out of college! To some extent, Dudley and, to a greater extent, Henry were guided by Cyrus' investments in the market, Henry stating trustfully, "Do with my stock as you'd do with your own."

His association with Gould was making him suspect in many quarters of Wall Street. When he retired from the directory of the Mercantile Trust Company, rumors immediately circulated that he had borrowed extensively from the company and found himself embarrassed. Actually, he was severing official connections with most of the companies he was engaged in, chiefly for the sake of greater freedom. His *Mail and Express* was suspect, too, perhaps justifiably, and the *Times* continued its attacks, calling the paper "a subsidized tout for all the crooked schemes in Wall Street. The *Mail and Express* is owned by Cyrus W. Field, the partner and associate of Jay Gould.... We labour as hard to protect the public against Gould's schemes as Cyrus W. Field's sheet labours to entrap them into those schemes."

On May 16, 1835, the *Mail and Express* featured a story headed "Striking Facts in Regard to Railroad Property—Remarkable Growth of the Elevated System." It rehashed an interview that Field had given on returning from his world tour in 1881, in which he had predicted a sharp break in the market *except* in shares of the New York Elevated Railroad Company. Figures, notably those of railroad stocks, were tabulated to prove his predictions sound. The article stated:

> In view of the correctness of Mr. Field's prognostications at that time, his opinion that good stocks will rise and worthless ones almost entirely disappear will, no doubt, be regarded with great respect by investors.

There was left no doubt what was meant by "good stocks." The article went on to say:

> In face of the great decline in railway property generally.... Manhattan Elevated has advanced from 15¼ to 95½, or over *five hundred percent*. This remarkable advance has been due to the steady increase in the earning capacity of the elevated system, which has demonstrated its ability to pay 6 percent per annum on its capital stock, and earn a surplus besides.

The story served notice that Field was about to support and invest heavily in the Manhattan Railway Company—a bit of news which Gould, as largest stockholder in the firm, must have relished.

By January, 1886, Manhattan stock had risen from the 70's to 128 and was pushed to 164 by Field's support. Throughout the year this "genial friend of canons and earls," as the New York *Times* delighted in reporting, had "his couriers flying around Wall Street offering 163 for thousands of shares." It was true; he was buying all the stock he could. By the time his bullish program had lifted the price to 175, he was reported as boasting "that the Manhattan's franchise alone was worth $50,000,000 and that this, apart from any other property of the company was worth about $200 a share."

He placed most of his transactions, especially in commodities, through Field, Lindley, Wiechers & Company (Edward's firm had taken on another partner), which held most of his securities, and through T. W. Pearsall, a close friend of Edward's and Dan Lindley's. The connection with Edward was natural. Unfortunately, however, Edward fancied himself a young Jay Gould, who, if ever cornered in an indiscretion, could extricate himself in time. But he was far from having Gould's resourcefulness and ingenuity.

There were other dubious omens on Field's personal horizon. He had been forced to caution Cyrus junior on his reckless speculations and to request from his youngest son a promise "to do as you may desire in regard to my family expenses, etc. I will not borrow any money of anyone." Edward's domestic life was shaky, he was complaining of headaches, and his doctor had written Cyrus: "I believe his imprudent indulgence in stimulants contributes to his melancholy." His daughter Fanny was ill at Menton with a severe case of gout, and he was obliged to finance both a nurse and carriage for her care. His daughter Alice was hovering on the fringes of schizophrenia. In one of her frequent periods of lucidity she had written a small volume called *Palermo,* published by G. P. Putnam's, a revealing mixture of fact and fancy, romance and poetic imagery.

These worries forced him into still more strenuous activity and, for some curious reason, an increasing recklessness. His holdings in the Manhattan Railway Company climbed from 10,000 to 70,000 shares, which, at his estimated price of $200, would have represented a tidy fortune of $14,000,000. However Pearsall was forced to warn him that his margin on shares acquired through their office was, although legal, more than 80 percent. Wrote Pearsall: "I do not think it probable that Manhattan will be seriously attacked, but it may— and if you can, I think it wise you make arrangements to meet it at once, for with a bad break, it would be most unfortunate."

He ignored these warnings, even though he must have known that Gould and Sage were waiting in ambush. The time was right for sweet revenge on Cyrus Field for lowering the elevated railway fare six years before. Early in 1887 they began unloading their Manhattan holdings. As fast as the shares became available, Field bought them up at the now inflated price.

The selling pressure overweighed Field's buying, and the stock began to slip. He unloaded his Western Union shares, which had also dropped in value owing in part to Gould's manipulation, and kept on buying—up to well over 80,000 shares. Simultaneously, the bottom dropped out of the commodity market. On Friday morning, June 24, 1887, Manhattan opened at 156 and, by 10 point drops, slid to 114 in the first half hour's trading. Wall Street panicked, and the rumor circulated that Field had sold out to Gould at 90. The squeeze was on. Field started borrowing to hold onto the shares he owned on margin. Quickly apprised of this, Gould withdrew his funds from the banks which lent Field money. The banks began calling in Field's loans, and he was in a hopeless trap.

By now he must have known who his opponents were, and he decided to sue for peace. It was a bitter decision. He had no friends behind him in this battle for survival—no one to turn to but Jay Gould.

June 24, 1887, was not just a black day in Field's life. It was a date engraved on tombstone granite.

Through an intermediary he appealed to Gould. He had no alternative but to offer 78,000 shares in Manhattan, which he had purchased at $175, to Jay Gould for the latter's price of $120 a share. In that single transaction he lost more than $4,250,000. The balance of his stock, some 10,000 shares, was forced to follow—some at as low a price as $90—and with the repayment of his loans, the total twenty-four-hour loss reached close to $6,000,000, virtually his entire net worth.

Russell Sage told a reporter from the *Times:*

> Mr. Gould is a noble-hearted generous man. Mind you, I don't say a word for myself; I'll leave my own praise to somebody else. Mr. Gould saved Mr. Field from teetotal ruin, and in his broad-minded, open-hearted way he put himself in the breach and saved Wall Street and the whole country from overwhelming panic. . . . But . . . the newspapers pitch into him, Wall Street reviles him, and he gets no credit anywhere. And Mr. Cyrus Field, what does he do? Why he doesn't even raise his voice to defend the generous man who rushed to his rescue.

Field was as angry as a wounded lion. He confronted Sage with the *Times* report, and forced "Uncle Russell" to eat his words—a retraction Sage consented to "in the interests of peace."

Meantime, John T. Terry, the broker who had acted as an intermediary between Gould and Field, gave his report to the *Tribune,* and for its particular color one should keep in mind that Gould had lent Whitelaw Reid money after Horace Greeley's death to keep the paper afloat:

> Mr. Gould was applied to for aid, and he generously loaned $1,000,000 of bonds, taking therefor no security whatever. This not being sufficient he purchased most reluctantly and at much personal inconvenience $5,000,000 of the stock of the Manhattan Elevated at 120. A few days later he stated to me that he feared this was not sufficient to afford all the relief needed, and he thought he would be obliged to take the remaining $2,800,000, which he did at the same price, and distributed all or the greater portion of it among his friends. But this was not the end. A few days later I was again asked to his office, when he said to me, "More assistance is needed, but I have declined to go any further. Won't you please look at their papers [Field, Lindley, Wiechers & Company] and see if you can suggest any way for them to obtain money."
>
> After looking into the matter, I said, "Mr. Gould, you have already done more than could be reasonably asked of any man, but I am assured that $300,000 more will be sufficient, and I think you can loan it safely, although the securities are not otherwise available." He replied, "Very well, I will draw the check." Here was assistance rendered of over $9,000,000 and although the stocks were purchased upon thirty days' time, the necessities of the case required immediate payment which Mr. Gould made at much personal inconvenience. . . .
>
> The transaction not only saved the parties, but beyond question saved a panic in New York.

There is one closing scene to this sad business. Alice Northrop Snow, Gould's niece, recounted an evening at Lyndhurst, Gould's estate next door to Field's, when his desperate neighbor called in a last, humiliating plea for help:

> Mr. Field—it is largely my remembrance of Mr. Field that day that invariably brings back the scene so clearly—sat slumped in his chair. He was pale and spent. He looked physically sick. He spoke very little, and, when he did, everything about him, his words and gestures, especially his gestures, made me think of a drowning man

beseeching a rope. I don't think I have ever seen a picture of more abject despair.

Later Field was shown to his carriage, and "when he was seated, virtually collapsed against the cushions."

He was back where he had started more than fifty years before. Almost everything—his Manhattan stock, his shares in Western Union, all his railroad securities and investments in coal, steel, and utilities, along with all his cash reserves—was gone. True, there were some assets left, in property and bank stocks, and he still had his Anglo-American holdings. But it took no seer to predict that these would vanish in the final reckoning. In prospect, he was as thoroughly wiped out as it was possible to be.

29

Years of the Locust

➤➤➤➤➤✕◄◄◄◄◄ Perhaps in no other period was failure more intolerable. Success and wealth, which were synonymous, had a peculiar virtue in that Gilded Age and the man who was without them —or, even worse, had once possessed and later squandered them— slipped from grace. Kind rallied to kind, and society protected those it had to. But there is no charity more devastating than that born of pity, and Cyrus Field was now reduced to charity.

His first thought was for Mary, and although she could have hardly escaped awareness of his fall, he kept things running as before—as long as he was able. She did her part of keeping up a front of affluence and hospitality. At a luncheon in honor of Mrs. Franklin B. Lord, the wife of Field's attorney, the *Home Journal* noted:

> The table decoration consisted of fourteen baskets of rare roses, which were distributed among the guests after the repast. The daintily devised menus were printed in white and gold. During the entertainment delightful music was discoursed on zithers and mandolins concealed behind a lattice of carved wood grown over with ivy, which, with the lights from lamps of different colors, the interchange of friendly toasts and the genial flow of conversation, contributed to render this luncheon especially charming.

Cyrus was living, he knew, on borrowed time. Both his country place (the house and immediate grounds) and the Gramercy Park residence were in Mary's name and thus secure for her lifetime. Everything else would have to go, if it had not already gone. This meant most of Ardsley Park, with its 700 acres, forty-one dwellings, church and school, which he now began to put "in the most attractive possible condition" preparatory to the auction block.

With Mary assured of a place to live, his next concern was for his sons. Ten thousand shares of Manhattan stock had gone to cover their losses when he found that ever since 1881 they had borrowed on securities they were holding in his name. He also covered their loans from the banking house of Drexel, Morgan & Company, which owing to Morgan's friendship for the family were handled without pressure. Most of his wealthy associates he could not turn to; they were his enemies. Pierpont Morgan, Junius Morgan's son, was an exception. There was a rectitude about young Morgan, as there had been about his father, that, whatever rumor said, kept him above shady dealings. He was capable of being ruthless with the best of them, but his name was rarely linked with Sage, Vanderbilt, or Gould.

Field placed himself in Morgan's hands with a letter, written on September 6, 1887, that was essentially a swan song to control of his own destiny:

> DEAR MR. MORGAN,
>
> No words of mine can express my thanks to you and Mr. Drexel for your kind and generous treatment of Messrs Field Lindley & Co. and for your many acts of friendship for years past in regard to myself.
>
> My doctor has informed me that it is absolutely essential that I be free for a time from all business cares, and have perfect rest. I have felt for several months quite unable to give that attention to my business affairs that they required; and in order to have perfect freedom from all matters of this kind, and to obtain, by going away, the rest I need, I desire to sell the following properties, and hope you will be willing to form a syndicate to purchase any or all of them. Of course you will be paid your commission.
>
> 1. The Washington Building.
> 2. United States Bank stock.
> 3. The Mail & Express.
>
> The Washington Building I estimate is worth to any party as an investment, $3,000,000.
>
> The United States Bank stock, including its surplus and goodwill, at least $225. a share.
>
> The Mail & Express, with its one-seventh ownership of the Associated Press, $500,000.
>
> As I desire to get away as soon as possible, I shall esteem it a very great favor if you will give this business your personal attention, so that all debts of Field Lindley & Co. can be paid before I leave New York.
>
> I remain, Dear Mr. Morgan,
> Very truly your friend,

For once he forgot to sign his name to a letter; possibly his unconscious mind resisted that finality. He also overlooked a matter which he may not have been aware of: as president of the Washington Building Company, John Lindley had borrowed $1,000,000 against the property some years before. That Field did not include his real estate in the inventory of his properties for sale was due to the fact that Drexel, Morgan had, with his instructions, taken care of that. Two weeks earlier Morgan had written him that he had received from John Jacob Astor $125,000 for Field's properties on the East Side and in Harlem, adding: "Have paid the balance to Field, Lindley & Company."

His mention of leaving New York and seeking rest and quiet meant simply retiring to Ardsley, a resolve strengthened by a letter he received the following day, September 7, from Charles Lindley, who was Edward's and, to some extent, the family's physician:

> Having anxiously watched the effects, upon you, of business cares I have often wished that you would go away for a rest, as I saw that your nervous system was suffering very much from continued strain. Now I feel that the time has come when it is absolutely necessary for you to have a change of scene & air. If you do not take a complete rest now, you soon will be so ill that you cannot attend to business & a much longer absence will be necessary.
>
> Whatever reasons you may have, to keep you here, would not influence me at all in my judgment, for rest is absolutely necessary & that at once. It is over two months that I have watched your case & you know my opinion has not been hastily formed.

He could retreat to Ardsley, as he did, but he could not escape the consequences of the last few months. His own downfall was difficult enough to face. But greater distress lay in the knowledge that the whole family had suffered. They had entrusted their investments to him, or been guided by his judgment, or simply followed his example. They had looked upon him as possessing an unfailing Midas touch and had gone along with Henry's faith: "Do with my investments as you'd do with yours." And he in complete faith had done so. Even his old friend Mark Hopkins had become involved, writing to an acquaintance, "As to my Elevated Railroad stock, I trust to Mr. Field's good judgment. . . ."

From others who had followed his advice, from beneficiaries of estates he had administered, he received letters of bitter acrimony and sometimes of desperation. Pitilessly they demanded of him: What was he going to do about it? To one such, he could only answer: "Your letter of yesterday wounded me so deeply that I could not trust myself to answer it then, but will do so within a week."

The consequences to his children hurt him most. He was forced to write to Fanny and James in Menton, who were largely dependent on him: "It will be impossible to let you have any more money at present." Knowing how this might affect her in her illness, he added: "Most earnestly do I pray that God will comfort, sustain and bless you in all your trials." It was a prayer he could have well directed at himself, and, like his father, he turned now to the Bible for his consolation. Among his papers at this time, becoming less ordered, less coherent, are noted the lines from Hebrews 12:6: "For whom the Lord loveth, he chastiseth [*sic*], and scourgeth every son whom He receiveth."

Edward and Cyrus junior had followed their father blindly to the same brink of disaster, but with even fewer precautions. Edward especially, his father's favorite son, had borrowed heavily from his own firm, and while Field had helped him out by covering his losses—believing his embarrassment was only temporary—he began to realize that Edward was in serious trouble. In addition to his reckless transactions, Edward was showing marked signs of irrationality. His doctor had prescribed that he strive for "peace of mind," but (Edward wrote his father) "how to do this with you so unwell, I know not. If you could only be your natural self again how happy we all would be. If you were only well and strong everything would be so bright, and business so easy, to carry on from this time forward."

It was too much to ask that Cyrus be himself again. He was forbidden even to see his daughter Alice, on the doctor's warning that a visit might upset her. Alice had escaped the custody of her nurses and managed to make her way by train to Buffalo and then Niagara Falls. They had found her in a hotel room overlooking the cataract, and she begged to stay, saying she could not sleep unless she heard the roaring of the falls. They indulged her until she talked of leaping into them. Then they were forced to put her in a private sanatarium in Pleasantville, New York.

Although Edward's mind too was clouding, he did his best to carry on. At the turn of the year, in early January, 1888, he wrote his father that he was consulting almost daily with Drexel, Morgan & Company and that they had been "most friendly" and "asked most kindly after you. . . ." He went on to say:

> Mr. Morgan went over everything most fully with me, and says he has not the least doubt of our carrying everything through and that you can stay away as long as you could desire and that all would turn out well. . . .
>
> This is his proposition. He, Mr. Morgan, will loan us 300,000 on such securities as we are able to give, such as the Mail & Ex—and any other securities which are convenient for us to give him. . . . The present 150,000 can remain as long as we desire. Mr. Morgan . . . said "by my doing this for you everything should be easy for your firm as well as your Father. . . ."
>
> Please telegraph on receipt of this letter if you are willing to accept Mr. Morgan's offer and if you are pleased. With warmest love to Mamma and yourself and all the dear ones.
>
> Ever your devoted son
EDWARD

From his other son, Cyrus, Field received what may have been an equally heartening communication. It read *in toto:* "To Cyrus W. Field, Esq. I hereby promise on my word as a gentleman not to enter into any speculation what-so-ever from this date. (Signed) Cyrus W. Field Jr."

He was now financially pretty much in the hands of Pierpont Morgan, and if he had to be indebted to anyone, he could not have chosen one of greater sympathy. Morgan advanced him the money to keep in force the premiums on his life insurance policies and during 1888 disposed of half his interest in the heavily encumbered Washington Building, although Field insisted on an option clause in the contract that would allow him to buy it back. Ardsley Park, for which he estimated he had spent $1,000,000, went to Charles Henry Butler for subdivision into building lots. Mary kept the house, of course, and the twenty-one acres which surrounded it.

In March the *Mail and Express* was sold to Elliott F. Shepard for $500,000—twice what Field had paid for it—but Cyrus somewhat surreptitiously withheld five shares worth $19,000, and it took Shepard several months to get them out of him. As was the case in the option to repurchase the Washington Building, Field clung with naive, unshakable faith in ultimate recovery; he could not let go completely.

By 1890 neither Cyrus nor Mary was altogether well. Field had grown nervous and moody, his blood pressure was high, and Isabella remembered that in March his doctor told her and her brothers that any excitement might be too much for him. His brothers were considerate and attentive. Henry, now editor and proprietor of the Protestant religious publication *Evangelist,* and Dudley, retired and living nearby in Hastings, were frequent visitors at Ardsley. Stephen had used his Coast connections to help Cyrus dispose of his Western railroad and mining stocks. He had reason to be grateful to Cyrus. When Stephen purchased a house in Washington at the corner of A and First Streets, Cyrus had helped him clear up debts involved in that transaction. At that time the Supreme Court Justice wrote:

> My dear brother—You will live, I am sure, until you are a hundred years old. So good an act, so generously done, can only be compensated by a century of happy years. You have taken a great load off my mind and heart. Thanks, a thousand thanks for this gift.... Though my bread tossed upon the water does not often come back— yours will, I am certain—a hundredfold.

It was not coming back a hundredfold to Cyrus. He was scraping the bottom of the barrel and in July, 1890, was obliged to sell four of his carriages at Ardsley for a paltry $365 to a New York livery stable.

In that winter of his discontent there was one shining interlude. On December 2, 1890, he and Mary celebrated their golden wedding anniversary. Fifty years before he had brought Mary to the city to begin life in a third-rate boardinghouse, and three months later he and the firm for which he worked were bankrupt. Through incredible trials and sacrifices they had reached the top rank of their generation. Mary had given him two things he prized highly in those years: loyalty and utter faith.

The invitations, reading simply "At Home," had gone supposedly to only family and intimate friends, yet the *Tribune* reported, "A thousand or more people were present, and hundreds of messages were received at their door.... Their spacious house was crowded. ... There were no brighter looking people in the whole assembly than Mr. and Mrs. Field. On Sunday Mr. Field was seventy-one years old, but yesterday's happiness took off almost twenty-five years if Mr. Field's looks and acts account for anything."

The reception lasted from four to six and was followed by something more to Field's taste, a family dinner, which included his three brothers—Dudley, Stephen, and Henry—his and Mary's six children, and fifteen grandchildren.

A letter from James Anderson noted:

> it was also fifty years since I went to sea as a sailor boy, and it was just twenty-five years since we made our first voyage in the *Great Eastern*. . . . The days and years are rolling away, and we may well cling to the memory of exciting and active days when we were twenty-five to thirty years younger and the future filled with nervous uncertainty.

Sir James enclosed an illuminated scroll, signed by eighty-five friends of Field's in England, expressing "to you and to your amiable and devoted wife our earnest and heartfelt congratulations on your golden-wedding day." Anderson admitted that he had had trouble gathering the names, for "oh, how many have passed away! It's like calling a roll after a battle—so few could be found." Yet the four-score names included many of the great men of the cable-laying days —Samuel Canning, Josiah Latimer Clark, Douglas Galton, the Duke of Argyll, Henry Clifford, Willoughby Smith, C. V. De Sauty, John Pender, Robert Dudley—and names less intimately associated with the venture, such as Julius Reuter, Samuel Cunard, Frederic Farrar, the widows of William Gladstone and Richard Cobden, and even Oscar Wilde.

The anniversary was the final bright spot in Cyrus' life, and its cheerful overtones were quickly smothered by his wife's increasing illness. Mary seldom came down to dinner now, and that summer when the family gathered for her seventy-fourth birthday on August 28, 1891, they dined together for the last time. Dudley, himself a venerable eighty-seven, proposed the toast: "Mary Stone Field, the wife of Cyrus W. Field, the mother of seven children and of sixteen grandchildren, a perfect wife, a perfect mother, a perfect grandmother. God bless her."

Less than three months later Mary was dead of a lung congestion. She died as she had lived, with patience and without complaint. After simple services, attended only by her family and friends, she was buried in the family plot in Stockbridge Cemetery. The press took only casual notice of her passing, but the Reverend Dr. Arthur Brooks, a longtime friend of the family, wrote truly of her:

> The position in which life placed her was one which made great demands, and she met them all. As the center of a large family circle,

involving wide and important interests, and also as the intimate friend of men and women of leading position, she never failed to manifest the ready wisdom and large sympathy for which each occasion called. She was calm under all trouble, reasonable in all perplexity, and thankful in all happiness.

Cyrus never rallied from her death. His brother Henry wrote:

> From that moment he lost his interest in life. He had no heart to go anywhere, but once came to us with Dudley on my birthday. It seemed to comfort him to be with his brothers, and we tried all our gentle arts to cheer him. He brightened a little and once or twice a smile passed over his sad face. But his heart was in the grave. . . .

There was to be no release from grief. His daughter Mary was extremely ill with tuberculosis. His other daughter, Alice, moved in a curious dreamworld of French aristocracy and did not recognize her father. She was transferred from the private sanatarium in Pleasantville to Bloomingdale, in White Plains, New York, where the doors closed on her rational existence.

On Saturday, November 28, 1891, the *Tribune* broke the news of the bankruptcy of Edward's firm, of which Cyrus was, of course, a nominal partner:

> The suspension of the firm of Field, Lindley, Wiechers & Co., yesterday brought a double blow to Cyrus W. Field, who is already crushed by the weight of the loss of his wife, who died on Monday. His eldest son, Edward M., is the head of the house, and with its collapse comes the revelation that a mental disorder has seized its senior member. Only one consolation remains to the afflicted family, the fact that this mental illness may prove to be the explanation of proceedings in the conduct of business that otherwise might raise the suspicion of disgraceful irregularities.

The suspicion of irregularities was quickly confirmed. "It is no longer doubtful," the New York *Herald* reported on December 1, "that wholesale rehypothecation of securities was indulged in." Edward's firm—or more exactly, Edward, since Daniel Lindley appears completely in the clear—had pledged securities held in trust against loans which Edward had negotiated to finance his market speculations. Specifically, a block of Union Pacific bonds which had been offered as collateral on a loan of $700,000 had disappeared completely.

If there were extenuating circumstances, they were perhaps best summarized by an anonymous friend, who told the press that "the firm has been virtually without a head for some time. The death of his mother and the illness of his sister have been enough to bring to a crisis any mental weakness that may have been developed by Edward's overwork." There was widespread belief that this plea of mental illness was a shield to cover gross misconduct. The *Tribune* report of November 28 continued:

> A still further affliction to the Field family is the probably mortal illness of the daughter of Cyrus W. Field, who married Daniel A. Lindley, a partner in the failed firm. Mrs. Lindley has been ill for some time, and the death of her mother aggravated her illness. . . . Lying at the point of death, it is feared, she may be in ignorance of the sorrows which are multiplying about her father. The elder Mr. Field was brought from Ardsley, his country home, to his home in Gramercy Park yesterday morning, overwhelmed by the misfortunes so closely heaped together.

Overwhelmed he was, but still impelled to do whatever he could to extricate Edward and save the firm at least from permanent disgrace. With Mary gone, her property was in his name, and this he mortgaged for $500,000 to help cover Edward's debts. It proved to be very little. There seemed no possible help for Edward and no relief from his own sense of guilt. He had speculated rashly, and the result was summarized in the news report: "Well informed persons believe the Field firm was virtually wiped out when the collapse of the Manhattan Elevated 'Corner' occurred five years ago. The house is said to have been interested in a pool of 25,000 shares."

Edward's physician, Charles Lindley, had him taken to "a more quiet neighborhood," and he was kept incommunicado for a while. Cyrus had his daughter Mary Lindley moved into his home and brought Edward's wife, Clara, distraught and all but destitute, to the Gramercy Park house. Beyond this, there was not much he could do. He was "ill from shock and suffering from nervous prostration," according to his city doctor, Eugene Fuller. On December 2, four days after Edward's failure had been announced, he collapsed completely and was confined to bed. The *Tribune* noted on that day:

> Mr. Field sank under a load of affliction such as few men are called upon to bear, and his age—he was seventy-two years old yesterday— has deprived him of much of his power of resistance to the mental and physical strain. His son is wrecked in mind and ruined in fortune; his wife has just been laid in her grave; his daughter is on a

sickbed from which she can never arise in health; his daughter-in-law is prostrate from grief and worry. Small wonder it is that the late autumn of his life finds him broken in health by the force of these blows.

Needless to say, speculation on Edward and his condition was rife throughout the city, and not always kind. The more scurrilous members of the press recalled that a French maid in Edward's household, named Marie Arigasei, had committed suicide some years before, an event now vaguely linked to Edward's character, and newspaper reports suggested that the Field scion was being blackmailed by her husband. Detectives picketed the Gramercy Park house, awaiting Edward's reappearance and apparently intending to arrest him, but refused to say on whose orders they were acting. It was also rumored that Edward had rifled his father's strongbox of securities. The *Tribune* reported:

> It is asserted that he exhausted his father's resources before the collapse came. The elder Mr. Field was badly crippled by the Manhattan "deal," and this property was not readily available to his son.

The New York *Herald* was more specific:

> Cyrus Field, led to suppose that comparatively moderate sums would save his son's firm and that the use of his securities would enable him to tide over the disastrous results of unfortunate but not criminal speculations, gave his son the key to his strong box at the safe deposit vaults and told him to help himself to what he needed to carry his firm through the period of storm and stress.

Field confirmed this, asserting that "any securities he may have obtained were freely given to him." But it appears true that Edward made away with everything he could lay his hands on—a fact which convinced the Fields of his insanity and led Dr. Matthew Field, Cyrus' nephew, to uphold this verdict when it was challenged by other reputable doctors.

On December 15, 1891, Edward was arrested and, under the protest of Dr. Granger at the Mount Vernon sanatarium, taken to the Ludlow Street jail. Among the charges now brought against him was that of forgery; he was accused of raising large sums of money on false bills of lading drawn against mythical cargoes of wheat (one of the steamships on which he pretended to have made shipments was in China at the time). The question of his sanity was up to the courts;

he had not yet been proved legally insane. The amount of money missing from the firm was raised by rumor to $3,000,000, later authenticated as total liabilities of $2,151,000 against assets of $30,000.

Field was considered too ill to be told of his son's arrest and imprisonment, but he heard of it anyway and took a turn for the worse. At times he was dangerously close to death. On Christmas Eve, Edward was pronounced legally insane, and this seemed, in a grim way, to relieve his father's mind—Edward had not been conscious of his actions. Young Edward was confined to Bloomingdale (where Alice was in the women's wing) with little hope of recovery.

After his death, an autopsy showed that Edward's mental deterioration resulted from the horseback-riding accident during the Christmas holidays of 1866. Now it was Christmas again, but no wreaths hung in the windows of the Gramercy Park house. Mary was fighting for her life against pneumonia. Two weeks later, on January 11, 1892, the fight was over, and the shades were drawn.

30

Return to Stockbridge

⤙⤙⤙⤙⤙⤚⤚⤚⤚⤚⤚ "Mr. Field's Acre of Sunflowers" the New
York *Sunday Times* headlined it after a reporter visited Ardsley and
found Field hovering tenderly over a meadowful of the tall plants with
their giant yellow heads. They had a double purpose, Field explained.
Besides their beauty, they provided seeds to feed his hens, saving him
the cost of grain.

Precisely a quarter century before, on the deck of the *Great Eastern*
he had told Willoughby Smith that he would gladly settle for a small
farm in the country with a cow and chickens. That was about what
he had finally settled for. The New York *Herald* noted at the close
of 1891:

> By his own magnificent and untiring genius he had climbed to the
> very top rung of the ladder of fortune and fame. By others' acts he
> had been plunged down to the bottom rung of ignominy and poverty.
> What wonder that he called for peace! And the peace of death would
> have come to him long ago but for the tenacity of his nature which
> made him cling to life as he had often clung to purpose, when there
> seemed nothing left to cling to.

Now he began to put his personal affairs in order, these affairs concerning largely the mementos of Atlantic cable days. On the walls of
his house and in Gramercy Park hung oils and watercolors of the ships
at sea and the activities on deck, some by Robert Dudley, some by
Henry O'Neil. These he gave to his old friend General Cesnola, who
acted as recipient for the Metropolitan Museum. With this collection
went his various medals and awards, of which he made the last of his
habitual lists:

1. Large gold medal from U. S. Government (in mother-of-pearl box).
2. Engraved gold snuff box from City of New York.
3. Gold medal from Chamber of Commerce.
4. Gold medal presented by "a few friends in New York."
5. Gold medal presented by Chamber of Commerce of Liverpool.
6. Gold medal presented by State of Wisconsin.
7. Gold medal, Grand Prix of French Exposition of 1867.
8. Decoration: Order of Knightly Commanders of Italy.

He went to Stockbridge in early April, 1892, for his brother Henry's birthday. Of that reunion Henry wrote that "we could not repress the foreboding that this family meeting might be our last, and so it proved." On his return to New York he transferred his townhouse to his daughter Isabella and, with the financial help of Pierpont Morgan, moved his few possessions to the house in Ardsley. The family thought the country air would do him good, and, as Henry wrote, "the beautiful scenery for a time delighted his eye, and the change of air brought a touch of the old spirit, as if perchance his strength were about to return. But it was only a momentary flush. . . ."

It would take more than country air to conquer his malaise, and his decline grew more pronounced. Dr. Coutant recorded:

> I saw a great change for the worse. The most trivial business matter caused him to become extremely irritable, and often completely unbalanced him. His ambition was gone, and it was with the greatest difficulty he could be made to take exercise. If his troubles were spoken of by any of the villagers, he would weep like a child, and as a consequence have a delirious night.

His brother Dudley, close by at Hastings, was with him for a while each day. Beyond that, he had little company except for the faithful servants who attended him. The townsfolk knew him mostly as a distant and benevolent old gentleman, who in the heat of past summers had sent his gardeners home for fear of sunstroke. From time to time he would go for carriage rides about the countryside; but even this began to tire him, and he spent his days on the veranda overlooking the Tappan Zee.

His family moved him to an upstairs bedroom in the northeastern corner of the house, from which he could see the Hudson and, if he chose, Gould's graceful *Atalanta* riding at her anchorage (the *Inanada* had long since been sold). He was so weak now that he never left his bed, his mind began to wander totally, and on June 29 Dr. Coutant wrote to Franklin B. Lord, one of his attorneys:

> In reply to your inquiry concerning the condition of Mr. Cyrus W. Field and the effect that the discussion of business would have upon him, I have only this to say: Mr. Field, by reason of his mental condition, is utterly incompetent to transact business of any kind or to converse intelligently upon any subject. He has been delirious for the past thirty-six hours. This state is not of sudden origin; it has been developing for many weeks. During the preliminary stages he was able to rouse himself and to give attention to whatever was presented to him and to form an intelligent judgment concerning it—but now his attention cannot be fixed and all his conversation is irrational and incoherent. He has in addition delusions and hallucinations of various kind. These symptoms may disappear in a few days—but they are more severe and more persistent than any that have preceded them.

The symptoms never disappeared, except for brief moments of lucidity. Between those moments he would lapse into unconsciousness or, what was worse, delirium, when they were forced to give him morphine. During periods of irrationality he stood with the captain on the bridge of the *Great Eastern,* shouting directions to the fleet, or found himself deserted on the shores of Valentia, and cried wildly, "Hold those ships!" He no longer recognized his family: Dudley became William Gladstone, while Henry and others peopled his room with the ghosts of Frederick Gisborne, Edward Archibald and Finley Morse.

By July 6 his weight had dropped to eighty pounds, and Dr. Coutant told the family, "His magnificent constitution is making a desperate fight against death, but death is sure to win," adding later: "He will never feel the sting of his afflictions; he will be in a mental slumber, and it is best that this is so." It was in slumber that he died on the morning of July 12, 1892. The attending nurse found his breath increasing sharply and his pulse so rapid that it could not be counted. Available relatives were quickly summoned, and by his bedside at the end were Dudley, Stephen, Henry, and his daughter Isabella—a majority of all the family that was left to him. The immediate cause of death was an internal hemorrhage.

Simple services were held at Ardsley on the fourteenth, with a special train engaged to bring the mourners from the city. It was asked that floral tributes be omitted, but the casket was blanketed with white carnations sent by the Anglo-American Company, with two lengths

of cord across them to represent a broken cable. Present was a correspondent for the New Hampshire *Sentinel,* alone reflecting the interest
of New England in its famous son, who wrote:

> ... Even in death the face showed the marks of the terrible suffering
> through which he had passed, and of consuming grief, bitterer than
> Marah's water. Hardly anything more sorrowful in our history than
> this. Griefs there are in the lives of every man and woman that ever
> hath been; there is no escape from them, they follow us through life
> to death.
>
> In one corner of the room with heads bowed sat three old men—
> the eldest had passed fourscore—these were the brothers of the dead
> man. David Dudley, the great jurist, whose fame has extended to all
> the law courts in this land; by his side was Stephen J., a judge of the
> Supreme Court of the United States and once a prominent Dem-
> ocratic candidate for the Presidency, and next to him Henry M., for
> many years a prominent evangelist. Cornelius Vanderbilt, the owner
> of many millions, sat near by, his face pale and sorrowful, barely
> two weeks having passed since he stood by the coffin of his favorite
> son, in whose grave lies buried the brightest hopes of his house.
>
> On the green outside was Robert Ingersoll, the great iconoclast,
> and many others equally famous. Notably absent were two other
> millionaires who, a few years ago, nearly compassed the dead man's
> financial ruin—Jay Gould and Russell Sage. One is wooing health
> in the Far West, which all his hoarded millions will not bring back;
> they do not purchase for him surcease from pain, nor banish the
> dread spector that follows him into his dreams at night, making sleep
> a hell more terrible than Dante's pool. Russell Sage was absent though
> he knew Cyrus Field quite well; possibly he remembered the day
> when Cyrus Field was cornered on Manhattan, and the operators
> swept away five millions of the dead man's money. No, it was just
> as well they stopped away, for neither he nor Jay Gould would have
> been welcomed at the funeral.

Also among the crowd was "a venerable old man with a white
flowing beard and white hair," who attracted the attention of reporters. He was found to be James Richardson of Wales, one of the cable
ship crew who had anchored the shore lines at Valentia before the
Great Eastern set out on her epoch-making voyage.

Dudley later wrote:

> The next morning we went in a funeral train to Stockbridge, where
> we rode slowly through the village street, so beautiful with its long
> avenue of maples and elms, to the old Congregational Church, in

which our father had preached for so many years, and the beloved form was laid in the aisle before the pulpit. The service was very simple: only a prayer, with reading of the Scriptures and the singing of one or two favorite hymns; and the procession formed again and moved across the green to the burying ground where our father and mother lay, and where his wife had been laid but a few weeks before. There, in the sweet summer afternoon, we laid him to rest in a bed of pine boughs and covered with flowers. Peacefully now he sleeps where he so often wished to sleep, by the side of his wife and close to his father and mother, his sister and his oldest son. Long as any of us survive, shall we cherish the memory of our beloved brother.

The inscription above his grave read simply:

CYRUS WEST FIELD
TO WHOSE COURAGE, ENERGY AND PERSEVERANCE
THE WORLD OWES THE ATLANTIC TELEGRAPH

The story of Field's life, in a sense continues—no longer wrapped in gutta-percha but in modern polyethylene, and flowing through the oceans not only in code or letters, but also in spoken words. A New England contemporary summed it up:

Every message that flashes through the Atlantic cables is his eulogy. His virtues are written in water in a new sense; and the memory of his indomitable courage; of his just sense of the right means to the right end; of his enthusiasm, and of his power of generating enthusiasm in others; of his fortitude; of his wise generalship; of his large views, and of much else, will endure.

Bibliography

Albion, Robert G., *The Rise of New York Port*. New York, Scribner, 1939.

Annual Register. London, Rivington, 1858, 1865, 1866.

The Atlantic Telegraph, Its History. London, Bacon, 1966.

Bates, David Homer, *Lincoln in the Telegraph Office*. New York, Century, 1907.

Bishop, C., and Bucklin, J., *The Chronicle of One Hundred and Fifty Years: New York Chamber of Commerce*. New York, Scribner, 1918.

Bolitho, Hector, *Albert, Prince Consort*. Indianapolis, Bobbs-Merrill, 1964.

Brett, John Watkins, *On the Origin and Progress of the Oceanic Electric Telegraph*. London, privately printed, 1858.

Briggs, C. F., and Maverick, A., *The Story of the Telegraph and a History of the Great Atlantic Cable*. New York, Rudd & Carleton, 1858.

Bright, Charles, *The Story of the Atlantic Cable*. New York, Appleton, 1903.

————, *Submarine Telegraphs, Their History, Construction, and Working*. London, Lockwood, 1898.

Bright, E. G., *The Life Story of Charles Tilston Bright*. London, Constable, 1910.

Britton, B. S., *History of Paper Manufacturing in the United States*. New York, Howard, 1919.

Brown, Henry Collins, *Valentine's Manual of Old New York*. New York, Valentine's Manual, Inc., 1919–1927, Vols. I–XI.

Brunel, Isambard, *The Life of Isambard Kingdom Brunel*. London, Longmans, Green, 1870.

Clarke, Arthur C., *Voice Across the Sea*. New York, Harper, 1958.

Clews, Henry, *Fifty Years in Wall Street*. New York, Irving, 1915.

Collins, F. L., *Moneytown*. New York, Putnam, 1946.

Collins, Irene, *The Age of Progress*. London, Arnold, 1964.
Cruikshank, R. J., *The Roaring Century*. London, Hamish Hamilton, 1948.

Davis, C. T., *The Manufacture of Paper*. Philadelphia, Baird, 1886.
Dibner, Bern, *The Atlantic Cable*. Norwalk, Burndy Library, 1959.
Dix, John Adams, *Memoirs of John Adams Dix*. New York, Harper, 1883.
Dugan, James, *The Great Iron Ship*. New York, Harper, 1953.
Durham, John, *Telegraphs in Victorian London*. Cambridge, Golden Head, 1959.

Field, David Dudley, *History of the County of Berkshire*. Pittsfield, Bush, 1829.
Field, Emilia R., *David Dudley Field, His Ancestors and Descendants*. Denver, privately printed, 1931.
Field, Henry Martyn, *The Story of the Atlantic Telegraph*. New York, Scribner, 1892.
———, *The Life of David Dudley Field*. New York, Scribner, 1898.
———, *Record of the Family of the Late David D. Field*. New York, privately printed, 1880.
Field, Rufus C., *The Persistent Fool*. New York, privately printed, 1962.
Field, Wells, and E. D., *Ancestors of David Dudley Field and Submit Dickinson*. Hartford, privately printed, 1966.
Flick, A. C., *Samuel J. Tilden*. New York, Dodd, Mead, 1939.
Forsyth, D. P., *The Business Press in America, 1750–1865*. Philadelphia, Chilton, 1964.

Garnham, S. A., and Hadfield, R. L., *The Submarine Cable*. London, Low, Marston, 1934.
Garratt, G. R. M., *One Hundred Years of Submarine Cables*. London, Science Museum, 1950.
Great Eastern Log, 1865, 1866 cable expeditions. Property of Submarine Cables Ltd., Greenwich, England.
Grodinsky, Julius, *Jay Gould, His Business Career*. Philadelphia, University of Pennsylvania Press, 1957.
Gurney, Samuel, *Epitome of Proceedings at a Telegraph Soirée*. London, Piper, 1862.

Halstead, Murat, *The Life of Jay Gould*. New York, Edgewood, 1892.
Harlow, A. F., *Old Wires and New Waves*. New York, Appleton-Century, 1936.
Haswell, Charles, *Reminiscences of an Octogenarian*. New York, Harper, 1896.
Hewitt, E. R., *Those Were the Days*. New York, Duell, Sloan & Pearce, 1943.
The Diary of Philip Hone, 1828–1850. New York, Dodd, Mead, 1936.

Huntington, David C., "Landscapes and Diaries: The South American Trip of F. E. Church." *Brooklyn Museum Annual*, Vol. 5 (1963).

International Telecommunication Union, *From Semaphore to Satellite*. Geneva, 1965.

Josephson, Matthew, *The Robber Barons*. New York, Harcourt, Brace, 1934.

Judson, Isabella Field, *Cyrus W. Field, His Life and Work*. New York, Harper, 1896.

Ketelbey, C. D. M., *A History of Modern Times*. London, Harrap, 1958.

Latham, Jean, *Young Man in a Hurry*. New York, Harper & Row, 1958.

Lawford, G. L., and Nicholson, L. R., *The Telcon Story*. London, Telegraph Construction & Maintenance Co., 1950.

Mabee, Carleton, *The American Leonardo, a Life of Samuel F. B. Morse*. New York, Knopf, 1943.

McDonald, Philip B., *A Saga of the Seas*. New York, Wilson-Erickson, 1937.

Mack, Edward C., *Peter Cooper, Citizen of New York*. New York, Duell, Sloan & Pearce, 1949.

Merrett, John, *Three Miles Deep*. London, Hamish Hamilton, 1958.

Mullaly, John, *The Laying of the Cable*. New York, Appleton, 1858.

———, *A Trip to Newfoundland*. New York, Strong, 1855.

Muzzey, D. S., *James G. Blaine*. New York, Dodd, Mead, 1934.

Nevins, Allan, *Abram S. Hewitt*. New York, Harper, 1935.

———, *Hamilton Fish*. New York, Dodd, Mead, 1936.

Ocean Telegraphy: The Twenty-Fifth Anniversary. New York, privately printed, 1879.

O'Connor, Richard, *Gould's Millions*. New York, Doubleday, 1962.

Pierce, Frederick C., *Field Genealogy*. Chicago, Conkey, 1901, 2 vols.

Pine, J. B., *The Story of Gramercy Park*. New York, Gramercy Park Assn., 1921.

Prescott, G. B., *History, Theory and Practice of the Electric Telegraph*. Boston, Ticknor-Fields, 1860.

Proceedings at the Banquet to Cyrus W. Field (London, July 1, 1868). London, Metchim, 1868.

Reeves, W. F., *The First Elevated Railroads in Manhattan and the Bronx*. New York, New York Historical Society, 1936.

Reid, James D., *The Telegraph in America*. New York, Doubleday, 1886.

Rolt, L. T. C., *Isambard Kingdom Brunel*. New York, St. Martin's, 1959.

Russell, William Howard, *The Atlantic Telegraph*. London, Dawson, 1866.

Sarnoff, Paul, *Russell Sage: The Money King*. New York, Obolensky, 1965.

Saward, George, *The Trans-Atlantic Submarine Telegraph*. London, privately printed, 1878.

Sedgwick, Sarah, and Marquand, Christina, *Stockbridge, 1739–1939; a Chronicle*. Great Barrington, Berkshire Courier, 1939.

Shaffner, Taliaferro P., *The Telegraph Manual*. New York, Pudney & Russell, 1859.

Simonton, J. W., and Field, Cyrus, *Atlantic Cable Mismanagement*. New York, privately printed, 1871.

Smith, E. E., *The Life and Times of Daniel Lindley*. London, Epworth, 1949.

Smith, Matthew H., *Twenty Years Among the Bulls and Bears*. New York, American, 1871.

Smith, Willoughby, *A Resumé of the Early Days of Electric Telegraphy*. Paper read at the Paris Exposition, 1881.

———, *The Rise and Extension of Submarine Telegraphy*. London, Virtue, 1891.

Snell, R. M., *The Story of Papermaking in the United States*. Holyoke, Mass., Paper Makers Chemical Corp., 1929.

Snow, Alice Northrop, *The Story of Helen Gould*. New York, Revell, 1943.

Strong, George Templeton, *Diary, 1835–1875*. New York, Macmillan, 1952.

Swanberg, W. A., *Jim Fisk, the Career of an Improbable Rascal*. New York, Scribner, 1959.

Swisher, C. B., *Stephen J. Field, Craftsman of the Law*. Washington, Brookings Institution, 1930.

Taylor, Bayard, *Egypt and Iceland*. New York, Putnam, 1874.

Thompson, R. L., *Wiring a Continent*. Princeton, Princeton University Press, 1947.

Tuckerman, H. T., *Book of the Artists*. New York, Putnam, 1870.

Van Deusen, G. A., *The Jacksonian Era, 1828–1848*. New York, Harper, 1959.

Wallace, E. S., *Destiny and Glory*. New York, Coward-McCann, 1957.

Warshow, R. I., *Jay Gould, the Story of a Fortune*. New York, Greenberg, 1928.

———, *The Story of Wall Street*. New York, Greenberg, 1929.

Weekes, L. H., *History of Paper Manufacturing in the United States*. New York, Lockwood Trade Journal, 1919.

Williams, Frances Leigh, *Matthew Fontaine Maury, Scientist of the Sea*. New Brunswick, Rutgers University Press, 1963.

Wilson, James Grant, *Memorial History of New York*. New York, New York History Co., 1892.

Woodward, Llewellyn, *Oxford History of England: The Age of Reform*. London, Clarendon, 1962.

Yglesias, J. R. C., *The Cable Story*. London, Quinn, 1957.

Young, G. M., *Victorian England, Portrait of an Age*. London, Oxford University Press, 1936.

Index

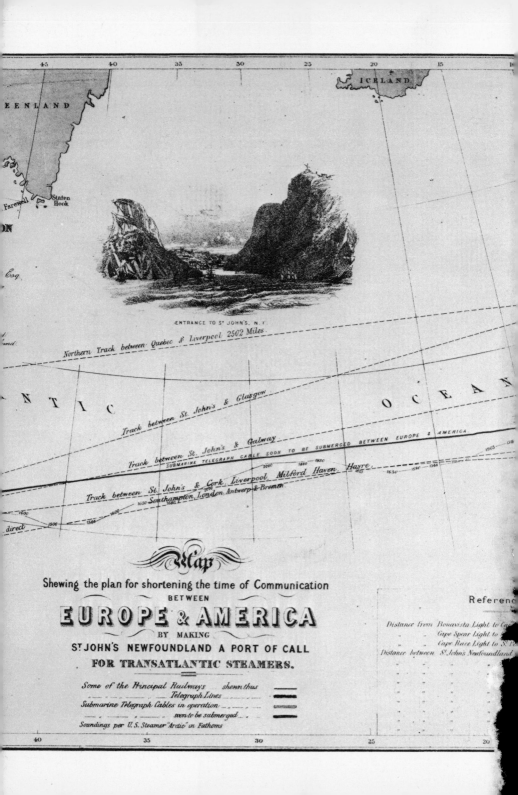

GREENLAND

ICELAND

Farewell   Staten Hook

ENTRANCE TO S.T JOHN'S, N.F.

Northern Track between Quebec & Liverpool 2502 Miles

ATLANTIC   OCEAN

Track between St. John's & Glasgow

Track between St. John's & Galway

SUBMARINE TELEGRAPH CABLE SOON TO BE SUBMERGED BETWEEN EUROPE & AMERICA

Track between St. John's & Cork, Liverpool, Milford Haven, Havre
Southampton, London, Antwerp & Bremen

Map

Shewing the plan for shortening the time of Communication

BETWEEN

EUROPE & AMERICA

BY MAKING

St. JOHN'S NEWFOUNDLAND A PORT OF CALL

FOR TRANSATLANTIC STEAMERS.

Some of the Principal Railways   shewn thus
Telegraph Lines
Submarine Telegraph Cables in operation
soon to be submerged
Soundings per U. S. Steamer "Arctic" in Fathoms

Reference

Distance from Bonavista Light to Cape
Cape Spear Light to
Cape Race Light to St.P
Distance between St. John's Newfoundland